MOUNTAIN PEOPLE

Gurung shepherd. Photo by Brot Coburn.

MOUNTAIN PEOPLE

EDITED BY MICHAEL TOBIAS

FOREWORD BY GEORGINA ASHWORTH

INTRODUCTION BY JACK D. IVES

UNIVERSITY OF OKLAHOMA PRESS : NORMAN AND LONDON

BY MICHAEL TOBIAS

(editor) *The Mountain Spirit* (New York and London, 1979–80)
Deva (San Diego and London, 1981)
(editor) *Deep Ecology* (San Diego, 1984)
After Eden: History, Ecology, and Conscience (San Diego, 1984)
Voice of the Planet (Los Angeles, 1984)
(editor) *Mountain People* (Norman, 1986)

Library of Congress Cataloging-in-Publication Data

Mountain people.

  Bibliography: p. 203
  Includes index.
  1. Mountain people.   2. Mountain life.   3. Mountain
ecology.   I. Tobias, Michael.
GN392.M68   1986   305.5′63   86-40085
ISBN 0-8061-1976-4 (alk. paper)

For Tessa

Contents

Illustrations

COLOR

BLACK AND WHITE

MAPS

Foreword

GEORGINA ASHWORTH

Historically, desert and mountain peoples are the last to be conquered by intruding local or imperial powers. The reason is evident; what is less evident is why the local or imperial invaders finally decide to overcome the physical barriers to their advance. Conquest and invasion, of course, may not be by sheer force of arms. The gradual infiltration of trade, religious fervor, and accompanying alien diseases have undermined societies from the Alaskan highlands to the Himalayas, across the atolls of the Pacific up into the Andes, and over to the Ruwenzoris. The instabilities these new impulses have engendered may or may not incur military intervention at a later stage.

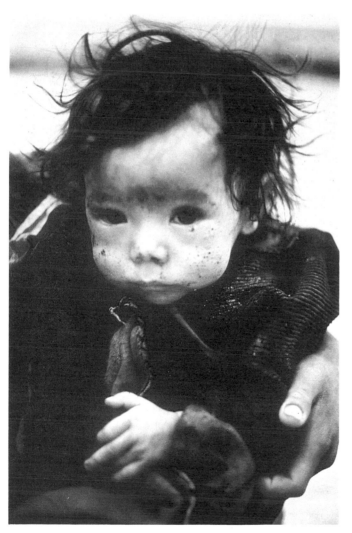

Tibetan malnutrition. Photo by M. Tobias.

It is difficult to suggest that no contact with the outside world is a tenable idea in the twentieth century, but what the remote peoples of the world do suggest to the outside world is that adequate protection in international law does not exist. The protection of mountain fastnesses is rendered useless when the interests of the outsiders—interests that may include oil or mineral-bearing rock, timber, agriculture, access to water, or a strategic utility—overwhelm those of the insiders. The illness of relations between China and the Soviet Union has colored their policies toward the Kirghiz, Uighur, Tadjik, and other groups in the vast plateau of Sinkiang and Soviet borderlands, while benign neglect of mountain peoples in southern China has been replaced by more positive policies following border tensions with Vietnam and the influx of a quarter-million montagnards. The Indochinese montagnard groups themselves—especially the Hmong in Meo, Laos—bore the brunt of ten years' war, swept up in CIA guerrilla training and then abandoned, without culture, land, or livelihood, to the antagonistic victors' mercy. The Baluchi problem, working behind the tenuous national unities of Iran, Pakistan, and Afghanistan, has been brought into international daylight again by political events and strategic responses in that region. Across India, the Naga independence issue in the sensitive border uplands has dogged every fragile government elected by the "world's largest democracy," while the Chittagong hill tribes have been more severely repressed by elements in Bangladesh, itself newly autonomous.

The remote Ifugao of the Philippines find that their steep valleys are to be flooded when a dam, financed by the World Bank, is completed. They were at no time consulted, nor were the social or economic effects measured—the townsfolk's water will wash away Ifugao livelihood. Upland timber forestry in many other parts of Southeast Asia promises the same; the result will be a drift of upland people to cities, where a climate of hostility towards "mountain goats" may prevent them from acquiring alternative forms of self-support.

Across the world, in the Americas, the stalwart poverty of the Andean groups contrasts with their historic wealth. Past military conquest cannot be undone, but the savagery of discriminatory policies, of utter economic neglect, can be analyzed and overturned. The circularity of remote deprivation is reinforced when urban interests are themselves fluid and must be fulfilled to ensure votes that keep administrations in power. In the immediacy of political crisis, the needs of the mountain villages will be neglected; the long-term effects are that institutional assistance (research on higher-yielding mountain agricultural produce, water conservation, or child welfare programs) is deflected. Protest may lead to repression and dispossession; these lead on to protest.

These people could hardly be directly protected by international law, but the indirect impact of an effective international sanction could bring greater safety to them and their welfare. This noninterference in the affairs of another nation is a most sensitive area of concern, but it is indeed broached daily, not only by the questionable activities of big powers, but also by trade itself and intergovernmental activity. Even the World Health Organization (WHO) is a form of interference. The arguments against intervention in any form on behalf of minorities are set in history, but they have trapped groups under unconcerned or vindictive governments, leaving them with inadequate recourse to benign intervention or protection. Until World War II many mountain peoples may have been saved from the very issues and conflicts that set those arguments, but the hardening of the nation-state as the political entity, the sophistication of stategy and arms, expanding populations, and conflict over resources of all kinds have brought the encroachments of modernity and potential destruction to their doors ever since. The omission of "ethnocide" (the cultural as well as physical attrition of a group) from the Genocide Convention of 1948 and the inadequate powers of the UN Subcommission on the Prevention of Discrimination and Protection of Minorities are both cause and effect.

The romantic response to the threats to highland minorities is almost as dangerous to them as realpolitik. The handsomeness of the Kurds and the stunning beauty of their mountains may obtrude in many minds between the problems of their long-betrayed promised autonomous state and the fact that five governments surround them and obscure internal conflict or political intransigence. The docility and stature of the Zairean pygmies make them photogenic and photographed but do not reflect the corruption and semislavery that is encircling and endangering them— for the threat of extinction to them is less directly obvious than that which faces their more publicized mountain neighbors, the gorilla species. The beauties and decorative clothing of the remote Himalayan Kalash are admired, but the sudden danger to them

Gadi child, Zanskar. Photo by M. Tobias.

comes both from interideological conflict with the interest of three big powers and from the roused bellicosity of other mountain neighbors, the Pashtun and Tadjik.

No one political system can be said to have truly evolved satisfactory responses to the existence of ethnic minorities within the frontiers of a state. Ethnicity itself has subjective elements that are often underrated and may be roused by many uncalculated factors. It can not be accommodated comfortably by proletarian structures nor justly where free enterprise prevails, particularly when the ethnic group is physically as well as spiritually on the periphery of the nation's institutions. I once envisioned but long ago abandoned a map of minorities that would have had a multiplicity of factors to convey to the observer. If these could have been projected, such a map could have contributed to our very necessary widening of knowledge, interest, and concern for mountain peoples of the world, which in turn must be translated into effective and understanding action.

MOUNTAIN PEOPLE

INTRODUCTION
THE FUTURE OF THE EARTH'S MOUNTAINS

JACK D. IVES

Modern development in the high mountain areas throughout the world is proceeding at many levels and at many rates, depending on the degree of industrialization, the extent of mountain population pressures, and the proximity of large lowland population centers in the countries concerned. Differences in both kind and degree of development vary greatly among countries, but especially between those nations of the industrialized world and those of the so-called Third World. At the same time there is a growing awareness of the accelerating environmental degradation that results either directly from technological development or more spontaneously from indigenous population growth, deforestation, and overuse or abuse of the soil.

The full range of factors that affect the mountain environment is immense, but it includes massive development of tourism, with financial control frequently exerted from outside the mountain region, as in the European Alps; rural agricultural pressures and attendant deforestation and soil erosion, as along the southern flanks of the Himalayas; and major mining, hydroelectric engineering, and strategic highway development in many other areas. Frequently the damaging effects in the mountains travel downslope and have disastrous consequences for the neighboring lowlands, inducing complex feedback mechanisms, in terms of both human and natural processes, that further compound the problem.

The world's mountain lands provide the life-support systems for about two hundred million people, and the effects of environmental degradation in mountain areas, moving downslope to devastate adjacent rich lowlands, touch on the welfare of several hundred million more. It can be argued, for example, that the destruction occurring today in a single great mountain range, the Himalayas, and its assumed effects on the heavily populated Indo-Gangetic Plain, is a problem of such magnitude that, unabated, it can destabilize the sociopolitical structure of the entire world.

In the temperate latitudes of the industrialized countries, millions of people find recreation and inspiration in neighboring mountain resort areas. This trend is spreading to the mountain regions of many developing countries, where tourism has become an important source of income. Mountains are important providers of renewable and nonrenewable resources, inspiration

and creativity, gene-pool preserves, wonderment, and peace. They are a fundamental part of the world heritage. They also appear to be suffering serious damage as population pressures, whether from indigenous people, migrants, refugees, or tourists, continue to grow and as demands for their products continue to escalate.

Before the middle of this century the mountain regions of the world and their peoples were isolated, largely inaccessible, beyond the mainstreams of our planetary affairs. Thus they harbored a wealth of human tradition and culture more varied and more intricately related to nature than could be found anywhere else. It is only with the recent massive development of communication systems, the spread of medicine and health care without thought for their effects, and the population explosion at large that ruin and desolation have appeared in the mountains. There is nothing especially new about man's misuse of renewable natural resources; serious problems resulting from the impoverishment and destruction of vegetation, soils, and water supplies have overwhelmed sectors of civilization since classical antiquity. What is new is the exponential rate of increase in destructive activities as a consequence of relentless population increase throughout the world, and the sometimes misguided attempts by bilateral aid institutions, international assistance agencies, and indigenous "Western-trained" elites to apply inappropriate technologies to fragile and marginal environments.

The damage that early civilizations did to their environment was of minuscule importance compared to the terrain that remained unimpaired in the unexplored and unknown world of that time. Today we see the destructive madness reach out until its tentacles encompass all livable land. Among those areas suffering overuse and abuse, our mountains are some of the most vulnerable, if only because the all-pervading force of gravity causes man-induced problems to descend the mountain slopes.

Much of the burgeoning development of the mountains is proceeding more or less spontaneously; adequate full-scale planning and assessment of the effects of land use are unobtainable, unknown, or deliberately ignored. Frequently the works of man are placed where they are subject to natural catastrophe or slope instability. The results are enormous costs in resources and damage to the environment and human health.

While much remains to be learned about the natural and human sciences of mountains and mountain peoples, a vast amount of existing knowledge is scattered across the world, some of it in very obscure places. The scientist must join hands with the planner, politician, mountain inhabitant, and tourist to arrest the prevailing slide into environmental degradation. New knowledge and the collation of existing knowledge can go far toward achieving such an objective, but perhaps one of the most important contributions that the scientific community can offer is to challenge the facile assumptions that are generally made about mountain environmental degradation.

While such assumptions may be broadly correct, they are based on grossly inadequate knowledge about the complex human and physical processes that are molding the mountain landscapes. We simply do not know, for instance, the sources of the silt that is being deposited in the Bay of Bengal by the floodwaters of the Ganges and the Brahmaputra. Nor can we assume that the widely accepted cause of mountain deforesta-

tion—the increasing demands for fuel wood by a growing population—is the real cause. Mountains and mountain societies are among the most complex elements of our planet. They are also among the least known.

This introduction represents something of a personal odyssey through many of the world's mountain regions. It was undertaken as a series of separate yet interrelated travels in support of the UNESCO program "Man and the Biosphere," Project 6 (MAB-6), a study of the impact of human activities on mountain ecosystems, and of a United Nations University program on systems of highland-lowland interaction. My travels are continuing with studies of deforestation and soil erosion in Yunnan, the Khumbu Himal, Nepal, and Ecuador. Beginning in the Alps (where I spent a year's sabbatical leave in 1976–77), I proceed to the central and eastern Himalayas and move on to the mountains of northern Thailand, almost enfolded into Burma and Laos, to a Papua, New Guinea, where the last of the Stone Age village communities were discovered by the outside world as recently as thirty years ago. For the New World, the central Andes form an ap-

Chamonix, France. Photo by Olivia Dolfuss.

propriate example, and I conclude in my own backyard, the Colorado Rocky Mountains.

John Muir's concerns about the mountains have really only recently come into their own: there is much devastation, yet much to preserve. Balances among resource development, mountain environment, and human welfare can be struck. We must not fail, and it is worth remembering what our spiritual forefathers clearly understood and wrote down in the puranas, the ancient legends of India: "As the sun dries the morning dew, So are the sins of man dissipated, At the sight of Himalaya."

ALPS

Much of Westerners' mountain lore, science, and sense of adventure derives from the Alps. Classic French mountain geography emanated from Grenoble, home of the venerable Institut de Géographie Alpine. Berne, Zurich, Innsbruck, Salzburg, Munich, and Vienna have produced generations of scholars to ensure a Germanic counterpart. The mixture of languages, cultures, forms of economic activity, and related mountain architecture stretching through southeastern France, northern Italy, Switzerland, Liechtenstein, Austria, Bavaria, and Yugoslavia, evolving from centuries of human occupation, provides us with a wealth of information and understanding that cannot be surpassed. Yet despite centuries of careful husbandry of the Alps, the future of that most closely man-adapted of mountain ranges is uncertain. The excesses of human attraction to those lovely and awe-inspiring mountain landscapes over the last thirty years have brought wide sections to the sorrowful brink of despoliation. The grandeur that attracted so many from the large population centers of Europe is being harmed by the very infrastructure established to accommodate them.

Certain problems had already arisen, however, long before the current tourist boom. During the preceding three centuries, expansion of mountain agricultural communities had induced the destruction of high-altitude forests to provide more space for animal grazing. Lowering of the tree line by up to sixteen hundred feet (five hundred meters) in extreme instances increased the frequency of avalanches and in many valleys proved self-defeating. Such was the case in the Oetztal Valley of the Tyrol. Population pressures in the Oetztal had reached such critical proportions by the 1840s that dramatic measures were introduced. Marriage was banned for twenty years, and unwed mothers were punished with deportation.

The real crises, however, developed after World War II. Growing affluence in Europe set off a tourist boom,

Ancient cabin in the Alps. Photo by Olivia Dolfuss.

based on winter sports and summer recreation, that in one generation reached critical proportions. A number of interrelated activities seem to have gone virtually out of control: rural depopulation, particularly of the higher valleys and alp pastures; conversion from farming to service occupations in the hotels and restaurants and on the ski lifts; and an intricate road system, which in turn seduced more agriculturalists into a suddenly more effective means of moneymaking. Shortage of land, or at least safe land, resulted in widespread construction in areas subject to avalanches, mountain torrents, landslides, and related natural hazards.

Since this process began ahead of the introduction of effective zoning and other forms of land-use planning, structures already built needed protection, especially from avalanches and torrents. Construction of supporting structures in avalanche starting zones and deflection structures and reinforced buildings in run out zones (the usual paths of avalanches), consumed a significant proportion of the economic resources of the Alpine countries. It also left many hitherto beautiful mountain slopes looking like battlefields, with miles of reinforced concrete and metal. And yet life and property losses have continued to mount as more development occurs. This crisis has only recently been fully recognized. The Swiss avalanche zoning plan, Austrian legislation against uncontrolled construction in areas subject to mountain torrents and avalanches, and similar, if less rigorous, responses in adjacent areas are slowly ensuring abatement of the losses. Nevertheless, human, economic, and environmental costs have already been unjustifiably high.

The tourist industry, of course, has not been the only form of economic activity with such a mixture of advantage and loss. Hydroelectric developments and reservoirs, in a Central Europe increasingly short of water and energy, have rearranged large areas. The

Power lines near Salzburg. Photo by M. Tobias.

spread of industry into mountain valleys has produced scars of enormous dimensions on the landscape and a disconcerting level of air pollution.

The future of the Alps is understandably in doubt. When tourism and other economic activities cause such a level of environmental deterioration that tourists themselves begin to look for more distant and untainted mountains, the very system may be sowing the seeds of its own collapse. It was this concern that, through the UNESCO MAB-6 program, led to the development of the Obergurgl model and placed the Oetztal in the role of experimental mountain world in miniature. The Austrian advances in mountain research were taken up by the Swiss, who provided large sums of federal money, formed a large interdisciplinary team of scientists, and established what is probably the largest single mountain-research program ever attempted. Their broad objective is to greatly improve our understanding of mountain dynamics through holistic evaluation of four test sites—Grindelwald, Dischmatal, Aletsch, and Pays d'Enhaut—as a basis for the development of land-use policy. Other projects inspired by the UNESCO MAB-6 program have been set off in many of the world's other mountain regions.

HIMALAYA MOUNTAIN RANGE

I had the privilege of gazing at Kanchenjunga from the doorstep of my friend Choni, a Tibetan refugee from Gyangtse. It was my second visit. The twenty thousand landslides of my first visit in the autumn of 1968 had been controlled somewhat by vegetative regrowth. Tea was still king, and the closed-crown montane forest had receded to a slightly greater altitude. Choni remarked that, although poor and deeply concerned about his five dependents, he was yet rich. He nudged my shoulder. It was close to sunset; heavy clouds, with great turrets of cumulus pushing up from the valley floor, had veiled the mountain throughout the day. Now the cloud tops had flattened and lowered so that the mountain floated on a sea of vapor as the sun sank into it, turning everything bloodred, gold, purple, and stark green. Choni turned to me and explained why he felt rich: he was one of the world's privileged few who could drink in such an unsurpassable view from the doorstep of his hut.

Afterward, as we drank yet more Tibetan tea, my mind returned to that place in 1968 where the Tista River surged out of the Singalilas onto the plain.

Bridges, houses, rice fields were gone; a vast delta of gravel, sand, and silt stretched gray to the southern horizon, it seemed to Calcutta. Twenty thousand landslides had occurred during one morning following 25 to 50 inches of rain in three days at the end of the monsoon. Thirty thousand lives had been disrupted. Why? Was the cause massive deforestation? Or was it just the nature of the eastern Himalaya Mountains? Our weather-station superintendant indicated that climatic events of such magnitude had occurred only once before in the more than one hundred years of record. The answer probably lies between those two explanations—a disastrous event with a return period of more than one hundred years, its effects accentuated by deforestation and road building on a grand scale. Some of the facts we know: for example, the sixty miles of road between Darjeeling at 7,600 feet (2,300 meters) and Siliguri on the plain had been cut in ninety-two places.

That had been my first experience with the Himala-

Leh Bazaar. Photo by M. Tobias.

yas, and the shock, grandeur, devastation, and sense of human persistence I felt then will remain with me for the rest of my life. On that autumn evening as I sat on Choni's doorstep, a painful question kept me from giving myself fully to the beauty: Can this scale of devastation be occurring along the entire length of this immeasurable mountain range? I am afraid the answer may be yes. I should have known; many could have told me.

What of Nepal? We hear that within twenty-five years of the opening of Nepal and the first ascent of Everest approximately half the country's forest cover was destroyed. For a while tourism, with heavy accent on mountaineering and trekking, was believed to be the answer to the country's development and foreign exchange problems. Today the trekking route to Sagarmatha (Everest) is locally known as the "garbage trail." It is said that the timberline trees are being felled for firewood for trekkers and mountaineers and that the forested, malaria-ridden tracts of the Tarai have become a Mecca for the burgeoning population of the middle mountains (and illegal immigrants from south of the border), a temporary respite now almost used up.

As the population of Nepal's middle mountains grew, it was necessary to add more agricultural terraces on steeper and steeper slopes; migration to the Tarai was not enough. So the forests fell, but also to the ax of the cook. Soon, it was claimed, more than half the villages of Nepal had pushed back the sources of fuel wood so that two days' labor each week was required to supply a family's needs. At that stage the effort is too much and an increasing proportion of animal dung is used for fuel. Thus the agricultural terraces are deprived of fertilizer, and yields are reduced. But even that is not the worst result, for as the terrace soils become impoverished, their holding capacity is weakened, and landslides become inevitable. The life-sustaining soil slips down into the valley bottoms and is washed down the rivers to the rich farmlands of the Gangetic Plain. Bangladesh pushes southward as more silt enters the Bay of Bengal, and the Indian and Bangladeshi military vie for the "new land"; villages are buried; rivers meander in anastomosing patterns; fields disappear; floods are more disastrous and last longer, while river flow in the dry season is reduced. Nepal continues to export to India and Bangladesh in ever-growing quantities that one commodity it cannot afford to trade, and the one commodity, in that mode of delivery, that the two neighboring countries cannot afford to receive.

Six years of intensive research in two small areas of Nepal (Kakani, in the Middle Mountains, and the

Agriculture in the Indus Valley. Photo by M. Tobias.

Khumbu Himal) have produced a number of potentially controversial conclusions with important implications for policy in resource development and the
form of foreign aid. First, while our initial reaction to
the large number of landslide scars and other evidence
of soil erosion and deforestation paralleled that of Erik
Eckholm (*Losing Ground,* 1975) and the conclusions
drawn from one-time visits of "experts," the experience based on several years of intensive involvement led
to some significant qualifications. Although losses of
land from landslides are serious, the local villagers,
using traditional strategies, were achieving a remarkable level of reclamation. Landslide areas, completely
unstable in 1979, were carefully tended and highly productive wet rice-paddy terraces in 1983. Second, shortage of fuel wood cannot be classed as a primary cause
of deforestation: population growth in a subsistence
farming community forces the clearing of forests so
that more agricultural terraces can be cut for the production of food. Third, the hill farmers, so often
faulted as ignorant despoilers of the mountain landscapes, had evolved extensive environmental knowledge and land-management strategies over generations. They were severely handicapped by oppressive

Nepalese Woman. Photo by James H. Katz.

Paro Valley, Bhutan. Photo by R. Radin.

patches of available land in the valleys and intermontane basins and on the terraces and foothills for irrigated rice paddies and for upland rice at the slightly higher levels. But in the adjacent mountains, which exceed 6,600 feet, (2,000 meters), tribal groups such as the Hmong, Lisu, Lahu, and Karen still had room to practice slash-and-burn (swidden) subsistence agriculture and to maintain a virtual independence— independence both from the governments of the nations across whose unsurveyed and unmarked frontiers they ranged and from each other. Under these circumstances, with periods of forest fallow often exceeding twenty years, subsistence forest agriculture, with some cash income from opium-poppy cultivation at the higher elevations, helped maintain a balance between traditional cultures and the local environment. In fact it can be reasonably claimed that in areas of tropical rain forest, or monsoon rain forest, that are devoid of the disturbing influences of "civilization" slash-and-burn forest agriculture is an ideally balanced economy. Certainly the system, in a large variety of forms, evolved

Namche Bazaar at night: The first electricity in a Sherpa village. Nepal. Photo by Brot Coburn.

levels of rent and taxation that are as much factors that force deforestation as is hunger. Although the data supporting these conclusions are derived from small test areas and thus cannot yet be generalized, such data pose many challenges to the way in which foreign aid is dispensed.

THE MOUNTAINS AND THE HILL TRIBES OF NORTHERN THAILAND

There are indeed mountains in northern Thailand. Although they are not comparable to the Himalayas, the prospect of a three-thousand-foot climb there will always be enough to allow me to believe I am in mountain country. Thirty years ago the rugged, forest-wreathed mountains of northern Thailand were a veritable no-man's-land that, together with neighboring sections of Burma, Laos, and Chinese Yunnan, formed what has come to be known as the Golden Triangle. Ethnic northern Thais were meticulously using the last and persisted for centuries throughout the humid tropics. There was enough land, or low enough population, that fifteen to twenty years of fallow were possible, and that was enough time to guarantee forest replacement and the reestablishment of soil fertility after the initial burning. Such conditions are now only a memory of past times.

Today's population pressures, both among the ethnic northern Thai and among the hill tribes themselves, are threatening to destroy the traditional patterns of land use together with related tribal behavior patterns. The first effects were felt after World War II. As in many other parts of the developing world, suppression of malaria and the general introduction of health care and medicine with a rudimentary communication system began the process. This process has been accelerated by the aftermath of the Vietnam War and growth in national awareness and concern for more secure frontiers. Migrations of hill tribal people out of Laos, Kampuchea, and Burma into Thailand have added to the population pressures in the mountains; so too has the progressive uphill push of the ethnic Thai as their lowland rice paddies become overburdened. Government concern for security, especially with hill tribes scattered across national frontiers, prompts an effort to induce consciousness of Thai allegiance. This frequently takes the form of military conscription and further thrusts the mountain people into the international market economy, increasing the need for cash income to buy T-shirts and transistor radios and, ironically, to increase the production of opium.

Now the slash-and-burn practices, which vary in detail from one group to another, are being continued with such a reduced period of fallow that the forests

Deforestation in Northern Thailand. Photo by Jack Ives.

cannot revegetate, and soil fertility cannot be restored. Tribal groups impinge on each other's territory. Land has become a cash commodity. This last is particularly distressing because Thai law does not allow for ownership of land by non-Thai people. Thus the hill tribes are being dispossessed of land, the no-man's-land they have been using for centuries, by Thai entrepreneurs, some of whom do not hesitate to claim and sell traditional hill-tribe land only to move on to other and richer pastures, leaving behind growing confusion, hardship, and environmental disaster.

The reduced period available for forest fallow has ensured the progressive and widespread destruction of the forest. Almost all of the primary forest has been destroyed, and the second growth is giving way to *Imperata* grassland, producing a landscape of greatly reduced yield. Despoliation of the teak forests of lower elevations, being completed by innumerable small acts of illegal cutting, and deforestation of the mountain belt are making themselves felt in the now expectable fashion: reduced river flow in the dry season followed by inundation and exceptionally high waters during the monsoon. In addition, part of the mountain soil finds its way downstream to add to the process of silting that clogs irrigation works and overruns rice paddies.

The beautiful country of Thailand, military pressures notwithstanding, is being brought to the brink of environmental, cultural, and economic upheaval. The Thai people are still exquisite and graceful, and their smiles and bright colors join with the equally attractive impressions one gains of the hill-tribe peoples. Yet northern Thailand needs immediate help in the form of problem assessment, environmental mapping, and techniques for appropriate development instead of the transfer of inappropriate technologies. The problems, as elsewhere, are immense and extremely complex. The massive mountain reforestation program of the Thai Royal Department of Forestry is an example of sectoral response that may be causing as many new difficulties as it resolves old ones. Thousands of hectares in the mountains are planted with neat rows of pine seedlings, frequently that breathtakingly quick-growing native tree *Pinus kesiya*. The plantations transcend the swidden lands of the hill tribes, but soil erosion must be reduced. Nevertheless, pine plantations interspersed with traditional slash-and-burn agriculture create obvious problems when "controlled" fires get out of control. In April, the climax of the dry season, the haze of forest fires sometimes reduces visibility at northern Thai airfields below safety limits for several days at a time. But the hill tribes constitute a fire culture. During times of stress, such as the death of a village headman, it appears that virtual pyromania becomes a formidable method of releasing mental tension. A rough estimate is that at least 40 percent of the pine seedlings are lost to fires.

Pisit Voraurai, vice-rector of Chiang Mai University, an agriculturalist with a doctoral degree from the University of Nottingham, England, is representative of a group of committed Thai scientists who are combining agricultural and horticultural skills with almost fanatical devotion, sensitivity, and imagination and an essential holistic approach to the development of a courageous project that could become a major force in effecting a practical solution. Voraurai, with his many helpers, has fostered a Thai Royal Forestry Department–Chiang Mai University research project based on the Huai Thung Choa field station, situated at 3,600 feet (1,100 meters) and some forty-five miles (seventy kilometers) northwest of Chiang Mai. This enterprise, which involves experimentation with and introduction of cash crops that will serve as alternatives to opium, as well as reforestation, practical education of tribal adults, health care, and training of the youngsters from four different ethnic groups in the vicinity, was identified in 1978 by the United Nations University (UNU). It was perceived as a strong base upon which to found an encouraging international effort.

The Huai Thung Choa project was originally set up by Voraurai to examine the possibility for commercial production of cut flowers, bulbs, and seeds. This was to be the basis for converting local Karen and Lisu villages from opium production and from their rapidly destabilizing slash-and-burn agriculture. A school was built, and an unprecedented mix of Karen, Lisu, Hmong, and Thai children began to study and prepare for a future village life based on "adjusted" agricultural practices. During my most recent visit I learned that two entire Lisu villages and several Karen villages are totally committed; forest burning has ceased in the immediate area, and the income from flowers sold in Chiang Mai, Bangkok, Singapore, and Hong Kong and seeds sold in the United States is exceeding that obtained from opium production.

The UNU involvement includes introduction of a wide range of agroforestry practices, including cultivation of coffee, tea, live hedges, firewood species, and temperate fruits. It also incorporates anthropological studies, soil and vegetation mapping, soil-erosion assessment on traditional and new croplands, and establishment of a network for the collection of microclimatological and hydrological data. Additionally, young Thai scientists, as UNU fellows, have been sent for special training to Turrialba, Costa Rica; Berne,

Switzerland; and Boulder, Colorado. Austrian, Swiss, Japanese, Costa Rican, and American specialists are collaborating on expansion of the Huai Thung Choa project. Will such a scheme become a prototype for widespread application to other areas of the humid tropical mountains?

Before we can answer that question, an intermediate response is required. What have we learned from the Huai Thung Choa project research itself? By the early 1970s several concepts had developed concerning land use in humid tropical hill countries in general and in northern Thailand in particular. These concepts included the popular beliefs that (1) swidden agriculture was inherently bad and that the highlanders were primarily responsible for the massive deforestation and associated downstream effects; (2) the spread of *Imperata* grassland resulted from highlander population pressure, led to the production of wasteland, and was extremely difficult to eradicate; (3) massive reforestation, involving in Thailand the large-scale planting of *Pinus kesiya,* was a necessary emergency response; and (4) the introduction of alternate cash crops and various forms of agricultural intensification provided a possible solution to a broad array of problems. The Huai Thung Choa project and the international workshops associated with it prompted the conclusion that many of the preexisting schemes to resolve problems of environmental deterioration and improve the subsistence levels of the highlanders are based on false assumptions or are in conflict with each other instead of reinforcing each other. Thus monoculture, in the form of reforestation with *Pinus kesiya,* often increases the land pressure facing hill peoples; existing swidden economies will support six or seven times the population per unit area. Also, formal attempts to intensify agriculture are having little impact on the Hmong system of hill swidden and opium production. Successful introduction of agroforestry systems among the Karen will be severely inhibited by the shortage of labor, even though agricultural intensification can be undertaken without augmenting absolute soil losses.

From these and other studies some broad issues have emerged: (1) existing Thai development policies may not be adequately based on the behavioral patterns and perceptions of the local people; (2) the perceptions of highlanders by Thais and outsiders are not necessarily accurate, and in particular the ethnic northern Thai may be responsible for more of the deforestation than are the highlanders; (3) the role of *Imperata* grassland is not perceived clearly, and the problems are neither technical nor scientific but social and economic; and (4) agroforestry, if appropriately applied to existing subsistence systems, has considerable potential for resolving the traditional conflict between forester and farmer. The overwhelming conclusion, however, is that the problems of the hill country of northern Thailand, and of many similar areas, are neither scientific nor technical. Instead, they are "people problems." Throughout the developing mountain world, solutions imposed by outsiders will frequently fail. Success will depend on the degree to which the mountain people are enabled to take the initiative.

THE HIGHLANDS OF PAPUA NEW GUINEA

The large equatorial island of New Guinea extends for 1,600 miles (2,500 kilometers) in a roughly west-northwest to east-southeast direction between the equator and latitude 11° south. It provides a bulwark of Asian-Australian transition north of the predominantly white island continent. Today its western half, Irian Jaya, is part of Indonesia. Its eastern half is one of the world's newest nations, Papua New Guinea. Its backbone is formed by an impressive mountain range extending above tree line and, despite its equatorial location, supporting small glaciers on its western culminations. Anthropologically, it is known for the Stone Age villages that were discovered by Australians as recently as 1955.

The main precontact population centers have been the central highlands, where a large population prospered. These people regarded themselves as alone for centuries in their island-highland world—the sole members of *Homo sapiens.* They were separated from the island coasts by steep mountain slopes covered with dense rain forests. Uncertain contacts for trade involved many days' journeys, articles passing through many pairs of hands so that source and destination of such trade were mutually known.

The aftermath of World War II (a phrase repeated many times in these pages) caused the opening up of the central highlands of Papua New Guinea under Australian tutelage. The hitherto isolated highland belt, from the upper forests to the snow line, a land of equitable temperature, healthy and productive, exploded into environmental crisis as medicine and health care ensured rapid population growth. Coastal populations also expanded. The previously untouched and barely populated land between was one of steep slopes and impenetrable forests.

The opening of the highlands has been accomplished largely with the bush plane, and the area has some of the most spectacularly steep landing strips in the world. The completion of a major highway from

Lae to beyond Mount Hagen has accelerated the conversion to cash crops and has facilitated the movement of people.

Population growth in both the highlands and the coastal areas has induced an assault on the middle altitudinal belt of steep slopes and rain forest. As is usually the case, enforced population movements of this kind occur after the source areas of the migration have already exceeded their carrying capacities. Migration downslope is particularly severe. In these instances a mixture of traditional highland subsistence agriculture and recently introduced cash cropping is being transplanted into rain-forest areas of much lower fertility. Deforestation and further reduction in soil fertility are a bleak prospect, both for the immediate areas and for the coastal valleys that are affected by increasing irregularity of river runoff and silting. This situation is exacerbated by deforestation in the lowlands themselves.

The Papua New Guinean scene is particularly fascinating and tragic. The situation is a complex of very recent and partial transition from Stone Age subsistence to participation in a world-market economy, a movement toward nationhood handicapped by the persistence of many tribal affinities and competition among them, and a minute educated class. Walking through dense midaltitude forest to inspect new coffee plantations in June, 1978, was an experience in itself. To have a traditionally dressed (perhaps best described as suitably undressed) hunter leap out on us and, in friendly pidgin, offer to sell his hunting arrows emphasized the problem of overcoming a socioeconomic gap compounded by a time gap. It is a measure of the education shortage that when a Papua New Guinean obtains a B.A. from the university at Port Moresby, his prospects for a high government administrative, if not a subministerial, post are secure. When will the pool of educated men and women be large enough to facilitate development of corps for research in environmental land use?

THE CENTRAL ANDES

The Andean Mountain system is usually classed as the most complex and intricately varied mountain range on earth. Stretching from well north of the equator almost to the ice fields of the Antarctic, the Andes offer an infinite variety of vegetation, microclimates, and human adaptations. They embrace lush tropical and equatorial rain forests on the middle-eastern flanks, Pacific coastal deserts of extreme aridity, rolling prairies, and subhumid coniferous forests. Some of the most fascinating Andean landscapes are in the highlands and mountain ranges stretching from Ecuador through Peru and Bolivia to northern Chile and Argentina. This is the fabled El Dorado, the Altiplano, land of the Inca and the conquistador, the inhabited roof of the world where centuries of human adaptation have produced the ultimate in high-altitude living.

The Altiplano is a rolling land above the upper tree line perhaps best developed around Lake Titicaca. It is bordered by spectacular mountain ranges, in Bolivia the Cordillera Real and the Cordillera Occidental. Even before the development of the great Inca civilization, this high mountain land supported a highly developed and densely settled civilization based on the llama, the quinoa, the potato and highly productive agriculture. Land use and organization probably reached their culmination under the Incas, only to be rudely gutted by the Spanish conquest.

Since the Spanish imperial period ended, the Andean mountain world has been beset by unstable and rapidly changing political structures, which over the last thirty years have been augmented by that region's own variety of population explosion and resultant environmental pain. The population densities of the ancient Incas have only recently been surpassed; however, the former period of high population appears to have been one of high, sustained agricultural yield. In the present period the carrying capacity of the land has been far exceeded.

The peoples of the Altiplano are predominantly derived from pre-Conquest Indian stock. Impoverished land, with communities still dependent on the potato and the quinoa, in all their multitudinous varieties, and the llama, has begun to compel emigration. This process takes several forms. For example, in Bolivia there is movement from (1) rural highlands to urban highlands (primarily La Paz), (2) rural highlands to rural humid lowlands (primarily the Ungas of the Amazon Basin), (3) rural highlands to rural lowlands along the Pacific Coast, and (4) rural highlands to urban lowlands. Frequently such movement is multiphased. In any event, it results in the younger, fitter, and more intellectually vigorous leaving behind a physically and mentally impoverished older population. It also often causes the transfer of highland, above-tree-line agricultural practices to devastate humid forestlands. Tropical diseases, morbidity, and a sense of desperation are often the end products of both the source and the target areas, and the impingement of elitist, affluent minorities on the highland societies is graphically depicted in the following poem. It is translated from the Quechua tongue (the author uses the term "doctors" as synonymous with "technicians" or "developers"):

They say that we don't know anything
and we are backwards,
that our hearts do not match the times,
and they'll exchange our heads for others, better ones.

They say that some doctors tell this about us,
doctors who multiply in our own land,
who grow fat here
and get golden.

But doctor, do you know of what my brains are made
and of what is the flesh of my heart?
Start your helicopter and climb here, if you can,
Take out your binoculars, your best lenses, and look.

Below five hundred kinds of flowers of as many different
        potatoes grow
on the balconies of the canyons unreached by your eyes.
They grow in the earth, mixed with night and gold
silver and day,
Those five hundred flowers are my brains, my flesh.

Come close to me, doctor, lift me into the cabin of your
        helicopter, and
I will toast you with a drink of a thousand flowers,
        the life of
a thousand different crops I grew in centuries
from the foot of the snowfields to the forests of
        the wild bears.

No!
Did I work for centuries of months and years, in order
that someone I do not know, and does not know me,
misshape my face with clay and
exhibit me deformed before my sons?

We don't know what will happen, let death walk toward us.
Let these unknown people come, we will await them,
For we are the sons of the father of all the mountains,
Sons of the father of all the rivers.

These processes of migration are both a consequence and a cause of overgrazing, soil erosion, deforestation, and general environmental and social devastation on a massive and growing scale. The migration is sometimes spontaneous, sometimes government-sponsored or even "forced." The possible future consequences should cause us to grave concern. The irony of the situation, as well as the tragedy, can be illustrated by the following brief anecdote: In June, 1974, I was a member of a UNESCO MAB-6 reconnaissance group traveling by bus from La Paz across the Cordillera Real down to the Yungas. Long before coming down to the tree line, where innumerable species of broad-leaved trees began, we passed a magnificent small stand of pine. "Why," I asked our Bolivian host, "doesn't your government sponsor extensive reforestation?" North American pine will obviously do well for more than 500 feet (150 meters) above the "natural" treeline. The answer was that, in a country where the government has been overthrown on average once every eighteen months, it was unlikely that the present administration would invest in reforestation with the prospect of sixty to one hundred years before harvest. Such action lies outside the realm of political reality.

COLORADO ROCKY MOUNTAINS

The Rocky Mountains of my home state, like many other mountain areas of the American West, have experienced two major periods of human activity. The mining boom that continued from about 1860 to 1920 witnessed extensive cutting of coniferous forests at high altitude. In many places those cut areas have subsequently nurtured many fine stands of aspen. A related effect was the digging of holes and tunnels and the construction of buildings in outrageously out-of-the-way areas. Even fifty years, however, was enough to turn such scenes of human devastation into picturesque landscapes of ghost towns, gaudily colored mine tailings, and superb autumn foliage—a veritable tourist Mecca.

The second period of human impact began about 1965. At that time Colorado was about fifteen or twenty years behind the Alps. Skiing and the associated construction of superhighways, mountain holiday homes, and summertime recreational activities triggered the mushrooming growth of old mining towns like Aspen and the overnight creation of new towns like Vail. Old mining towns, such as Telluride and Steamboat Springs, that had almost degenerated into ghost towns suddenly acquired ski resorts and a curious mixture of mountain wild West and après ski, attracting armies of Chicagoans, Texans, New Yorkers, and Europeans to the high-altitude winter gymnasiums. Crested Butte followed the same course until discovery of one of the world's largest deposits of molybdenum ore there brought a massive conflict among conservationists, ski buffs, and large-scale mining developers. Within the last several years there has also been great interest and activity in uranium mining and exploitation of coal and oil shale.

Before the penetration of European-derived communities in the second half of the last century, the scale of human activity in the Rocky Mountains had been minuscule. Even today the Swiss visitor marvels at the vast expanses of "empty" mountain landscape, compared to the vistas of his closely settled and intensively used Alps. Certainly a very large proportion of the Colorado Rocky Mountains is publicly owned in the form of national parks, national forests, and wilderness areas. But the geometric growth of the ski industry and the vast reserves of uranium, molybdenum, coal, and oil shale have set the stage for the establishment of complex priorities and massive competition.

Despite a high tree line of 11,500 feet (3,500 meters), a large proportion of the total mountain land lies above tree line, displaying attractive mountain meadows, high-altitude rolling summits of great beauty that are a paradise for backpackers. It is hard to imagine this landscape as one of high mountains except when hypoxia affects the hiker.

Many of Colorado's recreational transients, especially the winter skiers, are from outside the state. But Denver and the so-called Front Range urban corridor are one of the fastest-growing population centers in North America. Denver has moved into second place in its air-pollution problem, a phenomenon of high altitude and too many automobiles.

The stage is set in Colorado for massive conflicts over land use and, depending on how those conflicts are resolved, for wise use of nonrenewable resources and reclamation and well-planned recreational development, or the opposite, with its accompanying mountain disaster. As the relatively small amount of suitable level or gently sloping terrain available for buildings and highways is used up, Colorado's ten- to twenty-year lag behind the Alps will evaporate. Already, despite good first steps in mountain land-use planning legislation with the passage of Colorado House Bill 1041 in 1974, the hazards of avalanches and mountain torrents are heightening. There is a chance, given further resolute legislative action and adequate supportive research, that these natural hazards will be handled passively by zoning. The alternative is the heavy deployment of retaining and deflecting structures and the round of environmental effects associated with them. Is there still time to learn from the Alpine experience?

My personal odyssey could be extended almost indefinitely, but the general conclusions that can be drawn would not likely be changed significantly. Mountain landscapes and mountain people are best characterized by their infinite variety and great complexity. Despite a rapidly increasing research effort, they remain virtually unknown. All generalizations but two are both difficult and dangerous, if not downright irresponsible. The exceptions: that they are under enormous pressure and that change through "development" *will* occur. The more effectively such development can be based on a full understanding of the behavior patterns and perceptions of the mountain people, the greater will be the opportunity to reduce unnecessary damage. All of us—scientists, artists, bureaucrats, politicians, and citizens alike—face an obligation to help reduce the damage.

PART ONE   THE UNITED STATES

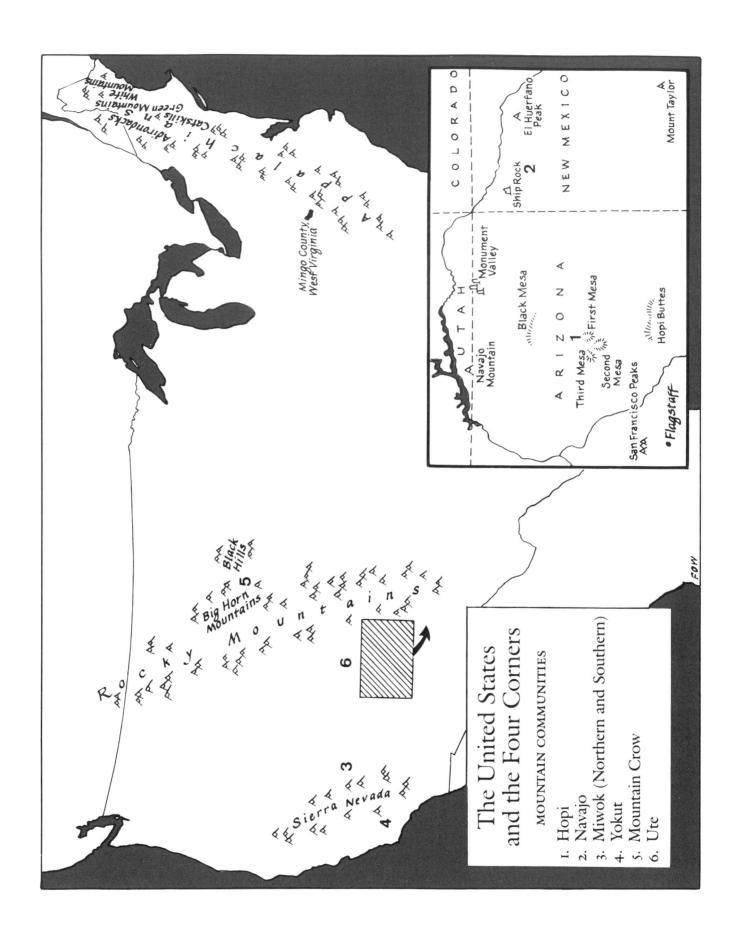

The United States
and the Four Corners

MOUNTAIN COMMUNITIES

1. Hopi
2. Navajo
3. Miwok (Northern and Southern)
4. Yokut
5. Mountain Crow
6. Ute

1. APPALACHIA'S MORAL LIFE

ROBERT COLES

What possible connection can there be between the moral life of a given region's children and adults, on the one hand, and the particular terrain they happen to call their own, in this case the hilly stretches of Appalachia that dominate the state of West Virginia, the eastern section of Kentucky, and the western part of North Carolina, to name the parts of a particular "mountain range" I happen to know best? That is a fairly long, if not long winded, question of a kind I was emphatically not trained to ask. I came to Appalachia not completely unmindful of its distinctive territorial characteristics: the high elevation, the hollows that go up and down, the valleys (and streams) that work their way around or through land at times mightily resistant. But it is one thing to know that one is in a particular place and quite another to connect that set of geographical circumstances to a child's mental life, let alone his or her moral life.

In fact, I spent years with the people of Appalachia in a wrong-headed pursuit of their various "problems," a search not exactly discouraged, I fear, by what people like me, in their self-importance, often refer to as "the literature"—a collection of books and articles meant to say what is important and truthful to be said. And that "literature," in its portentous, predominant, insistent sum, told me that the hill people of, say, Kentucky are, for the most part, a rather sad lot—hopelessly backward, not educated, suspicious, superstitious, even inclined to take offense easily and resort to quick violence. To be blunt, to be crude, when I went up those hollows I was going slumming—a Yankee doctor, full of degrees and theories offered by a shelf of books, intent on proving yet again what others had in their own ways documented. I am saddened as I look back and realize how long it took me to begin to change direction, so to speak—how stubbornly I tried to limit the human possibilities of the people I was getting to know. And the more "poverty" I saw (and I saw a lot), the more pity I felt (and I persuaded myself that my heart was bountifully compassionate) and the less likely it became that I would have a halfway decent chance of catching on to a few important moral as well as psychological facts that are, I believe, extremely important if we are to understand at least one mountain people.

It was, actually, the mountains themselves (or, at least, the subject of them) that finally began to undo, a little, my blind and ignorant habits of thought. One day, in the summer of 1968, I heard this from a young man of thirteen who was all too readily seen by me, at the time, as not well read, as uninterested in "learning," as lacking in "ambition," as in need of better dental and medical care, and on and on: "I do believe my people have been here so long, we'll never really leave, even if we do go to some city. I mean, you can go to places in Ohio, like some of us do, but you carry the hills with you; and you come back to die, if you have your way. My daddy says, if he was in Dayton or Cleveland, and he was lying on his death bed, and ready to meet the Lord, the last thing he'd think of, before he would go to get judged, would be our hills—the sight of them, and the sky beyond, and the woods below, and our hollow and the whole length of the valley you can see from up there, on top of yonder mountain."

He paused long enough to point. He wanted to make sure that I was following what he had in mind for me to see, to notice carefully, and, yes, to take into consideration. Then, as if doubtful, the yeoman lad continued, now more historically grand and dramatically instructive in his manner of exposition and clarification: "We came here a long time ago; we were going West, my daddy used to tell me, but we got cut off. It was hard, fighting the mountains. After a while, we must have stopped the fighting and started looking around, and figuring what to do. Then we decided: why go any further, when it's as fine as can be right in this spot! Sometimes you're blessed when you run into trouble!

"We've had our troubles ever since; I know that. The teacher tells us we've got to study, because there's a lot that needs doing and changing hereabouts. My daddy says, sure, that's true—but don't get lost worrying about all the bad. There's good, he says. He'll remind us at the table, before we eat, of the good: being here, near our kin; being up this hollow, and with our land to work the best we can—and not someplace off there in a big city, with nothing but people everywhere, and they can't go take a walk without getting into a heap of trouble. We hear what's going on, you know!"

19

That last comment was made with a touch of sharp irony, as if to remind me, the smart cosmopolitan one, that I may be in more jeopardy of ignorance and cultural insularity than I seemed likely to know. Then he continued, now in a more personal, confessional vein: "I like to go up the hollow, as far as the big path will take me; then I have my own path, and soon I'm on top of the hill, and I can see as far as the eyes were made to see! I remember looking at the mountain with my granddaddy; I'd ask him what's beyond them, and he'd say that here we are, and we can see way over, and our eyes weren't made by God to see any more! I'd lower my head and say I'm sorry. Then, he'd give me his sermon: he'd say that we're lucky to be able to get this close to God. I'd say yes, Sir. Then he'd say we should pray, and we did. I guess he was the one to speak the prayers. I was smaller than I am now, and I'd listen. He'd say that God sends us here, and then He calls us back, and before He does the sending, he stops and thinks, and He decides who needs sending where, and then He makes the big decision for each of us. If you end up here, then it means God wants to have you nearer to Him than it would be if you were way below and off someplace else.

"I was never clear how granddaddy figured all that out. I asked my mom one day: How do we know about God's thinking? She said I should explain myself, and I did, and then she told me that no one knows for sure what the Lord has in His head, but each of us is put someplace, and you have to stop and ask yourself why it's *this* place, and that's what my granddaddy does, and that's what I should do—because if you don't humble yourself and ask why, then you're taking this life for granted, and that's bad. We're sent here to ask, and to find, the right way to live. Christ told us, and He went on a mountain when he told us, remember. In the Bible they don't just let something happen. The people of Israel went up the mountains to get to hear God, and feel Him near them, and hear what He said. I don't think He can pay attention to all of us, but He tries His best, and He must have a reason for scattering us.

"My mother has always told all of my brothers and sisters not to get 'puffed up' with ourselves, though! She says if we're here, it's because there's a purpose. You don't just be tickled with yourself. You should think of your mother and father and your kin, and everyone you see, anywhere, and you should ask what you can do to help them. You have to prove yourself before God, and you can't forget that He's watching you, and He's right up there, and it's not so far away. Sometimes, when the clouds are real low, they almost touch you, standing on the big mountain. Then there'll

Farmhouse in Vermont's Green Mountains. Photo by M. Tobias.

be the mist, and the drizzle, and my grandmother says they are messages from God; He's touching you, He's so close by. So you go back down the mountain and you remember. Yes, you remember where you are, and what you've got to do! There's all those chores, and they're for you to do, and God is watching!"

I find it hard to convey to outsiders the importance of religion for Appalachia's people. They are a God-fearing people. They feel close to Him. They don't overlook, in that regard, the elevation of the land. They also live close to history—their history: the eighteenth- or nineteenth-century trek West; the confrontation with those hills, those mountains; the decision to yield, to surrender to the apparently impassable; and the life since then—a persisting, dedicated, resourceful and eminently proud accommodation to the realities of a given topography. "One thing I know," that child's father used to tell me, and then he spelled out what he did indeed "know," but also lived with—even, it can be said, lived for: "If I don't feel good when I wake up; if I'm in some trouble over cash; if someone's ailing; if one of my dogs looks to be nearing the end of life—I can always look up yonder, and there it is, God's land. The mountains are fingers pointing to Him. Don't misunderstand me, He's up there in Heaven, I know; but He's here with us, and it's up the mountains that He stays. You go down into the valley, and people there will tell you that. So I'm not boasting, I'm just saying! Moses went up the mountain; I think Abraham did, and Christ was there, teaching us; so we'd better do the best we can up here!"

There is a wry side to him; he is not about to become self-important. He knows how marginal his social and economic life has always been, and will continue to be. His capacity to abstract Biblical moments and connect them to his own life is an act of piety, not talkative pride. And maybe, too, a measure of the desperation he and other mountain people of the region have to contend with all the time. It is not fun ekeing the most modest of livings out of those stubborn hills, so fetching from afar to tourists. Subsistence farming, hunting and fishing, occasional jobs in towns not brimful of employment opportunities—those are hardly the ingredients of a comfortably affluent life. A number of Appalachian mountaineers have told my sons and me not only how hard and long they struggle, just to get by, or how little they can take for granted, but also how ironic they find life: their daily difficulties on the one hand and on the other the tourists who come through, staring at hills and valleys, camping near streams, full of enthusiasm for stretches of woods and pathways and waterfalls and flora and fauna. "I wish we could take it all in, the way they do," a resident of a Mingo County, West Virginia, hollow told me. He was trying strenuously to keep himself under control—to restrain his resentments and envies—but he could not quite manage to do so: "I'd try to behave myself, if I went into *their* places. If I did stare and take pictures and roar my car's motor and use the horn all the time and ask silly, silly questions, I'd at least try to remember to say please, say thank you, say I'm sorry to bother you. I'd ask if there isn't some help I can be, after being given some help myself. I wish some visitors would show that they love the mountains, instead of being so greedy about them."

What does he mean by that last comment? Is it a somewhat nasty rebuke of litterbugs, of pesky tourists? Is it a more portentous bit of social criticism of the demanding, self-centered, presumptuous nature of so many well-to-do travelers, who hungrily devour with their peripatetic movement all they can lay their hands on? (Or should one say, their feet?) Or is it a cry of self-defense on the part of someone genuinely afraid that a particular region will lose its own sovereignty and integrity if it becomes nothing but an "attraction" for hikers or people shuttling between the North and the South, the East and the West, and anxious, on the way, to get a bit of a bonus? Maybe it is all those—or maybe none. Many mountain people in Kentucky or North Carolina or West Virginia are genuinely glad, even flattered, that their fellow citizens should be taking such obvious interest in a rather spectacular and historically significant part of the United States. They also recognize that they need tourism, a major source of income, even if the cost is some hassles: the awkwardness of dealing with intruders and, even worse, the evidence of their more than occasional thoughtlessness, carelessness, and selfishness that almost invariably comes in the wake of their departure.

I rather suspect a youth of fourteen told my own son what really troubles many of our so-called Southern highlanders as they contemplate not only the present but also the immediate or long-term future: "You're lucky; you have a home, and you can stay there, and you don't have to show it off to people. I don't think we'd mind the showing off, though, but for the fact we think, even so, we'll have to depart these mountains. There's no living here for all of us. My daddy says we'll soon be saying goodbye to the mountains. We'll try Ohio. We'll try a city. We'll save. We'll hope to come back; surely we will. We'll be sad, I know, but we'll eat, my mother reminds us. And we can dream, she tells us; we can picture our hollow and the ridge of hills, and we can picture the clouds, and the lightning coming from them, aiming at a tree on the side of a hill, and the thunder going back and forth, booming from hill to hill. My grandparents won't leave, they'd sooner die. But we'll probably leave. I just hope we can come back and visit. Meanwhile, we can have our memories.

"But I wish we didn't have to go. I wish I could stay here all my life, and run with my dog, and carve my initials on every tree I take a fancy to, and do my target shooting and hunt and fish. In Ohio, when I grow up, I may be making lots of money, but it won't be no fun, and we won't be who we are. We're part of these mountains, and when we go, there's something that will die here—we'll die. We'll be someone else as soon as we leave. We'll be on our way to turning into people like the ones who come by, and they want to get 'a scenic view' before they go back to their graveyard lives. I guess we're headed in that direction, and no wonder I catch my momma and my daddy staring out at the mountains and fighting back the tears."

2. REMNANTS OF THE MOUNTAIN CROW IN MONTANA AND WYOMING

LAWRENCE L. LOENDORF

Among the Crow Indians of Montana, Henry Old Coyote is often a representative in matters that require a spokesman. In the early 1970s, Henry was filling such a role as an emissary from the Crow Indian tribe to the National Park Service, where he served as a liaison between the tribe and the Bighorn Canyon National Recreation Area.

It was my good fortune to get to know Henry during that time and to hear his stories about a multitude of things that usually included how the Crow Indians lived in the past and live in the present. With a group of students, I was completing an archaeological reconnaissance project in the Bighorn Mountains and Pryor Mountains on lands administered by the National Park Service, the Bureau of Land Management, the National Forest Service, and the Crow Indian tribe. Our task was to walk over the land, find the remnants of former Indian campsites or other evidence of past activities, and record these locations in order to aid planning efforts. Henry Old Coyote helped us tremendously in our task. He knew the land well, and in his evening visits to our field camp he would ask about our plans for the next day. He would then tell us to watch for a certain location where he knew of a former site. If he did not know any specific locations, he offered other clues, such as telling us the landscape would have once been a good area for bison and to watch for evidence of former hunting sites.

On many occasions Henry came with us to show us site locations; on fewer occasions he came with us to see a site that was unknown to him. On one of these latter expeditions, near the end of the field season, we were showing a group of federal land managers the sites found during the summer. Henry was along, but he was clearly staying out of the explanation for each particular site as we visited it.

We stopped on the side of East Pryor Mountain at a long, linear ridge confined by two canyons. Named Commissary Ridge, it terminates abruptly at its western end in the junction of the canyons. Overall, Commissary Ridge is about three miles (five kilometers) long with a vertical elevation of about seven thousand feet (twenty-one hundred meters). The sloping ridge is only about a quarter of a mile wide at its upper end, and it constricts between the two canyons to a few hundred feet in width at its lower terminus. The canyons are sheer-sided, with drops of several hundred feet to their bottoms, and the lower end of Commissary Ridge is actually a peninsula of broken limestone cliffs that ends in a sheer canyon drop. A bison skull was found on this constricted point. Excavation revealed the remnants of seven bison that had been killed and butchered by hunters from a Stone Age culture.

I stood at the site of the kill explaining to the federal managers what was believed to have happened. The hunters likely first saw the bison on the upper end of the ridge where there are open meadows for grazing. Knowing they could trap the animals on the lower end of the ridge, the hunters probably first checked the direction of the wind. Bison, which have poor eyesight but a keen sense of smell, will bunch together and move into the wind when they are frightened. Possibly it was mid-morning, when the warmer air from the lowlands makes its daily transfer to the cooler mountains by flowing upslope, and the rising sun had just cleared the main mountain to blind the bison as they looked back at the hunters.

Probably the hunters moved the bison slowly down the ridge, since any stampede would have forced the animals over the precipitous canyon sides. Finally, having trapped the bison at the end of the ridge and having blocked their retreat, the hunters had killed them from a small patch of trees that offered both vantage and protection. The six small triangular stone arrow points recovered in the excavation were a style believed to have been made by former Crow Indians. Since there were no iron arrow points or other evidence of contact with Euro-American peoples, and since the style was dated in other sites, the kill likely took place about A.D. 1700.

The assembled group of managers was genuinely interested in the reconstruction of the kill. Several asked questions about the arrow points or the butchered remnants of bones. Henry asked if he might say a few words. What followed was an extremely eloquent presentation delivered by an orator who showed a total understanding of the land and its components. He talked as if he were a weaver who strung his loom with biophysical warp threads while weaving his story in a cultural weft.

He first suggested that our explanation of the kill was quite correct, but there was more. He impressed upon us that we were on a mountain ridge made up of limestone bedrock with a soil covering that grew trees and grasses. The constricting ridge between the canyons was the perfect place to trap bison. This knowledge was important to the ancient hunters, but it was more important to realize that these mountains included the livelihood of the Crow Indians. He pointed out that he did not know how this ridge got its name, but it was appropriate because this ridge and these mountains were the commissary to the Crow. Bison were an important staple in that commissary, but there were many, many more products, living and nonliving, that were part of the Crow commissary.

Within a radius of a few feet, Henry identified the plants that were edible, those that had medicinal use, and those that had other uses, such as the straight pines for tipi poles. He identified a reddish clay ochre used for paint and a piece of purple-colored chert as the crystalline material used to make stone tools. He wove together the inorganic and organic parts of the mountains while constantly reminding us that this was the commissary, the storehouse of life to the Crow Indians. He finished by telling us that we must remember the Crow were but the veneer or the finish to the story. Countless generations had lived in these mountains before the Crow—peoples who also earned their livelihood from these mountains. He spoke for no more than ten minutes, but when he finished we all had gained a small part of his reverence for mountains.

Henry Old Coyote's description should not have been surprising, since various Crow Indians had been saying the same things for generations. Arapooish, a Crow chief in the early 1800s, explained that the Great Spirit put Crow country in the right place:

> The Crow country is exactly in the right place. It has snowy mountains and sunny plains; all kinds of climates and good things for every season. When the summer heats scorch the prairies, you can draw up under the mountains, where the air is sweet and cool, the grass fresh, and bright streams come tumbling out of the·snow-banks. There you can hunt the elk, the deer, and the antelope, when their skins are fit for dressing; there you will find plenty of white bears and mountain sheep.
>
> In the autumn, when your horses are fat and strong from the mountain pastures, you can go down into the plains and hunt the buffalo, or trap beaver on the streams. And when winter comes on, you can take shelter in the woody bottoms along the rivers. . . .
>
> The Crow country is exactly in the right place. Everything good is to be found there. There is no country like the Crow country. [Irving 1961: 165].

Several hundred archaeological sites were found and recorded during the research project in the Pryor Mountains. Most of those sites were former living areas. After the sites were compared and analyzed, it was learned they fit a pattern that showed the occupational use of the area. This use pattern was one of transhumance in which the former occupants moved up and down the mountain slopes according to a seasonal cycle that was nearly a precise replica of the seasonal use described by Arapooish. This match between an oral description and an archaeological model may reflect the geographical advantages of mountainous terrain for hunters and gatherers.

Mountains are excellent places for hunting and gathering cultures. Different elevations on the mountainsides create diverse ecological zones for a great variety of flora and fauna within a relatively small area. Hunters and gatherers can take advantage of the various ecological zones by searching for food in the areas where it is most abundant. When a particular resource fails, hunters and gatherers simply divert their efforts to secondary or tertiary resources. If the buffalo berries are infested with insects, the gatherers will put more emphasis on another collectable such as chokecherries. If it gets hot and dry, the gatherers will move upslope to cooler and more moist places where they can collect edible species at, for example, eight thousand feet (twenty-four hundred meters) in August that were available at five thousand feet (fifteen hundred meters) in May or June.

Mountains also offer hunters concealment and vantage, two features that are much more difficult to find on open plains. The mountain topography allows for combinations of trapping or impounding of herds of animals, yet at the same time a solitary hunter can lie in wait for animals along a trail.

The seasonal use of the area related by Arapooish may simply reflect a worldwide phenomenon. Nevertheless, it is an example of an oral description of a cycle of use that was verified by archaeological research.

For the most part, historians and archaeologists have not put much faith in oral description or oral traditions. Too frequently when written facts are compared with oral facts about past events, the written data are far more accurate. Perhaps this has led scholars to distrust all oral traditions or to consider them interesting but not to try to verify them.

In many ways archaeologists have greater opportunities to verify oral traditions than do scholars in other areas. Excavation of archaeological sites reveals what is termed "real culture," or that which a group of people really did, instead of "ideal culture," which is what a group of people said they did.

Some groups of American Indians may have kept more accurate oral traditions than others. Some appear to have used mnemonic devices such as pictographic records to aid the storyteller. In any case, it seems that the Crow Indians are extremely good at remembering unwritten facts. They may recount general information such as the seasonal use cycle or specific facts about a particular event.

For example, the Crow today remember a battle with the Piegan that took place about A.D. 1830. This battle was in the Grapevine drainage to the east of the Pryor Mountains. The Piegan, who were trespassing in Crow territory, retreated to the top of a low hill when they were discovered and built a series of rock walls or fortifications for protection. In the battle, the Crow killed fifty-eight Piegan. The Crow of today remember the details of the battle, including the names of some who participated.

On the spot where the Crow say the battle took place it is still possible to find the rock walls built by the Piegan. On a low hill there are twenty-three rock fortifications, meaning that more than one Piegan was protected by each structure. The oral tradition of the Crow is accurate, suggesting that oral history may be of more value to archaeologists than previously credited. One might argue that modern Crow found the fortification site and then fabricated the story about the battle or fit an oral tradition about a battle to the spot. However, it is possible to independently verify the story from several Crow Indians.

Although this site has not been excavated, more than likely artifacts will be found there that will confirm the story. In any case it would be foolish for an archaeologist to undertake excavation of the site without giving full consideration to the oral explanation for it.

Many times the oral traditions of the Crow contain place names that identify a particular location important in the story. The Grapevine Creek drainage is known as the "Place Where Men Pack Meat." As explained by Joe Medicine Crow, the Crow tribal historian, that area was used intensively for communal bison hunting. Today there are no fewer than a dozen bison drives or buffalo jumps found in the area. These communal hunting systems have complex drive lines constructed of piles of rocks that terminate at the edges of canyon walls. In these hunts the bison were stampeded through the drive lines and over the canyon walls to their death. The name "Place Where Men Pack Meat" is descriptive of the archaeological remains and an example of a verifiable oral tradition.

Another example of a place for which oral tradition has been used to explain archaeological remains is "Where They Saw the Rope," located near the top of East Pryor Mountain in the area known by Euro-

Americans as the Dryhead Overlook. Stuart Conner (1982:106) has recorded the story:

> Once when a band of Crow Indians was camped on upper Dry Head Creek between the Pryor Mountains and Big Horn Canyon, they were able to look high up at the rim of East Pryor Mountain and see the ropes with which a faster was dragging a buffalo skull. The ropes were attached to skewers stuck through the faster's back muscles, or chest muscles by some accounts. Because the line of sight distance is 5.5 km or more, modern Crow Indians believe it doubtful that the faster himself was visible from the Crow village, but they assume that the ropes had shone in the late afternoon sun. One oral account indicates that the ropes were pelts, and might even have been bloody when they glistened in the sun light.

On that spot one finds the remains of ten or more vision quest structures. Although none of these structures was likely built by the person described in "Where They Saw the Rope," they are the remains of fasting beds, and they are best explained through the oral tradition. Rock structures on many western mountains may be the remains of such fasting beds.

Vision quest structures are usually constructed of stones piled to form low rock walls in ovals, rectangles, or U shapes. The rock walls are usually about two or three feet (sixty to ninety centimeters) in height, and each structure is seldom more than six to ten feet (two to three meters) across its maximum horizontal distance. The person seeking a vision fasted for several days, sometimes inducing pain, as by dragging a bison skull, in order to receive a visit from a guardian spirit. This spirit instructed the person in ways to be successful in life.

One of the most fascinating prehistoric mountain structures in North America is located near the top of Medicine Mountain in the Bighorn Mountains of Wyoming. This large rock feature, called the Medicine Wheel, was discovered by EuroAmericans in the 1880s, and the identity of its builders and its purpose have been debated by dozens of authors.

The Medicine Wheel is an outline of piled stones with a circular shape, seventy feet (twenty-one meters) in diameter, flattened on one side. This outline has twenty-eight spokes, also made of stones, that radiate from a central cairn of stones. To early discoverers it most resembled a wheel, and since they could not learn its use, they suggested it must be the result of Indian medicine or the supernatural. Its early name, the Medicine Wheel, continues to be used, although it likely was not intended to represent a wheel. There is little reason that anyone who used wheeled vehicles should have built such a massive structure before it was discovered.

In addition to the central cairn, the Medicine Wheel

Mandan sacred lodge. Photo by G. L. Wilson. Courtesy Department of Library Services, American Museum of Natural History, neg. #286505.

has six other rock structures, five of them arranged at various points on the outer rim of the wheel. The sixth structure is offset and attached to the outside of the rim by a short row of rocks. Detailed descriptions of the wheel are found in works by Don Grey (1963) and Michael Wilson (1981), both of whom undertook archaeological excavations at the wheel and made detailed maps.

Explanations for the Medicine Wheel vary from the ridiculous to the creditable. One of the ridiculous suggests that it has an ancient Celtic origin, while creditable authors believe it to be the work of American Indians, but with no assurance about which tribal group built it or when it was constructed. The Medicine Wheel became the subject of recent debate in 1974 when John Eddy suggested that the central cairn and the structure slightly off the main circle align with the rising sun at the summer solstice. Eddy also suggests several other alignments between cairns and rising stars, but none as compelling as the solstice alignment, since it is found on other rock features elsewhere in North America.

Eddy's suggestions that the Medicine Wheel was used as a calendar or an indicator of the summer solstice is not believed by many anthropologists, who argue that hunting peoples do not keep calendars or practice calendrical ritual. Hunters may refer to seasons in general terms, but not with the accuracy of a certain day in every year. Hunters use ritual or magic as the need arises, and their ceremonies do not occur on the same day each year. These same anthropologists agree that gardeners or peoples who live in sedentary permanent locations can practice calendrical ritual or ceremony, but no known group of people who inhab-

ited the Bighorn Mountains in prehistoric times maintained a sedentary life-style. All who lived there were nomadic, and as such all would have practiced non-calendrical ritual.

Michael Wilson (1981) presents a compilation of all the previous explanations for the Medicine Wheel as well as several new ideas. One well-reasoned hypothesis by Wilson is that the structure may have been related to the Sun Dance, which was important to the Plains Indians as a dance to bring summer rains to replenish the grasses that fed the bison herds.

Most prehistorians would agree that since its original construction the Bighorn wheel has been used for other purposes. The most apparent secondary use is as a vision quest area, and probably some of the cairn structures in the outer circle of the wheel have been altered to suit individuals seeking their guardian spirits. Some of the cairns may have been built specifically as fasting beds and not as part of the original plan. The tribal group most likely to have used the Medicine Wheel for vision quests is the Crow, who told Robert

Prehistoric medicine wheel on Medicine Mountain, Wyoming. Photo by Ron Mamot.

Lowie (1922:436): "Many of the Crow would go there to fast; the structure has been there as long back as any period alluded to by previous generations. Those who fasted there would sometimes hear steps of some one walking, but looking up would see nothing."

Wilson presents other examples of Crow use of the wheel for vision quests, but none that explain its original construction. In fact most explanations for the wheel do not consider the Crow to be its original builders. This exclusion is based on an early description by S. C. Simms, an anthropologist working among the Crow in 1902 for the Field Museum of Chicago. Simms (1903:107) wrote:

> I was told of the existence of what my informant termed a "medicine wheel" on the summit of a mountain which he called "Medicine mountain," situated just across the Montana-Wyoming boundary line, in the Big Horn range of mountains in the latter state.
>
> Although I made many inquiries of the old men of the Crow tribe regarding the "medicine wheel" and its significance, I found not one who had ever visited it. A few of them had heard of it through their fathers, but they could tell me nothing whatever of it excepting that "it was made by people who had no iron."

Important issues in the use of Simms's account, however, are how, and whom, Simms asked about the wheel. If he asked an older Crow to guide him to the medicine structure, he may have been turned down because of the difficulty of the trip. River Crow were more common in Crow Agency, where Simms was asking about the wheel, and they may not have known its location or its importance because of their later arrival in the mountains. The Mountain Crow may have known more about the wheel, but by 1902 even they may have lost knowledge of its original significance if it was built by "people who had no iron."

Simms did find a guide to the structure, a white trapper named Silvertip. They made a sketch map of the structure and reported a bleached bison skull placed facing the east on the central cairn.

Most explanations for the Medicine Wheel ignore a series of important facts that include the oral traditions of the Crow Indians and their early migration to the mountains. There is considerable debate among ethnohistorians, prehistorians, and linguists about when the Crow Indians first moved to the mountains. It is known that the Crow originally lived with the Hidatsa in large villages along the Missouri River in North Dakota. They grew corn, beans, sunflowers, and squash in garden plots near the river and supplemented these products with meat obtained in hunting. At some point in prehistory the Crow decided to abandon gardening and become full-time hunters.

At the time of Euro-American contact the Crow were in the west and divided into two main groups: the Mountain Crow and the River Crow. Several explanations for the division of the River Crow and the Mountain Crow differ about when and where the split took place. Alfred Bowers recorded the division as described in the oral traditions of the Hidatsa and their nearest neighbors, the Mandan. He explains that there were three separate groups of Hidatsa: the Awatixa, the Awaxawi, and the Hidatsa proper. The Awatixa had the longest tenure of residence on the Missouri River and a close association with the Mandan. The Mountain Crow divided from the Awatixa, and the River Crow divided from the Hidatsa proper. The exact times of the two divisions are unknown, but the Mountain Crow separated about two centuries before the River Crow. Both groups were living permanently in the west when Lewis and Clark traveled the Missouri River in 1804, but the River Crow made frequent return visits to trade with their sedentary relatives.

The Mountain Crow may have moved in the 1500s, when there appears to have been increased moisture, better pasturage, and larger herds of grazing animals in the areas west of the Missouri River. The improved hunting conditions might explain the move of the Mountain Crow into territory that traditionally belonged to Shoshonean groups—a region with sufficient territory and resources for both the Shoshoni and the Mountain Crow.

When the Crow left the Missouri River, it must have been difficult to leave behind their ceremonies. It was likely more difficult for the Mountain Crow than the River Crow, because the Mountain Crow left at a time when ceremonies were totally intact. In addition, the Mountain Crow divided from the Awatixa, who were more sedentary than other groups of Hidatsa and therefore more involved in calendrical ritual and ceremony. The importance of calendrical ritual can hardly be overestimated when discussing the Mandan and Hidatsa. George Catlin (1967:39), who described the important Okeepa ceremony of the Mandan, says that they attributed to it "not only their enjoyment in life, but their very existence; for traditions . . . instructed them in the belief that the singular forms of this ceremony produced the buffaloes for their supply of food, and that omission of this annual ceremony . . . would bring upon them a repetition of the calamity which their traditions say once befell them, destroying the whole human race, excepting one man. . . ."

The ceremonies practiced by the Awatixa were greatly influenced by Mandan ceremonies. In both there were elaborate rituals associated with sacred bundles, which contained objects that were unwrapped and used in the important ceremonies. Ownership of the principal bundles among the Awatixa was hereditary through either the matrilineage or a father's matrilineage.

The division of the Mountain Crow from the Awatixa probably included considerable debate about the ownership of the principal bundles. Since all of the important bundles had been received through visions and interchange with supernatural beings, it was not possible simply to create duplicates. Probably the resident Awatixa retained ownership of most if not all the important bundles, so the Mountain Crow were without much of the material aspects of their religion when they moved west to the mountains. Anytime a bison hunt failed or there was a dry year, one can imagine the conservative members of the Mountain Crow lamenting the lack of sacred bundles.

At such a time the Bighorn medicine structure may have had considerable significance. It may have been a calendrical feature through which the Mountain Crow practiced some of the scheduled ceremonies from their days on the Missouri River. This explanation for a calendrical use of the Medicine Wheel is believable, because the Mountain Crow were using scheduled ritual before their move, and just as they retained their system of clans, they probably kept some of their calendrical ritual. Some ceremonies were left behind, but those that were needed, the ones directed toward improving the herds of animals, were likely kept.

The Bighorn medicine structure may have been a calendrical reminder of when ceremonies were being held on the Missouri River, but a better explanation is that it served as the site of an actual ceremony. Any of the three or four ceremonies practiced in A.D. 1850 by the Hidatsa are possible candidates. These ceremonies have long histories, as Alfred Bowers has demonstrated by combining oral traditions with archaeological research. The most logical series of ceremonies that might have been practiced at the Medicine Wheel are those for Buffalo Calling or those of the Old-Woman-Who-Never-Dies. The Buffalo Calling series is associated with improving the herds and seems to be a logical possibility because the Mountain Crow had given up gardening to depend wholly on hunting. The Old-Woman-Who-Never-Dies ceremonies seem possible because the Crow retained considerable folklore about the Old-Woman-Who-Never-Dies. The ceremony is also appropriate because it was associated with world renewal. As stated by Bowers (1965:338):

> The myth of Old-Woman-Who-Never-Dies provided the basis for native beliefs and practices for the propagation of the cultivated crops and she was considered the "goddess" of all vegetation. It was probably with this latter belief that she was associated by non-agricultural groups in the area such as the Crow and Cheyenne. The Hidatsa thought of her as the custodian of all vegetation that ripens or sheds it leaves in the fall and is "rejuvenated" in the spring with the northern flights of the waterbirds which she accompanied. She was equally regarded as the "producer" of wild fruit crops. . . .

In these ceremonies there is interchange between various characters and the Sun, the Moon, and several stars, who are intermarried or linked in some way.

The Bighorn medicine structure may be the plan for a ceremonial lodge and represent an actual ceremonial earth lodge as was used on the Missouri River. Ethnohistorical data regarding the orientation of the large ceremonial lodges of the Mandan and Hidatsa are lacking. However, the downriver tribes that lived in earth lodges, the Arikara and the Skidi Pawnee, erected structures according to a plan that was oriented to the sun and the stars. Melvin Gilmore (1930) describes the Arikara sacred lodge as a community structure erected for ceremonies. This earth-covered circular structure had its door to the east so that the rising sun could shine into it to illuminate a bison skull on a sacred altar. The support posts for the domed roof were equated with various aspects of Arikara cosmology.

The Skidi Pawnee have an even more elaborate cosmology. Von Del Chamberlain has shown that all Skidi earth lodges, those for living and those for ceremony, were oriented completely to the sun and the stars. The Skidi lodge was a replica of their universe. As explained by Chamberlain (1982:162) the "earth lodge contained features that reminded those dwelling there of the following sky-related objects and phenomena: the earth and horizon; important direction, especially the cardinal and semi-cardinal directions, and the zenith; the sky itself, life-sustaining weather phenomena; the sun; day and night; and the stars and planets, especially the Evening Star, Morning Star, four world-quarter stars, and Council of Chiefs." The Council of Chiefs was a Pawnee constellation represented by Corona Borealis, a circular series of stars that symbolized the zenith of the lodge and the zenith of the sky.

Although there are no ethnographic data for the cosmological orientation of Mandan ceremonial lodges, some archaeological data suggest they had fixed orientations. Several large village sites along the Missouri River in North Dakota that were once occupied by the Mandan typically have the remains of seventy to one hundred living houses and one large ceremonial lodge. The Huff site, for example, on the west bank of the Missouri River south of Mandan,

North Dakota, contains the remains of more than one hundred rectangular houses with a single large ceremonial lodge. This ceremonial structure was oriented with its door to the southwest. A series of central posts held the roof atop the structure, and these posts appear to have been oriented with the summer solstice. Emery Meher (1980) believes the rising sun may have come up directly over the ridge line of the roof on the morning of summer solstice.

The rectangular ceremonial lodge at the Huff site does not resemble the outline of the Medicine Wheel, but the shape of the ceremonial structure changed, as described by W. Raymond Wood (1967 : 156): "The form of the ceremonial lodge itself was changed after about A.D. 1500. As late as Huff it was a long-rectangular structure resembling the common dwelling type but of larger dimensions. In the historic sites at the Knife River it was a circular lodge distinguished by a flat front—a seeming retention of the front and entry of the older religious structure." The floor plan for a circular lodge with a flat front would have resembled the Bighorn Medicine Wheel, with its flat side, almost exactly. The orientation of the flat side on the southwest of the wheel is the same as that of the ceremonial lodge. The offset cairn structure connected to the outside of the wheel is in the position where the ceremonial lodge had an extended doorway entry. The radiating rock lines in the wheel are in the same positions as the rafters of the ceremonial lodge, and the central circular cairn is at the location of the lodge's smokehole. The bison skull found by Simms in the Medicine Wheel was found on the altar in every ceremonial lodge on the Missouri River. In essence, the Bighorn Medicine Wheel is a precise replica of the floor of the semiround ceremonial lodge on the Missouri River.

These comparisons to a Mandan ceremonial lodge still do not explain why such a replica would exist several hundred miles west in the Bighorn Mountains. The most logical explanation is that it was built by the Mountain Crow after they moved to the west. As stated above, the Awatixa from whom the Mountain Crow divided were closely associated with the Mandan and likely used a similar floor plan for their ceremonial lodge. Bowers (1965 : 21) writes that a few Mandan families actually moved with the Awatixa to become the Mountain Crow.

Another earth lodge site on the Missouri River that may be related to the Medicine Wheel is Grandmother's Lodge. This site, now inundated by Garrison Reservoir, was originally in Mercer County, North Dakota, on the south bank of the river. Archaeological investigations at the site were reported by Alan Woolworth (1956). The site consisted of the remains of one

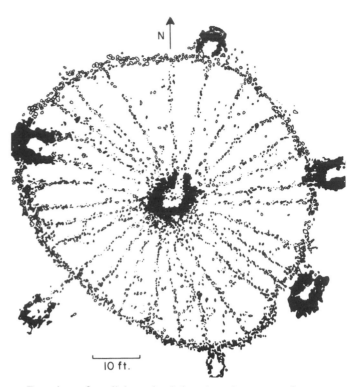

Drawing of medicine wheel showing placement of stones.

lodge believed by the Hidatsa and Mandan to be the former home of the Old-Woman-Who-Never-Dies, or Grandmother. The floor plan of the lodge is rectangular with a southwestern entrance and a roof ridge line that may have been oriented with the rising sun at the summer solstice.

The most interesting fact about Grandmother's Lodge is that it was highly revered by the Crow Indians. The Crow never failed to visit the site on return trips to the Missouri River to leave offerings for the Old-Woman-Who-Never-Dies. They followed this practice from the 1830s until 1952, shortly before the site was inundated.

It is clear that the Crow did not consider the Medicine Wheel to be the remains of another lodge of Old-Woman-Who-Never-Dies. If they had known it as such, they would have told the early ethnologists about the association. Instead they told the ethnologists that it was the home of the sun. Robert Lowie writes (1922 : 436), "According to Flat-dog this monument was regarded as the sun's lodge, i.e., as a lodge made for the Sun and used by him as a camping place." It does not seem unreasonable to believe that a ceremonial lodge among the Crow was the legendary home of the Sun. The Sun plays a prominent role in many of their stories, but most appropriate to this discussion are the series of Old-Woman-Who-Never-Dies legends.

In those stories the son of the Sun comes to earth by

running away with his mother, the wife of the Sun. The Sun discovers the two escaping the heavens on a rope and throws down a rock that kills his wife. The son, on earth with neither mother nor father, is raised by the Old-Woman-Who-Never-Dies. In his life he engages in many heroic feats in which his father the Sun usually helps. The Crow believe the son finally returned for all time to the sky, where he is represented by a star. The identity of the star varies from legend to legend. Perhaps it is one that John Eddy has charted in the Medicine Wheel.

One other Crow legend deserves mention because it has an association with the Medicine Wheel. That legend, about Scarface or Burntface, is a story about a young and handsome man who fell into a fire and destroyed his beauty with an ugly burn scar. He was so embarrassed by his appearance that he moved to seclusion in the mountains. There he met the Sun and undertook various deeds at the suggestion of the Sun. In the end, Burntface was cured by the Sun and returned to a happy life. In the version of the story told today, Burntface was instructed by the Sun to build a medicine wheel. The one he built was a much smaller structure near Fort Smith, Montana, about one hundred miles north of the one on Medicine Mountain. Other versions vary, but most contain the Sun and Burntface's interchange with the Sun to cure his deformity. The legends are compatible with the Medicine Wheel as symbolic home of the Sun.

Several dozen explanations have been offered by various authors for the Medicine Wheel. Most of these authors should have used a bit of practical sense. If the Crow Indians have oral traditions that say the Medicine Wheel is the home of the Sun, than we should believe they mean what they say. Other oral traditions are substantiated, and it appears this one is also. When the Mountain Crow moved to the west, they left behind a tradition for ceremonial lodges oriented to the solstice and symbolic homes for various persons in their mythology. It is not surprising that they took their ideology with them and constructed a replica of a ceremonial lodge when they reached their new home.

3. SACRED MOUNTAINS IN NATIVE AMERICA: THE FOUR CORNERS

DANIEL FELDMAN

Utah homestead. Photo by M. Tobias.

Historical and ethnographic analyses show that throughout the world, people with land-based economies who live in the mountains tend to develop an intimate relationship with those mountains. Prominent landmarks breed familiarity and a sense of place and eventually become incorporated into the oral history of a society as important elements of its cosmology. The people's dependence on the immediate topography for survival fosters respect for that land and its ecological cycles, particularly the water cycle. It becomes obvious to such people that the mountains play a crucial role in this cycle. During the winter, moisture is stored in mountain snowfields, and the rains always seem to originate in the heights. Because of these observa-

tions, the people may include mountain spirits in their magico-religious beliefs. In short, the mountains become sacred.

Today, respect for the land, the mountains, and their sanctity is being subverted by a desire for the mineral wealth they contain. Energy resources are in high demand, and powerful corporations are scurrying to recover them wherever it is economically feasible. In North America, much of those resources are on lands belonging to Indian nations. And in many cases those resources lie beneath spots that are sacred. In some places, such as the Black Hills, the land is no longer controlled by the Indians, in this case the Lakota, but still remains sacred to them.[1] Of all such regions, probably the most intensely exploited one is the Four Corners.

The Four Corners is home to several Indian nations, the most prominent of which are the Dine (Navajo), the Hopi, and the Pueblo. Within these nations are many Indians who are carrying on the traditional culture of their people. Naturally they are at odds with the "progressive" politicians on their tribal councils who favor the development of energy resources. For the traditionals, such development means relocation, disruption of subsistence patterns, and the desecration of their sacred shrines. For those who face relocation to urban areas, it is a fate akin to death. Many consider the hardship such development brings to be cultural genocide. In the context of the traditional Indian system of beliefs, the act of mining is simply inconceivable. To see it being done on such a massive scale is to witness an unprecedented and irreversible atrocity.

In comparison, consider the sacred places of Judeo-Christian tradition: Jerusalem (Mount Zion), Mount Sinai, and the many other holy mountains mentioned in the Bible. Imagine a dragline with a bucket thirty feet wide ripping through one of those shrines. Even for the nonreligious, an act of such profanity is, I'm sure, unthinkable.

THE LAND

To some, the Four Corners is little more than a desert. To a people such as the Hopi, it is their home, the one they have inhabited for more than a thousand years. It is a land of indescribable beauty that attracts thousands of visitors every year.

Geologically, the region is a plateau. Shaped like a dinner plate, it is rimmed with snowy peaks. Within it are innumerable high mesas, deep canyons, buttes, arroyos, and pinnacles that cast eerie shadows in the evening light. Because vegetation is so sparse, little impedes one's view. The horizon is often dominated by mountains of sandstone with banded cliffs towering a thousand feet or more above the desert floor. Volcanic necks, such as Shiprock (also a sacred place), rise like ghostly cities partially buried in the shifting sands. The escarpments are fossils of time reflecting eons of changing environments. They are the petrified remains of a landscape preserved by the encroachment of a warm, inland sea and subsequently revealed by erosion.

From another vantage point, the Four Corners assumes an entirely new identity. Satellite photographs of Sacred Black Mesa in Arizona reveal the dark scar of an enormous coal strip mine. Nearby, a telltale plume of smoke reveals the Four Corners Power Plant, where that coal is burned.[2] At Laguna Pueblo in New Mexico

is Anaconda Corporation's Jackpile Mine, the largest uranium strip mine in the world. Now inactive, it remains a moonscape of terraces five miles long. Radioactive tailings (a byproduct of uranium milling), remain too, either as "cheap fill" for reservation housing construction or to blow in the wind and seep into the ground. This is what the traditionals and elders mean when they speak of the rape of "sacred Mother Earth."

A BRIEF HISTORY

The first contact between the Indian people of the Four Corners and Europeans was in the first part of the sixteenth century. Before that both the Dine and the Pueblo had lived in the same area for more than a thousand years. In the case of the Pueblo, archaeological evidence confirms their ancestors' occupation of the region as early as 10,000 B.C.[3]

In 1540, Francisco Vásquez de Coronado arrived in the land that is now New Mexico. His two-year stay and mistreatment of the Indian population set the stage for the first period of Spanish domination of the region. By the seventeenth century the Pueblo had been colonized. Atrocities committed under Spanish rule were so severe that in 1680 the Pueblo revolted and drove the Spanish out. The effects of colonization were already devastating. More than half the Pueblo population had died as a result of disease or violence, and seventeen hundred Pueblo villages had disappeared.[4]

In 1696, led by Don Diego de Vargas, the Spanish reconquered the Pueblo. Their rule was again severe. However, much to the frustration of the missionary friars, the Pueblo refused to convert. Eventually, with the decline of Spanish power, the Pueblo reestablished most of their own religious rituals.

After more than a century of Spanish rule, New Mexico became part of the Republic of Mexico in 1821. Then in 1848, by the Treaty of Guadalupe Hidalgo, Mexico ceded that territory to the United States. At the same time, the destruction of the Dine became a prime objective of the U.S. military.

Before that time, the Dine had lived outside the control of Spanish and Mexican authorities. The only contact they had was skirmishes and reprisal raids.[5] The Americans were eager to quash such militant Indian resistance, so in 1863 Kit Carson was dispatched with specific orders to destroy all Dine crops and livestock. These scorched-earth tactics were effective; by early 1864 the Dine had begun to surrender.

What followed was the bleakest episode in Dine history and one of the most shameful acts of the U.S. government. Eight thousand Dine, young and old, sick and maimed, were forcibly marched 180 miles to Fort

Sumner. Those that survived the Long Walk remained imprisoned there for four years. In 1870, those who could returned to the portion of their home that was given back and began the struggle of rebuilding their lives.

Today the Navajo reservation covers 16,000,000 acres (6,500,000 hectares), still but a fraction of their original territory. The seventeen Pueblo villages control an additional 1,492,197 acres (604,128 hectares).[6] Beneath the land, joining these people together like an underground chain, is the Grants mineral belt. And within the belt are vast deposits of coal and uranium worth millions of dollars.

DEPENDENCE ON THE LAND

Both the Dine and the Pueblo have an ongoing tradition of dependence on the land for their subsistence. In the arid Southwest only specifically adapted plants and animals can be grown without irrigation. With their long history in the area, the Pueblo developed a method known as dry farming in order to survive. By combining these techniques with specially evolved varieties of melons, beans, squash, and maize, they produced surplus crops under conditions described as being "more rigorous than those found in the dust bowl."[7]

The basis of Pueblo agriculture is, nevertheless, the limited rainfall of the area. The preciousness of that moisture cannot be overstated. Nor can the fact that without the surrounding mountains, rain would be scarcer still. Recognizing this, Pueblo religion focuses on the mountains and mountain spirits as providers of moisture.

The Dine, in comparison, are relative newcomers to the area. It is believed that they augmented their hunting and gathering subsistence with agriculture learned from the Pueblo. Sometime between 1630 and 1700, with the advent of the Spanish, their acquisition of sheep and horses encouraged a gradual transition from sedentary farming, hunting, and gathering to a more mobile life of herding, traveling, and raiding. Farming was not entirely given up, though. When Kit Carson arrived in Canyon de Chelly, he found flourishing Dine peach orchards, which he promptly set ablaze.[8]

In the twentieth century the Dine experienced another major economic change as a result of the Indian Reorganization Act of 1934. Part of that bill required a reduction of Navajo stock to prevent overgrazing. Consequently, whole herds were lost and stock raising, the major source of Dine income, was replaced by government benefits and wage labor from energy development. As a result, large tracts of productive grazing land began to be opened up for mineral leasing. Political manipulations of this sort continue today in areas such as Big Mountain.

Statistics illustrate the dramatic effects of such policies. In 1940, stock raising accounted for 58.8 percent of the total Dine income. By 1955, that figure had shrunk to 9.9 percent. At the same time, social security, welfare, and railroad compensation payments increased from 0 percent to 16.2 percent of the total income.[9]

Throughout their history the Dine, like the Pueblo, recognized their dependence on the earth's precious moisture. Although they never developed a complex ritual calendar, they evolved numerous other ceremonies. Many of those ceremonies, still practiced today, emphasize the mountains as life givers and bringers of rain.

THE MOUNTAINS

In his study of sacred mountains throughout the land of the Old Testament, R. J. Clifford describes the "cosmic mountain": "a center of fertility, the primeval hillock of creation, the meeting place of the gods, the dwelling place of the high god, the meeting of heaven, hell and earth, the monument effectively upholding the order of creation, the place where man meets god, a place of theophany, and the battle ground of conflicting natural forces." In addition, a cosmic or sacred mountain usually defines the spiritual center of the world. Implicit in this notion is the metaphorical union of the three world levels along what is known as the axis mundi.[10]

Dine and Pueblo origin myths tell of their ancestors' migration through a series of successively higher underworlds. At each stage they committed some act of profanity and were beset by natural disasters such as floods and fire. They were then forced to ascend to the next stage, where they had to begin life anew. This ascension is analogous to a people progressively climbing the mountain of consciousness. It is a pattern of continual corruption, purging, and redemption or annihilation common to the mythologies of people throughout the world.

Part of the Dine origin myth describes their emergence into the present world. That tale also relates the history of the four sacred mountains, cornerstones of the Dine world view. These cardinally oriented peaks were already in place when the Dine arrived in the last underworld. Soon they became familiar landmarks, which, when sighted, signaled to the Dine that they were in their homeland. When, according to the myth, the First People arrived in the present world, they carried with them a pinch of soil from each of the four mountains. By planting that soil, the present mountains were made to grow.[11]

So significant are the four sacred mountains that they even figure in the great seal used by the Navajo tribal government. In the 1960 Indian land claims hearings, lawyers for the Dine argued that the four sacred peaks, as well as other sacred places, are evidence of their ancestral territorial boundaries. They have even been referred to by one Dine elder as the Navajo Nation's constitution.[12]

The four peaks are also of great significance as the basis of Dine religious ritual. In Blessingway, the most important of these ceremonies, earth from each of the four mountains is used to prepare the focal religious article, the Mountain Soil Bundle.

Navajo singers are the repositories of the ceremonial traditions handed down orally from generation to generation. According to contemporary Navajo singer Frank Mitchell, "Blessingway is used for everything that is good for the people. It has no other use than that."[13] All other Dine rites are designed with the purpose of curing a specific illness or ailment; Blessingway might be considered as general therapy. As such, it is said that Blessingway controls all the rest of the chantways.[14]

Sacred world quarter mountains also figure in the Pueblo world view as territorial markers. Each village may differ in its conception of just what those markers are. All do agree that they are cardinally oriented and that they are mountains and/or bodies of water. In the Tewa origin myth, the four mountains were discovered by four pairs of sibling dieties who had been forth to explore the world before the emergence of the rest of the people.[15]

THE MOUNTAIN SPIRITS

Almost by definition, sacred mountains are associated with gods or spirits. Mount Olympus and Mount Sinai are familiar examples of this relationship. The former is considered home to the pantheon of ancient Greek dieties, and the latter is famed for Moses's encounter there with the Judeo-Christian god, Jehova. Likewise, through oral tradition and ritual drama, the Dine and the Pueblo have invested their sacred mountains with the powers of living spirits.

During the summer months, Pueblo ceremonials and the prayers associated with them are directed toward the mountains and to the mountain spirits. Included in their ceremonies are the famous kachina dances of the Hopi. In the words of Frank Waters, "The kachinas are the inner forms, the spiritual components of the outer physical forms of life . . . not gods, but rather intermediaries, messengers. Hence their chief function is to bring rain, assuring the abundance of crops and the continuance of life."[16] The earthly home of the kachinas is considered to be the San Francisco Mountains.[17] Located on the western border of the Navajo reservation, these peaks are also sacred to the Dine as the cardinal mountains of that direction. Significantly, it is often the clouds forming above these peaks that first tell of an approaching storm. Thus they have earned their reputation as centers of fertility and the homes of the gods.

Mountains also play a crucial role in other aspects of Pueblo religion. By observing the position of the sun in relation to certain mountains, a priest, or cacique, as he is called, is able to determine the coming of the winter solstice. This marks the beginning of Soyal, a ceremony intended to strengthen and redirect the sun.[18]

In Dine religion, the concept of mountain spirits is slightly different from that of the Pueblo. According to the Dine, each mountain, as well as every other natural phenomenon, is imbued with an inner form or animating spirit. These spirits are also known as Holy Ones. It is the Holy Ones that are the object of the prayers and offerings of Blessingway and other Dine ceremonies. The Dine also associate figures represented in their mythology with particular mountains. The most notable of these figures is Changing Woman.

Changing Woman is the principal figure of Dine mythology. She is the embodiment of the earth, its seasonal variations, and its fecundity. She derives her name from the annual cycle she experiences, changing with the seasons from birth to youth to maturity and finally to death. She was born at the foot of Mountain Around Which Moving Was Done, also identified as Huerfano Mountain. It was Changing Woman who gave the Dine their first Mountain Soil Bundle. She is also credited as being the mother of Monster Slayer and Born of Water, the Dine culture heros. Their exploits are retold in the story called "Where the Two Came to Their Father," which further sanctifies many mountains in the Four Corners.[20]

Still another example of mountain sanctity on the basis of deification is illustrated by Tewa beliefs. Alfonso Ortiz says their cardinal mountains "are the source of knowledge and life sustaining blessings, the homes of the gods, definers and protectors of group space, dangerous for those uninitiated and unprepared, and finally, not subject to claims of dispute by any people!"[21] The Tewa mountain spirits are known as Dry Food Who Never Did Become. They include not only all the Tewa dieties, but also the spirits of the Made People, who were real people of high social and spiritual distinction. Like their Hopi and Dine counterparts, the Tewa mountain spirits are considered to be the harbingers of rainfall and game.[22]

PILGRIMAGE

Clearly, the traditional Dine and Pueblo owe much of their religious affirmation to their sacred mountains. They know that within those mountains is the germ of life waiting to burst over their heads in a peal of thunder and a flash of lightning only the gods could conceive. However, it is an assurance resting on the presumption that the people maintain a proper relationship with the spirit powers. When they do not, it is believed that good blessings will fail to descend upon the people and upon the land.

Retribution for improper actions may manifest itself as a severe drought resulting in parched earth and starving livestock. Occasionally, unsuspected cloudbursts flood the land with such alarming swiftness that an entire crop may be wiped out in seconds. For some, such acts of nature bring with them a fear that somewhere things are out of equilibrium. Perhaps a crime has been committed or a ritual desecrated. Whatever the cause of the imbalance, traditional belief says it must be corrected. Often this means a pilgrimage to the mountains must be undertaken.

In 1972, following a prolonged drought, the Navajo Mountain community held a ceremony atop Navajo Mountain. Naatsis aan, the Dine name for this sacred peak, means "Head of Earth Mother." Earth Mother is the Corn Pollen Range spoken of in Blessingway. The range itself represents a female figure of which Black Mesa is the body, the heart.

The pilgrimage involved most of the spiritual leaders of the area. Prayers were said and ritual objects were placed at the summit, just as they had been in previous times of need. One singer explained, "There used to be rain makers long ago. There were four men who were very good; when they were alive there was plenty of rain, but then they died. No more rain. Now there is no one who knows the proper way."[23] In that man's mind there was no doubt that the climatic repercussions being felt by his people were directly related to their loss of touch with a sacred mode of conduct.

The same feeling emerges in Leslie Marmon Silko's novel *Ceremony.* In her characterization of an Indian war veteran named Tayo, he returns from the jungles of Indochina, where he cursed the incessant rains, only to find his Laguna home suffering from drought. In an effort to reconstruct part of his cultural heritage, Tayo prepares to make a pilgrimage:

> He knew the holy men had their ways during the dry spells. People said they climbed the trails to the mountaintops to look west and southwest and to call the clouds and thunder. . . . he got up at dawn and rode the bay mare south to the spring in the narrow canyon. . . . He waited for the sun to come over the hills. . . . He had picked flowers along the path. . . . He shook the pollen from them gently and sprinkled it over the water; he laid the blossoms beside the pool and waited. . . . The things he did seemed right, as he imagined with his heart the rituals the cloud priests performed during a drought.[24]

Aside from being places to seek spiritual assistance, sacred mountains in the Four Corners are noted for other reasons. Special pilgrimages are routinely made to specific peaks in order to obtain certain herbs, minerals, and other ritual articles. For example, to gather the materials necessary for a Mountain Soil bundle requires up to three years of intermittent pilgrimage to various sacred places.[25] Some of the less well known of these shrines will fall prey to shovel and disappear. Others, like Mount Taylor, are already being disturbed.[26] Gulf Corporation is presently digging the shaft of a uranium mine into Mount Taylor, one of the four sacred peaks of the Dine. It is Gulf's largest investment and the deepest such mine in the world. Talk of reclamation in such cases is a fantasy. Sensitive ecosystems supporting rare life forms can never be recreated.

THE SACRED VS. THE PROFANE: CONFLICT IN THE FOUR CORNERS

Few Americans know what it is like to live in a national sacrifice area, as the Four Corners has been designated. Yet several controversies there have brought the plight of the traditional people to national and international attention. Probably the first major battle concerning the desecration of sacred land was the Blue Lake case.

Blue Lake sits atop Taos Peak, and together those landmarks are the spiritual center of the universe for the people of Taos Pueblo. Every year for centuries, the Taoseños ascended to this shrine, where they held their annual rite of renewal. Then in 1906 the U.S. government appropriated Blue Lake for inclusion in Carson National Forest in direct violation of the Treaty of Guadalupe Hidalgo, by which the United States was bound to respect the Taos peoples' property rights. It took sixty-five years of legal struggle before Blue Lake was returned to Taos Pueblo.[27]

A more recent battle is being waged over Black Mesa, sacred to the Dine and Hopi. Located in northern Arizona, Black Mesa covers hundreds of square miles. To the north it is inhabited by Dine, and on the smaller mesas to the south are located the Hopi villages. It has been described as "an island of forest and grass in the desert, last outpost of ancient cultures."[28]

In a sense, Black Mesa is a true oasis: drainages on its flanks direct water to Hopi and Dine farms, and water beneath its surface feeds desert springs.

Also underneath Black Mesa is coal. Between 1964 andf 1966, Peabody Coal Company signed leases that entitle it to mine 56,000 acres (22,672 hectares) of the mountain. Those leases were signed without consent of the majority of the Dine and Hopi under whose land that coal lies. But those people and their descendants will feel the impact of this project for generations.[29]

Probably the most serious environmental threats at Black Mesa concern water. Any water flowing through the mining debris carries in solution undetermined amounts of sulfuric acid and other contaminants. What these pollutants will do to nearby people, their livestock, and crops is, as yet, unknown. Water that does not flow into surface drainage will leach into the ground, where it may enter the water table and get into wells. The amount of water consumed by the Black Mesa mine is astonishing. In order to run the mine and push the coal in a slurry to the Four Corners Power Plant, 2,700 gallons (10.23 kiloliters) per minute are pumped from the underground aquifer. Again, the effects of such dewatering are untold.[30]

Other consequences of Black Mesa's destruction are all too evident. The mine itself stands out like a huge abscess on the earth's surface. Pollution from burning the coal has already significantly reduced visibility in the area. In 1969, before the Four Corners plant was at full capacity, it was emitting about 383 tons (348 metric tons) of fly ash, 1,032 tons (936 metric tons) of sulfur dioxide, and an undetermined amount of nitrogen oxides per day.[31] Pollution of this magnitude constitutes a serious health hazard to anyone within its reach.

There is a sad irony to the situation at Black Mesa. The people who are suffering directly from the exploitation also have no access to electricity. Unfortunately, they are like many other land-based indigenous people who have had to watch their land exported as a raw material. One community, the Big Mountain Dine, even faces forcible relocation. Big Mountain is one of the most remote and traditional communities in all of Indian country, and the situation there is particularly volatile.[32] Tensions are so high, in fact, that it has been compared to Wounded Knee, South Dakota, before the 1973 occupation there.

PROGNOSIS

Clearly, the future of the traditional Dine, Hopi, and Pueblo people is uncertain. The delicate balance of their relationship to the land has already suffered irre-

versible damage. While the public is becoming increasingly aware of and vociferous about their problems, and politicians and venture capitalists move ahead with their plans to develop this national sacrifice area.

Many believe the controversy surrounding the Joint Use Area on the Navajo reservation was invented as a means to open up more land for development. Allegedly, the Dine and Hopi who live in that area are in conflict. To settle the supposed dispute, the area has been partitioned, and residents are being moved to their respective sides of the border. In total, some fifty-seven hundred people are involved in what has become

Hopi Second Mesa. Photo by M. Tobias.

the greatest mass relocation of Indian people since the Long Walk.[33]

It is within the Joint Use Area that the Big Mountain Dine intend to make their stand. If there is a direct conflict with law enforcement officials, it would certainly focus public attention on the situation. Whether it would change anything is impossible to predict. Either way, the Dine could lose everything they value. With resistance at least there is hope.

On the other hand, many traditionalists believe that things have already gone too far. The Hopi, in particular, maintain a sense of fatalism, in part because of their prophecy, which, like Christian prophecy, predicts a series of events culminating in a cataclysmic apocalypse followed by rebirth and eternal life for the righteous. It is agreed among the Hopi that this process has already begun.[34]

In retrospect, the attitudes of traditional land-based people carry tremendous wisdom and foresight. In their eyes, we are the stewards of the land. We must care for it if we expect it to support us. They see the earth as a living entity, as complex in its working as the human body. In the words of one Dine, "Each mountain is a person. The water courses are their veins and arteries. The water in them is their life as our blood is to our bodies."[35] In essence, it is this vitality that makes the earth and the mountains inherently sacred.

The struggle between the sacred and the profane has plagued human existence at least since the beginning of recorded history. Then, it was a matter of social and ethical questions that had no direct bearing on our survival. Today it is different. We have allowed ourselves to develop the technology that gives us the power to bring about our extinction. I refer not only to the threat of nuclear destruction. By altering the face of the earth on a massive scale, as we have begun to do, we initiate changes beyond our control. It is quite possible that we will someday upset the balance of nature so severely in some areas that they will become lifeless deserts. It is ironic that the Four Corners could become such an area and that those who may witness the destruction include the few whose cultures would never have permitted it.

Stok Kangri, Southern Karakoram. Photo by M. Tobias.

Woman working in late afternoon, Nepal. Photo by James H. Katz.

Stok Palace, Ladakh. Photo by M. Tobias.

Hogan, southwestern United States. Photo by M. Tobias.

Canyon De Chelly, Arizona. Photo by M. Tobias.

Bolivian terraces. Photo by Joe Bastien.

Runas father and son. Photo by Bruno Roissart.

Imazighen girl, Atlas Mountains, Morocco.
Photo by Bruno Roissart.

Mountain, Nepal. Photo by James H. Katz.

"*Juk bya,* the last crowing of the cock, herald of the dawn." Photo by Richard Emerson.

Bhutanese monks. Photo by R. Radin.

Gurung sheep dog. Photo by Brot Coburn.

Indus Valley and Lamaist funerary, Ladakh. Photo by M. Tobias.

Nepali Ama. Photo by Brot Coburn.

Man giving blessing. Nepal. Photo by James H. Katz.

The mountain Su-Meru, the Sherpa metaphor of the universe. Photo by H. Downs.

Tibetan Monk. Photo by M. Tobias.

Along the Li River, China. Photo by G. Johnston.

Tasaday boy, Mindanao, Philippines. Photo by John Nance.

Monastery above Mulbeck. Photo by M. Tobias.

Meteora monastery, northern Greece. Photo by R. Radin.

PART TWO   SOUTH AMERICA

PART TWO   SOUTH AMERICA

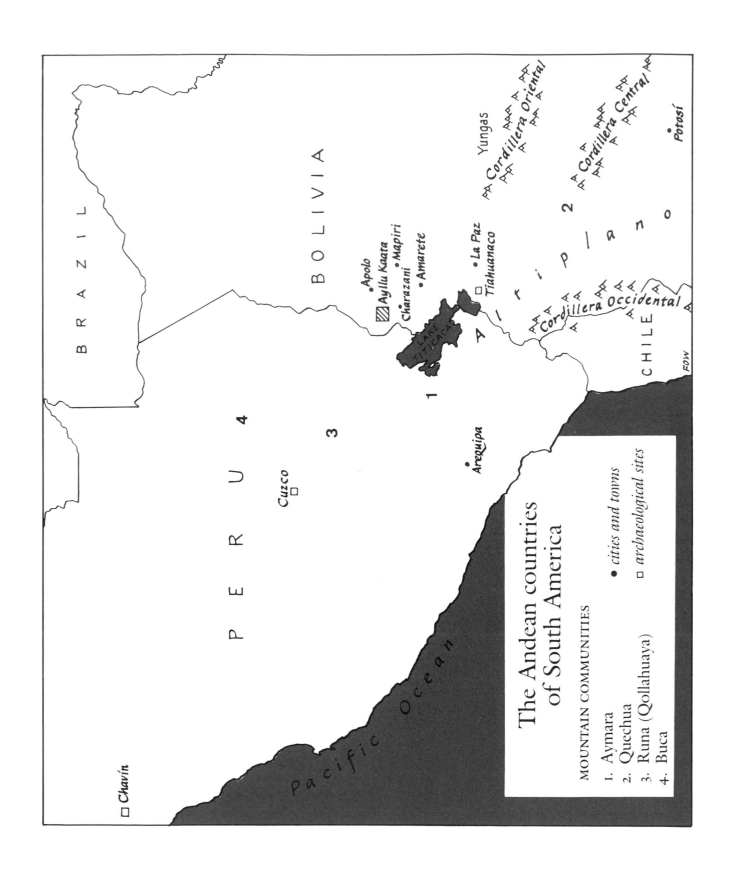

The Andean countries
of South America

• *cities and towns*
□ *archaeological sites*

MOUNTAIN COMMUNITIES

1. Aymara
2. Quechua
3. Runa (Qollahuaya)
4. Buca

BRAZIL

BOLIVIA

P E R U

CHILE

Pacific Ocean

Arequipa

Cuzco

□ *Chavín*

□ *Tiahuanaco*

• La Paz

• Amarete

Charazani • *Mapiri*

Apolo •
Ayllu Kaata

LAKE
TITICACA

Yungas

Cordillera Oriental

Cordillera Central

• *Potosí*

Altiplano

Cordillera Occidental

FGW

1

2

3

4

4. FARMING ON HIGH

ROBERT E. RHOADES

By birth and upbringing I am a "flatlander" who through accident of profession has spent many years in mountains throughout the world. My job is in the "Green Revolution," the worldwide effort of planned technical change in agriculture that has developed and disseminated high-yielding crop varieties and improved practices to millions of Third World farmers. The potato is my speciality.

In North America, Europe, and the Soviet Union we grow potatoes most productively on flatland; in the tropics, they do best in the highlands a mile or more above sea level. But wherever you go in the mountains, from the Andes to the Alps to East Africa to the Himalayas, you will invariably find the nutritious potato. This means that to speak knowledgeably about potato farming, I have had to learn not only my crop, but about mountains as well. This has been no simple task for one with a seemingly incurable "flatland" mentality, and I certainly would have failed had it not been for some unusual teachers. I am referring to the highland farmers of the world, often illiterate and impoverished but unequaled in their down-to-earth knowledge of mountain reality.

"Save the Mountains" is assured of becoming the slogan of yet another important development movement. No fewer than a dozen international symposia have been held over the past decade on the problems of mountains and hills. We have specialists, computer-based planning models, interdisciplinary projects, and even our own science, montology. Soon, I'm sure, there will be an international institute devoted to mountains. But unless scientists and planners draw their inspiration and ideas from as many sources as possible, they—like counterpart workers in deserts and tropical rain forests—will fall miserably short of providing solutions to the complex problems at hand. For that reason, it will be a tragic mistake if we ignore the world's greatest reservoir of knowledge about highland life, the traditional mountain peoples.

My suggestion that scientists and planners can learn from highlanders may seem at first misplaced. After all, mountain folk are seen as part of the problem and rarely as part of the solution. The image imprinted in our mind's eye is that of the shortsighted peasant caught in a vicious cycle of having unwillingly to over-exploit his land to feed his growing family. His behavior understandably comes from dire necessity, we sympathize, but in the end the mountain dweller is an involuntary villain on the slopes. Even in a general sense, mountain cultures are often considered the inferior "backwaters" of human history, hidden away in a remote valley or on some high point seemingly more accessible to eagles than to man. Yet such a view, I contend, is that of the uninformed lowlander who has never bothered to understand the world of mountains.

At the outset, I must assure the critical reader that what follows is not a romantic discourse on a rustic, mountain peasantry. I am the first to admit that highlanders have made ecological mistakes similar to the lowlanders' dust bowls, oil spills, and waste pollution. What is needed is a realistic appraisal of the human factor in mountain ecology. First, if we are going to plan for the destinies of highlanders, we need to understand and know them in a face-to-face way. Second, we need to cull through their ages of experiences to see what they have learned that might be of value to sustained mountain preservation. I have been looking into those experiences now for twenty years and have come away with a deep appreciation for their insights. Despite normal human shortcomings, mountain people of the world are neither as destructive nor as backward as we flatlanders think. They may well be conservative, but, as we will see, this is for some very good reasons.

Many kinds of people have come to the mountains, each for a different purpose. Some have come temporarily to fulfill a dream, others to reside forever. And each group has left behind its own legacy. Archaeological evidence indicates that man's aversion to mountains as a place to live—as opposed to a place to visit—may have come about only recently in the human drama. Prehistoric hunters and gatherers preferred mountains because of great plant and animal diversity within short distances; year-round water, wood, and shelter; and conditions favorable for self-defense. Ironically, such early mountain dwellers set the stage for lowland civilization by domesticating the five most important food staples in the world today; wheat and barley in the Zagros Mountains of the Near East, corn in highland Mexico, the potato in the Andes, and rice in the Southeast Asian highlands.

With the evolution of lowland civilization, man came to have a new relationship with the remote uplands. Mountains more and more took on the character of regions to be temporarily exploited by lowland dwellers whose interest was short-run extraction of resources with little to be returned. This was especially the case with the nomad who came only for the summer pasture, the miner for the minerals, the lumberjack for the wood, or the engineer who built dams and roads for the benefit of the lowlands. Yet out of the many approaches to the mountain, one kind of mountaineer did learn to meet the highlands on their own terms, to treat the environment so that it gave sustenance year after year. This was the mountain farmer-herder who chose to build his home in the remote valleys and raise his children there generation after generation. This permanent mountain way of life is known by many names. I refer to it simply as the "traditional mountain economy."

I have intimately experienced this way of life in the Himalayas, Alps, Andes, and Spanish Sierra Nevada and observed it in many other mountain ranges. This highland life-style has evolved in virtually every major mountain region in the world and is strikingly similar wherever it is found. Agriculturally, it combines in a carefully regulated manner both herding and cultivation by seasonally using different altitudinal zones for different purposes. In lower areas, permanent villages are frequently surrounded by rock-walled fields, corrals, and kitchen gardens. Zones immediately above are used for hay making or the cultivation of hardy grains or tubers, although the higher the fields, the greater the difficulty with productive farming. The alpine pastures are mainly suited for grazing, but then only when forage bursts forth in response to the seasonal rains, as in the Andes, or the warmth of summer, as in the Alps or Himalayas. During these periods the Quechua of Peru, the Sherpa of the Himalayas, or the Spanish peasants of the Sierra Nevada drive their herds upward to capture nature's moment. The seasonal migrations between the high pastures and the valley floors lend mountain agriculture its unique design.

The traditional mountain economy has been self-sustaining in some areas for centuries without doing extensive ecological harm to the habitat. This is the result of many things, but above all of a finely tuned agricultural calendar, a technology and landownership pattern adapted to the mountain conditions, a belief system that restricts reckless exploitation of community lands by individuals, and a social arrangement that demands cooperation of all members. This approach is an outgrowth of centuries of trial and error resulting in a degree of harmony between men and mountains.

In many regions, land has actually been reclaimed from the slopes, soils productively built up, and erosion sufficiently checked. This is not to say that these mountaineers have not had an effect on their habitat. Man, like all species, alters his environment for his own goals. Whether to our liking or not, most mountains of the world are inhabited, and unless we drive highlanders from their homes, we must learn how to achieve a relatively stable mountain ecology that includes the activities of humans. Our choice is not, nor has it ever been, between the extremes of total wildness and complete environmental destruction. The solution must involve a man-habitat interaction that both sustains man and preserves nature. In this respect, the traditional mountain folk deserve our attention for what they can teach us about their successes and failures in attempting to strike a workable balance.

Any highland economy must be appreciated against the special demands of the mountain landscape. Human survival over long periods depends on the ability to effectively use rough, precipitous slopes. High mountains characteristically contain within short distances a number of tightly compressed belts of natural vegetation that range from warm valley floors through grasslands, coniferous forests, tundralike zones, and finally a level of permanent snow. Added to this is a broken terrain oriented at different angles to the sun, wind, and rain, creating a thousand neighboring microniches. More biological and topographical diversity can be found in a few thousand feet of mountainside in the Andes or Himalayas than in over thousands of flatland miles. High mountains are like islands in the sky; although physically connected to the lowlands, the great heights create a distinct ecology.

In asking myself the question of how mountain peoples have survived so successfully under harsh mountain conditions, I have come to appreciate that these cultures are as finely tuned to their specialized habitat as the Eskimo are to the Arctic, the Polynesians to the sea, the Australian aborigines to the desert, or we to our modern, postindustrial world. The traditional mountain way is a special art, a science, a technology, and a religion all wrapped into a single life-style. Whether or not we take advantage of this knowledge depends upon our willingness to get to intimately know highland peoples. If our planning takes place at sea level, far removed from the realities of the mountain world, our efforts are certain to end up as another chapter in the sad history of well-intended but ill-conceived development projects which failed.

Today, for example, there is a lot of talk about appropriate technology in developing countries. For the mountains, no better place can be found to look for

Andean terraces. Photo by Robert Rhoades.

ideas, principles, and even the technology itself than in highland villages. The tool kit of the traditional highland farmer is simple, rustic, and often unchanged for centuries, but lowland mechanical devices have never been of much use on the slopes. Mountain technology is locally hand-made and well adapted. The short-handled hoes, scythes, items for handling animals, such as milking utensils; weaving and cloth-making machines; and basic food processing equipment all are geared for living or working efficiently in the desolate uplands.

An example of such a highland implement is the Andean foot plow, the *chaquitaclla,* frequently considered a primitive tool by outsiders. It has been used in Andean valleys for centuries, although since the 1930s farmers have been aware of tractors used at lower elevations. Certainly the failure to take up the tractor cannot be attributed to lack of awareness. The fact is that the foot plow is extremely efficient on the rugged slopes, which are too steep for tractors and even oxen. The "*chaqui,*" as it is known for short, is ideal for turning over grassy sod in fields that have been fallow for several years and that would be virtually impenetrable by the drawn plow. It might be added that planting with the *chaqui* involves a form of "minimum tillage," an ancient Andean practice that has recently become a "flatland" rage using the tractor.

The mountain tool kit is complemented by specially adapted grains, tubers, and animals capable of withstanding altitude and frost. In the higher parts of the Andes the foot plow is used to cultivate or harvest frost-resistant varieties of Andean tubers such as the potato and oca as well as hardy grains like quinoa or *cañihua.* Animals such as the yak in the Himalayas, the alpaca and llama in the Andes, or the Swiss highland cattle are likewise specially adapted to the harsh conditions of high altitudes.

For other necessities of everyday life, mountain cultures have developed and refined methods of working with wool and leather or in special food preservation techniques. The first successfully preserved foods were developed in the Andes in the form of freeze-dried potatoes, called *chuño,* and *charqui* which we know as jerky, both readily transportable items that, along with the use of llamas, gave the Incas the mobility and speed to conquer the Andes and establish a civilization. Elsewhere, production of cheese and milk and curing of meat are highland specializations.

While the tools of mountaineers may readily be judged as relevant to highland conditions, I have met very few "outside" observers who would say the same about land conservation practices in the mountains. Indeed, flatlanders are frequently shocked by the farming techniques of highlanders. A foreign agricultural adviser working in Peru once explained to me the absolute irrationality of Andean farmers, who prepare furrows that slope down the hill instead of running in horizontal contours. This, he explained, is the worst conceivable way to construct furrows since water runs down the ditch, cutting deeper into the mountain and washing soil away. His argument seems logical, but I have learned from Andean potato farmers that they use vertical furrows for some very sane reasons. First, unless they allow for sufficient drainage, water stagnation will cause potatoes to rot. Second, heavy rainfall against poorly drained horizontal furrows could build up pressure and cause landslides, thus completely destroying the farmer's field. Moreover, most farmers use vertical furrows in areas where erosion is not a serious threat and gently sloping furrows in steeper areas.

The natural pull of gravity in mountains fosters erosion, avalanches, and mudslides that can destroy fields, paths, irrigation ditches, and even entire villages. Mountain land tends to be of poor quality for agriculture, and farmers face a never-ending battle against continuous loss of soil. Yet mountain men have fought against incredible odds in stopping erosion and even building up the soil on otherwise unproductive land. The elaborate stairway terraces, for example, found in mountains from China to Peru are marvels of the world. Mountaineers have reclaimed land from the precarious slopes just as the Dutch reclaimed land from the sea, and the highlanders' accomplishments are no less herculean than those of the Dutch. In the Andes and Himalayas, the terraces sometimes climb a thousand feet or more on slopes of 45 degrees or steeper. One wonders how man can still cling to the ground to cultivate the fields. In many areas of Switzerland and Peru, soil has been collected and actually carried up the slopes and put in place. Peruvian farmers today, so the story goes, know their own soil so well that each year they go to the lower terraces and sort out by smell their soil from that of their neighbors and return it to the proper fields.

The struggle against loss of soil nutrients and build-up of harmful pathogens to crops is also universal in highlands, and over the centuries mountain communities have developed ingenious ways of dealing with this problem. They mainly counteract nutrient loss through manuring, composting, complex field and crop rotations, and reliance on a great variety of native crops. The agronomic techniques now used by native mountain peoples are poorly understood by modern science, although evidence suggests they are quite effective and environmentally safe.

Take the example of a community in the Andes where I work with potato farmers. The village territory is divided into seven areas or "sectors," which are worked by what are called "turns." The community concentrates its planting in one area for a period of one or two years, during which time herds or flocks are exiled to other sectors that serve as pastures. Every household owns fields in each sector, and according to village law no outsider may purchase village land. The farmers pursue a strategy of complex rotation of crops within sectors under cultivation. The potato always leads off the rotation cycle after fallow because it is the most sensitive to soil pathogens, and it is followed by a soil-enriching Andean crop but rarely by another Andean tuber. Temporary corrals containing sheep or other livestock are moved daily over the prepared soil to fertilize the land next in line for cultivation. Despite low yields, a mixture of many native varieties of potatoes is grown as a way to "spread out" risks, as each variety responds differently to disease, insects, or climate. Although potato "late blight" has long been a problem in the Andes, nothing like the Irish potato famine has ever occurred there mainly because farmers guard against total crop loss by maintaining variety.

At least seven or eight years may pass before a sector is used again, until a complete turn has been made through all the sectors. Why is the cycle so long? During the fallow period, the soil builds up a layer of organic matter crucial for future production. Insects and harmful fungi decline while pasture is provided for animals. A colleague of mine, an expert on a nematode potato parasite, argues that the length of the cycle roughly corresponds to the point of time in which the parasite populations become so low that they do no damage. This particular nematode is a serious problem in the highlands, and it seems doubtful that the correlation is pure coincidence. Interestingly, when corn blight swept the U.S. corn belt in the 1970s, recom-

Potato cultivation, Andes. Photo by Robert Rhoades.

mendations similar in principle to the practices of the Andean community were made: more reliance on crop variation, with systematic rotations. Modern agronomy has much to offer highland farmers, but it has much to learn from them as well.

Another aspect of indigenous mountain agriculture frequently considered irrational is the large number of unusually small and dispersed fields. "Why do they have so many postage-stamp-sized fields scattered from here to kingdom come?" people often asked me in Peru or Nepal. Indeed, I have known farmers who have had as many as ninety tiny fields scattered over a valley and frequently located several days' walk apart. The common flatland solution would be to lump all these into a single field. Yet many reasons for the dispersion can be offered. First, scattered fields reduce the risk of total crop failure. Because of the practice of planting a wide range of crops and varieties in different localities and at various altitudes, a poor yield in one part of the valley does not imply a loss of the entire crop. Mountain farmers opt for one main strategy: diversification. If frost, hail, or an avalanche destroys the crops at one level, it may affect only one of a family's many parcels. Second, since crops are planted and ripen according to altitude, cultivation and harvesting can be a family or community affair carried out without hiring outside labor. A few feet of elevation can make a difference of one or two days in the maturation of the crop, allowing a stepwise progression of harvesting activities. A family can follow a staggered work schedule that would be impossible on flatland, where several crops may ripen at about the same time. Finally, the dispersion of holdings makes sure all families have access to soil types of varying quality and are not restricted only to low-yielding fields.

The need to regulate village lands is reflected in the close watch community members keep over all land, including that privately held. Outsiders, for example, are usually prevented from acquiring any village lands. Most traditional mountain communities allow private ownership or rights to fields and gardens in the lower zones, which are perhaps more efficiently cultivated by individual households. Upland forests and pastures are generally always held in common. The pastures and high forests are carefully regulated by local law, and in the Alps and Himalayas special forest wardens are elected to make sure that unwise cutting of the forest or abuse of the high pastures does not occur. Communal decisions are made annually about how many animals the pastures can support. Informal sanctions are applied, and anyone who steps out of line is subject to ostracism, gossip, and public criticism or is fined by the wardens.

The fact that high pastures and forests are communal property has frequently been seized upon by national governments to justify the alienation of such lands from communities. These lands have been turned over to outsiders through land reform or used to establish national parks, in many cases with disastrous effects on the mountain communities that depend on the high zones for grazing and wood. The holding of communal lands in the upper areas is not, as has been argued, a survival of "primitive communism," but rather a practical matter of the mountains. Successful grazing in the high pastures and use of the forest require a coordinated, community-wide effort. Uncontrolled cutting of timber could leave the entire community without essential firewood or building material. Overgrazing of alpine pastures could destroy the vegetational cover and lead not only to erosion but also to dangerous landslides above the village. Moreover, if high pastures were parceled out to private owners,

Andean Festival. Photo by Robert Rhoades.

some households might be blocked from access to that crucial zone.

Such adaptive agricultural practices, however, would be impossible without a corresponding village social consciousness. Every effort is made in alpine communities to build a civic awareness and involve all members. High pastures must concern everyone if successful pasturing is to take place. Irrigation ditches or paths must be repaired by communal effort. Landslides and avalanches can be averted only if everyone is sensitive to ecological conditions on the mountain slopes above the village. The movement of animals between the village and the high pasture requires the cooperation of all members. The nature of self-sufficient farming in isolated highland regions demands an elaborate system of reciprocity in the exchange of labor, tools, supplies, and seed. In short, mountain agriculture is coordinated agriculture.

Even the colorful festivals of highlanders, now tourist attractions in many mountainous regions, are important for building social solidarity and providing a framework for the agricultural cycle. High-altitude communities have learned to avert disaster by fixing dates between which certain tasks should be started and finished. Typically, saint's days or religious festivals are used as a rough guide, although tasks may be conveniently postponed if the weather is not favorable. The festivals serve to keep things on schedule and to prevent, for example, the herds from entering a harvest zone too soon. The boisterous festivals are further complemented by a rich lore of the farmers that helps villagers make difficult day-to-day decisions about practical matters.

The essence of government in mountain villages is that authority and responsibility are shared by all. From among their own ranks one or two "majors" are elected to serve a one- or two-year term, rarely longer. The rotating office serves to draw all families into the decision-making process. Annually, the leader calls a community meeting in which everyone is expected to participate. Democratically, they vote on crucial matters such as when, how far, and how many animals will make the migration to the alpine meadows. Likewise, the community often casts ballots on which crops will be planted when and where. The open community meetings allow for the accumulated experience of everyone to be presented, discussed, and judged.

Flatlanders have sometimes seen such social demands as a strangling of individual initiative. Yet in this environment of great risks and harsh elements, a single irresponsible decision could spell disaster for the entire village. Without careful timing of agricultural activities, the village herds could get caught in the deadly grip of a sudden fall storm or the crops could be lost or damaged unnecessarily. If a herdsman neglects his duties and loses control of his animals, they could wander into the village's unharvested fields and deplete the year's grain reserves within a matter of hours. In essence, strong social demands are mere reflections of the stringent physical demands of the mountain itself.

The fragile nature of the traditional mountain economy became suddenly clear to me in the Andean winter of 1979 when I visited an elderly friend, Don Maximo Poma, who lives in a Peruvian village on the eastern slopes of the Andes. He was troubled, more so than I had ever noticed before. "Today," he explained, "we have a community meeting, and for sure there will be a bad fight." When I inquired further, he set forth his community's dilemma, one that throughout this century has affected mountain villages throughout the world:

> We have already allowed some outsiders to own land in the valley floor, and today others want us to give up control of the higher lands. Some people want to sell their fields to outsiders who can pay more. The young farmers are crying to stop the "turns" and plant year after year in the same fields. It is foolish, they say, to let the land lie fallow so long when we can make so much more money by selling our produce in the Lima market. They say don't worry about the old ways. Today we have fertilizers and pesticides And it's true, *ingeniero,* we can produce many tons more.

Inevitable winds of change have come to my friend's village. Is that change bad? Is it good? I, for one, do not know. If history repeats itself, this village may soon fragment into a community of more or less independent commercial farmers. Those with the energy and finances will progressively control the land of the poorer families, who will probably leave the village. In this respect, fewer people in the mountains may mean a healthier mountain environment. Human population pressure against limited resources has and will always be a key ecological problem in the highlands. By the same token, in some mountainous areas, such as in alpine Europe, the ecology has become so dependent upon human activities that rapid withdrawal could lead to environmental deterioration. On the other hand, we know that unless the new mountain economy develops adaptive social controls to prevent overexploitation of the land for individual gain, the end result could be devastating.

Since most upland communities are caught between two worlds, the traditional and the modern, mountain policy makers will be faced with the difficult task of converting the old into a new system that will not lead to the destruction of the fragile mountain environment. I believe that incorporating the principles, if not the substance, of the traditional highland economy into the planning of mountain communities of the twenty-first century is a first step. I am referring to an ethic of nature, a concern with land management, a civic responsibility, a low-energy technology, and a great will to return to the mountain as much as is taken away.

However, students of the mountain must act now if they are to understand properly the traditional way of the mountains. My advice to those concerned with the mountains' future: go, and go soon, to the mountain people and involve them in planning their destiny. Highland villages have survived across the millennia, while nations, governments, and even cities have faded from the human stage. But today there is an erosion in the mountains that cuts silently and unseen. Like the erosion of the precious soil, this erosion is equally irreversible and just as costly. I am referring to the demise of traditional insights and practices. Perhaps it is inevitable that such culture should join the graveyard of extinction along with most of the native cultures of the world. But if we who propose to save the mountains let the insights of the existing traditional mountain people escape us, we have lost a great deal.

Aldo Leopold, the famous American conservationist, once wrote: "Man has not learned to think like a mountain. Hence, we have dust bowls, and rivers washing the future into the sea." Leopold was right. Most of us have not learned the art of vertical thinking, or perceiving the balances of nature in the highlands. However, if any people have approached this understanding, it has been those who have struggled to survive on these islands in the sky. Only they, among all men, have learned "to think like a mountain."

5. The Human Mountain

JOSEPH W. BASTIEN

My love for Andeans began in 1963. I had worked as a missionary priest among the Bolivian Indians and, for six years, had directed a leadership school in a tiny Indian village on the Altiplano. I taught Indian leaders how to start credit cooperatives and raise chickens, which, I thought, would benefit their communities. Dressing in a poncho and sandals, I spoke with them in Aymara and Quechua. Many people at that time saw these Indians as backwards or as obstacles to progress, and I wanted to incorporate them into the mainstream of Bolivian life.

Most of the projects I undertook, such as providing potable water, electricity, and consumer cooperatives, were not accepted by the Indian communities. My evangelistic activity was even less effective. The Catholic religion was as foreign to them as I was; the Indians put up with it because they had to.

By the end of the sixties, I realized that my endeavors had failed because I was oblivious to an ancient Andean religion, rich in symbolism and ritual. Deeper symbolic patterns governed the lives of these Indians, who preferred to worship land instead of spirits. It appered to me that anthropologists had been successful in interpreting those patterns, so I decided to become an anthropologist to better understand Andean Indians. I resigned from the priesthood in 1969 and began studies in anthropology at Cornell University.

After I completed graduate course work in anthropology, my wife Judy and I journeyed to the Qollahuaya Andeans of Bolivia in January, 1972. Beginning a year of fieldwork for a doctoral dissertation, we wanted to understand Andean behavior and personality in terms of deep symbolic patterns, and to do that we became engaged with the Qollahuayas in their way of life. Qollahuayas are a special cultural subgroup of the Aymara nation (Tschopik 1946:569).

Even though many Qollahuayas speak Quechua, as a result of Inca influence, they have been classified with the Aymaras because of their association with pre-Incaic Aymara traditions and because of their role in contemporary Aymara culture as herbalists and ritualists (see La Barre 1950:40−45, Cárdenas 1979:10−11, Oblitas 1978:20−21, Tschopik 1946:569, and Wassén 1972:28). However, they were probably a distinct ethnic group with their own language, the vestiges of which appear in a secret language still used for curing (Oblitas 1968; Stark 1972).

The province of Bautista Saavedra, northeast of Lake Titicaca in midwestern Bolivia, is a mountainous area about the size of Delaware. Americans and Europeans rarely ventured into the remote Qollahuaya region before 1948, when a dirt road was completed from La Paz to Charazani, the capital of Bautista Saavedra. Two hundred miles long, the road crosses a high plateau, the Altiplano (12,500 feet; 3,800 meters), and a mountain range, the Cordillera Oriental (about 18,000 feet; 5,500 meters); consequently, the trip takes from ten hours during the dry season, April to November, to several days during the rainy season, December to March, when the roads become muddy and impassable. Even today, few non-Andeans endure the uncomfortable trip in the back of a crowded truck from La Paz to Charazani. Because of Bautista Saavedra's inaccessibility to non-Andeans, Kaatan diviners there still practice Andean rituals that in more accessible areas of the Andes have been suppressed by missionaries. For this reason, an early ethnographer to South America, Bandelier (1910:103), described the Qollahuayas as the "wizards of the Andes."

QOLLAHUAYA AYLLUS

Qollahuayas distinguish their communities according to the mountain on which the community is located. They call these mountains *ayllus,* and each *ayllu* has communities on low, middle, and high levels of the mountain. Qollahuayas have nine *ayllus,* namely, Amarete, Chajaya, Chari, Chullina, Curva, Inca, Kaalaya, Kaata, and Upinhuaya. Although valleys and rivers separate the mountains of the Carabaya Range, resource exchange unifies the Qollahuaya *ayllus.* According to an *ayllu* division of labor, the communities on each mountain specialize in some profession. The *ayllus* exchange services and supply each other, as well as other parts of the central Andes, with necessary resources. Ayllus Amarete, Chajaya, and Upinhuaya, for example, provide the potters, jewelers, and tool and hat makers for the province. The people of Ayllu Amarete mold pottery and carve wooden tools, and Ayllu Chajaya, famous for jewelers who once fashioned ornaments for ruling Incas, furnishes most Qollahuaya jewelry. According to a unique technique, Upinhuayas press sheep wool into the white dress hats with wide brims and rounded crowns that Qollahuayas wear for fiestas. The craftsmen from the *ayllus* practice skills learned from their ancestors, who, following a long tradition, developed a technology tested through time. As a consequence, the complexity of each craft encourages specialization among the *ayllus,* and this specialization, in turn, requires exchange between *ayllus* for complementary resources.

Qollahuayas not only trade crafts but also balance their diet. Since vegetational zones change with altitude, the *ayllus,* situated at varying altitudes, grow and exchange a variety of foods. In the eastern and lower area of Bautista Saavedra, for example, Ayllu Chullina borders the rain forest region of the Yungas. On the lower slopes (7,000–9,000 feet; 2,000–2,750 meters), Indians cultivate peach and orange orchards. Near the center of the province, the people of Ayllus Inca and Kaata cultivate wheat on lower slopes (9,500–10,500 feet; 2,900–3,200 meters) of their mountains and grow potatoes on the central slopes (10,500–14,000 feet; 3,200–4,300 meters). And on the highest moun-

tains in the western part of Bautista Saavedra, herders from Ayllus Chari, Chajaya, and Kaata graze alpacas, llamas, and sheep from 14,000 to 17,000 feet (4,300–5,200 meters). In other words, the vegetational zones of the Carabaya Range provide the *ayllus* with the necessary carbohydrates, cereals, minerals, and proteins for a balanced diet.

After the Indians harvest their crops, the people of the *ayllus* come together at fiestas, which are sponsored twice a year in each community. They bring their community's produce and trade it for other necessary goods. The herders from Ayllu chari, for example, swap dried meat (*charqui*) for bread, fruit, and potatoes from Ayllus Inca, Chullina, and Kaata. Furthermore, the people of the *ayllus* gather at fiestas to share a meal. The people pool their food, and the Indians feast upon the products from the Qollahuayas' mountains. As a balance of diet and as an exchange between *ayllus,* the banquet is also an important symbolic gesture for Andean rituals. While the variety of food and people at a banquet symbolizes area specialization, the common meal symbolizes area integration.

Ayllu specialization, moreover, is an efficient strategy for using the resources of Bautista Saavedra. Farming

Mayan agriculture. Photo by P. Veggars.

and herding require great skill in the Andes, where the soil is marginal and the climate is variable, and the people of each *ayllu* must study the climate, soil, and plants of the *ayllu's* levels. The elders of each community, for example, know agricultural methods that are successful on their land. They can read signs of nature to determine when to plant and harvest in places where frost sets two hundred days of the year. Breeding seeds to grow in barren and high places, they carefully select and cross-fertilize plants that can resist the frost and snow. Consequently, the people of each *ayllu* adapt to the vegetational zones of their levels. By specializing and trading, then, the Qollahuaya *ayllus* are able to skillfully use complex resources within Bautista Saavedra.

Recently, however, verticality and resource exchange have become diminishing factors for cultural and social unification of Qollahuaya *ayllus*. By verticality Murra (1972:429–68) means the strategy of controlling as many distinct niches as possible; in the Andes, altitude is the great ecological variable. Through resource exchange, upper and lower levels are held together by their participation in an ecosystem wherein there is a sharing of specialized resources from different microclimates, necessary for each level's and each society's energy demands (Thomas 1972). Vertical exchange is being replaced by horizontal links (roads and trucks) to economic centers, where goods are purchased at competitive prices and sold by middlemen at profitable gains. There is a trend to produce the same cash crops, the most profitable, and to compete with each other for the best price. The selling of goods to middlemen at national centers decreases the social ties created by exchanging goods within and between the *ayllus*. As a result, the Qollahuaya *ayllus* are slowly changing from specialized and complementary units of an integrated region to similar and independent units of a nation state.

Qollahuayas also take advantage of resources found outside Bautista Saavedra. The people of Ayllu Upinhuaya, for example, travel three days by foot to the Yungas, where they harvest incense. Loading the incense on their backs, Upinhuayas carry hundred-pound sacks up the tumultuous Ayllu River to the Qollahuaya Mountains. They market the incense in Bautista Saavedra and the southeastern Altiplano; Andeans burn large quantities of incense in their rituals. Upinhuayas reek with incense, and they are known throughout the Andes as the "walking incense pots."

More than incense, however, Qollahuayas use coca not only for their rituals but also for survival in the Andes. Andeans divine from coca and serve it to the earth shrines during rituals. But magical qualities of the "divine leaf," as Andeans call coca, are interrelated to its physical properties; dried coca leaves contain the bitter alkaloid of cocaine, the anesthetic properties of which are also used by dentists to deaden dental nerves. As fortification against the higher altitudes, Andeans masticate coca for its narcotic effect; cocaine alleviates the pains of cold, hunger, and tiredness, and it protects Andeans against hypoxia (altitude sickness). Not surprisingly, then, Andeans use coca as a symbol in all rituals. They say that Pachamama (Mother Earth) gives them power through coca.

Since 1969, the United Nations, the United States, and governments of South America have tried to abolish coca in the Andes. A UN commission superficially studied the issue in 1956 and concluded that coca was harmful to the health of Andeans. In addition, drug enforcement agencies believed that the solution to the illicit use of cocaine in the United States was to prohibit coca production in the Andes. The U.S. government then encouraged certain governments of South America to destroy coca fields and to punish the Indians who chew it. Finally, they wanted to abolish coca from the Andes by 1983.

At the American Anthropological Association meetings in Los Angeles in 1978, Andean scholars gathered for three symposia on medicine, malnutrition, and morbidity in the Andes. Eighteen speakers presented papers on environmental, biological, cultural, and sociological aspects of health and sickness in the Andes. The following are some of their conclusions (Bastien n.d.*a*): (1) coca has important medicinal uses for sick Andeans; (2) coca has salubrious biological effects that counteract altitude stress, modify carbohydrate consumption, and increase work capacity; and (3) coca is an integral part of curing rituals and Andean religion. After the papers, the participants of all symposia concluded that the use of coca was an integral part of Andean health and culture. Moreover, the U.S. government's interference violates the human rights of Andeans and interferes with their culture and religion.

Traditionally, Qollahuayas of Ayllu Kaalaya have harvested coca in the Yungas and marketed it in the densely populated areas of the Puna. (Coca does not grow in the Qollahuaya region.) The Yungas is the rainy and heavily forested slope of the Cordillera Oriental. A line drawn north of due west from Santa Cruz to the edge of the Altiplano, passing north of Cochabamba, marks the southern end of the Yungas (James 1959:209). South of that line stands a high-level surface (12,000–14,000 feet; 3,600–4,300 meters) known as the Puna. Above this surface are high mountains, and below it are valleys and basins. Most Bolivian Andeans occupy the northern basins of the Altiplano and the basins and valleys of the Cordillera Oriental along the line of transition between the very wet Yungas and the very dry Puna (James 1959:211). Qollahuayas live between the Yungas and the Puna.

The trip, nevertheless, from Kaalaya to Apolo, a coca center of the Yungas, takes seven days by mule. Kaalayans travel this journey three times a year to exchange coca for Qollahuaya products: hats, jewelry, pots, tools, *charqui,* potatoes, and salt. When they arrive in Apolo, Kaalayans trade with their relatives who have settled in the Yungas and grow coca in that area. The coca traders are linked to the coca producers by *ayllu* and kinship ties that guarantee exchange. The coca traders transport the coca to Bautista Saavedra, where they barter it for items marketable in Apolo. The coca traders are important links between the Puna and Yungas zones because they provide the Yungas area with crafts and the Qollahuaya area with coca.

Like the coca traders, Qollahuaya medicine men link the Puna and the Yungas; they descend to the Yungas, where they gather natural remedies, and then ascend to the Puna, where they cure the sick. Qollahuaya curers live in Ayllus Chajaya, Curva, and Chari, the valleys of which descend to the Yungas and the mountains of which ascend to the Puna. Skilled wildcrafters, these herbalists travel to the Yungas; gather animal products, herbs, and minerals; and dispense them throughout the central Andes. Qollahuaya curers can, for example, calm mental illness with *guayasa* (*Ilex guayasa*), set bones with plaster casts, and stretch muscles with frog skins. Their pharmacy includes more than one thousand remedies (Girault 1972), some of which are nature's equivalent of aspirin, penicillin, and quinine, and others of which have yet to be discovered by modern medicine.

People unable to be cured by doctors have been healed by Qollahuaya herbalists. Domingo Flores, a famous herbalist, cured the daughter of Augusto Leguia, former president of Peru (Oblitas 1969:11–18), within fifteen days although she was diagnosed as incurable and dying by Lima's best doctors. Leguia awarded Flores an honorary M.D. diploma, and the former president, moreover, publicly acclaimed the competence of Qollahuaya medical practices.

Medical doctors and missionaries, nevertheless, have tried to extirpate Qollahuaya pharmaceutical practices. Doctors and missionaries inculcate doubts among the Indians about the spiritual and material powers of the Qollahuayas. At the turn of this century, for example, curers stopped bloodletting and trepanning because of pressure from doctors, who said these practices were dangerous. At the present time, according to Andean informants, Methodist missionaries preach that Qollahuaya herbalists do the Devil's work in the Garden of Eden. At the Methodist clinic in Ancoraimes doctors refuse to admit Andeans who have been cured with herbs. Because of this discrediting, Aymaras from Ancoraimes ridicule Qollahuayas and deride them as they travel by. "Hey you dumb Indian with the medicine bag," they shout at Qollahuayas, "What tricks you got to cure me?"

These mysterious medicine men, rapidly passing from the scene, still remain the hope of all incurables and the healers of the Indian. Doctors and missionaries are scarce in the Andes, and traveling curers treat sick people in places where doctors refuse to live; they travel throughout five Andean nations and cure all classes of people. As hope for incurables throughout the world, Qollahuaya medicine men have remedies for diseases that Western medicine cannot cure. For this reason, Andeans call the land from which these herbalists come Qollahuaya or "Land of the Medicine."

Qollahuaya also means "Sacred Land" and refers to Mount Kaata, an *ayllu* of diviners. Anthropologists and historians have emphasized that Qollahuaya curers are famous throughout South America; these scholars, however, have seldom mentioned Qollahuaya diviners and their religious influence upon the Andes. Nonetheless, Qollahuayas consider diviners to be different from and more important ritualists than medicine men. Qollahuayas distinguish the two specialists according to curers (*curanderos*), who cure with natural remedies, and diviners (*yachaj*), who not only cure with supernatural remedies but also arrange tables to feed the earth. Qollahuayas do not mix the two professions; an herbalist, for example, never feeds the mountain blood and fat, nor does a diviner cure with herbs. Although several herbalists perform earth feeding rituals outside Bautista Saavedra, Qollahuayas frown upon this practice and call them *farsantes* (quacks). Each profession requires such specialized expertise that rarely can anyone master both skills. It takes years of apprenticeship before an herbalist can know the interrelationship between the properties of plants and the symptoms of sicknesses or the ritualist can successfully divine from coca the signs of nature when to plant and harvest. If crops fail in the Andes, Indians die of starvation, and divinatory skills, as curing, determine the fate of Andeans. Qollahuayas, consequently, have *ayllus* specialized in each profession so that Andeans have competent curers and diviners. Chajaya and Curva are *ayllus* of curers, and Kaata is an *ayllu* of diviners.

AYLLU KAATA

After Judy and I learned about the Qollahuaya *ayllus,* we decided that the best way to learn about the Andean religion would be to live in Kaata. Carmen and

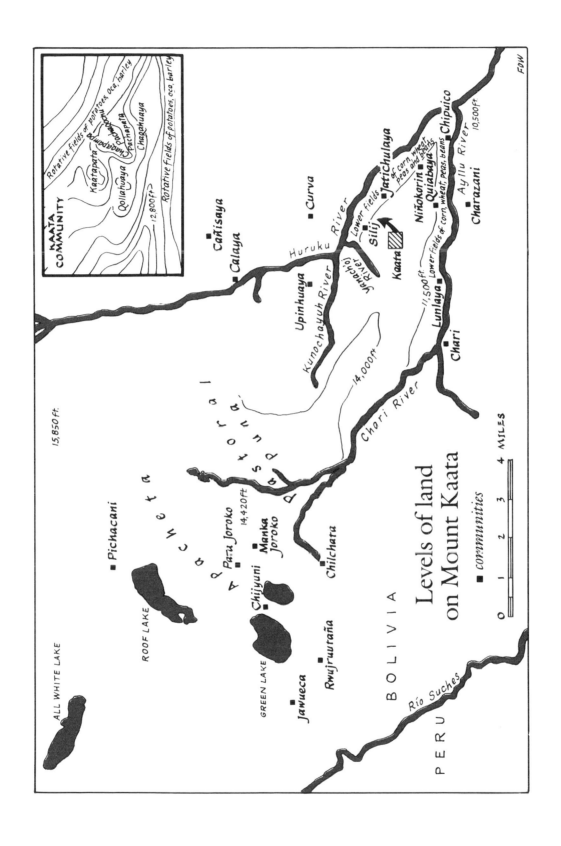

Levels of land
on Mount Kaata

■ communities

0 1 2 3 4 MILES

KAATA
COMMUNITY

Rotative fields of potatoes, oca, barley

Kaatapata
Qachapampa
Qollahuaya
Pachaqota
Pachapata
Chaqahuaya

12,800ft

Rotative fields of potatoes, oca, barley

15,850 Ft.

ALL WHITE LAKE

ROOF LAKE

GREEN LAKE

■ Pichacani

■ Jawueca

■ Rwjruutaña

■ Chijiyuni

Para Joroko

Manka Joroko

14,420Ft

A p a c h e t a   P a s t o r a l

■ Chilchata

Cañisaya ■

Calaya ■

■ Upinhuaya

Kunochayuh River

Huruku   River

Yanachoj River

14,000ft

Curva ■

■ Niñokorin

Sitij ■

Kaata

11,500ft

Lower fields of corn, wheat, peas and beans

Lower fields of corn, wheat, peas, beans

■ JatiChulaya

of corn, wheat, peas and beans

■ Quiabaya

Lunlaya ■

■ Chari

Chari River

Ayllu River

■ Chipuico

■ Charazani

10,500ft

B O L I V I A

P E R U

Río Suches

FDW

Mercelino Yanahuaya invited Judy and me to live with them in Kaata, a community of 205 families on Mount Kaata. The Yanahuayas, suspicious at first, after a while grew to love Judy and me. We lived in a small hut alongside their courtyard and shared meals with them. Our participation in Andean activities was very important to the Yanahuayas; Carmen taught Judy weaving, and Marcelino taught me farming. I learned how to plow with oxen, and Judy wove a Qollahuaya belt with a design finer than Sophia, Carmen's ten-year-old daughter, could weave. Carmen was proud of Judy because she had mastered the technique and design of Qollahuaya weaving.

Ayllu Kaata has three major communities (see map, Levels of Land on Mount Kaata).

The community of Kaata is nestled on the central slopes (11,500–14,000 feet; 3,500–4,300 meters) above the community of Niñokorin (10,500–11,500 feet; 3,200–3,500 meters) and below the community of Apacheta (14,000–17,000 feet; 4,300–5,200 meters). The people of Niñokorin and Kaata speak Quechua, and those of Apacheta speak Aymara. The communities differ in settlement and subsistence patterns and are quite far apart; from Niñokorin to Kaata takes a two-hour climb, and from Kaata to Apacheta takes a full day. Nonetheless, social principles and the cultural understanding of the mountain unite these different and distant communities into one *ayllu*.

Near the base of Mount Kaata, Niñokorin rests on the lower fields of the mountain. The northern and southern slopes of Mount Kaata ascend abruptly from the gorges of the Ayllu and Huruku rivers (10,500 feet; 3,200 meters), and between these altitudes narrow riparian strips produce corn, wheat, barley, peas, and beans. These fields lie within the upper zone of corn cultivation entwining about the Andes from 8,000 to 11,500 feet (2,400–3,500 meters). During the frost-free rainy season from December until March, the moist, ashy loam of these fields permits yearly wheat and corn rotations, the vegetables growing around the corn and wheat. Lunlaya, Quiabaya, Chipuico, and Jatichulaya, each with about ten families, are also scattered along both riverbanks. The four settlements are economically and politically independent of each other, yet they comprise a single cultural part of Mount Kaata. They all speak Quechua. Moreover, they are agriculturally, socially, and symbolically the lower people of Mount Kaata, as the name Niñokorin means "Lower Son."

The highlands of Mount Kaata are called Apacheta, and 120 Aymara-speaking families live there. These herders graze alpacas, llamas, sheep, and pigs on Mount Kaata's high level. The high level is between the upper limits of potatoes at about 14,000 feet (4,300 meters)

and vegetation at about 16,000 feet (4,900 meters; Troll 1968:35). Animals graze on clumps of tough, strawy bunchgrass (*Festuca scirpifolia*) that grows in this freezing zone. Apachetans go with herds and as a result live far apart. Although these herders are spread apart in dispersed settlements, they are culturally united by language and by living on the high level of Mount Kaata. As part of Ayllu Kaata, furthermore, Apacheta is culturally united to the communities of Niñokorin and Kaata.

Apachetans farm an occasional plot of bitter potatoes and the grain called quinoa (*Chenopodium quinoa*) in places protected from the frost and cold. An astute folklore enables them to discern the place and time to plant hybrid seeds specifically developed for an area where there is frost more than 250 days of the year. Because of the altitude and proximity to the equator (17° south), the highland pastures are warm, bright, and comfortable during the day, when temperatures soar into the eighties, but once the sun sets, icy winds sweep down from glaciers, bringing frost and lowering the temperature to below freezing. In the northern United States, the contrast of cold winter and a warm summer affects the ecological activity of all organisms, while in the central Andes the daily fluctuations of a warm day and cold night not only curtail plant life but also influence cultural themes of reciprocal exchange between contrasts.

The Andeans are an ingenious people. They use frost and sun to dehydrate potatoes (*ch'uño*) and oca (*khaya*), for example, so that these tubers can be preserved and transported. The Indians freeze potatoes at night, crush them with their feet in the early morning, and then dry them in the sun. This process of preserving food allowed Andeans to settle permanently in the high mountain country (Troll 1968:33).

Every day, Kaatans are able to see mountains miles away, be enclosed within a cloud, hear the whistle of the wind, perceive a stillness, and feel intense heat during the day and severe cold at night. Even greater than the contrast between day and night in the Andes is that between the rainy and dry seasons, which corresponds to winter and summer in North America. From about November until March, clouds climb the Carabaya valleys, bring rain to the slopes, then dissipate over the mountains. The eastern side of the Andes of Bolivia and Peru draws rain from southeast tradewinds, and the Qollahuaya region receives an estimated 30 inches (76 centimeters) yearly (Sauer 1963:339). The valleys are also enormous wind gaps through which dry and moist air are exchanged between the moist tropical forest of the Amazon Basin and dry Puna highlands. A galelike wind, capable of carrying small stones, begins suddenly each morning and blows along the valley floor and up the mountain slopes, often leaving the Qollahuayas in fog.

The central fields also follow a cycle every eight years. Extensive tracts of land (*qhapanas*) produce potatoes, oca, and barley during each rainy season for three years, and then lie fallow for five years. As Kaatans say, the fields are put to sleep. The fields slowly replenish their nutrients by the fertilization of the droppings of grazing sheep. Night frost decreases as the rainy season advances, and tuberous plants are able to grow in the upper region of the mountain's temperate zone above 13,500 feet (4,100 meters). On the lower fields where there is less frost, from about 11,000 to 12,000 feet (3,400–3,700 meters), barley grows.

These central fields nestle around Kaata community like swatches of a patchwork quilt: the white and yellow flowers of potatoes and oca, the green stems of barley, and the tan grass of those fields resting for the year. The people of Kaata farm these rotative fields, supplying the potatoes and oca for the peoples of the highlands and lowlands, who exchange their own produce with the people of the central lands.

Until recently, the communities of Niñokorin, Kaata, and Apacheta exchanged produce from level to level and provided each other with the necessary carbohydrates, minerals, and proteins for their balanced subsistence. Exchange of produce, however, has become less a uniting factor on Mount Kaata since the Bolivian Agrarian Reform of 1953. The administrators of the reform insisted that Apacheta, Kaata, and Niñokorin become autonomous communities, each with political leaders subordinated to Charazani, the provincial capital, and to La Paz. In 1956, the Bolivian government surveyed Mount Kaata, defined the boundaries of the three levels, and generated endless border disputes between them. Roads to each of the three levels encouraged horizontal selling and buying in Charazani and La Paz in preference to exchange between levels. The reformists looked to the external diversity of Mount Kaata without considering its territorial, social, and symbolic integrity. They divided Mount Kaata into three separate zones: lower corn and wheat fields; central rotative fields of potatoes, oca, and barley; and pastoral highlands with alpacas, llamas, and sheep. There were notable differences among the human groups who lived at each of these altitudes. Apachetans spoke Aymara, lived apart from one another, and herded llamas. Kaatans spoke Quechua and lived together in a large community. The peoples of Niñokorin spoke Quechua and lived in smaller communities along the river. The reformers, therefore, concluded that the three communities were independent of each other and that they should compete with one another as autonomous societies.

Yet for Kaatans, there is a wholeness in their mountain, which is an *ayllu*. In their context, *ayllu* refers to a mountain with thirteen earth shrines and with communities on low, middle, and high levels. And if history is an indicator, then Ayllu Kaata will remain intact for years to come. The Indians of Mount Kaata remain united to each other by social and cultural principles. Kaatans argued, in 1598 against the Conquistadores and in 1953 against the agrarian reformists, that like a human body, the mountain is composed of parts organically united to each other. The lands of Mount Kaata belong together because they are parts of a social and human mountain.

HUMAN MOUNTAIN

We were approaching the end of our third month in Kaata when Marcelino Yanahuaya first spoke to us of the mountain. He led us to the edge of a terraced field, a balcony overlooking a vertical world. To the north, Aqhamani mountain towered over us, and a tumbling white stream ran through a valley below us. The wind rustling the trees temporarily suspended the stillness. We looked across the valley and then at Marcelino. A tall Indian, Marcelino was dressed in a red poncho woven from alpaca threads and brilliantly layered with designs of animals and people. The poncho sloped down the length of his arms almost to his hands and covered coarsely woven black pants, worn over another white pair. His rough, sandaled feet stood firmly on the ledge as he raised his hands with coca to Aqhamani.

"Aqhamani, Lord of the Harvest, grant us food as we give you coca," Marcelino prayed. His wide face was faintly marked from smallpox and slightly wrinkled from age, wind, and sun. He smelled of smoke and earth.

Marcelino helped us offer coca to Aqhamani, slowly speaking the Quechua prayer so that we could follow. He was as patient with us as he was gentle with the plants and children around him. A careful observer, he loved to reflect on nature and society, always examining, questioning, and verifying the nuances of the weather, land, and community. He could collect countless herbs for curing, plant many varieties of potatoes, and list the genealogies of all the families living in his hamlet.

"The mountain is like us, and we're like it," Marcelino explained. "The mountain has a head where alpaca hair and bunchgrass grow. The highland herders of Apacheta offer llama fetuses into the lakes, which are its eyes, and into a cave, which is its mouth, to feed the head. There you can see Tit Hill on the trunk of the body." He pointed to a large knoll high on the central slopes surrounding Kaata. "Kaata is the heart and guts, where potatoes and oca grow beneath the earth. The great ritualists live there. They offer blood and fat to this body. If we don't feed the mountain, it won't feed us. Corn grows on the lower slopes of Niñokorin, the legs of Mount Kaata." In other words, Kaatans understand Apacheta, Kaata, and Niñokorin, the high, central, and low communities, according to the head, trunk, and legs of a human body. It was then that we realized the continuing importance of the mountain metaphor to Kaatans, and to other Andeans as well (see map, Ayllu Shrines and Anatomy of the Mountain's Body).

Kaatans look to their own bodies for an understanding of the mountain. How they see themselves is how they see their mountain. For a long time, Andeans have personified their land, and Kaatans still do. They name the places of the mountain according to their positions within the human body, and these places, set far apart on Mount Kaata, are organically united.

The anatomical paradigm for Ayllu Kaata does not correspond entirely to geography, ecological zones, and communities. The metaphor involves imagination, ability to understand meaning of three languages, embellishment by oral tradition, and, most of all, the external application of the metaphor in ritual.

The organic wholeness projected on the communities originates from Kaatans' understanding of their physical bodies. The body (uqhuntin) is all the parts and only those parts which form one inner self. Kaatans do not conceptualize interior faculties for emotions and thoughts as distinct from corporal organs. Rather, they refer to their bodies as within or inside (uqhu). The body includes the inner self, and experiences are not dualistically perceived as those of the psyche and those of the body.

Without this dualism of material and spiritual or corporeal and interior, then, Kaatan ritual does not intercede with the spiritual in behalf of the material; rather, ritual composes both terms into one. Kaatan religion is not conceptual, nor does it contain a world of spirits, but it is a metaphorical relationship with their land. Kaatans do not pray to the mountain to appease its spirit; rather, they feed the mountain blood and fat to vitalize and empower it. Ritual involves them physically with the mountain. The mountain is their land and their divinity.

Andeans understand their body as a gestalt, and the suffix ntin of uqhuntin expresses this completeness. When Andeans add ntin to a word, it means transformed wholeness. Tawantinsuyo was the Andean name for the Inca empire. It meant the four (tawa) places (suyo) insomuch as they were distinct yet united (ntin). The solidarity of the Inca empire was its similarity to a human body, as Garcilaso de la Vega, an early part-Inca chronicler wrote (1961):

> The Inca Kings divided the Empire into four districts, according to the cardinal points, the whole of which they called Tawantinsuyo, which means the four parts of the world. The center was Cuzco, which, in the Peruvian language, means the navel of the world. This name was well chosen, since Peru is long and narrow like the human body, and Cuzco is situated in the middle of its belly [57]. . . . . The inhabitants of Upper-Cuzco were to be considered as the elder, and those of Lower-Cuzco as the younger brothers. Indeed, it was as in the case of a living body, in which there always exists a difference between the right and left hands.
>
> All the cities and all the villages in our Empire were subsequently divided in this way into upper and lower lineages, as well as into upper and lower districts [45].

The communities and land compose the parts of Mount Kaata's body, and they form the mountain's inner self, which is like a center whose axis simultaneously touches every point. The points suspend the axis and yet are always in touch with the center. Apacheta, Kaata, and Niñokorin are different levels on the mountain body, and their position is what constitutes the mountain's inner self. The inner self then gives its life to the parts.

Blood and fat empower the body: blood (yawar) is the life principle, and fat (wira) is the energy principle. There are different bloods: strong, weak, frightened, and exhausted. Qollahuaya medicine men always feel the sick person's pulse to determine the type of blood. Juan Wilka, a Kaatan curer, said that Elsa Yanahuaya's blood was weak because a landslide had taken it and replaced it with water. Landslides, floods, and turbulent streams wash the land away, and water, instead of blood, flowing through the body is associated with loss of land—as well as with death. The association is that Kaatans refer to their ancestral line as blood neighbors (yawar masikuna) and that blood is a symbol of claim to land. An important gesture of the agricultural ritual is to sprinkle the earth with blood, vitalizing the land with the animal's principle of life as well as ratifying a kinship relationship with the mountain body (Urioste 1976).

The most important part is the heart (sonqo), which pumps the blood through the body. The heart is thought, intentions, and emotions. Sonqos are sad, happy, and sick, and to determine the heart of another person, the diviner places a guinea pig's mouth next to the person's heart to read its content. The person's heart is symbolically transferred to the pig's heart,

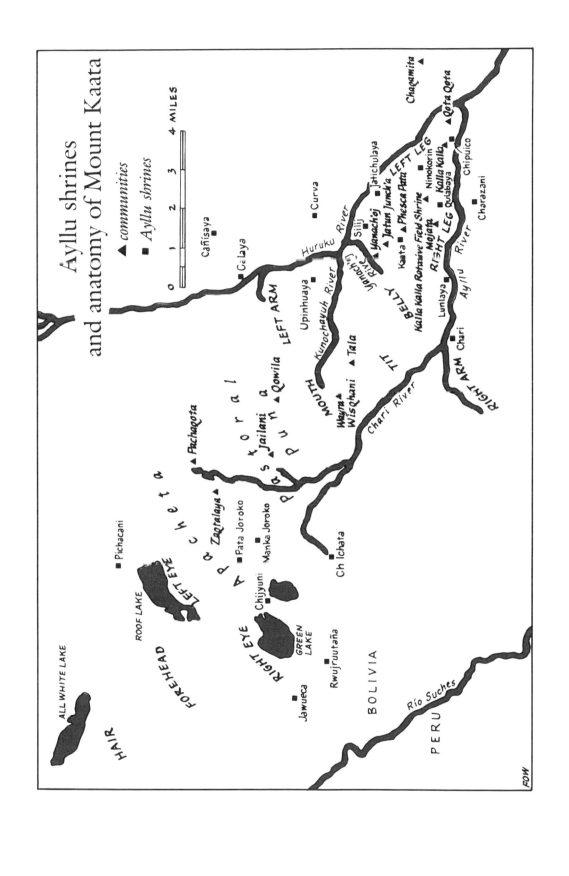

Ayllu shrines
and anatomy of Mount Kaata

▲ *communities*
■ *Ayllu shrines*

0 1 2 3 4 MILES

which is then read, revealing the type of heart in the person.

Fat (*wira*) empowers the body and is produced in the bowels. Viracocha ("Sea of Fat") was the name of an important divinity and emperor. The powerful Spaniards were called Viracocha, and today Kaatans call white people by the same name. The bowels include the liver, pancreas, kidneys, stomach, and intestines. At New Earth, Sarito, chief ritualist, reads the llama's heart and bowels to determine the agricultural life (blood) and political authority (fat) of the *ayllu*.

Kaata is the viscera of the mountain body. Its central lands yield potatoes and oca, root plants grown inside the earth, just as the viscera give vitality and power to the person. The hamlets are joined together as are the vital organs surrounding the heart: Kaatapata, the oldest and highest of these hamlets, forms the liver where the *ayllu*'s central chapel is located, and the secretaries (the dominant political leaders for the entire *ayllu*) constitute the heart. The eight large rotative fields fold like thick layers of fat around Kaata community.

Kaata's place on the mountain geographically qualifies its people to be the major ritualists for the *ayllu* body, the Qollahuaya area, and the Andes. These ritualists can best circulate blood and fat, because they live where the vital organs of the mountain produce these charged symbols of life and energy. Kaata's symbolic position does not mean, however, that communities outside of Ayllu Kaata conceive of it as being the center of the universe, but that Kaatans' conception of their *ayllu,* according to three levels and a human anatomical paradigm, places Kaata community at the center and the inside of the whole.

From the center of the mountain, the slopes slant up to form the mountain's chest (*kinre*). The right breast is called Tit Hill (Nuño Orqo), with its knob shaped like a nipple. Sophia, Carmen and Marcelino's fourteen-year-old daughter, was born on Nuño Orqo, which became her place on the mountain. It will make her fertile if she feeds it blood, fat, and coca.

The highlands are the head (*uma*). Bunchgrass grows near the summit of the mountain, as hair on the head. The wool of llamas that graze on this grass resembles human hair. As new hair grows after cutting, so do llama wool and bunchgrass continually grow in the highlands. Similar to the regeneration of human hair, llamas originate in the highland lakes, or its eyes (*ñawi*), according to Kaatans' belief. The sun dies into these eyes of the highlands, but from the reflections within the lake come all living creatures. The lake's reflections (*illa*) are the animals and people returning from inside the earth.

Animals and people originate from and return to the head of the mountain. It is the place of origin and return, like the human head, which is the point of entry and exit for the inner self. The dead travel by underground waterways to the mountain's head (*uma pacha*), from where they can arise to the land of the living. The living emerge from the eyes of the mountain, journey across its head, chest, trunk, and legs, and die in the lowlands. They are buried and return with the sun to the *uma pacha,* point of origin and return.

Apachetans' home near the summit of the mountain qualifies them to be the ritualists of the lakes and the dead. These highland herders travel to Kaata and Niñokorin for the Feast with the Dead. After praying for the dead and receiving bread, they carry the dead's food to the highlands. A highland herder feeds Lake Pachaqota a llama fetus during the major herding ritual of All Colors. Kaatan diviners assist Apachetans in this ritual by prophesying from guinea pigs, and Niñokorins bring *chicha* (corn beer) to the highlands.

The dispersed settlement pattern of pastoral Apachetans resembles the differentiated face: Jawueca is the hair, Ch'uyuni (four families) is the right eye, and Zaqtalaya (six families) is the left eye. Water holes are necessary for livestock, and alpacas need the softer marsh areas to keep their hooves from cracking.

Wayra Wisqhani ("Door of the Wind"), a cavity within the earth from which air arises, is the mouth. Whenever it rains too much, mountain ritualists feed a llama heart into Wayra Wisqhani so that its breath will blow the rain clouds away.

Flowing from the summit, the Chari and Kunochayuh rivers form the *maki* (hand to elbow) of Mount Kaata. The right arm is Ayllu Chari, and the left arm is Ayllu Upinhuaya. Chari and Upinhuaya women are the major ritualists for dispelling misfortune and inflicting curses. During the Misfortune Mass, Rosinta Garcia washed a rat fetus into the Kunochayuh River to remove sickness from the Yanahuaya family. Upinhuayas are ritualists of the river who can remove, as well as cause, misfortune.

Mount Kaata's lower fields are the *chaqi* (foot to knee), and the indentations on the river are the *sillu* (toenails). The long, narrow fields run parallel to the rivers descending to the jungle, and the mountain appears to be standing on them. The left leg is Niñokorin (eighty families), and the right is Quiabaya (fifteen families). The *sillu* are at the periphery of Mount Kaata where it joins at its lowest points with Ayllus Chari and Upinhuaya. The two small settlements of Silij (four families) and Jatichulaya (thirteen families) are the left toenails, and Lunlaya (fifteen families) forms the right toenails. Many more *sillus,* however, naturally arise every time the rivers subside after flooding.

The lower fields produce corn, which is fermented

into *chicha*. *Chicha* is the sacred drink of the Andes, although it has more recently been replaced by sugarcane alcohol. The mountain and its people drink *chicha* during all ritual occasions. Niñokorin's people take care of the lower fields, not only by agriculture, but also by ritual to guarantee abundant corn for the mountain. The lower peoples annually feed their shrines at the feast of Corn Planting, which is similar to New Earth. Apachetans contribute a llama, and Kaatans bring blood and fat to the corn planting ritual at Niñokorin.

Kaatans perceive of their *ayllu* as an identity between the mountain and the human body. They love metaphors between people and nature, and the association may be a resemblance of parts, similar use, or identical words. *Uma*, for example, means "head" in Quechua and "water" in Aymara. This double meaning fits their symbolic understanding of Apacheta. Kaatans are alive to the multiple interpretations of behavior, words, and natural phenomena. They compared my beard to the rays of the sun, but they also associated it with heart, because I always confused heart (*sonqo*) for beard (*sonk'a*). They later explained, however, that I had spoken correctly, since Kaatan pictographs depict the sun with a beard for its rays and a heart for its center.

The mountain is the unifying and holistic metaphor for Kaatans. Judy and I participated as members of the Yanahuaya family in twelve rituals that dealt with sickness, death, lineage, and land. In some way, every ritual centered around the mountain metaphor. Sickness, for example, was cured by symbolically putting the body of the mountain together. Marriage rituals gathered together people and produce from three levels of the mountain to symbolize that marriage unites the people of the mountain. Furthermore, statistical patterns from 24 marriages in the eighteenth century as well as 205 in the twentieth century verified that the people of Mount Kaata evenly exchanged spouses in marriage among low, middle, and high communities on the mountain. Metaphorically, then, social principles corresponded to a mountain understood as a human body with three parts: head, trunk, and legs. Agricultural rituals symbolically awoke and fed the mountain so that the mountain was kind to Kaatans and gave them food and life.

Rituals, moreover, reminded Kaatans of the integrity of their mountain, especially when the parts of Mount Kaata did not correspond to the human metaphor. The governor of Charazani usurped the lower lands of Mount Kaata in 1592. He turned that land into a hacienda and forced the Indians to work as serfs. As a record of their battle to regain the land, Kaatan Indians hold in Kaata legal documents dating from 1592

until 1799, validated replicas of originals now in Seville. The Indians, testifying in these documents, argued that the land on the lower part of Mount Kaata belongs to the middle and high communities because it is part of the mountain's body. Not only by this argument, however, but also by legal strategy did Kaatans convince the Crown to restore the lower part of the mountain in 1799. For two hundred years Kaatans have been reminded of the wholeness of their mountain by metaphors and rituals that lend cultural solidarity to distant and divided communities (see Bastien n.d.*b*).

The Indians' battle for their mountain continued into the twentieth century. Four centuries of litigation gave them a mastery over the legal-bureaucratic Spanish "sense of justice," the intricacies of which many Spaniards and Republicans never understood. Charazani officials usually bypassed legal arguments and employed racial slurs against Kaatans by calling them "rebels, savages, barbarians, naturals, devoid of reason, and unenlightened." In 1919, Eduardo Pasten of Charazani, for example, forced two Indians to give him their house plots in payment for a loan. Kaatans reclaimed this land and sent their leader, Vicente Vega, to authorities in La Paz. Vega astutely argued that according to article three of the Law Fifth of October 1874, and article fifty of the Supreme Court of the Law First of December 1880, commoners held indivisibly and in common all lands corresponding to their communities. The sale of land to Pasten was, therefore, invalid, since no Kaatan commoner had total proprietorship over communal land. The La Paz prefect agreed with Vega's arguments, even though, in his conclusion, he referred to Kaatans as members of the disgraceful indigenous race. Pasten ignored the decree, threatened Vega's life, and had him arrested. Vega, however, sought asylum with Ulla Ulla's subprefect, and the argument was resolved in Kaata's favor. The Charazani mestizo used prejudice and violence against the Indians, and they resorted to justice and the law.

This century's concern has not been so much the removal of *ayllu* land as the division among its communities brought about by boundary disputes. Bolivian laws (1833, 1874, 1888) emphasized proprietorship and indivisibility for the community rather than the *ayllu*. Whereas during the Crown and early Republic the Qollahuaya *ayllus* were united against the mestizos, presently they are internally divided by boundary disputes. Such disputes resulted in inter-*ayllu* wars, as illustrated by an eyewitness account of Upinhuaya's invasion of Kaata: "Six Kaatans were fixing their terraces, clearing brush and removing rocks. Forty Upinhuayas crossed the Kunochayuh River. They beat and stabbed the workers. The Upinhuay(as) claimed that land to be theirs" (Kaatan ms. 1904: October 27).

Kaatans regained their land shortly afterward, but the crossing of the Kunochayuh is still remembered by Kaatans.

Since 1953, Agrarian Reformists have tried to incorporate Qollahuaya communities into the social, political, and economic life of Bolivia. These reformers have disregarded the more traditional cultural unit of Ayllu Kaata. Apacheta, Kaata, and Niñokorin were legally incorporated into the statutes of the reform as independent, autonomous, and territorially defined communities. Each community now has its own leaders who are linked to Charazani and La Paz instead of to its neighbors on the mountain. The Bolivian government, moreover, requires that each community build a school where Indians should learn the "new" language, economics, politics, mathematics, civics, and Spanish and Bolivian history. New links have been formed between the communities by a common civic pride as well as by competition between them with soccer matches and tournaments that rank the winners and losers with trophies and awards.

The definition of boundaries has split the communities of Ayllu Kaata not simply by stating that levels are distinct to the communities, but also by making these differences explicit in relation to external sources of authority. Especially after the Bolivian laws of the 1880's the communities defined and redefined their boundaries. The Agrarian Reform further insisted on clearly defined community boundaries. The resultant feuding has been a strong centrifugal force that has separated the parts of the *ayllu* body from each other and has made them dependent on the legal chicaneries of La Paz. The Indians complain that they have spent six thousand pesos (a day's wage for twelve hundred laborers) in legal fees against Chari and Apacheta within the last twenty years. They explain it simply by recalling the day when the surveyor "photographed their mountain."

Laws of supply and demand determined by national and international markets create new relationships on Mount Kaata. Apachetans, for example, have linked themselves economically with the pastoral herders of Chari; they realize the advantages of consolidating pastoral lands and flocks, as well as utilizing Chari's truck to ship hides and wool to La Paz. Apacheta has sided with Ayllu Chari in another land battle with Kaata. Niñokorin now ships more resources to La Paz than it exchanges with the central highlands. The three levels of Ayllu Kaata are exchanging fewer resources than before; they prefer to sell them in La Paz, where they can buy the traditional goods and the "new" world products such as clothes, sewing machines, radios, Japanese wool, and plastic pots. Competition between sellers and buyers slowly discourages the amiable ties of reciprocal exchange among levels as these farmers compete with their neighbors in an economic world of supply and demand.

Airports and roads have created new economic relationships among sectors of Bolivia—relationships that are different from traditional exchange patterns within the Qollahuaya area. Before the advent of trucks, roads, and airplanes, the Qollahuaya area was an important central level between the highlands (Altiplano) of Bolivia and Peru and the lowlands of the Yungas. Coca, incense, quinine, and fruit traveled up to the highlands in exchange for meat, salt, wheat, and pots, which were sent down to the Yungas. In contrast to the present time, fifty years ago Charazani was a village of muleteers exchanging the produce of the Yungas (as well as gold and rubber) with the highlands of Bolivia, Peru, and Argentina. The traveling curers and ritualists followed this expanding exchange. The Chaco War of the 1930s cut off the supply of mules from Argentina by tightening national boundaries between Bolivia and Argentina. More direct routes to the Yungas were made from La Paz, bypassing the Qollahuaya region. The airplane has made direct contact with large urban centers and the productive Yungas easier. Now, as a result, intermediate marketing communities are on the decline.

Kaalaya and Cañisaya, neighboring communities of Kaata, illustrate these new economic relationships. These people travel to Apolo to exchange coca for the produce of the Qollahuaya *ayllus*. Ten years ago they traveled three times a year to Apolo, a journey of seven days each way by mule. Kaalayans and Cañisayans distributed coca to the southeastern parts of the Altiplano in exchange for *charqui*, potatoes, pots, and salt. Today, half the Cañisaya coca traders now live in La Paz, and they fly to Apolo, often renting a DC-3 for some 1,750 pesos ($700) a flight. They buy and sell the coca for cash and control a large part of the La Paz coca market.

For many Andean areas, colonialism, republicanism, and modernization have obliterated the *ayllu*'s integrity. Many people consider the Aymara pastoral people of Apacheta, who are politically and economically associated with Chari, and the lowland people of Niñokorin, who are associated with Charazani. The people of Charazani consider Ayllu Kaata to be nonexistent; they argue that the three communities are no longer linked to one another, but instead to Charazani. These observers, and many anthropologists as well, have identified Andean unification with political and economic associations, and consequently they have overlooked deeper symbolic ties. At different historical periods, Mount Kaata's land and people appeared to be divided, yet they were metaphorically united. This symbolic solidarity spurred them on to restore the mountain integrity. Their rituals, for example, continued to feed Mount Kaata as a whole body, even though its legs had been expropriated for several centuries.

In conclusion, metaphors were, and still are, unifying principles between ecological levels and groups within the Andes. The mountain/body metaphor of the Qollahuayas continues to unite distant and distinct Andeans into an *ayllu*. This metaphor has enabled these communities to maintain cultural units despite divisive external political forces. The metaphor is essentially a comparison of analogous qualities between Andeans and their environment. They understand their own body in terms of the mountain, and they consider the mountain in terms of their own anatomy. The mountain/body metaphor provides Qollahuayas with an ecological/natural model for their identification of self. It provides them with a symbolic system and religion that is ecological and earth-oriented.

6. The Runas of Bolivia

BRUNO DE ROISSART

Translated by Françoise Dumonceau and Mónica Weiss

The Runa Indians live in the Bolivian Andes, an extraordinary mountain range with peaks as high as 21,300 feet (6,500 meters). The Aymara Indians, harsh and hostile to strangers, live in the high plateau (Altiplano) between 13,100 and 16,400 feet (4,000 and 5,000 meters). This area is a steppe alternately swept by the icy gales and parched by the unrelenting sun. The Quechua Indians live in the valleys extending from the snowy mountain range down to the luxuriant vegetation of the Amazonian plains. Owing to their milder climate and more fertile land, the Quechuas' outlook on life is more joyful and carefree than that of the Aymaras.

The pre-Columbian religion of the Runas, which still persists inextricably mixed with Catholic worship, has as its supreme god and creator Viracocha. Then came the Father Sun (Inti-Tatay) and the Mother Moon (Quilla-Mamay). This holy couple presided over the life of everything on Mother Earth (Pachamama)—a sensible world, on a human level. Above the Pachamama is Hanaj Pacha (heaven), a resting place for those who have come to a spiritual life. Under the Pachamama is Uku Pacha (hell), the dwelling place of inferior beings. The path for every being goes from Uku Pacha to Hanaj Pacha, through the incarnation in the Pachamama goddess who dispenses good and evil to the beings living within her.

Animals, natural phenomena, and the elements also enjoy a worship still expressed in the dances: the Dance of the Condor (animal-head), the Dance of the Puma or of the Jaguar (animal-heart), and the Dance of the Bull or of the Cow (animal-stomach), which has become integral since the introduction of cattle into the Andes by the Spaniards. The trilogy thus becomes complete, like the Egyptian sphinx, which is simultaneously eagle, lion, and cow. But the arrival of the Spaniards has drastically changed the structure of the ancient religions by forcibly imposing Catholicism: one God; one representative on earth, the Christ; and one law, the Bible. To safeguard the worship of their gods, the Indians gave them the names of Catholic saints. For example, the Pachamama became the Holy Virgin; Waira, the god of the wind, became Saint Peter; and Illapa, god of thunder, became Santiago.

To illustrate the mixing of two religions, this is how I saw the feast of Santiago in 1977 in the remote community north of Potosi. Santiago or Illapa is generally represented by a rider brandishing a sword as resplendent as the lightning. He also substituted himself for Tatay Wamani, god-protector of the livestock. According to the ancient tradition related by the author Pablo José de Arriaga, "Illapa was a man in heaven formed from stars, carrying a club in his left hand and a sling in his right hand. He was dressed in brilliant attire which gave the spark to the lightning when he turned around to draw his sling, while snapping would cause the thunder."

Sabine Hargous in *Les Appeleurs d'Ames* tells us: "Concerning the transformation of Illapa into Santiago, numerous explanations have been given. It is believed that the Incas gave to the Spanish blunderbuss the same attributes as the thunderbolts because of its snaps which resulted in the striking of the victim. According to Father Arriaga: Perhaps it is because when it thunders, the boys from Spain say that the horse of Santiago gallops. During the battles, the Indians saw the Spaniards shooting with the blunderbuss and they named it Illapa, thunderbolt. They heard the Spaniards screaming, Santiago! Santiago! No matter what Illapa or Santiago is called, this deity can explode with anger and cut off ten human or animal heads in a single swipe of his sword of light, if one fails to respect him or neglects to make the offerings that are due him."

The best sacrifice that we can offer this demanding god is of course the llama, preferably red (like fire?). Let us witness a typical ritual: Silverio, the *yatiri*, is already at the sacrificial site and has placed his special cloth for coca on a small stone altar. He is sitting behind it, on a seat also made of stone. Little by little, the members of the different *ayllus* (totemic clans on mountains) arrive with alcohol. We exchange coca leaves, and we all chew it with a small piece of *lejía*, made of solidified quinoa ash and some other substances, to better extract the cocaine. The bag of coca and the bottle of alcohol are passed around the group several times, and we are soon in a state conducive to communication with the divinities. Here we have the miracle of the little mother coca.

Then Silverio starts the reading of the coca leaves spread in front of him. Everyone holds his breath. We can hear the fall of every coca leaf on the ancient square of fabric that is reserved for this purpose. Silverio's eyelids squint slightly, and his eyes are reduced to brilliant slits in his shriveled ochre skin. The magic word falls from his lips, "*Sumaj*" ("Everything is all right"). He moves his head slightly in the direction of the llama, which is then roughly dragged into the center of the circle of spectators. It is a magnificent animal, and its red fur shines in the sun. It is shaking with fear, resisting the rough treatment of the Sicuyas—the shamans performing the sacrifice. Illapa will have every reason to be satisfied with this sacrifice.

Silverio is now standing. His wife has brought him a

Runas Shaman. Photo by Bruno Roissart.

terra-cotta brazier. He kneels towards the East, the sacred direction, and while his wife sprinkles some copal resin over the incandescent coal, he lifts up his censer and smoke rises straight toward the sky. While he is reciting a prayer, four men lay the llama on the ground and hold it there, knife at its throat, ready to slaughter. Silverio, the smoke of the incense half concealing his face, is invoking all the deities one by one. At that moment we get the impression of being sent back very far in time to the time when the Aymaras were free to worship their gods and were masters of their sacred ground, of the Sacred Earth.

At a given signal, they slice the llama's throat, and its blood pours down into a large ceramic bowl. Our eyes are riveted on the bright red blood. I stiffen, on the verge of nausea. Nevertheless, nothing is barbaric or savage in this sacrifice, which allows for the equilibrium of the community below with the world above, the divine domain. The sacrificed llama rejoins the gods in their eternal race, and its blood fertilizes the earth. Silverio removes a small amount of blood with a wooden spoon and walks off to offer this magic fertilizer to the Pachamama, goddess of the earth, in particular places determined by tradition. Before the men cut up the beast, the sorcerer plucks out its heart; he will use it to cure the teacher's epileptic son. The coca and the alcohol are again circulated, and everybody congratulates each other warmly. The year will be good.

We anxiously wait for nightfall. Silverio will no doubt use his *hantis,* wooden sticks, which he clicks against each other when he reaches a state of trance, putting him in communication with the supernatural. These sticks help him "take the step," the bridge over which his voice will "reach the other side" and awaken the occult powers. Last year Silverio wanted to use the sticks to cure me of a serious case of dysentery, but he did not succeed in attaining the second state, which is absolutely necessary for the use of his *hantis.* Therefore, I did not see them. But this night, Panfilo asks him to take advantage of the fact that he has the heart of a sacrificed llama to try to cure his little boy, who is epileptic.

At 8 P.M. we are all gathered at Panfilo's house with his wife, their little boy, Silverio, and Miguel, the *hilanko,* or traditional chief. We have large quantities of coca, *lejía,* cigarettes, and alcohol. The llama's heart is on the *mesa* (altar) with *cuti* (kernels of corn that are used for divination) and some medicinal plants. Everything is ready. The door is bolted so that neither spirits nor human beings may enter or leave. We begin to chew the coca and drink the alcohol in silence, interrupted only by a few words uttered by the sorcerer. He reads our futures in the coca leaves and warns me that the soul of one of my grandparents is constantly watching over me, but he demands that the soul be worshiped. Apart from that, his divinations are *"suerte, suerte,"* or luck, lots of luck.

Four hours later, nothing has happened yet. We are a little high, and the combined effects of the alcohol and the large quantities of coca have created an atmosphere of unreality. We are all drifting. It is then that the shamanistic ceremony actually begins. Formerly, it was prohibited by the Catholic Church, and practicing it was punishable by death, but the Indians have kept it in the strictest secrecy for centuries. Silverio and Miguel leave with two censers and pray to the moon (Pfarsi Mamay), their arms extended toward the heavenly body. They also implore the famed Virgin of Copacabana; it is better to have all the luck on your side, and two divinities are more powerful than one. Shortly after they return to the shelter of the small hut, I sense that the sorcerer is going to enter a trance. He kneels facing the four cardinal points, turning himself at a great speed on one knee and calling upon the gods. Without pausing, he insults all the devils, making gestures to chase them away, then runs screaming from the room, leaving us astounded. The door bangs, and his screams vanish into the night.

The next morning we wake up very early because Silverio, according to the ritual, must offer the heart of the llama to the rising sun in order to obtain the recovery of Panfilo's son. The sky grows pale and we are getting worried when Silverio finally appears with his usual smiling face. He greets us, laughing, as if nothing had happened the night before and immediately sits in front of his *mesa* beside the little boy. In a small bowl he grinds the kernels of corn that have been used in the divination ceremony and mixes them with some clotted blood of the llama, which he carefully examines for a long time. He adds the tip of the llama heart and a few coca leaves, all without ever stopping drinking alcohol or chewing more leaves. Then he stands up and, murmuring in a low voice, turns the bowl three times around the child's head and passes his hands over the child's whole body without touching it. Then he walks towards the parents and performs the same liberation rite on them.

As a fine psychologist, Silverio understood that the child's sickness came from unconscious conflicts with his parents, and he deals with them separately. However, he does not discount the supernatural origin of the sickness and takes some kernels of corn (*cuti*) to read in them a message that he delivers to us with his smiling slanted eyes: "Suerte, suerte!" The child will recover. He grabs the bowl and leaves, takes some steps toward the church, kneels in front of the portico, and turns to face the sun. He kneels again, and finally he throws the contents of the bowl towards Inti, the morning star. The ceremony is over, and in fact it later turned out that the child did recover.

How can we explain this trance? A shaman has the power to put himself in contact with the supernatural world by means of the state of trance brought on by the consumption of certain drugs (San Pedro cactus, cocaine, and the like) and an extreme concentration. The voice of the spirits is manifested through the sound of the magic sticks, which can be replaced by a rattle or a bunch of leaves.

However, there is a basic difference between the shamans of the Andean high plateaus and those of the Amazonian tribes. The latter, as is the case of the shamans of the Siberian communities, are the center of religious, and therefore of community, life. In the Andean communities they are simply part of the group, have their role to play, and are not called upon except in certain cases. In the Andes, the shamans are sorcerers, soothsayers, and healers, but they are not the only ones who possess these powers; numerous *yatiris* can foretell the future without entering into a trance. This shows the developing Andean evolution towards a specialization of the function of the representatives of the gods, in contrast to the situation among the forest tribes.

Like the shamans, the "clergy" comprises practitioners of white magic (the *pakos*) and practitioners of black magic (the *laikas*). The *yatiris* devote themselves to the prediction of the future, and the *collasiris* to medicine. The shaman can be at the same time *pako, laika, yatiri,* and *collasiri.*

One can find a variety of functions in he who is called the "healer," but it is important to note that not all healers are shamans. Here, the healing is above all magic. The scarcity of medicinal plants in the north of the Department of Potosí forces the healers to overcome illness by fighting the evil spirit that brought it on, because illness is almost never considered natural. Either the patient has had a spell put on him by a sorcerer or an evil spirit, or his soul has been possessed. This harmful force must be fought by the magic force. Therefore, the medicines are almost always magic. It is only in another region of Bolivia, that of the Qollahuaya healers, that one can attend a healing ceremony where magic and the science of plants are of equal importance and blended into one single ceremony, as we shall see further on.

The society of the Runas (the Quechua and Aymara Indians) is characterized by an absolute democracy on the traditional community level; one could even say that we have come onto a case of perfect communism, but reserved for men.

The numerous systems of mutual aid and economic compensation (*ayni* and *minka*) within the Indian community, or *ayllu*, make capitalism and personal enrichment at the cost of other members of the community impossible. Land was (and sometimes still is) communal property and evenly redistributed every year among the heads of family. The agrarian unit inside the family is the *aynoka*, made up of several *topus*. The *topu* is the agrarian unit at one ecological level.

It is mandatory in theory for all men to pass through the hierarchy of ranks in the community, and elections are held every year. Any danger of deterioration of power is thus avoided. No economic advantage is gained from being in power; on the contrary, it sometimes results in a slight impoverishment but is compensated by prestige. The systems of mutual aid by free labor (*minka*) and by payment in kind and in money (*ayni*) permit the authorities to carry out their duties and at the same time ensure their own subsistence and that of their families.

The patriarchy is almost absolute. The Indian woman has little authority and is submissive to her father and then to her husband, except in cases of extremely strong personalities, but these cases are overcome by social pressure. The Indian women who want to live an independent life are forced to flee their community. They usually go to live in the city as servants of a bourgeois family, which is still worse, but there is at least the illusion of being able to walk freely down the streets of the city.

There is not a lot of sexual freedom, although virginity is not a requirement for marriage. We must not be misled by the fact that youngsters in early adolescence already share a life together, often with the approval of their parents. This is *sirwiñacu*, traditional cohabitation that inevitably leads to marriage except in extenuating circumstances. Incidents of free love are not customary among the Indians of the Andes except in decaying communities depraved by the influence of the vices of the city. This should not be referred to as free love, but instead as prostitution.

The Runas, before the Spanish Conquest, deserved without a doubt the prize for ecology. Traditional agriculture as practiced by the Quechuas and Aymaras on the slopes of the Andes required the construction of huge structures that are probably unequaled on all five continents; millions of kilometers of terraces and irrigation canals were built on the steep Andean slopes or in the rocky mountains, as well as on the desert slopes facing the Pacific Ocean. They permit the use of enormous extensions of land, and without them that land would have remained either steppe or desert.

The technique used in the construction of terraces was also remarkable; the steep land, after being formed into steps, was reworked in the following manner: one layer of waterproof clay was laid down, then a layer of stones and permeable gravel or sand to facilitate the drainage of any excess water, then a layer of earth, and then a layer of humus. It was all held in by remarkable stone walls, placed with extreme caution and containing small openings at the lower level to let water pass through to the level of the humus of the terrace below. This ingenious system allowed for the irrigation of the corn crops of the lower terraces by the nitrogen-enriched water coming down from the leguminous crops of the upper levels.

The tools used by the pre-Columbian Indians and still in use in the region of Copacabana and also the whole Apoobamba Mountain Range and its continuation north to Cuzco do not cause erosion and are respectful of the microbiological life and structure of the terrain, since, unlike a plow, they are not used to dig up the land completely. They are called *chaquita-jilla* (a type of long-pointed spade) and the *laukana* (a small hoe). With these two tools and their hands the Indians accomplish these incredible feats without ruining the land.

The edible plants chosen and constantly improved upon by the phytogeneticians of the pre-Inca and Inca empires are highly nutritious—once again, unmatched on earth. *Tarwi* (a legume richer in proteins than soya) and *cañihua* and quinoa (grains that are richer in proteins and vitamins than any other grains on earth) are among the specialties of this agricultural region. There are also tubers: potatoes (more than three hundred varieties), *illacos, isaños,* and ocas. The vegetables grown (varieties of *Rumex* and *moutarde,* for example) are more nourishing than the Euro-Asiatic vegetables, and there are fruits, too, such as *chirimoya* and *sinchua*— again, richer in vitamins and proteins than all other known fruits. Regarding the conservation of natural resources, the Incas were once again in the vanguard. One who cut down a tree without permission in the Upper Andes was simply punished by death.

The collective ownership of land facilitated better land management and intelligent rotation, avoiding depletion of the land and the spread of plant diseases. The Indians never hesitated to take long trips to the Pacific Coast in search of guano and to the banks of the Amazon for humus. They carried back those two types of fertilizer. The earth was priceless, and time did not count.

The Spaniards changed all this, and since their arrival, the practice of agriculture began a period of rapid and continuous decline that accelerates even now. The famous conquistadores began by destroying the irrigation canals, causing famine and providing the Spaniards with considerable manpower for their silver and gold mines. The extraction of those metals resulted in the clearing of entire forests of *queñuas, queshwaras,* and *kholas* of the Altiplano and the Cordillera. The land was abandoned by the victims of massacres (especially the intellectual elite, among them the famous Inca agronomists), and famines and epidemics racked the population (in fifty years the Indian population of Alto Perú went from ten million persons to one million, according to the most reasonable estimates). This extensive land, once fertile and cultivated, became grazing land. These impressive "civilizing" measures by the Spanish brought the Altiplano and Cordillera to the point of desertification.

Currently, the southern Altiplano resembles the Sahel, and Lake Poopo runs the risk of suffering the sad fate of Lake Tchad in the Sahara. But the Spaniards, and their creole descendants, "liberators" of Alto Perú (present-day Bolivia) did not stop there. They appropriated the lands of Indian communities, and by the time feudalism was ending in Europe, it was starting in America. The Quechuas and Aymaras were left the hilly land. The Incaic organization, which would have aided in the construction of new terraces, no longer existed, and so erosion began. The Andean peasants then adopted the practice of outlining furrows in the direction of the slope, and the erosion is catastrophic, though such vertical furrows have been shown to prevent potato rot [Ed. Note: however, see R. Rhoades, page 41]. This sad history of the Andean land continued until 1952, the date of the agrarian reform in Bolivia.

The lands of the large estates were redistributed to the Aymaras and Quechuas. But the land was given to them individually, not communally, as ancient custom would have dictated. This results in the loss of ancient traditions of mutual aid and so, in turn, the possibility of rebuilding the terraces or the irrigation canals or of programming rotation of the crops. Moreover, the sons of large families saw their portions of inherited land progressively diminish; they could no longer let the land rest. They were advised to use chemical fertilizers, but those are costly and they "burn the land," as the Runas say. The 1952 agrarian reform also forced the peasants into a desert-producing "commerce agriculture" (planting for selling).

Other "improvements" were introduced after the arrival of the Spanish. Introduction of the Egyptian-style *araire* resulted in the upheaval of land structure and, again, the loss of fertility and land by erosion from the slopes. For economic reasons (commerce with the city), since the agrarian reform the peasants are involved in the monoculture of plants like potatoes, corn, or wheat, which debilitates the soil and produces deserts.

Livestock breeding did not follow a better path. It was extremely well organized during the Inca empire. Immense herds of vicuñas, alpacas, and llamas grazed in the Andes on rich natural pastures carefully kept up by irrigation. The results were protection of the vicuña, a wild llama with exceptionally fine wool that has become very scarce today, and protection of the land, since Andean camelids do not have hooves, but instead padded feet that adapt perfectly to the topography and do not make the land crumble. Their teeth cut the grass but do not pull it out. A large assortment of grasses is used as pasturage, because the llamas eat all grass, even the coarsest. Andean camelids have a wool finer than sheep's wool, with longer threads that therefore can be woven into more durable clothing.

The imported herds have all the disadvantages. The heavy cows make the terraces crumble, and the sheep and goats increase the erosion with their hooves. Since their incomplete dentures cannot cut the grass, they must pull it out by its roots, thereby leaving the ground barren.

The pre-Columbian houses (which can still be seen in the north of the Department of Potosí and in the south of the Department of Oruro) were round, made of stone or adobe. The round shape, as opposed to the square, preserves heat most efficiently and resists earthquakes. Its roof is conical, requiring only the use of branches and straw in spiral form. It does not need tree trunks like those used in the construction of houses with right angles, now very common in the Andes. Besides, the latter, with their aluminum-sheet roofs, are more expensively wasteful of heat at night than are the round houses. The cutting down of the most beautiful *queñuas* and *queshwaras* for the roof beams necessitates the replantation of the eucalyptuses, which grow fast but wear out the planting ground and their water preserves by excessive evapotranspiration and heavy use of nutritive elements. Moreover, the eucalyptuses give back to the ground very little organic matter and favor erosion, leaving under them a barren ground.

To save what is left of the land of the Andes, gigantic reforms must be undertaken by the Andean nations. These reforms should have several different concerns: conservation of the lands, fabrication of compost, and a well-thought-out reforestation plan together with the use of nonviolent energy (solar, aeolian, and that produced from methane gas), the severe reduction and improvement of the flocks of sheep and goats, the reorganization of the country society based on traditional patterns, the reinstitution of all the knowledge and techniques used by the pre-Columbians in their agriculture and livestock breeding, and above all, a total and drastic reworking of the relationship of exploitation that exists between the city and the country. Therein lies the true origin of the extreme exploitation of the land and of the slow death of the Altiplano and the Cordillera. It is not yet too late, but for political reasons the development of the Andean lands is not a priority of the Bolivian government, which prefers to invest in the colonization of the Amazonian plains, the Great Illusion. In a few words: progress, as ever, means destruction. This is the "civilized way" and history shall repeat until. . . .

Good health requires pure air and water; well-balanced and healthy diet; periodic fasts; absence of drugs; a good natural pharmacopoeia drawn from mineral, vegetable, and animal kingdoms; no emotional disturbances; sufficient rest; and good body hygiene. Among the Runas, air, water, and rest are satisfactory, but nutrition and hygiene are actually at a regrettable stage. In Bolivia the Indians are not undernourished, but they are poorly nourished. The situation has not stopped deteriorating since the fall of the Incaic organization. Before the destruction carried out by the Spaniards, the Indians had an incredible assortment of food at their disposal.

Thanks to the cultivable ecological stages from 15,000 feet (4,600 meters) above sea level to the subtropical forest at more or less 5,000 feet (1,500 meters), the Runas could produce among other products:

—Tubers: three hundred varieties of potatoes, *illaco* or *ulluco*, bitter potato, *pinauttanta, yacón, racacha, quemillu,* oca, *isaño, yuca* (mandioca), sweet potato, *walusa,* and others

—Cereals: quinoa, *cañihua,* corn, amaranth

—Leguminous staples: *tarwi* (*lupino,* richer in protein than soya bean), broad beans, and the like

—Pre-Columbian vegetables

—Other products like *escariote, lacayote, chirimoya,* avocados, *sapote, lucuma, pacae,* Brazil nuts, *sank'ayu,* peanuts, tomatoes, cacao, *ayuramp'u, sinch'ua,* honey, and so on

—Meat of llamas, alpacas, guinea pigs, ducks, insects.

Even until the agrarian reform in 1952, there still existed in traditional communities numerous exchanges of products between the different ecological zones (vertical zones). In 1952 the lands were given back to the peasants mostly as private property, and exchanges are now made more "horizontally," that is to say, between the Indian peasant and the city via the mestizo trader. Indeed, a lot of goods come from the city (white sugar, white flour, noodles, alcohol, and the like), but most of them are useless and even detrimental to the Indians' health. The result is a complete impoverishment of the diet inside the Indian community, especially where the road goes through communities, this road that is said to be "absolutely necessary for the development of isolated communities." It is also said in government circles that the road provides the Indian community with the "advantages" of the city. These pompous words hide another reality: the road allows the city people to better exploit the peasants through the middlemen, who are the truck owners, the undisputed kings of commerce. And thus begins the vicious cycle of economic dependence. This ends with the "subproletarianization" of the landless peasant, who emigrates to the city, starving, searching in despair for a way to feed his family with the leftovers rejected by the "great machine."

In the mountains the Indian fights hunger and fatigue by chewing coca leaves, which also remain the essential element for numerous religious and social rites. The mixture of coca juices and the *lejía* allows for the extraction of the coca alkaloid in the mouth, in which case the dosage of cocaine is minuscule. But when the coca is chewed every day from morning to night, it becomes a vice. The Indian relies on it and does not try to escape his exploited condition. Without the help of the coca, he would feel the pain of starvation and would also feel too weak to work.

Alcohol, however, is the Indians' most harmful drug. At 90 or 192 proof, ethyl or methyl, cane or wood, any alcohol is used to burn the throat or the stomach in an attempt to forget misery and exploitation. Alcohol is slowly killing the entire population of the Andes. Knowing this, it is difficult to discuss health in the Andes. I am familiar with the situation, having spent several years in the Bolivian Cordillera, sharing the Indian way of life, trying to improve their living conditions without great expenses. There are very few healthy Indians, morally or physically. The two conditions go hand in hand.

Regarding natural pharmacopoeia, there is a fact to be mentioned in Bolivia. The herbalist-healers of the Bautista Saavedra province in the Department of La Paz, called Qollahuayas, are likely to have the richest variety of plants of all the herbalists in the entire world. Their pharmacopoeia includes more than a thousand medicinal plants, not only from the Saavedra region but also from every climatic zone in Bolivia, Peru, Ecuador, Chile, Argentina, Brazil, and Paraguay. They are nomadic physicians divided into three castes according to their specialty: Khutus, Jichastes, and Rekhas. They, like the Yatiris (soothsayers-wisemen) of every Indian community, know how to cure psychological illnesses that are inevitable in a primitive society where taboos are numerous and where man lives in perpetual contact with the spirits (elementary, benevolent, or malevolent). The Qollahuayas are known to the Indians and the mestizos in the whole Cordillera of the Andes and beyond. They were once the astrologer-physicians appointed to the Inca court, the only non-nobles authorized to approach the sovereigns. Having heard of their legendary reputation, I went to the region in 1977, and so I have had the opportunity to observe their healing techniques. The healers were extensively researched and well documented by the French scientist Louis Girault, whose study of seventeen years is yet to be published because of his untimely death.

Don Florentino is dressed in his ceremonial poncho and wears an unusual type of straw hat that his father, a renowned healer, had brought back from a medical visit to Panama. He has tied around his neck a finely embroidered white scarf, of course his *chuspa* (coca bag), and, hanging from his shoulder, his large *capacho,* a magnificent hand-woven bag, red, covered with designs of small white horses. He carries in this bag his medicinal plants and other medications drawn from the three natural kingdoms—animal, mineral, and vegetable. He is accompanied by his assistant, and they walk together, chanting in the holy language of the Qollahuayas.

Crossing the garden, the healer picks a few more fresh plants, since it is the end of the dry season and there are few green plants. Then he goes to the house of the tubercular patient. The patient's wife and sister, in honor of the occasion, have pinned onto their *mantas* (large squares of wool that cover their shoulders) their large silver *topus*. The *topus* are enormous pins ending in a large spoon. The most beautiful ones come from this region.

The healer and his assistant sit in front of a small stone altar over which they place a *chusilla,* cloth reserved for this purpose. To wrap the gift for the Pachamama, there is a piece of material called *istalla,* over which are placed all the "ingredients" of the altar, which usually include: one liter of pure alcohol; one liter of wine; one pound of coca leaves; red carnations; resin of copal; rough cigarettes of black tobacco; one handful of seedless cotton; two eggs of hen; two fetuses of llama; llama fat; a strip from fur of a wild cat (*titi*) and also of a vicuña; minuscule lead and/or stone

Runas shamans. Photo by Bruno Roissart.

amulets (*chichiricaros*), which represent domestic animals, trees, and many material symbols; one silver leaf (*kolke libro*); and one gold leaf (*kori libro*).

The two women are sitting at the healers' feet and like them place the coca, amulets, copal, gold, and silver according to the invariable ritual. The healer and his assistant each take a llama fetus, rub it with llama fat, and with the cotton attach the red carnations to its skull. Then they offer the fetuses to the seven cardinal points: the East, the South, the West, the North, the Above, the Below, and the Center, symbolized by the fire they just lit and into which they throw the fetuses.

"Pachamama, Santa Tierra, I am going to give you this altar; you are the Uyuriri who will protect this house. Do not let them succumb to illness; protect them from all harm. Pachamama, protect me from all evil and next year I will serve you even better." This is a prayer to consecrate a good luck altar, or "*kussi sami mesa*," collected by Louis Girault.

All the "ingredients" of the altar are now consumed by the flames. The white smoke of the incense rises in offering to the gods. It is now the moment, before taking care of the patient, to invoke the Achachilas (spirits): "Come, all of you, the Achachilas, Achachilas of Mount Hipi, of the Khapia, of the Huspaka, of Illimani, of Illampú. Mallku of Jhojhani, Mallku of Kakata, of Illampu, Mallku of Khapia, lord of wild geese, lord of the mines, of the silver poncho. Great Mallku of Quimsa-Chata, Mallku of Mount Alabaster, Achachila of Huayna Potosí, Achachila of Sajama, Achachila of Mount Santa Rosa. I salute you all, the Achachilas. I come to please you with alcohol so that our soul won't be taken from us" (free translation by Jean Vellard).

With a carnation dipped in alcohol in a shell, Don Florentino now makes libation to the seven cardinal points. Then he sits next to the tubercular patient, who is lying directly on the ground, covered by an old blanket. Don Florentino takes his hand and converses with him a few minutes:

"Tapukusjaiki" (I am going to ask you a few questions.)

"Imaangmi onkhoskhaikitchu, guaguai?" (What are you suffering from, my son?)

"Kaipi nanawasing, Tatai." (It hurts here, my Father.) The patient says this pointing to his chest. "Hampita kanchu manachu, Tatai?" (Is there a cure or not, my Father?)

"Tian" (Yes, there is one.)

Don Florentino now takes a live guinea pig out of his pocket and proceeds to the *limpia*, or cleansing of the patient, on whose body he rubs the animal. Then the patient blows on the guinea pig three times; he

is now, in theory, rid of the malign influence under which he has been. The Qollahuaya's assistant then slits the throat of the guinea pig and drips the blood into a shell. His master looks attentively at the way in which the blood coagulates and then throws it as an offering to the earth. Then he opens the visceral organs and interprets the composition of the small balls of excrement in the small intestines. Their composition is loose, which means that the patient will be cured. It is an omen that never fails.

He then administers an extract of *chuchuwasi* to the patient, then a tea made of lichens, and he advises the patient to drink the juice of three citrons without sugar every morning on an empty stomach. He also hands him a bunch of plants in order to continue the treatment.

The healer now gets up, turns his face to the Cordillera, and questions his fellow divinity in these terms:

"Kai hampiwang allingkachu manachu, Hatun Ankhamani?" (With this remedy, will he be cured, Great Ankhamani?)

The therapy of the Qollahuayas is trustworthy. First of all, they observe the ageless traditions, proof of an unquestionable reliability. They were chosen to be the private doctors of the Inca emperors and the high dignitaries of the court. This in itself was already a special distinction accorded to them because of their high qualification and their thorough, extensive knowledge of medicine and astrology. They care for their patients with the help of a therapeutic arsenal which includes, in addition to the principles of penicillin and terramycin that they have known for centuries (used in the form of a black pomade made from mold and spiderwebs), thousands of powerful remedies from the mineral, vegetable, and animal kingdoms. And above all, they give the highest importance to the psychological aspect of the illness and its treatment.

Don Florentino told me that he once arrived incognito in a village in northern Peru and learned that there was a patient in critical condition in a house. He waited for the night, then silently slipped into the adjoining garden and buried a dirty rag doll containing the corpse of a toad, some hair, and excrement. The next morning he made it known in the village that he was a Qollahuaya, and the family of the sick person did not waste any time requesting an appointment. He granted their request and gave his diagnosis: the sick person was the victim of a spell that had to be found and burned. After an hour of "searching," he triumphantly unearthed the cursed doll and explained to his patient that a sorcerer must have put it there to harm him. They burned it together, reciting formulas to break the spell. Because of this single act, the patient recovered his optimism and consequently his health.

Superstition? No, it is efficacy of a skilled psychological persuasion. There is still the magical aspect, the appeal to divinities. We must not forget an essential fact: if Cartesianism has contributed to impoverishing our universe to its lonely material dimension, the Indian cannot imagine a world without a spiritual dimension, without the gods. The sorcerer guarantees, saves, or restores the equilibrium among man, his soul, his community, and the divinities. The psychological treatment of illness evidently must be taken into account. Of course a part of this treasure is already lost, and the Qollahuayas no longer perform surgical operations, notably trephinations (brain surgery), which helped to spread their fame to the four corners of the Inca empire, Tawantinsuyu. But there still remains much of this precious wisdom. It is of inestimable wealth to the Bolivians, and to let it disappear would be an unpardonable sin.

PART THREE   AFRICA AND THE MIDDLE EAST

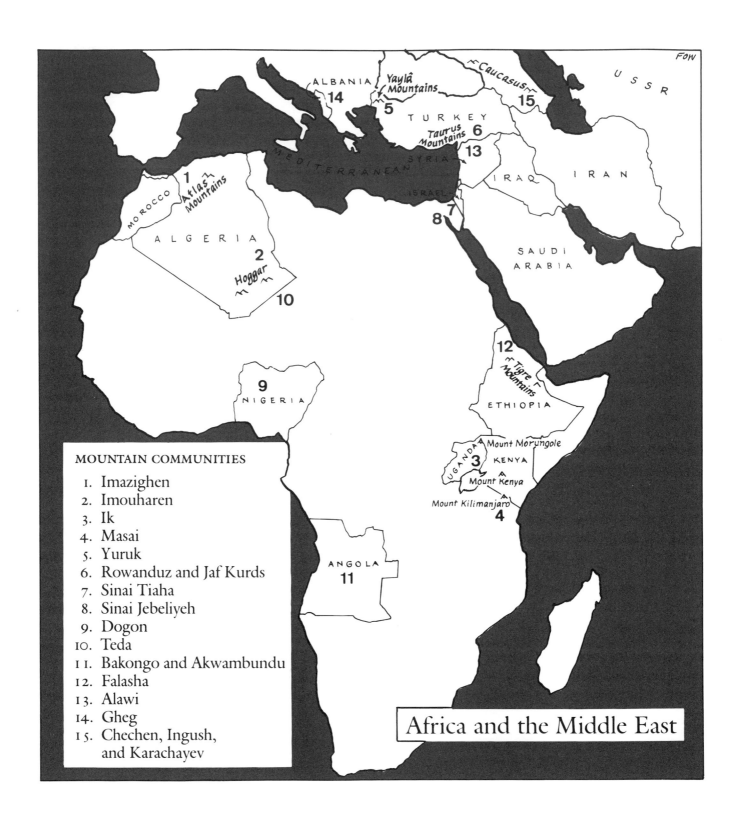

MOUNTAIN COMMUNITIES

1. Imazighen
2. Imouharen
3. Ik
4. Masai
5. Yuruk
6. Rowanduz and Jaf Kurds
7. Sinai Tiaha
8. Sinai Jebeliyeh
9. Dogon
10. Teda
11. Bakongo and Akwambundu
12. Falasha
13. Alawi
14. Gheg
15. Chechen, Ingush, and Karachayev

Africa and the Middle East

7. Man Makes the Mountains

COLIN M. TURNBULL

Environmental determinism happily can be ignored these days, but the recognized realities of the profound influence environment sometimes exerts upon man, his thinking, and his social organization have led to another equally dubious level of generalization that still seems to presume that the environment is the active agent, most often if not always. In fact it is questionable that it ever is. The interrelationship with man is two way traffic. Having lived and worked in the kinds of environments that are least permissive—deserts, tropical rain forests, and mountains—I am well aware of the intensity of the man-nature relationship and of man's perception of his dependence upon the particular world in which he lives, often defining himself as a person or child of a specific environment. However, in both material and conceptual terms it is plain enough that man makes his world what it is, for him, either by adapting to it or, more aggressively, by seeking to control it.

In all environments you get both kinds of adaptation, inclusive and intrusive, with correspondingly different kinds of social organization and value systems. With mountains perhaps more than any other environment we have tended to generalize as though by necessity that all mountain people must share certain characteristics by which they can be recognized and distinguished from others. Mountain peoples are generally considered to be freedom loving, enjoying their splendid isolation, lofty in thought, somber in mood, highly individualistic, and so forth. The Ik, with whom I worked in northern Uganda and who call themselves mountain people, would seem an aberrant exception, a disgrace to the mountain race. But all of that is so much nonsense.

To start with, there is no such thing as one kind of mountain. Technically speaking, anything over 2,000 feet (610 meters) may be called a mountain according to some authorities, but to others it is a question of geology rather than altitude that makes a mountain. And even the height is a questionable criterion and deceptive; Mount Everest is not as high as Kilimanjaro if measured from the surrounding plateau from which it rises, which reduces it to less than a puny 15,000 feet (4,600 meters). And surely a mountain range such as the Himalayas offers vastly different possibilities for human and social adaptation than does an isolated inland mountain such as Kilimanjaro, and both again are from the same point of view in no way comparable with the volcanic mountains that soar directly skywards from the waters of the Pacific. Mountains such as the latter, isolated from each other by huge tracts of ocean, afford their inhabitants a totally different experience than mountains connected by land, and elicit a different emotional response.

The cultural differences to be found among various mountain dwellers are as enormous as the geographical, topographical, and geological differences. At one end you have human populations living in dispersed, virtually autonomous hamlets with no trace of centralized chiefship, and at the other end you have some of the greatest civilizations we have known, empires and theocracies. Peru and Tibet are hardly comparable even at that one end, however, except in the contrast they offer both within their own environment and by comparison with other high-altitude populations. These two examples introduce another differential factor, that of human adaptation. In both cases an Asiatic people have undergone significant adaptive changes that have enabled them to survive and even thrive at an altitude where others would find mere survival problematic. The large rib cage alone, increasing the lung capacity; the structure of the lung; and the higher proportion of oxygen-releasing red blood cells all make possible the greater expenditure of energy that the altitude demands in the work of moving the body, let alone heavy loads, upwards and downwards. An adaptive capillary structure increases circulation at the extremities, lessening the danger of frostbite, enabling those people to walk barefoot in the snow with relative impunity.

But it is man's body that is being helpful, not the mountain. The mountain is the body's enemy, and both the rarified atmosphere and the vertical direction of movement combined with the force of gravity militate against an easy or successful livelihood. Other considerations of terrain and climate are equally hostile to human habitation, and mountain deities are by no means invariably friendly or benevolent, reflecting a certain human disenchantment with the mountain world. Dante's Inferno is a lowlander's vision of hell;

69

for others it is an icy eternity that threatens, and which they dread. High places may be holy, but the fact that mountains, high and low, are consecrated or deified throughout the world does not mean that they are considered friendly; indeed, they often are not. Their very consecration serves as a warning for mere mortals to stay away.

A sense of freedom and glorious independence of spirit are frequently associated with the cultural isolation that some mountain dwellers experience. The isolation, which is often not nearly as complete as it first seems, more often was not *sought* as desirable in itself; it was a last resort. Many a mountain has offered safety to peoples who, in return, had to give up their cherished and preferred way of life. The extreme cultural adaptation they underwent, let alone any psychological or physiological adaptation, in time rendered them victims of overspecialization and debarred them from return to lowland living. Further, when the geographical isolation does exist, together with the natural antipathy of lowland peoples to living in such hostile terrain, mountain populations may be further severed from cultural diffusion to a considerable extent, depriving them of technological developments that could ameliorate their living conditions.

Tibet seems to offer a rather rare example of a population that made a virtue out of an extremely uncomfortable necessity; thumbing their collective nose at the world they left behind, the Tibetans sealed themselves in and sought, for a time, to keep the rest of the world away. But this was only a continuation of their enforced flight from that world. They are to be admired for the ingenuity with which they developed a theocratic social system that added inner strength to the natural defenses afforded them by their mountain environment, enabling them to hold their Mongolian and Chinese enemies at bay. But we tend to forget that the recent Chinese invasion was not the first and that the Chinese have always left, finding Tibet not really worth the holding unless that could be accomplished by proxy. Even the present occupation is of questionable durability.

And Tibet is not all mountains. The Tibetans themselves seem to prefer the good farming life of their comparatively lush, almost tropical valleys to the hardships of pastoralism on the slopes and brigandry with its nomadic settlements at an even higher altitude. Further, it is a myth that Tibet has always sought to isolate itself from the outside world. Even while resisting wholesale incursions, Tibetans have throughout history welcomed and even actively sought contact with the world below them. But the rest of the world, other than for political or economic profit, has not reciprocated the interest. Distance lends charm. Our lowland culture looks to the sky for perspective, and our values are oriented upwards. Mountains are perhaps a prime tourist attraction for this reason, coupled with the fact that tourists do not have to live there.

Even where the mountains are much more readily accessible than the Andes or Himalayas, and where lowland man has found a way of exploiting those mountains for his economic benefit, the benefits are extracted by proxy, by the exploitation of the indigenous population for the welfare of the absentee beneficiaries. Whether the product is tea in Assam or gold in the Andes, the enormous economic potential of some mountainous areas does not seem to attract a large resident population the way we would expect if mountains were, indeed, such wonderful and friendly places. It has been clearly demonstrated throughout the world that even in the absence of an advanced technology mountains *can* support large populations at almost any level of political organization, yet they remain among the most underpopulated regions of our planet. Even if we confine our examination to one relatively small geographical area, East Africa, say, all of the above can be seen at work and should make us seriously question the common assumption that mountain living (or mountain people) is both different and superior. If it is different, it is largely in the degree of discomfort, danger, and difficulty the population must endure; if it is superior, it is largely only in the literal sense of elevation.

Throughout Africa the diversity of social organization matches the same difference between one "mountain" and another that we have been all too sketchily looking at on a global basis. In North Africa the Rif and the Atlas Mountains, as close and connected as they are, provide examples of very different forms of human adaptation, even among the same cultural group. Some Riffians are transhumant and pastoral, while others, like the Aith Waryaghar, are neither. While some live in concentrated settlements, the Waryaghar, sedentary farmers, live in widely dispersed households scattered, as they themselves say, "like stars in the sky" (Hart, *The Aith Waryaghar of the Moroccan Rif*, 1976). Some authorities hold that the Riffian settlement patterns result from the nature of the terrain and water supply, but Hart, whose study of the Rif is as extensive as it is intensive, suggests that the cause of specific patterns and settlement is social rather than economic. He relates it to the very specific place of women in Waryaghar society and to the crucial concept of shame and honor. Even irrigation patterns and water rights can not be held to be determined by terrain and the natural downward flow of water; instead, water and the mountain slope are adapted to War-yaghar social needs and hence differ significantly from the practices of other peoples in similar terrain but with different social values.

The various Berber peoples of North Africa relate to the same mountain environment, then, in very different ways, at different levels of social and political complexity, varying in subsistence patterns from sedentary farming to transhumant pastoralism, from permanent to seasonal occupation of the mountains. In my own limited experience the Berber I met, almost without exception, preferred the hot, seemingly barren desert end of their transhumant movement to the richer and cooler living back in the mountains. The equally indisputable "mountains" that rise above the plateau of northern Nigeria provide tribal experiences of totally different adaptation based upon a mixture of farming and hunting, with correspondingly different world views and with contrasting concepts of shame and honor. In addition, such tribes foster kinship systems involving sequential polygyny and institutionalized elopement that would be incomprehensible, if not abhorrent, to other mountain peoples. Yet although they, too, could be considered a refuge population as much as the mountain Berber, their relationship with their neighbors bears little resemblance. In East Africa alone, widely divergent forms of the man-mountain relationship can be seen, indicating that the mountain, in offering a refuge to a people in flight, by no means always offers friendship as well, nor does it necessarily, if ever, bring isolation, splendid or otherwise. The variety of mountain adaptations in this one area demonstrates that it is man who makes his specific kinds of terms with the mountain, not the other way around.

Atlas Mountain Berber child. Photo by Bruno Roissart.

Nor do the mountains of East Africa bear out the contention that mountains in a tropical climate are more friendly to man than those in a temperate zone.

Without doubt, Rwanda can be said to be a mountainous region, though it lacks the spectacular peaks of its three East African neighbors. Starting at 4,000 feet (1,200 meters), the country rises to a maximum height of about 14,000 feet (4,300 meters). Uganda, to the north, is similar in this respect, rising up to the perpetual snows of the Ruwenzoris at 16,000 feet (4,900 meters). But while man in Rwanda adapted the topography to his social convenience, with the Tussi as the cattle-owning highland overlords and the Hutu as lowland peasant farmers, distributed in this fashion throughout the nation, the adaptation in Uganda was quite different. In opposition to the southern kingdoms, each with its own hierarchical divisions of nobility and commoner, cattle herders were confined to the north while the royal southerners adjacent to Rwanda subsisted largely by farming. For farming purposes, especially for the favored combination of *matoke* (plantain) and coffee, the Ganda used the midway belt of land encircling each hill; this suited their political structure and their world view. But since the breakdown of the traditional system, coffee and *matoke* have spread both upwards and downwards. It is probably as impossible to prove that an already existing social system determined the manner in which the mountainous terrain was exploited as it would be to prove that it was the terrain that determined the social structure. But the latter would assume that the lower and upper slopes were unusable for settlement purposes, and that has now been shown not to be the case.

At the foot of the Ruwenzoris, the Amba farm satisfactorily at a mere 3,000 feet (900 meters), with the Konjo equally satisfactorily working the land above them. And again, while the Amba choose to build their settlements on the more or less level tops of the ridges that engulf them, making for a certain degree of autonomy and independence, in both qualitative and quantitative terms their pattern of social cohesion and their relationship with their environment are noticeably different from the patterns forged by the Ik, in the north, and the Kikuyu, say, in Kenya, two other East African peoples who similarly settle on the tops of ridges. And similar terrain right across the border, a few miles away in Zaire, is exploited in a totally different way by hunters and gatherers whose social system, values, and attitude toward the environment are different in almost every respect. In this case the difference might suggest that the nature of the ground cover, the degree of forestation, is of more significance than the mountainous nature of the terrain; but that would be an equally dangerous assumption, given man's adaptive potential.

In southern Kenya and in Tanzania, Kilimanjaro and Meru rise like islands out of the grassland ocean. The Chaga, living on the lower slopes, are divided into some thirty small chiefdoms. They irrigate fields, and they choose to stall-feed livestock in order to best use the manure. Not far away the Pare and Teita adapt to their mountains yet differently, but it would be dangerous to say that this is their preferred way of life, in face of their extensive migration down into the lowlands now that such migration is possible. Perhaps the clearest example of this ambivalence, in East Africa, is provided by the Pokot of western Kenya. For them their smaller mountains, similarly rising out of the grasslands, offered refuge in time of need. Mountain living was determinant to the extent that at the upper level their former cattle herding practices had to be abandoned. The Pokot took to irrigation farming, leading water around the mountainside by the ingenious and extensive use of aqueducts in a way that suited their organizational needs. And, as the threat from below diminished, they spread back downwards, taking up a form of mixed farming as they went until finally some of them returned to the open grasslands, resuming the

life of pastoralists. The mountains remained as a symbol of their salvation, however, and the focus of their ritual and spiritual life was the high-level farmland, even for the pastoralists. But the highland irrigation farmers who remained there do not form a separate people or class. The Pokot do not see themselves as divided horizontally by their different subsistence patterns or proximity to the sacred heights; they make a vertical division, and any one major Pokot unit consists of groups at each level with vertical affiliations linking the highland to the lowland, bound by ties that are affective as well as effective.

In northern Uganda, not many miles to the north but above the escarpment that forms the western boundary of the Rift Valley, the Ik, who call themselves Kwarikik, or "Mountain People," still defy satisfactory interpretation but without any doubt show us yet another possible form of the man-mountain relationship. In the literature we have nothing but a few sketchy paragraphs that effectively tell us only that half a century ago the Ik were nomadic hunters ranging through a large mountainous area in a cycle that led from Uganda, through the adjoining terrain of Sudan, into Kenya, and back up into Uganda. Oral tradition confirms this but does not tell us more, except that

Imouharen tribesmen, Hoggar, Sahara. Photo by Bruno Roissart.

"Winkelhaaksrivier," Western Cape, South Africa; rock painting reproduction by R. Townley Johnson.

once again they were far from isolated and actively sought political and economic relationships with the lowland cattle herders. My own two years with them were spent at a time when a combination of events (political, economic, and environmental) had reduced them to such an extremity of deprivation that nearly all vestiges of their former social system had been abandoned and a new system, better adapted to the exigencies of the current context, was being crystallized. The significance of this dramatic change from the highly social system of a group of nomadic hunters to what was essentially a nonsocial system of sedentary farmers is arguable, and has been argued enough on the data available. The data proved that the terrace farming developed by the Ik was in itself a temporary measure, and five years after my last visit they had abandoned farming in favor of scavenging and gathering, with a small amount of illegal hunting, continuing as before.

Many questions were raised by the incomplete data I was able to gather during my stay, and all subsequent efforts to get other researchers into the field, including the latest attempt at the end of 1979, failed because of political instability. Of these questions the most nagging one concerns their relationship with Mount Morungole, which legend says is the place of their origin, where God set the first Ik down on Earth. We are deprived of nearly all the kind of evidence that anthropologists normally amass. There was no observable ritual practice associated with the mountain. Their abortive attempts to make rain at the behest of the lowland cattle herders did not relate to Morungole, and in any case had all the appearance of being an economic ploy instead of being based on any traditional belief. Life-cycle rituals that formerly might have been practiced were no longer practiced, and only a very few of the oldest Ik had any store of folklore to reveal. This in itself was highly significant, for the legends and myths that existed seemed to fit well with what little I could reconstruct of the Ik's former existence, and they carried with them an intensity of feeling that affected all those who heard them except the young, who seemed to find the stories of the utmost insignificance. Without exception, tales of the sacred mountain were never told by social context itself, and despite concentrated efforts I was not once able to find any evidence of the lore being passed on to the children. Even the young adults were indifferent, and the occasional attempt by some of them to relate some mountain lore to me was plainly as much a ploy for my benefit (and their material gain) as was the rain medicine a ploy for the benefit of the cattle herders. Such attempts to pretend to a knowledge of sacred mountain lore only served to demonstrate their ignorance as well as their indifference.

And yet, something was there. The mountain *was* a force to be reckoned with, though they seldom verbalized it, and the reckoning was at an individual level, not a communal or corporate one. There was, for example, the prohibition, remarkable given their economic plight, against hunting on the sacred mountainside. And there were the constant looks bent in that direction by individual men and women when sitting at the *di*, with nothing to do but wait and hope for food, miraculously, to come their way. The sidelong looks are ethnographic fact; their interpretation, in the absence of other data, is hazardous at best. Yet, coupled with beliefs and myths as related by the old Ik, I can find no satisfactory explanation other than that, although all ritual practice had been abandoned, and although all communal manifestation of any ritual belief concerning the mountain was confined to hunting prohibition and to those head turnings, some kind of belief represented a potentially beneficent force.

This is corroborated by the persistent refusal of the Ik to relocate in other areas offered to them where their farming would have been both easier and more successful, and life a lot more comfortable and predictable. The incident in which one family took off for the relative ease and security of illegal hunting and gathering in the mountains on the Sudan side of the border, yet after a while returned to the known misery of living in sight of their sacred Morungole, further testifies to the very real power of the mountain over the people. But the people invested it with that power, and we have to remember that the legend of origin shows their recognition of the fact that the mountain can be malevolent as well as benevolent, for the same God that set them down on the mountain, whose seat it is, gave them life on earth but then deprived them of wealth and ease, giving the cattle to the less favored son, the ancestor of the lowland cattle herders.

Such evidence as there is suggests that on the one hand their self-perception as mountain people, and as a people related to this mountain in particular, enabled them to retain a sense of group identity despite the loss of anything resembling a social system—despite the overt, stated value of individual survival and nonreciprocity. They themselves state that their very existence is indissolubly bound up with the existence of the mountain. It is the one thing that seems to hold them together, conceptually, while the harsh realities of life that the mountain world imposes on them tend to split them apart. They might indeed cease to exist as Ik were they taken away from their mountain. But that same mountain, on the other hand, could just as well be said to have, in precisely this way, prevented them from moving to another location where they could have survived with much greater ease and where they could have regained some semblance of social organization, if not the form they knew before.

In point of fact the Ik, while showing us yet another way in which man can adapt to a mountain environment, show us a sociological parallel of dysfunctional (in the event of change) adaptation similar to that of high-altitude dwellers such as those found in the Andes, for whom a move to the easier life of lower altitudes would be as physically painful as it would be for us to live and work as they do where they live, getting only 50 percent of the thin air's oxygen into our bloodstream and suffering from frostbite in the bargain. In order to survive in the only territory available to them, the Ik adapted and lived well. How long they lived that way we do not know. But it was long enough for the adaptation to become so inflexible with respect to their self-perception as mountain people that while they could and did make ongoing drastic adaptations to match the thorough impoverishment of their mountain world, they could not bring themselves to leave and live longer, healthier, and more productive lives elsewhere as nonmountain people. Morungole did not make the Ik what they are. It is the Ik who have made the mountain that harsh, uncompromising taskmaster that it is.

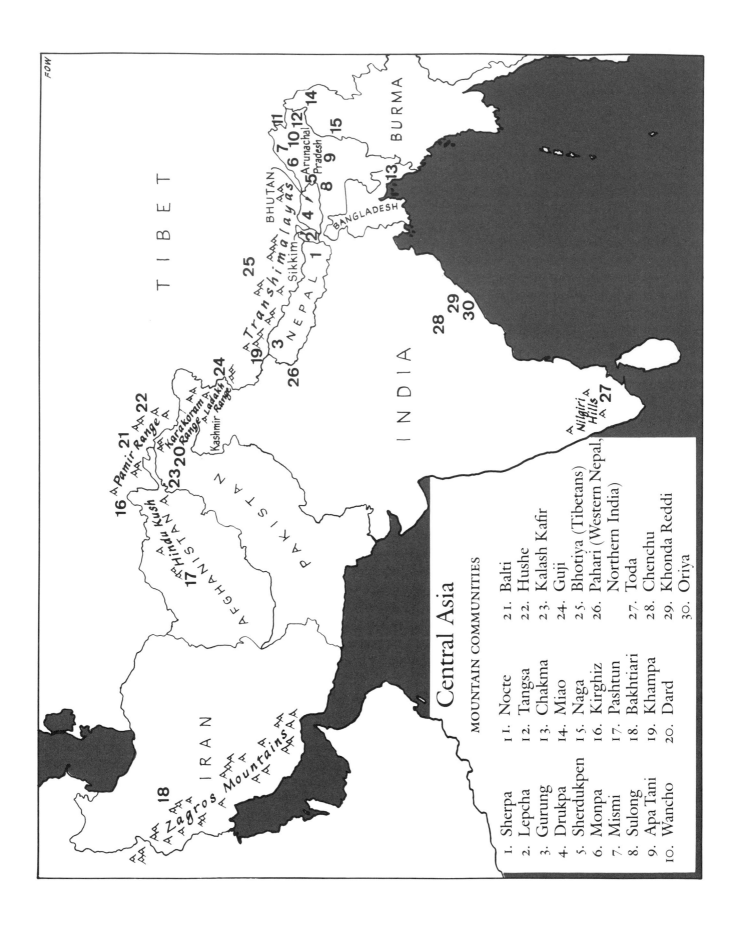

Central Asia

MOUNTAIN COMMUNITIES

1. Sherpa
2. Lepcha
3. Gurung
4. Drukpa
5. Sherdukpen
6. Monpa
7. Mismi
8. Sulong
9. Apa Tani
10. Wancho

11. Nocte
12. Tangsa
13. Chakma
14. Miao
15. Naga
16. Kirghiz
17. Pashtun
18. Bakhtiari
19. Khampa
20. Dard

21. Balti
22. Hushe
23. Kalash Kafir
24. Guji
25. Bhotiya (Tibetans)
26. Pahari (Western Nepal, Northern India)
27. Toda
28. Chenchu
29. Khonda Reddi
30. Oriya

8. Nuristan: Lost World of the Hindu Kush

SCHUYLER JONES

Tucked away in the Hindu Kush mountain range of northeastern Afghanistan is an isolated forested region more than 5,000 square miles (13,000 square kilometers) in extent. Since 1900 the area has been known as Nuristan (Land of Light); earlier it was called Kafiristan (Land of Infidels). From the early years of the last century when it came to European notice, it has been regarded as a particularly remote and mysterious part of Central Asia and has frequently, in books and articles, been the subject of fiction and speculation, from the romance of Kipling's "The Man Who Would Be King" to more recent and deservedly obscure fabrications by O. M. Burke and Peter King.

My own interest in the North-West Frontier in general and Nuristan in particular began in Germany in 1957 when I saw photographs taken among the Kalash Kafirs of Chitral by the Swiss traveler Hans von Meiss-Teuffen. A few weeks later in Greece a discarded copy of *Scientific American* came into my hands (actually, I picked it out of a trash can). Inside was an article by Robert Heine-Geldern on vanishing cultures containing a brief account of Nuristan. I was hooked.

In the summer of 1958 my wife and son and I set out overland from Greece to India in a Volkswagen with vague ideas of trying to get into Nuristan. Although we did not know it then, this "Nuristan quest" was to result in our spending six rewarding years in Afghanistan.

In that autumn of 1958 we soon found that getting into Afghanistan was one thing, and getting up into the Hindu Kush was quite another. No foreigners had been allowed into Nuristan since the Danish expedition of 1953, although Wilfred Thesiger and Eric Newby had traveled briefly along the extreme western fringes of the area in 1956.

With winter coming on, it was an impractical season for such an expedition anyway, so we went on to India and Nepal, returning to Kabul six months later. As it turned out, it was the summer of 1960 before we finally got into Nuristan. In the meantime we had studied most of the published sources on Kafiristan and Nuristan. There were not many of them: three books, one by the Scottish medical doctor, Sir George Scott Robertson (*The Kafirs of the Hindu Kush* [London, 1896]); one by a team of German experts who had traveled

widely and collected data in the area in the early 1930's (*Deutsche im Hindukusch* [Berlin, 1937]); and the other by Albert Herrlich, a member of the German team (*Land des Lichtes* [Munich, 1938]). The remainder of the published sources, in the form of articles and reports, was scattered through dozens of journals and British Government of India Records, most of them written in Victorian times. Aside from the reports of the German Hindu Kush expedition and those of the Danish expeditions (1948 and 1953), scarcely anything had been published on Nuristan in this century.

In the decade from 1960 to 1970 we made nine journeys into Nuristan to collect a range of ethnographic data. We also made one journey to visit the Kalash Kafirs of Chitral. In addition to taking many hundreds of still pictures, we studied arable agricultural practices, calendar systems, social organization, mythology, political systems, herd management, social change, kinship systems, and the material culture and technology of a dozen communities.

It quickly became apparent that Nuristan formed not only a kind of cultural "island" in south central Asia, but that it constituted an ecological "island" as well. Preliminary study also showed that both the cultural and the ecological characteristics of the region were vulnerable and liable to rapid change.

The cultural uniqueness of Nuristan, notably its languages, arts, crafts, religious beliefs and practices, and political systems, had survived, against all odds, several centuries of pressure by surrounding Muslim peoples. This survival is attributable to two main factors: extreme isolation caused by a rugged, inhospitable terrain, and the aggressive activities of generations of enthusiastic warriors.

This isolation was only partly broken down in the years 1895–1900 when Afghan troops, armed with British breechloaders, finally managed to invade, conquer, and force the "kafirs" to become Muslims. So vanished the old pagan religious beliefs and practices. But aside from temporarily wrecking the economy, the Afghan invasion did little to change other indigenous institutions. For one thing, the Afghans did not stay; they withdrew from what they now called Nuristan, leaving the new converts to Islam to rebuild their economy and to get on with most of their traditional activities.

Winter in Nuristan. Photo by Schuyler Jones.

For another thing, communications did not really improve. Roads were not constructed, bridges were not built; all the natural and most of the cultural barriers remained, with the Nuristani hatred of Afghans not only maintained but also reinforced by their recent experiences.

The landscape in Nuristan is for the most part one of steep, narrow valleys separated from each other by high ridges. In many areas the slopes are covered with evergreen oak trees from about 4,000 to about 6,000 feet (1,200–1,800 meters) above sea level. Between 6,000 feet and the timberline, forests consist mainly of coniferous trees. In the four main inhabited valleys on the southern slopes of the Hindu Kush live approximately seventy-five thousand people, though no one really knows how many. They live in compact villages, most of them approximately 6,000 feet above sea level. The trails in and out of Nuristan, like those connecting one village with another, are mostly so steep and rocky that pack animals cannot be used. Travel is by foot, and goods are carried on men's backs.

Five related but mutually unintelligible languages are spoken in Nuristan: Kati, Paruni, Ashkuni, Wai-

ala, and Tregami. Together, they form the third branch of the Aryan languages, the other two being Indian and Iranian.

The people of Nuristan engage in a specialized form of mixed farming that involves the raising of cereal crops on irrigated hill terraces and a system of transhumant livestock herding that makes seasonal use of alpine pastures for the making of dairy products. These two branches of the economy, although mutually interdependent, are quite separate, requiring entirely different skills and different seasonal activities. The difference is reflected in the division of labor in Nuristani society: women are entirely responsible for all arable agriculture. They not only plant the wheat, millet, barley, and maize, but they also harvest it, weed the fields, irrigate the terraces, carry manure from the winter stables to spread on the arable land, and, in addition, do domestic chores such as fetching wood and water and caring for the children. For their part, the men are responsible for the care of the goats, sheep, and cattle, especially the seasonal movement of livestock from one grazing area to another, milking, and the making of butter, ghee, and cheese.

Both sets of economic activities are governed by rules enforced by a body of annually elected men who are given specific responsibilities. These men supervise the seasonal movement of livestock, control the allocation of water in the irrigation systems, set the various dates on which different fruits may be harvested, control the cutting of trees, and settle disputes arising from any of these activities. Each village has its own set of laws covering not only agricultural activities, but also other areas such as theft, injury, and property damage. In each village on the first day of spring an elder recites the laws publicly. He then ritually plants seed in a small plot of ground, a cow is killed, and a public feast is held. These ceremonies mark the beginning of the year's agricultural activities.

The division of labor in Nuristan, the special nature of the dual economy, and the rules that regulate seasonal activities all combine to form a system that not only exploits local resources, but also ensures that the bases of village life—that is, arable land, water, timber, and mountain pastures—are preserved for succeeding generations.

In 1959, after half a century of relative peace and quiet, a major threat to Nuristan's isolation occurred when the Afghan government began the construction of a narrow jeep track from the Kunar River up along the right bank of the Bashgal River into northeastern Nuristan. By the late summer of 1960, provided one had permission, it was just possible to drive (over an extremely rough, rocky trail) up as far as Chapu, a distance of 35 road miles (56 kilometers) from the Kunar River. Later this track was pushed on to Bragamatal, 43 miles (69 kilometers) altogether.

The resulting improved communications quickly led to the establishment of a weekly bus service, and, for the first time, it was possible to get on a bus in Jalalabad or Chaga Sarai and, during at least part of the year, get halfway up the Bashgal Valley. Even though the road was closed through much of the winter by deep snow and through the spring and early summer by rock slides and flash floods, it still allowed an increased movement of people and goods into and out of northeastern Nuristan. German-made kerosene lamps and the fuel needed for them quickly became popular;

Winter in Nuristan. Photo by Schuyler Jones.

portable radios made their appearance. Commercially manufactured cloth, snuff, rice, arms and ammunition, and various other traditional imports began coming in at an increased rate. Many villagers get into debt in order to acquire such goods and then borrow from Afghan moneylenders (at 100 percent interest rates for six months) to pay shopkeepers. Creditors who are unable to collect frequently take their grievances to Afghan officials, usually a subgovernor in administrative centers outside Nuristan, such as Barikot, Chaga Sarai, or Ningalam, where they swear out a complaint. The debtor is summoned (a day's walk, perhaps three). Almost certainly unable to pay the debt, he gains time by handing over a goat or two and perhaps 50 pounds (110 kilograims) of walnuts and some honey. This is done in the presence of witnesses and is noted, but in doing it, he is not even paying the interest on the loan. This situation, repeated again and again, month after month, along the borders of Nuristan represents a steady drain on the resources of the Nuristani people and serves to keep their antagonisms with Afghans and officialdom alive through disputes and court cases.

Between 1960 and 1980 the Afghan government made no attempt to build other roads into Nuristan. In the late 1960s it was proposed that a motor road might be constructed up the Waigal Valley of south central Nuristan. This led to bitter arguments and occasional shooting between rival factions in the valley, but the road was never built.

Another source of contact with the outside world is military service. Every other year each region must supply a certain number of men of military age for a two-year spell of duty in the Afghan Army. The quota is based on a rough approximation of area population. The men who actually go for military service are chosen by village elders in consultation with the senior male members of different lineages. The Afghan government does not interfere in this process as long as the quota is met.

Men who serve in the Afghan Army are given basic training, including literacy classes in Dari and/or Pushtu. With more than thirty languages spoken in Afghanistan, and with a national literacy rate hovering round 2 percent, this language education is essential. These men are then posted to various parts of the country for routine military duty. In addition to becoming familiar with automatic weapons, many of them learn to drive trucks and tanks. Since World War II, virtually all Afghan Army and Air Force equipment has been supplied by the Soviet Union.

One might expect either that a two-year stint in the army would result in emigration from Nuristan by those with such experience, or that men returning to village life after military service would introduce innovations. In general, neither happens. Emigration is rare and confined almost exclusively to a few members of the *bari* craftsman class, who see emigration as the only way to escape the social and economic restrictions imposed on them by the rigid class structure of traditional Nuristani society. The rest, constituting about 90 percent of the population, are landowning livestock herders, and they see no advantages whatever in emigration. Those who have been outside Nuristan know that most of Afghanistan is arid, with sparse natural vegetation, and they realize that the standard of living in Nuristan is very much superior to that of the average villager elsewhere. Furthermore, to the relatively prosperous Nuristani, ideas of wealth, status, and prestige tend to be linked directly to herd size and grain production at a level that would be extremely difficult, if not impossible, to achieve elsewhere in Afghanistan. The people of Nuristan are, moreover, extremely proud—to the point of arrogance—of their clear, sparkling springs, their rushing rivers, and their extensive forests. Nothing else that Afghanistan can offer appears half so attractive to them.

The same factors operate to minimize innovations that, in theory, might be introduced by Nuristanis with experience elsewhere. The Nuristani value system focuses overwhelmingly on its own special brand of wealth and has its own special sources of status and prestige. New ideas are judged in this context, and any proposed changes that are not perceived as contributing directly to the achievement of these goals is unlikely to gain acceptance. In short, if the change is not seen by villagers as something that will greatly increase grain production or enable them to produce more and larger goats, it is unlikely to interest them, unless it in-

Nuristani family. Photo by Schuyler Jones.

volves exchanging old British Army rifles for modern automatic weapons. None of these changes, of course, involve new concepts. They would just be improvements in well-established areas of interest and competition, and therefore readily acceptable.

In time, major changes might well come from a workable policy of compulsory education and a network of schools staffed by trained teachers. In Nuristan, although schools exist in some villages and although a few teachers have had some teacher education, attendance is not compulsory and schools are ill equipped and ill attended. In most villages, moreover, parents seem to feel that the education offered is irrelevant to traditional village life (which is where their interests lie) and of too short a duration and of insufficient quality to train their sons for anything else. Generally the "school" is a gathering of boys in the local mosque for instruction by a mullah. The instruction is heavily weighted towards memorizing passages from the Koran, supplemented by some instruction in reading and writing Pushtu. In a few villages there are also classes for girls, but there, too, attendance is poor. Even relatively young children are useful working in the home, the forests, and mountain pastures, and in addition to lack of interest on the part of parents, there

is the general idea, shared by most young people, that school is a waste of time. Given these circumstances, schools in Nuristan are not the source of change that they might one day become.

Certain themes are clearly discernible in Nuristani culture. Among the most prominent are pride and honor, with the emphasis on achieved status and a consequent male preoccupation with prestige. Before 1895 the main way for a man to gain a position of rank and honor in his community was through raiding and plundering neighboring Muslim communities. The more enemies he killed, the higher his rank and the greater his prestige. Following the Afghan invasion of Kafiristan (1895–1900) and the conversion of the population to Islam, these raiding activities were suppressed. But the attitudes towards warrior exploits and the prestige attached to them remained unchanged.

These attitudes help explain why in the recent confusion of coup and counter-coup in Kabul, followed by the Soviet invasion of Afghanistan, Nuristan quickly emerged as a center of guerrilla activity. Political unrest in the country was seen by village men as a heaven-sent opportunity to do what they enjoy most—sniping at the enemy from the rocks and trees of their mountain home. In short, the good old days are back again.

9. Axis Mundi: Living Space, Custom, and Identity among the Kalash Kafirs of the Hindu Kush

KENNETH HEWITT

In this essay I deal with the way a small society in the Hindu Kush interprets and organizes the spaces of its mountain habitat. Moreover, I try to present the geography of their life and land as they treat it rather than through, say, a Western conception of human ecology. The approach adopted here is, however, that of a personal encounter—the geographer thinking aloud in the face of a very different place and people—instead of an ethnographic report. As such it harks back to the style of Elisée Reclus's classic *History of a Mountain*. There are, however, some broader issues involved that should be dealt with first.

ALTERNATIVE GEOGRAPHIES

Geographical questions arise out of the variable distributions of phenomena over the earth and the experiences of different places. Geographical understanding requires a knowledge of the ecological and cultural forces that shape the distributions and of the ways distinctive places emerge within a world that is fully interconnected. Mainly, we work by inference from objective material conditions. However, of basic concern in the sense of place are the shared meanings, valuings, and motivations that bind human groups together in their approach to and shaping of their surroundings. In this it is doubtful if there is such a thing as a universal geographic framework. Every society formulates its own geography. As creations of human experience, action and thought are as distinctive as the adaptations of different biological organisms. To assume otherwise— for example, that Western science and its maps define *the* geographic realities—is both to violate the very "objectivity" in which science prides itself and, in a multicultural world, to practice an *a*geographic human geography.

The issue is the more relevant when we seek to understand the high mountain cultures and environments that seem marginal to and, so often, are destructively made marginal by the development of urban-industrial economies. Communities primarily adapted to mountain conditions are of special interest. Their ideas and behavior may be oddly at variance with those of the industrial world. Yet if they maintain a nondestructive, finely tuned relationship with their environment, it is instructive to study their achievements.

In the remotest valleys of the Karakoram Himalayas and the Hindu Kush one still encounters folk living largely off the mountain environment and maintaining an unusually harmonious relationship with it. This is striking in the case of the Kalash people of Pakistan's Chitral district in the Hindu Kush. It involves a strong, religion-based partitioning of the habitat.

The Kalash, barely three thousand in number, are a last remnant of the once extensive realm of Kafiristan. Scholars believe that forebears of the Kafirs fought with Alexander the Great and Tamerlane. If that suggests more than two millennia of cultural continuity, the Kalash give but a small indication of the larger Kafir world of the past. Even that is for us a world of legend more than record—a world physically apart in its mountain fastness, culturally separate in ways and beliefs whose origins may involve Persian, shamanic, and Hindu forms but remain lost or undecipherable. Because of their so-called polytheism, their wine drinking, and their open treatment of women, the Kafirs appear strikingly different from the surrounding Muslim peoples. The presence of fair-skinned and blue-eyed members fostered the legend that they were a "lost tribe" or descendants of Alexander's soldiers. If these are doubtful, even racist, propositions, they are partly redeemed in such fine fiction as Kipling's "The Man Who Would Be King."

The Kalash inhabit three valleys, called Birir, Bamboret, and Rombur, that lie deep within the vast mountain region where the Himalaya, Pamir, and Hindu Kush ranges meet and some 90 miles (150 kilometers) south of Tirich Mir (25,200 feet; 7,690 meters). Although set amid desert lands, the mountains here generate abundant moisture that sustains some large glaciers; the extensive alpine pastures where the Kalash graze cattle, goats, and sheep in summer; and perennial streams that irrigate the fields around their settlements. Thick forests cloak the sides of the three valleys. Corn is the staple crop in most places. Vegetables, grapes, walnuts, and wild pine nuts are among supplements that make for an excellent diet.

The landscapes around the villages have an intimate, human scale despite their setting among the formidable features of the Roof of the World. Houses of reddish brown timbers are stacked one above the other on rocky bluffs over the river or nestled among quiet groves. Water for irrigation is led along sheer valley walls in troughs of hand-hewn logs. Among the fields it flows in tree-lined ditches or froths down wooden pipes into the small mills where grain is ground. These landscapes usually have a foreground of small fields or the stepped, flat roofs of houses backed by groves of walnuts or dark holly oaks, and a more distant panorama of conifer forests and, far off, of some snow-covered peaks. Visually, the land is a living realization of the harmony of man and habitat, a subtle blend of the wild and the cultivated, of natural and man-made features. It is easy, therefore, to draw an overly romanticized picture of it. But Kalash life is not lacking in hardship or difficulty. Indeed, it is likely that the distinctive features of Kalash identity we shall describe have become more overt because of recent stresses and threats to their very existence instead of an idyllic feeling for their land working in isolation. We begin with an event that is central to the Kalash view of the world, though it may seem marginal to our materialistic perspectives.

THE SACRIFICE

Fall had come to Rombur. The river was low, flowing clear over a stony bed. A first snowfall dusted the nearer peaks, and cool, blue light lay upon the forest-covered mountainsides. On the roofs of the village, carpets of multicolored corncobs lay drying in the sun. With the harvest in, the fields round about bristled with yellow stubble. The grapes had been picked, too, and the wine pressed from them lay in stone vats underground until the great new year festival of Chitter-mas. For some days shepherds had been moving the flocks down from the high pastures, and the compass of activities was converging on the village in anticipation of the long winter.

We left the village with a crowd of men, others running to join us from houses in the trees. The circles of their white, homespun caps shone in the morning sun. Their voices echoed from the cliffs across the river and in the forest above. One man led a goat. Its large horns nodded from side to side in an uncertain rhythm, the clear light aglow on its thick brown and white coat and in its knowing amber eye.

After a while we entered a grove of holly oaks. It was a sacred grove, and reminded one of Zeus's shrine at Dodona in the Pindhos Range of northern Greece, also set among holly oaks. The voices subsided in the deep shade. It was an oppressive change from the fields we had left. The sunlight was completely shut out. The dark, almost black leaves contrasted sharply with the autumn yellows of the willow and apricot trees around the village, the brilliant reds of white-barked maples,

and the gray green leaves and carnelian berries of wild olives. Near the village, the holly oaks had shawls of vines over them. There nothing tempered the prickly, spiderish shade where no other plants grew. Yet it was the place of the god, a source and focus of all life.

We stopped in a small clearing beside a huge holly oak, larger than any I had seen before, even in "wintry Dodona." Two old men were tending an open fire, making flat cakes of dough and boiling a caldron of water. A few shafts of sunlight struck through the branches and smoke to fall on flat wooden statues whose stylized faces stared vacantly at us with pebble eyes. A pruned holly oak bent over the clearing, its arc hung with the horns of many goats.

Three other men moved to a low stone altar. It was decorated with branches, flowers, and offerings of food. From it stuck out two rough-hewn carvings of horse heads. One of the men was the priest; the tight-stretched skin of his old face was stained with red henna, the eyes rimmed with black paste. The other two, his assistants, were unmarried young men considered "pure" and fit to carry out the sacrifice. The three stood looking up into the great tree, arms outstretched, palms upward, intoning monotonously their supplication to the god.

Then one of the young men gathered some twigs of holly oak and set fire to them. They crackled fiercely as he circled the altar with them. The goat, tethered to a particular tree nearby, watched him and bleated feebly, but did not try to break loose. Suddenly, everyone was crowding around a slab of stone between the altar and the great tree. The priest seized the goat and thrust it forward onto the slab. In an instant, one of the young men threw it on its back and drew the knife across its throat. No more than a small nicker marked its dying, and bright, thick blood spilled over the stone.

The other young man cupped his hands under the wound. They filled with red, and he flung some onto the altar, the horse heads, and the ritual fire. Now the holly oak is set with splashes of red more brilliant than the berries of our northern holly.

Afterwards, the head was severed from the goat and tossed among young boys, who scrambled to win it. The horns were then cut from it with an ax and hung in the tree. A boy put the head on a spit and roasted it. The fleece, which went to the priest, was removed and hung upon one of the statues, its rich pile warm and bright against the blackness of the grove. The skinned carcass was hung from the same tree where the live goat had been tethered a moment before. After it had bled, air was blown into its stomach. Then the men cleaned it and butchered it, throwing the pieces into the boiling water of the caldron.

When the meat pieces were tender, the old men

fished them out and handed them around on pieces of bread. The stock they thickened to a gruel with flour, and we all scooped out a handful. The young boys grinned and joked as they ate, their fingers still stained with dried blood from the sacrificial stone. In time, all were well fed—the men, the dogs, and the god Sajigorr.

Outside the grove again, a boy took out a wooden pipe and played short, rhythmic tunes. But when he left the crowd, the music became more wistful, as if recalling something strong and alive that was gone; the shortness and uncertainty of life; the strong, pretty women who became worn and old so quickly even here with water sweet and plentiful, many fine trees, good harvests of grain and grape, and strong gods like Sajigorr.

SACRED AND PROFANE SPACE

This sacrifice was one of many such observances peculiar to the Kalash, though reminiscent of Eurasia everywhere in ancient times. What interested me particularly was how these and all other aspects of life were tied to a distinctive map of the meaning and uses of the landscape. While their activities are hardly irrational or impractical, the Kalash attribute the main lineaments of land and life to the agency of gods or the spirit world. Broadly, they divide the land into sacred areas that are and must be kept permanently pure and unpolluted—places such as the grove of Sajigorr—and two varieties of profane space.[1] Areas of ordinary social and economic exchanges such as fields, pastures, communal parts of the village, and homes are considered intrinsically pure but constantly and unavoidably tainted by impure acts or beings. Then there are thoroughly "polluted" areas, again in a religious rather than a physical meaning of the term. Access to and use of all areas is carefully prescribed by time and conditions and according to age, sex, or achievement. Disasters or individual deaths and injuries are believed to flow mainly from violations of these partitionings of space.

Some large areas of the landscape are wholly the domain of the gods and of the *parian,* who seem to be something like fairy folk. Peaks, remote gorges, and lakes are their favorite abodes. A flood or a storm is thought to happen when "impure" beings such as women or chickens molest these spaces. (The Kalash will not eat eggs or the flesh of chickens.) But sacredness attaches both to remote and to intimate spaces, including parts of the home. The groves, shrines, and "temples" of some gods are in or near the villages and are sacred spaces where the major observances of Kalash life occur.

A number of sacred areas can only be approached at certain times or after special achievements. On a rugged, barely accessible ridge in Bamboret Valley is Ju-nagar, a god's shrine for special celebrations of manhood. When a shepherd has killed a bear, the people take the skin there to feast and dance around it. The description is reminiscent of a similar ceremony of the Ainu of Japan, who would chant, "We kill you, oh bear! Come back soon into one of us!" But a priest told me Ju-nagar has fallen into disuse. The bear have been hunted near extinction.

In villages of the Birir and Rombur valleys the most important sacred place is Jestak-han, the house of the only female deity venerated by everyone, the goddess Jestak. Its door will be elaborately carved, often with horse or ram heads guarding it. Finely carved columns support the roof, in which the central opening is designed like the "whirling logs" of the Navajo hogan, a way not only for the smoke to escape, but also for souls to pass through and perhaps the spirit of the shaman when it flies off seeking knowledge of other worlds. Jestak-han is especially the focus of family life. Nuptials and the birth of children are celebrated there under the four horse heads that form the goddess's shrine, and it is the only sacred place women can readily enter. In winter the dead may be laid out there. The great festival of the winter solstice, Chittermass, ten days of torchlit feasts and sacrifices, dancing, and wine drinking, is centered there.

The two most feared of "polluted" spaces are the graveyards where the dead lie unburied in wooden coffins, amid wooden effigies of eminent ancestors, and the women's house called Bashaleeni. It is thought to be dangerous for men to visit the former, and they are forbidden to enter the latter. Women may visit the graveyards, and even sleep there for certain purposes, with relative impunity. Bashaleeni is where they *must* go during menses and childbirth. If a man accidentally steps over the stream separating the Bashaleeni area from the village, he is shunned until purified by sacrifices. The Italian anthropologist Professor Graziosi, evidently above such things, entered Bashaleeni and photographed the grim little hut where women must bear children even in winter.[2] He found a statue there, too, of the goddess Dezilak, quite distinctive among the Kalash images of gods: humanoid, highly stylized, and reminiscent of Stone Age fertility goddesses elsewhere. But if she is there, the sacred intrudes even in these polluted areas.

For peoples who are strongly aware of a spiritual substratum to nature and who attach ultimate meaning to actual places, having to move to a new place is potentially the most disastrous of events.[3] The Kalash have techniques to reduce the risks of such dangerous ventures. One of their stories describes how a village in Rombur Valley was founded, apparently when its people came across the mountains to avoid enforced conversion to Islam. Everything depended upon properly locating sites for the shrine of their god, Sajigorr, for the village, and for the women's house. The method was to fire into the air, respectively, an arrow with a red thread attached, one with white, and one with black. The extent to which such a method leaves this critical "founding of a world" to chance may be debated, since an arrow need not travel very far, but similar magical techniques are widespread and have profound psycho-social implications.

IDENTITY AND BELONGING

The organizing of space, the pattern of meanings given to natural and artificial features, must in turn be coordinated with the organization of society and patterns of human activity. And in that we find not only isolation and attachment to a particular land helping main-

Kalash Woman. Photo by Kenneth Hewitt.

tain Kalash identity through centuries of change and pressure around them. Equally important are uncompromising conditions for belonging. The Kalash do not appear to be bigoted toward others, yet not even birth is sufficient condition for the honor of being called a Kalash. One must also observe throughout his life the outward forms: dress, eating habits, labor, and use of the land. These reflect the imprint of one's "Kalashness." A general term they use for this is *dastur,* which combines something of the sense of our words *habit, custom, heritage,* and *religion.*

Paradoxically perhaps, it is the women who bear the exigencies of *dastur* most fully, despite, or perhaps because of, their relative subservience and unpureness. They must wear Kalash costume always. Every woman's daily life is channeled by custom and propriety. She will grind the flour and cook the bread but may not serve a meal or enter the (pure) part of the house where serving utensils are kept. Each day she will wash her long hair, treat it with olive juice, and braid it, but she must never perform these attentions within the village confines. Even her comb must be left under a stone by the river. Though not for menfolk, the floor is considered a fit place for her to sit. And if she dies in Bashaleeni, a special disaster which all mourn, she is buried apart without the normal ceremony. To us these seem degrading practices, though widely echoed in patriarchal societies. In other ways, such as the strict division of labor by sex, Kalash women appear to be independent and indispensable to their economy. For all that, their life is often harsh; they age with tragic swiftness, and many die young.

Thus far a rather static picture of Kalash relations to nature may have emerged. But their observances are much concerned with *processes* in human nature and the environment. Through blood sacrifice, recitation, music, dance, and orgiastic rite they join in and strive to influence the great flows of energy and control that they perceive around them.

THE DANCE OF LIFE

Perhaps the most remarkable achievement of Kalash culture lies in their festivals, which add to the sacrifice of goats and cattle, dramatic dances, song, and the recitation of their unwritten history and beliefs. These festivals occur at major conjunctions of the natural calendar: the spring festival called Joshi or Chilimjuisht, a complicated series of observances surrounding harvest time, and the new year festival of Chomass or Chittermass. For the last, people gather in the main villages, coming in procession on the first night, bearing torches, singing and dancing barefoot in the snow. Then there occur spectacular ring dances before Jestak, often continuing for many hours and re-forming day after day. Space permits me only to deal here with these dances and what they may add to our theme of the relations of such folk to nature.

For the ring dance, the women link arms in a great circle. At a signal from the "dance-master" the drummers begin, and the women move around with dirge-like singing that surges and fades in trance-inducing monotony. Much takes place within the circle, too, where there are musicians with pipes and strings. The village headman and others engage in mock battles. There are bursts of song, whistling, and capering. But what the long recitations of Kalash history and beliefs record they would not reveal to me.

All of this was said to be truly Kalash, of ancient lineage, not borrowed or copied as are some of the other dances the women perform, and more alien to the Western eye and ear. Nevertheless, I could get no satisfactory interpretation of its significance from them. Yet that circle at the time of the solstice is so suggestive of the whole world of nature myths and religion that we may offer some pointers.[4]

The purpose of such dances is obviously to encourage and cement the relations of nature and society, and not only nature "here below," but also in the eternal realm; and not just the society of the living, but also that of the dead and of the undying gods. Long before the circle became a wheel and the wheel what it is to us, it was perhaps *the* symbol unifying all these things. "What is eternal," says Aristotle, "is circular, and what is circular, eternal." Among innumerable peoples the moving circle has defined the frame of time and space. Each example of it is magically linked to the rest— from the millstone that grinds flour for bread, to the turning "mill wheel" in the sky grinding out the dust of the stars; from the cycle of the land's yearly course, to that of human life—a numinous and protecting symbol behind the welter of experiences.

Here lies perhaps the most important of all symbolism involving mountains. It stems from the sense that they are the link between earth and heaven. But as well as being an abode of gods or a ladder to the hereafter, mountains have also been seen as the *axis mundi,* yoking the turning of heaven to the seasons of the earth, the eternal and the temporal.

These "analogues," as we say, between terrestrial cycles and the circling of the fixed stars promise that youth returns, heroism endures, the Golden Age will come back to the fields of earth. For cultures such as the Kalash, this possibility of renewal is literally present at the solstices, times of birth or fruition, but also of crisis. Everything possible must be done to ensure a favorable outcome, including assistance to the

turning of the seasons and the heavens by the circling of humans.

Like all major mythological symbols, this one embraces and unifies time, place, and people, the realms of uranography, geography, and biology. The purpose is to encourage that which brings life and to put the people at the center, the axis of the world's turning. Such symbols can be effective without logical articulation and may, indeed, lose their force when stripped to the bare geometric bones. But they cannot be sustained unless imbued with the stuff of everyday experience in work, nature, and society. It is seemingly a world we have lost, though the ecologically sensitive keep reminding us of it. To be sure, the wheels grind and reign supreme, but the sense of connection among them and to our fate is severed by processes that begin, inexorably, with the economic logic of alienating people

Kalash dancer. Photo by Kenneth Hewitt.

from the land. It is a matter of pride with us and occasionally of regret.

When the Kalash women go to the water mill before each meal, many strands of meaning are drawn together; of the power of the stream, of rounded stone and ripe grain, guided by human hand and eye to serve the most ordinary needs, nourishment. When the Kalash men make sacrifices in the sacred grove of Sajigorr, they are "redistributing wealth," paying their "taxes" perhaps, but sharing directly in the proceeds with the arbiters of it all, the gods who ultimately keep the wheels spinning.

POSTSCRIPT

Some will regard these folk as "archaic," remnants of one stage in man's progress from animal society to technological civilization. Even if this dangerous myth has a grain of truth, the Kalash have not survived without constant struggle and change. Ninety years ago the majority of the Kafirs and their main centers in Afghanistan were conquered and forcibly converted to Islam. Today, on every hand there are signs of the erosion of the independence and means of life of the Kalash remnant. Much of their best land has gone. Roads are being built bringing more outside influences and pressures for change: government officials; tourists; devout Muslims looking for converts; merchants looking for timber, grain, and animal fibers; and geographers asking leading questions. There is a steady loss of men and women through marriage into Muslim families and a questioning of Kalash ways that are so often called harsh or primitive by outsiders.

This is, then, an interregnum, as in so much of the world beyond the urban-industrial frontier, including, now, the remotest mountain wilderness. For the Kalash it is a brief episode between the long history of their warring independence among the other peoples of the Hindu Kush and more or less total absorption into a wider world.[5] In the meantime, they are making a last desperate struggle to maintain their roots and identity, a more intense turning to the land that is still theirs, and a self-conscious effort to maintain Kalash consciousness and practices.

10. An Inhabited Wilderness

PAT EMERSON

In 1974, mountaineering exploded into the Karakoram Range of northeastern Pakistan. Climbers from developed nations who had "done" the Nepalese and Indian Himalayas during the earlier decades now found themselves standing before a plenum of unclimbed Karakoram summits. For fourteen years before, strategic military considerations had kept the region closed to all foreign travel.[1] Now, the government had discovered—as had other developing nations—an untapped, exploitable resource: wilderness. Here in Baltistan is the world's most densely concentrated cluster of unclimbed peaks and untrodden passes. The flood of climbing and trekking parties that ensued was astonishing.

I first went into the Karakoram in 1974 as a member of an expedition trying to climb a peak and intent on exploring 17,600-foot (5,400-meter) pass called Masherbrum La.[2]

I trudge along a hot, dusty track, my only drinking water being that which I can carry in two quart poly bottles. My ears are assaulted by the roar of the silt-saturated river that fills the deep, narrow gorge, leaving only a thin, precarious foot track across the loose scree slope, a slope that seems to rise forever above my left shoulder until it disappears into the steely sky. When I dare to raise my eyes from this constantly shifting path, I see spread before me miles and miles of snowfields, couloirs, stones and rocky pinnacles, range behind range of great mountains, glaciers glittering in the hollows of them, a weird, a beautiful, a desolate scene. There are no plants, no animals, only sand, river, rock, glacier, a vast vertical desert. I am exhilarated.

The day is long, and toward twilight, eyes burning, throat parched, I drag around a corner into mirage, into green trees, verdant fields, clear water, smiles, welcoming voices. Sitting in the soft grass under the flowering branches of an apricot tree, my pack and boots off, I am handed a cup of tea, a hard-boiled egg. I am smiling back at people: old people, young people, baby people. People! The transition is too abrupt. How did this happen? Who are these people, and what are they doing here?

During the next week of wilderness travel this incongruity occurs each day. I march through a mountain landscape devoid of any sign of life: no plants, no trace of man. Then, as the day of walking ends, I find myself in a village, in an oasis of houses, trees, crops, animals, and people.

In Askole, I ask the hereditary headman how many people there are in the village. About one hundred households, he replies. "How long have there been one hundred households?" It has been that way always, he says. There are *people* in the wilderness. They have not just arrived here; they have *always* been here.

Since 1974, I have returned again and again to the Karakoram. With each visit my motives have shifted more to curiosity and concern about the people than the romance and challenge of the wilderness they inhabit. I am motivated by the personal, perhaps selfish, need to understand how these people exist within so inhospitable (at first glance) an environment. What follows is based upon notes made while living in the Balti village of Hushe during the winter months of 1980. Without some historical background, however, my observations of one small cluster of households in the midst of those vast mountains would have little perspective.

The great Indian subcontinent is a land of dramatic contrast, gigantic and legendary river systems, immense deserts, violent weather, and mountains—a vast northern wall separating all of South Asia from the great plateaus of Central Asia and China. The western portion of this mountain barrier, the Karakoram Range, forms its border with China to the northeast, Ladakh to the southeast, and Indian Kashmir to the south. This area, known as Baltistan, is penetrated only a few short weeks a year by a few widely separated passes. The expansive chain contains the second highest peak in the world, the world's largest mountain glacier, the largest number of the world's highest peaks—the superlatives cascade—and 176,000 Baltis. These people of mixed Aryan and Tibetan ethnic stock express themselves in a form dating from the tenth-century Tibetan poet Milarepa, but their names—Mohammad, Hassan, Fatima, Khasim—are evocative of the *Qur'an* and *A Thousand and One Nights*. Living in subsistence-level villages carved out of alluvial fans made by streams pouring out of the rocky gorges of the high peaks, they have remained relatively unknown to the rest of the world, and unknowing of it. They were there when the armies of Alexander passed by on the west, when Genghis Khan came by on the north, Babar to the south, Mirza Haider to the east, passing by on journeys of more lucrative conquest. Only in the nineteenth century did the conquerors exploit them for the only thing they had of value, their sturdy backs. "These poor Baltis, robbed by the tax-farmers of their conquerors, dragged from their homes to do forced labour on the dreaded Gilgit Road."[3] The armies of the maharaja of Kashmir on their way to help fortify the British garrisons at Gilgit used them as human pack animals and then discarded them.

In the nineteenth century also came the solitary Western hunter, surveyor, explorer, and mountain climber: Vigne, Conway, Thompson, Cunningham, D'Abruzzi. Until 1974, the people of the Karakorams, in their small pockets of villages, watched the visitors come and go, apparently without much effect upon the tenor of their lives.

If the mountains kept the invaders and the world out, they also kept the Baltis in. The mountains exercise the control on their lives and are the source of their existence and its limit. The soil, the water, the food, even their marriage patterns are influenced by the presence of mountains. Battering against the barrier of this upthrust, the moisture-laden winds of the monsoon are forced to drop their burden of rain on the plains, leaving the Karakorams dry, arid, a desert, frozen in one season and baked in another. The snows that fall only on the highest peaks are the source of life, because the glaciers create the soil and provide the water; the human inhabitants provide the irrigation system and bring fertility to these small patches of ground.

Here in this barren landscape the rivers pour out of the snouts of the glaciers, carving deep, cliff-lined chasms between the 25,000-foot (7,600-meter) peaks, depositing silt along the banks of the main river. Here on these precarious perches the people of the Karakoram have, over centuries, patiently and laboriously carved out terraces, built villages. To the Western trav-

Peaks rising from Hushe village. Photo by Richard Emerson.

eler these villages that appear every ten or so miles are welcome shelters of vegetation and human habitation, all but lost in the surrounding land. Only the Baltis can know the constant, unceasing labor that goes into creating and maintaining those refuges.

The side stream has brought down a fan of ground-up rock. Then comes the arduous construction of miles of intricate irrigation channels. Anchored to the sheer walls by ropes of twisted goat hair, these uncommon engineers dig and shape with wooden shovels and pry out house-sized boulders with crowbars made from tree trunks. As many as twelve years may go by before water can run through the channel and out onto the slope. Then begins the task of building terraces, years of carrying and spreading dung, coaxing life into the sterile soil. Eventually the "capital construction" is completed, and the routine cycle of plowing, sowing, and harvesting begins. If the Baltis are controlled by their environment, they have learned to wrest a living from it.

Despite five hundred years of following the teachings of the prophet Muhammad, the Baltis persist in some remnants of an ancient pre-Islamic, pre-Buddhist mystical attachment to the mountains. In all the villages the people recite the epic of Lepo Kesar, legendary king of Ladakh, born in the high peaks and still residing there among the eagles and the ibexes.

If mountains are to be contended with, if the Baltis do not have the leisure to climb mountains for pleasure, if they do not fear or worship the mountains in any religious sense, they are nevertheless respectful and appreciative of the mountain beauty that embraces them. The peaks have no Balti names. All are referred to as *kha-ri,* "snow peak." But Abdullah, the most skillful hunter in the village, who spends much time alone tracking ibexes, shows us a slender obelisk that he has named, and with eyes shining beneath the primroses tucked in his hat he sings of its beauty. Ali watches the light on Masherbrum and suggests that I might get my camera. The rhythm of their days, their months and years, is orchestrated, fashioned by the light on the mountains. They may, now, in this new age, wear wristwatches (purchased with wages earned carrying expedition loads), but the watches are not wound. The Balti reckoning of time cannot be spoken of in terms of hours and minutes. The sun is the timepiece. Every villager knows well the time of the day by the light on the mountains, even when the sun cannot be seen. The passage of each day is expressed through the presence, and absence, of light, light itself.

It is *juk bya,* "the last crowing of the cock, herald of the dawn," when coming light gives the first edge between black peaks and a blue black sky. The fledgling

Porters at tea stop. Photo by Richard Emerson.

rooster throws his uneven voice into the lightening sky, and I hear the whoosh-whoof, whoosh-whoof as coals are puffed into flame. Soon the insistent thud of the tea churn reverberates through the village, "cha-dong, cha-dong, cha-dong." That faint thap thap is wheat flour cakes being mixed and shaped, to be seared over the fire and set on edge in the ashes and coals to bake. Outside in the shadowy alleyways, the men are pouring water for the ritual washing before morning prayers. The gentle murmur of the women's voices and the soft shuff, shuff of their yak-hide boots drifts by. They are on their way with copper pots to the spring, the first of many trips they will make today. They come back with a load of water and a bundle of hay for the animals, and through the rising light the men are returning from prayer, carrying warm, steaming balls of *zan* (whole-wheat dough) in their cupped hands.

It is winter in the village, perched on this 11,000-foot (3,400-meter) shelf near the banks of the Hushe River, which gushes out of the snout of the Masherbrum Glacier. Masherbrum, at 25,660 feet (7,821 meters), caps the end of the valley, always there, even when hidden by clouds or falling snow. It is a legend to the Baltis only because of the American expedition that came to climb it twenty years ago. Otherwise, they speak of its beauty as the "source of the winter winds."

The houses huddle on the extreme edge of the river gorge to get the earliest and latest rays of the sun. The houses share common walls in order to reserve maximum land for cultivation and to conserve heat. The village is, thus, a maze of passageways, rooms, apertures, and tunnels, and in summer the easiest way to navigate is across the rooftops. In warm weather much of the life of the village takes place on the roofs. In winter, however, the people live on the ground floor above the subterranean *balti*, where the animals are housed.[4]

Nam longpa, "rising of the sky," or "day-break," and the household gathers around the fire pit to breakfast on eight to ten cups of *paiyu cha* (salt tea) and the baked bread. Balti-Tibetan butter tea has a reputation among foreign travelers as being nauseating. It is when the butter has been stored for months in goatskin bags. But the Baltis, living at high, harsh altitudes on a diet of wheat and potatoes, have learned that the tea has important nutritional, even medicinal, value. Tea, milk, salt, soda, and butter combine into the same remedy recommended by Western doctors for alleviating fatigue, shock, stress, and even dysentery.

The snow is four feet deep, and there is no field work or herding to be done, for Baltis winter is relatively leisurely. Last summer I was quizzing Achmad about the winter to come. "It is very cold, Api Pat, the snow is high, *hlung tan-et,* the wind blows, it is icy and difficult to go for wood." While he was reciting this litany of hardship, his eyes were telling me another tale of reminiscent pleasure. When I prodded him, he permitted a small grin. "Well, we do not have to work so hard, we can stay warm and snug in our houses, and we can eat meat when the snows bring the ibexes down from the high crags." But wood does have to be gathered, and animals and people must be fed and watered. The only water source in winter is a mile and a half away, and fodder is stored in outlying fields.

During spring and summer from *juk bya* to *tshan* (dark), the villagers are trudging miles between their widely separated small plots, plowing, planting, irrigating, weeding. In late summer and early fall they are

Late winter afternoon in Hushe. Men of the village relaxing after Friday prayers. Photo by Richard Emerson.

at even harder labor, cutting every blade of grass, miles up and down the valley, hundreds of feet up the mountain walls. After "grass-cutting month" and until snow falls, the whole village is occupied with the wheat and potato harvest. The cured grass and the wheat straw are stored in small rock huts located in the outlying fields, and every winter day many loads of fodder are carried into the village.

At *braqtse phoqpa,* "direct sun's rays on the mountain tops," the high musical call of today's shepherd runs through the streets, and suddenly from every doorway a flood of goats and sheep fills the narrow passageways. There is no confusion. They know exactly where they are going, and there is no need for the herders to do more than prod the stragglers. The flock files sedately across the snowy flat, down the steep slope, and on to the spring. A short time later I press my back against the wall and such in my stomach to let the horns of the *hYaks* and *dZmos* go by, herded by the women as they go down for their second or third load of water.[5]

There is no unemployment in a Balti village; the subsistence-level technology in its variety is a demanding one. Everyone has duties, and for the most part there is no obvious division of labor; most tasks are performed by men and women alike. However, men *never* carry water. If a woman is incapacitated, then her female relatives add her water-carrying burden to theirs. Even the smallest girls make the trip with a miniature version of the carrying basket and copper pot. Much of the female socializing and supportive companionship goes on in connection with this chore.

Fatima stops at my door, *chu tanet-a,* "bringing water." I take my backpack and plastic water bottle and join the group. Dablatt is no longer young, the load is heavy, and her rawhide boots are slick on the icy 30-degree slope. Young Azima extends a hand and side-steps up the hill, supporting Dablatt. We stop to rest on the rock wall at the top to gossip and to banter with the young men who have come out to the edge to scan the slopes above for ibexes driven down by yesterday's snowfall.

The Pakistan government has banned the killing of ibexes (and snow leopards) as an endangered species, but the Hushe-pa have always hunted the wild alpine goat for meat. They are virtual vegetarians by necessity, not choice. Their animals are too important as producers (milk, butter, yoghurt, wool, eggs, and offspring) to be killed for meat. So in winter they continue to hunt with the only gun in the village, an ancient muzzle-loader.

"The sun's rays fall on the village"—*ngima sna phoqpa*—and some of the men have crossed the river and are breaking trail to the small juniper-poplar forest several miles upriver to cut firewood. Hushe-pa do not burn animal dung; they must hoard every scrap to fertilize the sterile glacial silt that is their only soil. So wood gathering is a continuous and often dangerous chore. Just the week before we arrived this winter, young Ali Hussain fell to his death gathering juniper snags from a high cliff near the village. His young widow, Amina, is not to be seen as she observes the forty-day Islamic mourning period. Her month-old daughter is carried about and amused by aunt, grandmother, and neighbors.

Death is a frequent visitor to the village. There is no woman of middle years who has not lost several infants. Fatal accidents happen often, and elders die of natural causes, but no death is taken for granted; every loss is genuinely grieved. When we returned this year, we brought photographs as gifts. When we gave Achmad Ali a picture of his eighty-year-old father, who had died during the intervening year, his mixture of pleasure and grief was patent.

The repeated clang of metal on metal attracts me to the sunny schoolyard to find a ring of men and boys warming their hands around the "smithy" fire. Although all Baltis can make and repair anything, the ancient tradition of an artisan class persists. Ibrahim, the master blacksmith, has "come up" from Thagas to sit in the schoolyard every day, making and repairing tools and utensils. Machmad's gnarled hands work the sheepskin bellows, and Rozi and Ghulam Hussain wield the heavy sledgehammer in alternating rhythm while Ibrahim turns the chunk of glowing metal. As small Karim watches the ax head taking shape, wishing he were big and strong enough to help, Machmad pulls him between his knees and with his large hands over Karim's small ones teaches him by letting him help. When Ibrahim goes back to his village in two months, he will carry on his back his wages: butter and wheat.

In another corner of the yard the "schoolmaster" sits on the only chair ever seen in the village, supervising the group recitation of the schoolboys. Baltis speak classical (literary) Tibetan but have no history of literacy. School is conducted in Urdu, the official language of Pakistan.

Master Abdul Rahim, a Balti trained in government schools in Skardu, has only twelve pupils. Out of the fifty boys eligible, only twelve families have the resources or the desire to send their sons to school. After completing fourth "grade," a boy must go down to Khapalu or Skardu for further education. A family must have a surplus of sons to afford to lose the labor of one for many months. Few boys get more than rudimentary reading and writing.

As the boys work out their sums on wooden boards reblackened with shoe polish between lessons, Anwar

Ali's twelve-year-old sister skirts the edge of the group with her ubiquitous carrying basket and water pot, prodding the family's *dZmo* calf ahead of her. If she is envious, *adad* ("custom") regarding women's role is so strong that she does not express it. Besides, she is betrothed and in another two years will move into her husband's father's house; she already thinks of herself as an adult.

The pungent scent of juniper and the busy sound of saw and hammer draw me away. In another sheltered corner the visiting carpenters are supervising the manufacture of wheat storage bins. The juniper logs, cut miles up-valley, are floated down the river on the spring freshet. Positioned at strategic points on and in the river, protected with goat-hair safety lines, the men retrieve the logs with remarkable skill. The spring log drive is high excitement for participants and spectators alike.

I sit against the wall with the other women, out of the wind, warming in the sun. Their hands fly, carding and spinning sheep wool. Against the opposite wall an elderly man sits, chunking, ka-chunking the loom, weaving a ten-inch strip of wool that will become part of a blanket or coat. A rhythmic counterpoint comes from a "well" cleared out of the deep snow, where three women with long, limber willow switches are whipping and turning the raw wool, cleaning it of burrs and dirt.

The sun is high at *ngima tro,* "midday." The wood gatherers and grass carriers have come back with their loads. Seeing her husband go by, a woodpile with legs, Rahima winds up her spindle and asks us to take *zantus,* "morning food," at their fire. Motivated in part by the prestige of having us in her home, she is genuinely pleased with our company and willingly shares her scarce resources. The wood has been dumped in a corner of the room, and Rahima, squatting on her haunches, with youngest son Ali resting on her thighs under her overblouse where he has quick access to her breast, moves, still squatting, swiftly and efficiently, to blow up the fire, mix and shape whole-wheat cakes, boil potatoes for stew, comfort three-year-old Ibrahim, and chat with me.

Her house, like all others, is low-ceilinged, partially below ground, with walls in common with the neighbors' houses. The fire is in a small pit in the middle of the 8-foot by 8-foot (90-centimeter by 240-centimeter) dwelling, with smoke escaping through a hole in the roof. That is, it is supposed to go that way. More often than not capricious winds swirl it fiendishly around my head. I am a true coughing, wheezing Hushe-pa with red and smarting eyes.

Wood is precious, and not a twig is wasted. Never

more than two slender pieces of wood are burning at a time. Whole meals are cooked on what Westerners consider fire starter. The large chunks of weathered and twisted juniper lie in the corner, and every time Rahima needs to feed the fire, she chops or whittles off a piece. I open my mouth to protest the inefficiency. "Why don't you chop up *all* the wood at one time?" Rahima knows what she is doing. She is tailor-making every piece to fit the state of the fire, and of the cooking, at each moment. I am, once again, brought up short by the persistence of my own Western cultural attitudes and wasteful habits.

Above the village is a small juniper grove that the people of this village have harvested and conserved for centuries. Now, however, they are faced with an attempt by the former raja to lay claim to their woodland. The influx into Skardu, the administrative center of Baltistan, of government and military personnel accustomed to the warmer climate of the plains has raised the price of wood to a premium. Despite their recently acquired desire for the appurtenances and prestige of modern technology, and the subsequent need for cash, the Hushe-pa resist the takeover. "If we give up our wood, what will our children, and their children, burn?"

The potato stew is seasoned with wild herbs, imported chilis, and carefully hoarded onions brought from down-valley. After stew, I drink my three-cup quota of *paiyu cha*. Into the last one I stir a special treat, finely ground parched barley flour. I eat the thick paste with my finger and wipe the cup clean.

We are all glad to escape the smoke into the clear air of *pishin*, "early afternoon," as the *bang-i*, muzzein, on the roof of the mosque sends out the call to Juma, the traditional Muslim day of prayer that comes about every eight days. Islam came to the Karakorams in the last days of the fourteenth century with a Persian Sufi proselytizer who fled into Baltistan when he fell out of favor with the court of Kashmir. Although the sect has disappeared from the rest of the Islamic world, the people of the Hushe Valley retain their identification as followers of Syed Hamadani and speak of his bringing them the Nurbakshi faith as though it were yesterday.

After prayers, the men gather in the mullah's house to drink innumerable cups of *paiyu cha*, sing religious songs, and listen to readings and exhortations by Syed Hassan. Excluded from gathering for prayers in the mosque, women are expected to say prayers privately. For the most part, however, they leave the ritual aspects of Islam to the men. They are not unbelievers, but they are the custodians and transmitters of old ways and old beliefs. They are forceful and self-respecting members of the community, and their importance to this subsistence economy and their clinging to their pre-Islamic cultural roots gives Balti women distinct personality and status in an Islamic society. In their independent attitude they resemble their Tibetan Buddhist relatives. Vigorous and earthy, they freely joke and debate with the men of the village; a comportment which has earned them a reputation as "loose" among Muslim visitors from urbanized down-country (Pakistan).

My husband is out of the village for several days, and as we meet at the spring, my friends chaff me about my single state and my empty bed, and with ribald laughter and pokes to my ribs they offer to lend me someone to fill it.

The large animals have come back from water and stand ruminating in the sun, steam rising from their backs. Marium and daughter move among them with small baskets, waiting for the droppings, which will be added to the "compost pile" attached to the side of every dwelling. I am suddenly aware that Bardool has been squatting on his haunches, hands cupped around his eyes, staring straight ahead for several minutes. Is he resting his eyes from the glare? Five minutes later he is still there, and then I see that he appears to have his "binoculars" focused on the hindquarters of a cow a few feet in front of him. What is he doing? A little later the cow has moved, and Bardool has moved with her to maintain his unbroken gaze. Naisip becomes aware of my puzzlement and explains that Bardool's cow is not *skya yod*, pregnant. He is "willing" the cow into a pregnant state, a ritual that appears to have its roots in some shamanistic time predating Islam in Balti history.

It is warm in the dry, clear air. The sounds are busy, cheerful ones of women gossiping, the musical chunk of the blacksmith's hammer, the rasp of the carpenter's saw, children laughing as they slide down the snow mountains made by yesterday's roof shoveling.

I seldom hear a discordant note in Hushe; babies and small children are welcome and tenderly cared for by all members of the family and village. The village is *not* utopia; there are factions and rivalries, disagreements and even lawsuits. But as people go about their daily chores they are friendly and courteous to each other.

As Sikeena and Gulsum, who are neighbors, meet in the sunny courtyard, they greet each other as if they are meeting after a long absence. Yet yesterday they made many trips to water together and spent the afternoon crushing apricot kernels in Gulsum's house.

As I sit on Marium's doorstep with my "work," writing, I can hear around the corner the rhythmic thud of the pestle in the communal grinding stone; wheat is being crushed for tonight's soup. Through the wall I can hear the slosh of Rahima's butter making.

Houses at summer pasture village named Andoro (14,000).
Photo by Richard Emerson.

She has tied one end of the milk-filled goatskin to the wall, and with a rope on the other is pulling it back and forth, back and forth, churning.

In ancient Chinese documents Baltistan was known as "Apricot Tibet," and the dried apricots were prized and traded all the way to Lhasa in central Tibet. The village of Hushe is too high to grow apricots, but its location gives it access to more extensive summer pasture than the lower or "apricot" villages. The Hushe keep larger herds and even provide summer pasture for animals from the lower villages in return for winter care or a share of the milk and butter. In the winter, the milk supply is scanty, but in the summer when the *dZmos* and *hYakmos* freshen, the women keep busy in the high pastures making butter and yoghurt. Although both men and women come and go carrying butter, wood, and dung from the "high pasture" *broq,* the summer pasturing is women's province. They revel in the break from the tedious routine of village chores and in the companionship of other women. Away from the observation of the mullah and their

husbands and fathers, they sing the old songs and dance for each other.

A special relationship often develops between the women and their animals. The small goats and lambs are picked up and fondled as though they were children. One day last week, as Fatima was taking her oldest *dZmo* to water, the elderly animal's stiff legs could not hold the slope. Fatima made a desperate lunge, catching one horn, attempting to hold all five hundred pounds from going over the edge. Her anguished cry for help was quickly answered, and both *dZmo* and owner were brought back up to safety. Fatima's immense concern and relief were unmistakable. As she fondled ears and muzzle, she turned to me, "You see, we have been together twenty years."

Fatima is telling me of her sorrow at having no daughters. Of the eight children she has given birth to, only two sons survive as adults. I try to comfort her by saying that when Ghulam and Machmad marry, she will have daughters in her house. She shakes her head: "There are no girls in the village of the right age for them, and women from other villages will not marry into Hushe. It is too high, too cold, there are no apricots, and women have to work too hard."

However, Hushe butter is prized and traded throughout Baltistan for apricots, barley flour, and onions, which cannot be grown at Hushe altitude. Stored in earthen pots and buried in the corner of the house to mitigate the problem of "seasonal supply," certain amounts of it are reserved for special occasions.

Yesterday, we had another *olchi-zan*. Apo Hussain,[6] who at seventy-six is feeling his years and his mortality, "threw a feast" for the entire village.[7] All the males in his kin group gathered wood, and the women carried water, filling the mammoth copper vats, and the whole clan contributed the wheat that the men cooked into a porridge so stiff that five men with four-foot tree trunks were needed to stir each pot. At the *bang-i* calls, all the men and boys gather in the courtyard of the mosque, sitting in groups of seven around large copper trays of the *zan,* dipping small hand-molded cups of dough into a crater of melted butter in the center of the mound. When they have eaten their fill, the women and girls eat, also in groups of seven. When all have eaten, prayers are recited for the giver.

Apo Hussain must be feeling particularly vulnerable, because this time we were treated to butter that had been stored away by his great-grandfather. Eighty-year-old butter has no color but does have impact. According to the Hushe-pa it has strong medicinal qualities. They may be right; it certainly cleaned out my intestinal tract.

Olchi-zan occurs regularly during January and February, always contributed by an elderly person in return for the villagers' prayers to Allah. Yesterday the thank-you prayer was perfunctory. The food and socializing were paramount for the participants. The event must have historical and functional explanations that predate Islam. It is apparent that only those who can afford it are expected to give. It may be a redistribution of wealth, the Balti version of a potlatch.

It is *ngima huba,* "setting of the sun on habitation," and suddenly the shaggy-haired, yellow-eyed goats are leading the sheep up the slope from the spring. At the edge of the village they divide, pouring into their streets, falling out of the parade to stand with heads butted up against their own door, waiting to be let into the *balti.*

Every day different households rotate the duty of guarding the flock from predators. The red fox is ubiquitous, his tracks criss-crossing the snow around the watering place. The *khlchan,* snow leopard, is seldom seen but takes a heavy toll. Just last week I was urgently summoned to apply my dubious medical skills to a *dZmo* that had been clawed in the neck by a leopard. The sharp, heavy horns and the size of the "cattle" are usually good defense against predators, but the calves of the hybrid are routinely slaughtered, considered to be of little value because (in inexact translation), "They do not know enough to come in out of the snow leopards."

With the "sun only on the hills," *gontakhs,* the men come into commons from their *cha-res* (tea session) with Syed Hassan. Without the sun, the chill descends, and the men sit watching the veil of dusk fall down the slopes, sharing the warmth of their blankets with babies and toddlers as the women make yet another trip to the spring. Giggles and chatter come from a gaggle of small children sitting in the warm ashes of the smith's fire. Swathed in his blanket, young Ghulam Ali sits softly, almost furtively, playing his brass flute.

In other years the sounds of the village day would have been punctuated with singing. In those rare moments of leisure some group would chant and clap and take turns dancing. Traditional fundamental Islam has always restricted nonreligious singing and dancing, but the traditional, pre-Islamic songs and dances have been a strong unifying element in Hushe. The Hushe people take pleasure and pride in their music; in this way they have preserved and passed down their culture and kept their history alive.

Islam is the other major cohesive force, and the elderly mullah, Syed Mahdi, is respected, as was his father before him. Now he is retiring in favor of his son, Syed Hassan, who has had the advantage of studying with a senior mullah "down-valley." Because the Nurbakshi sect exists only in the Hushe Valley, those who go out for religious training find themselves of necessity under the guidance of Shia mullahs. This is the case with young Syed Hassan. As a result of exposure to the outside world, he is bringing a more fundamental, conservative brand of Islam to the village and forbidding the people to dance or sing their traditional songs. There are rumblings of disagreement, but as yet no overt rebellion. It is ironic that Islamic fundamentalism is having a more immediate impact upon their traditional culture than is modernization.

At *gonphin,* "no sun, first stars appearing," a still, almost visible cold settles over the village. The sounds are muted and fading as everyone turns homeward, and except for starlight, the village is dark. The people retreat into their homes for the evening meal, and, sitting in a close circle around the fire that here and there highlights a feature, a copper ladle, they converse quietly. They pause to make room in the circle for visitors who stoop through the low doorway. Handed a cup of soup and a piece of bread, they are made welcome, as are all who come—kin, friend, and stranger.

All around this house are clustered ninety-nine other households, snowy roofs above, a warm, breathing layer of animals below, the whole village encircled by mountains. During winter nights, no Hushe-pa, no animal, is out of these narrow confines. Crowded into a 75- by 100-yard space of a Balti village are four hundred people and four hundred animals sharing body warmth. The limit of the environment is in the space as well as in the subsistence—space and subsistence wrung out of an inhospitable land. As I watch the firelight play upon the faces of my friends, I attempt to sort out my involvement and observations during these past months. Loads: loads of wood, water, fertilizer, milk, butter, babies, building stones, expedition boxes, snow from the roofs; no one is ever without a burden. Hands: hands weaving, spinning, carving, sewing, shelling, pounding, shoveling, planting, cooking; even in periods of apparent relaxation, there is constant activity. As the images of loads, constant activity, and struggle to stay ahead of the pressure of the environment pass before me, I realize that I have come to the resolution of my quandary over the question of habitation within wilderness. Wilderness does not have to mean the absence of human beings and technology. An inhabited wilderness exists when the forces of nature have the potential of overwhelming the technological capacities of the people who "live" there.

The dilemma, however, does not end here. The resolution of the paradox opens up a more profound dilemma—not one of definition, but one of another dimension, perhaps of morality. The increasing intrusion of modernization and technology (as well as conservative Islam) is bringing imminent and intensive change to this self-sufficient economy. The Balti people are, at this time in history, balanced between two potentially overwhelming forces: the always threatening force of nature and the intrusion of modern technology. While their material resources are meager, their self-sufficiency stands as a valuable resource in its own right. It is this resource that they stand to lose under the current technological change.

In the summer a road is completed, and the first jeep arrives in Hushe. Most of the men have seen jeeps down-valley, but the women and children have never even seen a wheel. In excitement, awe, and fear they flock to wonder. Api Hajira, blind and crippled, is carried out to share this momentous happening. She sees the jeep by touching and listening. When the motor starts, small Zohora tramples her even smaller brother in her panicky flight from the monstrous roar and smoke. Within three days, as the jeep makes daily trips carrying salt, kerosene, a pressure cooker, people no longer leave their work to marvel. The jeep has become, if not commonplace, familiar. The coming of the modern vehicular age may have tremendous impact on their future, but today they must get the potatoes planted if they are to have enough to eat next winter. Who knows if this machine will come again? They know, as did those one hundred ancestral households that were here before them, what will happen if the potatoes and the wheat are not planted, because here they live perpetually on the defensive in a constant standoff with their environment.

11. Himachal: Science, People, and "Progress"*

GERALD D. BERREMAN

In the end, the greatest challenge of all may be convincing the people of the plains that the future of the mountains cannot be isolated from their own.

ERIK P. ECKHOLM

Fourth-world colonialism, by which I mean the colonization or exploitation of indigenous minorities within third-world or "developing" nations, is as pernicious—as damaging to the colonized—as any other kind of colonialism, the more so that it often goes unrecognized. Ethnocentrism can be as narrow-minded and relationships as exploitative when India or China, for example, deal with Himalayan peoples within their borders (or when their elites decide what is good for untouchables or tribals, or when their men decide what is good for women) as when foreigners do so.

I shall give a brief example from the region of my own research in the outer and lower ranges of the Himalayas in India. Among a number of the Pahari ("of the mountains") societies of the western Himalayas—Hindu speakers of Indo-Aryan as distinguished from Bhotiya, who are Tibetan-speaking Buddhists of the higher altitudes—a system of marriage and family organization generally described as "polyandry" is the norm. The system is more accurately described as fraternal polygynandry, and as D. N. Majumdar and others have shown, it is a coherent, viable, and valued system there, apparently independent of Bhotiya polyandry (Majumdar, 1962; Berreman, 1962, 1975, 1978). When the chief minister of Himachal Pradesh, Dr. Y. S. Parmar (himself a member of Pahari society), reported it in 1975 in a sociological book entitled *Polyandry in the Himalayas,* he became the subject of a legislative furor in his home state. As reported in the Indian newspapers, "Four women legislators walked out of the Assembly, when their call-attention motion . . . was disallowed alleging that the book portrayed hill women in a vulgar and distorted fashion. A poster war has since been launched calling for the banning of the book" (*News INDIA,* July, 1975:10). The legislators "said the books should be banned and copies already in circulation confiscated" (*Overseas Hindustan Times,* May 22, 1975:3). The result was that a section was inserted at the end of the book, announcing that this marriage system had largely disappeared (Parmar, 1975:189–92)—although it had not. This is not only an example of perverse political pressure on scholarship, but also an ethnocentric derogation of the way of life of a Himalayan people, an uninformed denigration specifically of their women (perpetrated by women legislators, I might note). It is likely to be followed over the next few years by increased intrusion on their lifeways in an attempt to bring them around to alien ways of life adjudged superior by outsiders.

THE POLITICAL IMPLICATIONS OF ANTHROPOLOGICAL WORK

This example of ethnocentrism points up a related problem that is close to all anthropologists—namely, the political implications and uses of our work. Because of the political sensitivity of the Himalayan region, independent scholarship is likely to be compromised no matter how good the intentions of the scholars involved. Sources of research funds, be they governmental or private, tend to channel research by determining who shall work on what and where. The same end is achieved through the requirement of permissions, clearances, and visas and through the establishment of restricted and prohibited areas and topics. These hindrances are inevitable, no doubt, but their effect on indigenous as well as foreign scholarship should not be underestimated. The effect is exacerbated to the extent that there is official censorship and a climate of suspicion of scholarship and research, as American social scientists learned so vividly during their nation's disastrous military and political adventurism in Southeast Asia during the 1960s and early 1970s. Thus, apart from the relatively overt problems of research censorship are the covert problems of channeling research efforts into problems and places that are acceptable, noncontroversial, fashionable, and productive by the standards of those who give money, review proposals, employ researchers, and publish their works (Berreman, 1971). It is an acute problem and one sure to have long-range impact in the case of Himalayan research.

The relationship between the Himalayan people and their environment, the plans and prospects for their futures, and the role anthropological research may play in all of these suggest that we cannot expect research there to be free of political consequences or that we should regret that this is so. I think that in the last analysis there is no freedom from values and politics in science—there is no absolute objectivity—for even the decision to do science, and to study a particular problem, is a subjective one, and the decision to record evidence and report it truthfully is a decision based on values (cf. Berreman, 1968). Therefore, I turn to the great sociologist C. Wright Mills for a definition of the politics of the social scientist, which could as well be a definition of the politics of all people of knowledge. He described our legitimate politics as the "politics of truth," saying: "The very enterprise of social science, as it determines fact, takes on political meaning. In a world of widely communicated nonsense, any statement of fact is of political and moral significance. All social scientists, by the fact of their existence, are involved in the struggle between enlightenment and obscurantism. In a world such as ours, to practice social science is, first of all, to practice the politics of truth" (Mills, 1961:178).

Mills pointed out that the job of any person of knowledge "is the maintenance of an adequate definition of reality. . . . The main tenet of his politics is to find out as much of the truth as he can and to tell it to the right people, at the right time, and in the right way" (Mills, 1964:611). That is what I think we should do.

The Himalayas are shrouded in mists of myth, romance, and misinformation, and their people, no longer isolated from the impact of governments, entrepreneurs, tourists, and others, suffer as a result. For better or for worse, they are included in programs of community development, family planning, and education; they are reached by motor roads; they are pressured to change their ways of life; they are incorporated in national cash economies and party politics;

Ladakhi child. Photo by M. Tobias.

they are exploited for their land, labor, and income—in short, they are assimilated into the outside world from which their lofty environment, in simpler times, largely protected them. On the whole, those government servants who are invested with protecting the interests of the mountain people are benevolent in intent, I think, but are quite ignorant of their situation: their hopes and fears, their problems and satisfactions, their customs and experiences. Therefore, whatever we who study the Himalayas and their peoples learn from our research, honestly and publicly told and assessed with respect to its implications for the lives of these peoples, is in most instances more likely to help them than to harm them, and I think we should act accordingly. We should report what we find as we find it, as fully as we are able, in its full human context; not to advance our careers, but to enhance the quality of their lives; not to insure future research access, but to insure, or contribute to, future well-being of the Himalayan people. As our research is not value free, neither does it occur in a vacuum; it has consequences—often fateful ones—in people's lives. If instances arise when research appears to be potentially harmful in its effects, or likely to be used for devious purposes, it should not be undertaken or its findings should remain unreported. These decisions are up to the individual researcher, based on his or her best assessment of the situation and of the implications of the research.

The Ethics of Research are Ethics of Responsibility

The ethics of research are ethics not only of truth, but also of responsibility and accountability, which means that when we act as scientists, we are responsible for what we do and must be held accountable for its consequences. We may make errors, for it is only human to do so, but another aspect of our humanity is that we are accountable when we do so. During the Vietnam War, American scientists (including, I am ashamed to say, a number of anthropologists) served overtly and covertly as hirelings of military, quasi-military and political agencies, doing research and advising in support of U.S. military and political aggression in Southeast Asia. When finally called to account for their actions, there was no more frequent, no more hollow, no more evasive and disingenuous plea among them than the claim that they were simply scientists doing their job—pursuing knowledge, the context of which was scientifically irrelevant, the purposes and consequences of which were out of their hands and hence none of their responsibility (cf. Berreman, 1973; Condominas, 1973; Wolf and Jorgensen, 1970). I am reminded of the final conversation between a condemned prisoner and the hangman, who, in response to the prisoner's plea, commented defensively as he adjusted the noose, "This is only my job," to which the prisoner replied, "Then get another job!" Their assertion that science is not accountable overlooks the fact that science is done by scientists, and scientists are people, hence humanly responsible and accountable. I am proud to say that anthropologists, at least, were called to account for such actions in Southeast Asia by the Committee on Ethics of the American Anthropological Association on behalf of the membership in 1970, and that when an attempt was made to censure the Committee on Ethics—itself an exercise in irony—it was overwhelmingly rejected by the membership (cf. Berreman, 1973 : 51–55).

THE CASE OF THE HIMALAYAS

Beyond accountability, however, I think we all have a positive responsibility to the people we study, namely to attend to the problems and issues confronting them in their lives. The late Nirmal Kumar Bose, formerly India's commissioner of scheduled castes and tribes, exemplified the acceptance of this responsibility to a unique degree throughout his life as an anthropologist. In 1968 he chaired a conference in India on urgent research in social anthropology. Although all but two of the participants in that conference defined urgency in terms of what is often called "salvage ethnography" (learning the esoteric facts about dying cultures before they disappear forever), Dr. Bose indicated agreement with a more socially relevant definition of urgency. Let me paraphrase what I said then, substituting references to the Himalayas for those to India: "When I ask myself, 'what are the urgent problems in Himalayan research,' I immediately think of the urgent problems facing this region and its people, and of our claim to be students of 'the science of man.' Surely the most urgent problems for anthropologists (and all humane scientists) are those most urgent to all people: poverty, ill health, hunger, hopelessness, bigotry, oppression and war. Whatever we can say that is relevant to these vital problems is urgent" (cf. Berreman, 1969*b*:1).

It is scarcely evident from much of the writing on the Himalayas, I fear, that the fascinating people of this beautiful environment are afflicted with appalling poverty, ill health, high infant mortality, and short life expectancy; that those of low caste are subject to severe oppression with little or no recourse to the nation's protective legislation; that few of the amenities offered other rural peoples of the subcontinent, most noticeably modern medicine and schooling, are available in the Himalayas; that their lands and forests are being depleted by outside commercial interests, their privacy invaded by tourists and adventurers, and their ways of life subjected to planned and unplanned alterations

Ladakhi children. Photo by M. Tobias.

through governmental programs often with starkly deleterious effects. As one who has remained in touch with the people of a Pahari village for nearly thirty years, I can testify that these are agonizing problems to those who experience them (cf. Berreman, 1972, 1978). I hope that as our Himalayan research increases, we will report and analyze these and other problems facing those we study, and that we will propose and advocate solutions where possible—"to the right people, at the right time"—whether or not these reports, analyses, and proposals are recognized by governments, by sources of funds, or by colleagues as worthy scholarly activities. As scientists knowledgeable about the Himalayas, we have a positive responsibility to do so—a responsibility that is inherent in the "politics of truth," to which I think we are obligated. Otherwise we become chroniclers of an idyllic view of Himalayan life that bears little relationship to the existential realities of those who live it, or we become celebrants of a status quo so selectively reported that it is grossly misleading to those in a position to alter it. Either would implicate us in the impending destruction of the Himalayan environment—a grave disservice to the people whose welfare we identify with and whose confidence and good will we seek and rely upon for the success of our research and of our own careers.

A new mecca for tourists and climbers

Some time ago I attended the motion picture *The Man Who Skied Down Everest*, filmed in 1970 and released in 1975, in which a Japanese skier, Yuichiro Miura, skied and fell some eight thousand feet down the side of Mount Everest, in Technicolor (Crawley, 1970). This preposterous stunt, which took just over two minutes, was the culmination of a two-month trek involving 27 tons (25 metric tons) of baggage and equipment; a couple of dozen Japanese climbers, scientists, and cameramen; and over eight hundred Pahari and Sherpa porters, and it cost three million dollars (not much of which went to the porters; among Miura's musings was this rhetorical question, "Are there men in the Western world who would carry 30 pounds on their backs for a dollar a day for a living?"). It also cost the lives of six Sherpas killed in an avalanche. A spokesman says in the film, "A Sherpa will not be a Sherpa if he does not continue to climb," but one might add, as this expedition and too many others demonstrate, he may well be a *dead* Sherpa if he climbs for adventurers. In this regard, one may quote from the *Royal Anthropological Institute News* (1974:1):

> The number of major expeditions has increased so much that the more famous mountains such as Mount Everest, Annapurna and Dhaulagiri are booked for several years to come. The number of Sherpas capable of high-altitude work, on the other hand, has not risen. The population of Khumbu numbers about 2,200 men, women and children, and of these no more than perhaps 500 are able-bodied men of suitable age. The casualties suffered by this relatively small group over the past two decades must give rise to serious anxiety. . . . There exist no exact statistics of the accident rate, but in the worst years up to ten Sherpas lost their lives in the course of various expeditions, and few mountaineering seasons pass without the occurrence of some fatal casualties. In villages such as Khumjung and Khunde, from which many of the most skilled high-altitude porters hail, there is hardly a household which has not lost at least one member in a mountaineering accident. It goes without saying that it is the most enterprising and the physically fittest men who are placed in the most exposed positions, and a small village community cannot afford for long a steady depletion of those young men who would become its natural leaders.

In a moment of reflection in the film, Miura asks himself, "I wonder what will be the future of these tribesmen who have lived here for centuries almost unknown to the rest of the world. I hope their land will remain unspoiled by the ways of life we call progress." The simple answer evidently escapes him: their land has not and will not remain unspoiled, thanks in no small part to intruders and tourists such as himself.

No sooner had this film been released than (as reported in the *Overseas Hindustan Times,* May 27, 1976), "Four Indian skiers did the incredible last week when they skied or rather raced down 15,000 feet to the base camp from the top of the 23,360-foot-high Trishul mountain (in the Garhwal Himalaya) in 90 minutes." They were sponsored, incidentally, by Bharat Heavy Electricals, a private firm whose flag crossed that of India in photographs at the summit. Two days later, a

Tibetan pilgrim in northern Nepal. Photo by James H. Katz.

second team of four repeated the stunt. Filmed by the Indian government's Ministry of Broadcasting and Information, the stunt was reported to have cost Rs. 75,000 in addition to use of equipment worth over Rs. 505,000 donated by an Italian firm (*Overseas Hindustan Times,* 1976*a*, 1976*b*).

The July 9, 1976, issue of *India News,* published by the embassy of India in Washington, D.C., boasted that "The year 1976 has been one of the best years for mountaineering in the Indian Himalayas. A record number of both Indian and foreign expeditions have either gone or are booked to go to Indian mountain peaks. Before 1966, Indian expeditions used to be only three or four per year. . . . In the last three years, the number went up to an average of 24. The number this year is expected to be more than 35." Foreign expeditions were five in 1971, and five years later, in 1976, thirty-six had been registered. In the fall of 1976 a team entitled "The American Bicentennial Everest Expedition," with about twenty members, including a five-person television camera crew plus innumerable porters, scaled Mount Everest under the sponsorship of ters, scaled Mount Everest under the sponsorship of the Columbia Broadcasting System Television System. Tragically, at about the same time, Nanda Devi, an American student on an expedition led by her father, died near the summit of the mountain for which her father had named her. Like that ill-fated and widely publicized venture, more than half the mountain-climbing expeditions in India went to Garhwal, while one-fifth went to Kashmir and one-tenth to Himachal Pradesh. Speaking of Kashmir, the September 2, 1976, issue of the *Overseas Hindustan Times* announced that "A 25-kilometer narrow gauge railroad is to be laid around the Dal Lake in Kashmir by the end of next year for a joy ride train for tourists," at a cost of fifteen million rupees. In the 1970s the Japanese built a luxury hotel (now abandoned) on the flanks of Mount Everest, and less pretentious indigenously built hotels are now to be found in every Sherpa village on the trekking routes. The impact of mountaineering, to say nothing of wholesale tourism, can be suggested by a mountaineer's report: "At each place where our 600 porters had stopped for the night and gathered firewood, the hillsides looked as if a swarm of giant locusts had passed through" (Rowell, 1977:297). Litter has become an increasing problem in the Himalayas. Another veteran mountaineer, Bonington, commented, "The trail to Everest is littered with cans and refuse. Some years ago this was appreciated by mountaineers for it assured them that they were on the right track, but this no longer holds true" (*The Statesman*, 1973: 182). The Everest base camp has been described as one of the largest garbage dumps on earth.

In short, the Himalayas are being sold as a mecca for climbers, adventurers, and tourists. But the price is high. What will be the long-term consequences for the environment and the people? I can only think of Theodore Roszak's introduction to the book *Small is Beautiful: Economics as if People Mattered,* by E. F. Schumacher, the distinguished British economist whose thinking was influenced by Mohandas Gandhi, among others. In the introduction to that book, Roszak said: "Consider the poor countries that sell themselves to the international tourist industry in pursuit of those symbols of wealth and progress the West has taught them to covet: luxurious airports, high-rise hotels, six-lane motor ways. Their people wind up as bellhops and souvenir sellers, desk clerks and entertainers, and their proudest traditions soon degenerate into crude caricatures. But the balance sheet may show a marvelous increase in foreign-exchange earnings" (Schumacher, 1973:7–8).

As if to exemplify the point, the director of tourism of Uttar Pradesh said in a newspaper article: "The sturdy growth of tourism in the decade has transformed it into an economic giant. It has now become a major industry which earns considerable foreign exchange. It . . . provides innumerable benefits. It provides economic multiplications and generates employment. To promote this industry agencies of hoteliers, airlines, transport, railways, travel trades should work in co-ordination. . . . Now there is an increased scope of receiving more tourists (in the Himalayas) because of the opening of Yamunotri, Banderpoonch, Kedarnath, Badrinath, . . . Nanda Devi, the Pindari Glacier and Kauri Pass, for the foreign tourists" (*Overseas Hindustan Times,* 1976d).

Destructive development

Too much of the actual and proposed development of the Himalayan region is of this character. Tourism and mountaineering are not the worst of it. On the whole, the Himalayas have been regarded as an inexhaustible reservoir of exploitable and expendable resources without regard to the future of the fragile mountain environment, and especially without regard to the people of the Himalayas, who are treated at best as an unfortunate inconvenience in need of assimilation to the lifeways of the plains and incorporation into the national and international economic system.

Absolutely essential to the indigenous economy are the forest lands, which make possible the agriculture upon which the mountain people depend by providing fodder for their animals, which provide manure to enrich their soil, which in turn gives them the crops for their livelihood. The forest lands are the first to go when lands are exploited by outside interests. De-

Ladakhi yak herders. Photo by M. Tobias.

forestation has many causes. To be sure, the much-discussed lopping, cutting, burning, and clearing entailed in indigenous agriculture and animal husbandry play their role. But it is rare that these alone are sufficient to destroy the land, and in any case they proceed slowly. More commonly and rapidly destructive is commercial exploitation by outside contractors, who often devastate huge areas under government license for quick profit. They cut forests for lumber, paper pulp, and charcoal—I have seen large forest tracts cleared, the great logs piled high only to be burned to charcoal—and they denude the land for the development of mineral resources ranging from gravel and limestone to coal, oil, phosphorus, and valuable metals. Not to be ignored is the incidental destruction wrought by hydroelectric development schemes, by commercial crop and orchard growing (which is rapidly being expanded in the Indian Himalayas, not by the Himalayan peoples but by large industrial and commercial concerns that buy up their land for this purpose), and by the training and posting of military personnel, road building, and development of other transport and communication systems that facilitate and exacerbate other ecologically destructive activities. Similar consequences follow extension of the consumer-oriented market economy into the mountain regions, creating a demand for cash—hence cash-cropping, outside employment, and emigration (especially of young men), with its resultant inroads on traditional management of land and other resources (to say nothing of the damaging social effects of their departure). The encouragement of a cash and consumer/market economy not only jeopardizes the forests and other wild lands, but also drives out traditional subsistence crops and often drives out the indigenous peasant farmers themselves as commercial producers move in. Even community development and agricultural development programs aimed at increasing productivity at the local level have often had the effect of creating overdevelopment and the problems that go with it. In using the term *overdevelopment*, I am following Marriott, who so described the Indian plains region in which he worked; by that word he meant "the pressing of techniques up to and beyond the point of an optimum relation between man and environment. In an overdeveloped area, too many techniques are too exhaustively applied by too many people to too little land" (Marriott, 1957:423).

THE WELL-BEING OF PEOPLE VS. PROGRESS

One can only hope that measures will be taken to curtail the forces that make this process seem so inexorable in the Himalayas. These would have to be measures that place human values above technical and political ones. They would require a commitment to maximize the quality of life instead of the gross national product.

The qualify of life to be maximized would have to be, in this instance, that of the mountain people. This would require planning and implementing development in their homeland with their full participation, in such a way that it would enhance their well-being as they define and experience it, rather than trying to change them to make them more acceptable, manageable, or productive in the eyes of others.

As has been demonstrated by India's experience with the Green Revolution, the Community Development Program, and the Family Planning Program, planners in India as elsewhere have consistently failed to take adequately into account the existential, traditional, and material realities of the lives of the people they intend to change, with the result that these programs have failed either absolutely, as in the case of the latter two, or partially, as in the case of the first, wherein production increased but the well-being of most of the people did not (cf. Frankel, 1971; Sharma, 1973; Mamdani, 1972; Nair, 1961).

It is worth pointing out here that the reason the Green Revolution failed to improve the standard of living and availability of food for most people in India is simply that it required capital investments in seed, chemical fertilizers, pesticides, manual or mechanical labor, and water (usually construction of wells) that were beyond the means of most cultivators. As a result, the rich who owned substantial amounts of agricultural land and could afford the requisites for applying the new technology grew richer. The poor, who owned little or no land (in most cases tenant farmers or sharecroppers), could not afford the new technology and grew poorer as they dropped behind in productivity, losing markets for their grain and then often losing their lands to the rich, who bought them out when they fell far in debt. When they lost their land, they often became farm laborers, competing with the already existing surplus of landless and underemployed agricultural laborers, increasingly displaced from their jobs by machinery available to the prosperous farmers. Thus, the ranks of the rural unemployed swelled, and many drifted to cities to join the mass of urban poor. To be sure, governmental goals of greater agricultural productivity were attained in some areas, but the vast majority of poor farmers, farm laborers, and customers were not benefited—in fact, they were pushed deeper into poverty by the increased costs of agriculture, decreased employment, and increased consumer prices. Rich and poor were further polarized, and goods more unequally distributed.

The program to implement the Green Revolution in India, like that of family planning, directs our attention to a fundamental problem in national development, namely, that it is characteristically undertaken by governments in the name of an abstract entity, the nation. The interests of the nation are rarely perceived or treated as being congruent with those of the masses of the poor and the oppressed—especially when the poor use land or other resources that others prefer to use for their own purposes (usually described as "more productive"). Rather, national interests are conventionally regarded as congruent with the interests of elites who largely control their governments and who in any case are ignorant of the needs of the dispossessed and the economically marginal. As Conor Cruise O'Brien has noted, in the poorer nations of the world "the oppressed are not minorities but the masses, and they are confronted by ruling classes that cling avidly to their traditional large share of scarce resources. The interests of the ruling classes are simply not consistent with any social change in the interests of the people as a whole" (O'Brien, 1966:21). Therefore, the welfare of relatively powerless people, such as the Garhwalis of the village in which I have worked, and Himalayan peoples generally, is usually served only incidentally, if at all, by the actions of government. Ivan Illich addressed this issue in an important article fittingly entitled, "Outwitting the Developed Countries." He commented: "There is a normal course for those who make development policies, whether they live in North or South America, in Russia or Israel. It is to define development and to set its goals in ways with which they are familiar, which they are accustomed to use in order to satisfy their own needs, and which permit them to work through the institutions over which they have power or control. This formula has failed, and must fail" (Illich, 1969:22).

Illich calls for redefinition of development to benefit the poor rather than the short-run interests of the policy makers and those whom they represent. This is as important for the Himalayas as anywhere else.

Measures that would benefit the Himalayan peoples in substantial ways, therefore, would be politically difficult as well as unlikely. Such measures are not likely to be in the perceived interest of those who profit from exploitation of the Himalayas at the expense of the Himalayan peoples, and these are too often the decision makers, or are close to them. It should be clear in this instance, however, that in fact measures which preserve the mountain environment will in the long run benefit the peoples of the entire nation as well as those of the Himalayas because the mountains and plains are environmentally and socially interdependent. This is something planners and developers ought to realize and act upon. Erik Eckholm put it well when he said,

Nepalese Woman. Photo by James H. Katz.

"In the end, this may be the greatest challenge of all: how to convince the people of the plains that the future of the mountains cannot be isolated from their own" (Eckholm, 1975:770; cf. 1976:100).

Into their own hands

Himalayan mountain peoples of India—both Pahari and Bhotiya—have not waited for plainsmen to be convinced. They have taken matters into their own hands in response to the readily apparent destructive effects of wholesale exploitation of their homelands. This is not new, for in the 1920s there were protests against destruction of forests in the area which led to social movements and to governmental suppression, including at least one firing on protestors by the military on May 30, 1930 (Dogra, 1983:43–44; see also Berreman, 1983:308–16). Since that time there have been repeated demands for separate statehood for the mountain districts, resulting in the formation of Himachal Pradesh from the former Punjab Hill States, and for separate statehood for "Uttarkhand," comprising the districts between Himachal Pradesh and Nepal. These demands are sought on the grounds that neither the present state nor federal governments are responsive to, or even comprehending of, the needs and circumstances of the mountain peoples, with the result that poverty grows unabated among them. Advocates of statehood point to rampant deforestation at the hands of timber and charcoal contractors, the absence of serious afforestation and reforestation programs, and consequent destruction of ground cover leading to massive erosion, landslips, flooding, and other disasters that take vast amounts of land out of cultivation and endanger lives and livelihoods as they diminish the supply of trees for firewood, fodder, and construction materials for houses and farm implements and of the forest environment that harbors many of the other resources upon which these people depend, including the life-giving land and water. They note road building without attention to the devastating landslides and erosion it precipitates; mineral extraction that scars the land and enriches only outside companies, contractors, and governmental agencies; and the hydroelectric projects that damage rivers and mountains while designed to benefit only the people of the plains.

The most recent and most noted expression of these complaints has been a social movement called Chipko ("to hug, embrace"), or Chipko Andolan ("movement to embrace"). It had its origin in March, 1973, in Chamoli District, but it did not spring full-blown there. It followed accelerated road building, mineral extraction, military maneuvers, and commercial deforestation of the region over several years, the effects of which became disastrously apparent in the 1970 monsoon when the Alaknanda River, a major tributary to the Ganges and pathway to hallowed Hindu places of pilgrimage in the high Himalayas, "burst its banks in an unprecedented flood. Within two hours the river rose 60 metres, sweeping away entire villages, roads, bridges, cattle—and busloads of pilgrims" (F.A.O., 1977:20). Many lives, many acres of cultivated land, and many millions of rupees' worth of property were lost. Other major floods followed in other Himalayan river valleys. Among their consequences was increased resentment among the people whose lands, livelihoods, and very lives themselves were at stake. This resentment was exacerbated by governmental regulations that prohibited or drastically limited tree cutting by local people for subsistence use, but which gave permissions and contracts promiscuously to outside entrepreneurs, whose profitable and exploitative task was eased by newly built networks of military roads con-

structed in connection with the Indo-Chinese border conflict. Where the indigenous farming peoples had expected modernization and opportunity to come by way of the roads, nothing came but rapacious destruction of their environment. The little reforestation that took place saw oak forests, which hold water and protect the soil while providing valuable fodder, replaced by pine forests, which, unlike oak, are commercially valuable but leave the soil unprotected and unreplenished and provide no fodder. The loss of forests diminished livelihood and drove increasing numbers of mountain people to the distant and inhospitable plains in search of work, leaving homes and families unattended.

Chipko originated as a result of the building resentment surrounding these events. It was precipitated when contractors for a sporting goods manufacturing company in Allahabad (on the plains) were licensed to cut ash trees in Chamoli district—ash trees that the local people depend upon for construction of strong, light farming tools and animal yokes, but that they had been told by government officials were not available for their use. The people were advised to use unsuitable pine wood instead. Frustrated in their appeals, they decided to act.

There followed a well-planned and entirely indigenous nonviolent resistance movement participated in by both Pahari and Bhotiya villagers of the district, and in crucial instances led by women (Bahuguna, 1975). The technique of the movement was one in which local people, alerted by watchful villagers in the region, would interpose themselves between the contractors' workmen and the trees—in some instances literally hugging or clinging to the trees to prevent the axemen from felling or even approaching them. As a result of such actions and the sympathetic response they evoked, the felling was stopped, the contract expired, and the trees were saved.

From the success of these actions there followed an organized movement with full-time organizers, training camps, propaganda programs, action programs, and lists of demands on government. Governmental agencies have acceded to many of the demands, and nationwide respect has grown for the movement, for the people who created and enacted it, for their programs, and for their accomplishments. The acknowledged leader of the movement, Sri Chandni Prasad Bhatt, put it simply: "Saving the trees is only the first step in the Chipko movement. Saving ourselves is the real goal. Our future is tied up with them."

Now the movement has expanded its goals and has combined with other expressions of regional political and social awareness in mobilizing for conservation of the mountain environment and way of life, for elimination of poverty in the Himalayan region, and for statehood for the mountain districts of Uttar Pradesh, to be called Uttarkhand.

This is the most hopeful sign I have seen for the preservation of the Himalayas and the Himalayan peoples. Outsiders have not been inclined to take them—the mountains or the people—seriously heretofore except as resources for wanton exploitation. Chipko, and the political activity associated with it, has changed that.

Chipko has demonstrated that the Himalayan people are determined to act and that they can do so with effect. Yet it is clear that alone they are too few, too scattered, too poor, and too powerless to drastically redirect the course of national policy toward the Himalayas and its resources. They must approach this task with the cooperative assistance of their government and their fellow citizens of the plains.

Development for . . . . instead of development of . . .

To assure the future of the mountain environment and the people who depend upon it—which includes those of the plains as well as those who inhabit the mountains—will require nationwide efforts toward conserving the mountain ecosystem rather than continuing to treat it as an apparently (but deceptively) invulnerable, limitless resource to be exploited by and for others, and it will require protection of the culture, society, economy, and religion of the mountain people, with respect for the traditions and institutions with which they have adapted so successfully to their rugged environment for centuries—protection from demands and pressures for confirmity to alien standards of progress and nationalism. To meet that requirement would entail maintenance of a degree of cultural autonomy, even isolation, for mountain peoples—an isolation from exploitation similar to that devised by the anthropologist Verrier Elwin which for long protected the peoples of the former North-East Frontier Agency of India from devastating inroads by entrepreneurs and assimilationists (Elwin, 1957). This would be a relative rather than absolute isolation and autonomy, accompanied by cooperation by government and others with Himalayan peoples to develop the region with the welfare and wishes of its people the foremost consideration—development *for* the Himalayan peoples, not development *of* them and their environment for others.

When I refer to respect for the people, concern for their welfare, cooperation with them, and attention to their wishes, I mean *all* of the people: the heretofore oppressed, low castes as well as the dominant high castes; the poor as well as the affluent; women as well as men; Muslims and Buddhists as well as Hindus; nomads and transhumant peoples as well as agriculturists. To enhance social justice in the Himalayas, as anywhere else, would require outside initiative in many areas at present, because power and privilege are tightly interlocked, but I believe that it could be done by reallocating indigenous resources among indigenous people without fundamentally altering their environment or ways of life.

John Bodley has argued in his compelling book, *Victims of Progess* (1975:173): "If industrial civilization cannot exploit tribal cultures without destroying them and degrading their environments, then perhaps it should leave alone those that remain." And again: "The important point to remember is that tribal societies are not museum pieces to be preserved as curiosities, but they are composed of real people who have developed unique adaptations to unique environments. They have given every indication that they wish to continue pursuing their own life styles, and they should have that alternative." His argument is as applicable to the peasants and pastoralists whom governments and entrepreneurs are continually trying to develop, remove, resettle, exploit, and dispossess—including those who live in the Himalayas—as it is to the tribals of whom he was writing.

If the Himalayas are to become a showplace of technological ingenuity, cash cropping resource extraction, military invincibility, tourism development, and modernization—as seems all too likely—they will become overdeveloped, uninhabitable, and uninhabited, no longer contributing richly to the environment and the culture of the adjacent lowlands. Then the mountains will stand as sterile monuments to those hardy peoples who inhabited them, who in turn will be remembered only as another colorful chapter in the chronicle of victims of the destructive process some call progress.

I believe that those who do research in the Himalayas should dedicate themselves, their efforts, and their knowledge to trying to prevent that unhappy end for the people and the environment that they know so well, and to which they owe so much. This is consistent with the positive responsibility all research scholars have to those they study—a responsibility the American Anthropological Association has recorded as the first of its "Principles of Professional Responsibility," adopted in 1971 (and amended in 1976): "In research, anthropologists' paramount responsibility is to those they study" (American Anthropological Association, 1983:1). Let us all act in accord with that principle.

12.   Gurung Shepherds of the Nepal Himalayas

BROUGHTON COBURN

The Gurung are a tribe of Tibetan origin, a quarter million in number, who have herded sheep and goats on the south side of the Himalayas' Annapurna range for the last few centuries. In the face of falling demand for woolen goods brought on by cheaper Indian and Chinese textiles, and growing population pressure, they have migrated further into the lower valleys to adopt subsistence agriculture. The high-caste Brahmins of the valleys regard them as spiritually their juniors, but throughout their hilly habitat the Gurung retain an economic dominance over these later settlers. Many have earned a healthy income and notoriety through enlistment as mercenaries in the Indian and British Gurkha armed forces. From one valley to the next and from village to village their dialect varies enough for a Gurung to identify a stranger's birthplace from his accent and inflection alone. They practice a unique combination of Buddhism, Hinduism, and animism, and their social purview seems to expand to absorb more recent western beliefs as well, rather than being dogmatically exclusive. To take advantage of the verdant, protein-rich grass that grows to 15,000 feet (4,600 meters) on ridges between the glaciers, some Gurung still husband sheep and goats.

Shepherds, among the Gurung, are often the social misfits, the loners, or those disqualified from taking a leading role in village affairs as a result of physical handicap or slight mental aberration. Each seems to know why he is a shepherd, and each accepts the stigma of managing the village's sheep and goats with stoic resignation. The shepherds are personally accountable for every animal, though the many hazards to Himalayan livestock are generally beyond their control. "Fate," as the shepherds describe the ultimate cause of their frequent sheep losses, commonly takes the form of poisonous plants, leopards, freezing weather, foot rot, and sheepdogs too complacent to bother rounding up stray sheep. In addition to the inherent difficulty of maintaining herd sizes in an unpredictable mountain environment, the shepherds suffer endless rebuke and a reputation for ineptitude among the village livestock owners. Some Gurung suggest that the greatest threat to high-altitude herds is hungry shepherds. When speaking with outside visitors, however, the villagers proudly cite their shepherds as examples of the fortitude, sense of duty, and good humor that characterize the Gurung people.

One fall I met Ram, aged forty-two, on his way to the village of Rhiban, where he was to deliver a load of mutton and pick up supplies of corn flour and salt. At that time his hut, connected to that of his partner, cousin and brother-in-law Indra, was located on a ridge bordering the rhododendron forest a few hours' walk above Rhiban. Ram invited me to move with them as the spring thaws progressed to the high summer pasture, two vertical miles above the village at the base of the Himalayas.

"You have to let these crazy sheep and goats go off to the pasturelands on their own, in their own direction, at their own speed; we can't control them," Ram reflected as he poked the embers of a spartan rhododendron fire. "The Brahmin pundits from the lowlands can predict how many children you'll have or how the crops will do next season, but hook them up with a herd of these animals and there's no telling where those sheep will go. And the sheepdogs are almost worthless—the dogs are so dumb they've been known to bite us shepherds, their masters, when we step out at night to piss. They hardly seem worth their keep when they lounge around the fire pit in the hut all day and snooze."

The incessant monsoon mist and drizzle filter through the woven bamboo hut Ram and Indra had carried up from the forest two days' walk below. The flock of four hundred sheep and goats huddle in tight groups, the intensity of their bleats and cries varying proportionally with the rain.

Ram, hard of hearing and a shepherd since an ear infection in his youth, stirs the corn flour soup for the dogs over the smoky fire.

"I think that basically I hear okay," Ram says, "It's just that my ears are out of order. The left ear is out completely, and the right ear hears better sometimes than at other times—it must be the weather. The shamans have chanted to them and blown into them and I've eaten medicinal herbs from around here—supposed to be sure cures—plus some expensive western potions. But my lack of hearing just won't leave. I need good ears especially when the fog packs in toward the late afternoon. The sheep get lost out on some ridge finger, and I have to go look for them. And when it's wet in the afternoon and then clears up at night, it gets cold enough to freeze the sheep to death, if the snow leopards don't get them first. It seems as if we are forever chasing after lost sheep. We have to know every single one of these sheep and goats, who owns which ones, and how many lambs each ewe has issued. The villagers scold us if we lose track of any of them."

Indra pulls on his goat-hair rain cape and squeezes out the bamboo entranceway to call the dog or two that aren't asleep in the hut.

"AUHEEE . . . AU-AUHEEEEE. . . ." The dogs in the hut jump up howling, momentarily dreaming that they are out chasing leopards and must return to the hut for morning gruel. They refocus on the meal being lifted off the fire and fall over each other to take the warning blows from Ram's stirring paddle, sharp raps given out to keep them from burning their mouths on the hot soup. The last dog announces its arrival in the hut by shaking off a cloud of mist, sizzling the fire. Indra scrapes ankle-high sheep dung onto a rock in the entranceway, throws his cape over the woodpile by the fire, and sits down to warm his hands and feet. The fire smoke distorts his prematurely wrinkled features into a perpetual squinting smile. Ram pours steaming gruel into smaller pots, which the dogs are licking in anticipation. He keeps a stray eye on the bigger animals lest they monopolize a gruel pot by out-snarling the others. He leans back and pulls half a cigarette from his pocket and stuffs the end into a short bamboo cigarette holder. Finding a hot coal with the fire tongs, he joins it to the frayed cigarette end, takes a long draw, and exhales, hacking out smoke and curses. Ram sees that the butts Indra is nursing are getting smaller and wonders aloud when Raaila, the lone shepherd who herds sheep an hour down the ridge, will hike up to borrow the rest of their tobacco, carefully hidden in the woodpile.

"Its a bad day when we run out of tobacco and spirits both. If we could get down to the village during festivals, being a shepherd wouldn't be so bad. Festivals are certainly the last time that anyone would come up to relieve us. We don't get even a crust of bread or a drop of alcohol, just millet mush and this musty old sheep milk."

Taking a handful of ashes from the corner of the fire pit, Indra gathers the dogs' gruel pots to wash, stoops outside, and drops them by a small hand-dug pool of yesterday's snowmelt. He breaks the thin layer of ice with a thin cup and ladles it into the pots. Ten thousand feet directly above, the top of Macchapuchhare, the fishtail mountain, floats into view. The movement of a massive cloudbank across its base evokes the dizzying illusion of a windblown mountain sailing on a foaming cloud-sea. Indra had mused before that climbing parties were not allowed to actually touch Macchapuchhare's summit. Should they ever stand on top, it would bring endless misfortune to the villages of its watershed. Besides, anyone who did would be struck down instantly by the local gods for desecrating their resting place. Indra scrubs the pots with a wad of foliage and ashes, rinses them, and bears them back to the hut as two blinking dogs slip out and bark a warning to imaginary leopards. He sits down to warm his hands while Ram dagger-grips a paddle, turning and folding their morning millet-flour mush.

"That damn musk hunter Karna should be coming through here in the next couple days on his way back from hunting musk deer," Indra says. "He's been out over three weeks now on only half a bag of flour. He must have bagged a goat-antelope or an Impeyan pheasant and is sitting in a cave somewhere getting fat. We won't even see the bones."

Ram lifts the millet mush from the cooking tripod and puts an empty pot in its place.

"Musk is up over twice the price of gold, down in India where it's sold for medicine and perfume. But there sure aren't many musk deer left these days. I haven't seen one in two years now, but the hunters say they see them all the time—higher up near the rivers of snow and ice. They're hard to shoot at; you have to be lucky. The hunters have better luck setting snares. They'll spend a month or more setting traps along the snowline and then circle back to pick up the catch and reset the traps. The cold weather keeps the meat fresh, so they need only a warm cape, salt, and matches to survive. The hunters look for a watering hole where the *kasturi* might drink and then find the place with the most tracks and droppings. Then, along the trees that border the water hole they build a makeshift fence so the deer can get down to the water through only one opening—right at the spot where they most frequently drink. The trees that grow near water are small and flexible, so they bend one over, tie a noose rope to it, place the noose in the path, and cover it with duff. Of course snaring is easier than shooting, but with a gun you can be selective and let the females go; the females have no musk, and their upper fangs are shorter than the males'."

"To remove the musk gland you can't cut it right out, or all the juices escape. First, you must cut a wide area around the gland and then carefully peel back the skin. The pod is not in the testicles, as some people think, it's forward of them, in the navel. Once, after finding a deer caught in a snare, some lowland shepherds removed only the testicles, leaving the real goods for someone else!"

"With the 'pension' the hunters get from selling the musk, they can relax and eat mutton for eight months of the year," Indra sighs. "Some police are as corrupt as they are, so there's no trouble getting the musk out of the country, either."

Indra turns to show a deep scar on his arm where he had cut himself with a sickle. "I placed a drop of musk on the wound right after it happened; the bleeding stopped immediately and the wound healed overnight."

"But the way the musk deer stock has really been cut back," Ram explains, "is by dogs. Good dogs trained to track musk deer cost a lot more than our sheep-tracking dogs, but they can pay for themselves in no time. They can chase deer everywhere but the steepest terrain; when the deer get tired the dog starts barking and the hunter comes in for the capture."

"Dogs; and poisoned stakes," Indra adds. "Musk hunters use them to the west of here, around Dhaula-giri. On a steep scree slope angling down to a stream or lake where the deer come to drink, the hunters plant poison-tipped bamboo stakes directed with the sharp end uphill. Once the deer got moving down the slope, they can't stop in time after they see the stakes. The stakes are coated with juice from the roots of the monkshood plant, so the deer die quickly once they've been speared. I haven't seen hunters do this, but I hear that's how they catch them there."

"After building a hut at an isolated place like this, we can't turn away hunters when they come looking for game, herbs, or mica. But some of these scoundrels show up in the fall or spring when the sheep are down in the lower pastures, and they burn up all of our hut frames just to keep warm at night. We have to carry these frames up from the lower forests a few pieces at a time—this rhododendron wood right below here isn't any good for hut frames. We have no proof that any hunter did it for sure, but who else comes up here when we're not around?"

Ram paddles the sticky millet mush onto brass plates, dragging the flat stirrer across the plate rims to release the tenacious and unappetizing substance. Pulling meager strips of charred mutton from the fire, he hits them on a rock to remove the ashes and adds them to the mush piles. Indra pours goat buttermilk from the churn, and they begin to eat noisily with large hand-fuls. They toss the dregs of the second helpings to the wide-eyed dogs and clean their hands on the fur, soon to be licked off by the other dogs.

Each day in the alpine pasture requires a load of fire-wood for cooking and a shepherd to follow the sheep. Today is Indra's turn to descend 2,500 feet (760 meters) to the fog-bound rhododendron forest to hack at branches with his curved *khukri* knife, arrange and tie

the pieces with vines, and haul them back to the hut. Seeing that the firewood stock is low, he resigns him-self to a long day and a heavy load. He puts his knife and a pouch of roasted flour into his carrying sling and, throwing rocks at the dogs to keep them from fol-lowing, heads down the hill.

By mid-morning the sheep begin to move out to-ward the northeast. Ram stores the meat on the drying rack where the dogs can't get at it and sets out behind the sheep.

"HAAA HAAA HAAA . . . HAAA HAAA." Wav-ing his arms like an animated scarecrow, Ram wanders through the barely motivated herd, tossing sheep dung at the ones still munching grass and scooping into his sling the young lambs that will stay in the hut until the ewes and rams return in the afternoon. The four-hundred-strong pilgrimage in search of grass greener than that of the day before strings out in single-file lines across the hillside, eventually disappearing into the fog. Ram hangs back with the old and crippled, keeping an eye out for medicinal herbs.

"You find the most potent medicines up here where the sheep graze," Ram explains as a sweep of his arm takes in a hillside littered with flowers. "A lot of them have similar-looking relatives in the lowlands, but none of those have the curing power that these do. The most potent of them is a tree, I forget its name, that the shamans say grows right on the rivers of snow and ice, sometimes to a height of sixty feet. It is hard to see during the day because it is almost pure white—it blends right in with the snow. But near the top of this tree are flowers that glow in the dark, on their own, like lanterns. If you are crooked or have bad karma, you can't even approach it; you'll get sick and faint if you try. But if you can get the flowers from that tree, they make a good aphrodisiac and are used in a tonic that will let you live a hundred years. Or, for instance, the monkshood that the hunters use to poison musk deer. There's a kind that looks just like the poisonous one except that its habitat is different. If you think you have found it, cut its root open. It looks white inside, like the poisonous one, but within a minute or so it turns to a bright red color—that's the real medicine. Just a little bit of it will cure fevers and bad hangovers."

Ram steps off the trail and pulls a small digging tool from his sling. He hacks at the base of a broad-leaved flowering shrub. "We have a way to tell if a plant will work as an antidote for plant poisoning. First, if you see a flower that has no poisonous plants growing within a pace of it, it may be a 'poison-killer.' The most common variety is called 'one pace poison.' We can test this by grinding up some of the plant and putting pieces of it in a water vessel that has some slices of a

Gurung Shepherd. Photo by Brot Coburn.

poisonous plant in it. If the 'poison-killer' chases the poison around in circles, then you know it is a good antidote for plant-poisoned sheep."

The sounds of munching and bleating sheep are interrupted by Ram's occasional leopard cry, which keeps the herd from spreading out. Knowing the rocky creekbeds where the one-year-olds are most likely to detour, he wanders a circuit around the pasture, closely followed by Kaaley, the most enthusiastic of the dogs. He sends Kaaley to bark at the strays, but their meandering is little affected until Ram goes himself to throw rocks at them.

Toward later afternoon the herd lazily grazes its way back to the hut.

"One of Ganga's rams is lost at the far end of the northeast pasture," Ram announces as he enters the hut. "If it doesn't turn up tonight, maybe the dogs will run across it before it fogs up tomorrow morning."

Indra and Raaila, a visiting shepherd, squat by the fire, gnawing on strips of mutton cut from the drying rack. Ram warms his hands and takes a fingerful of butter from the lid of the churn to soothe his thorn stabs. He bundles the day's collection of herbs and hangs them from the wall as Indra and Raaila ramble on, exploring the more fertile grazing grounds of shepherd conversation.

"Next Thursday is the auspicious mid-summer full moon," Indra mentions. "Maybe we'll get another group of Hindus up here on their way to bathe at the Three Headwaters beneath the Maccapuchhare face. Ram and I led a party of fifty of them last year, and we were out three days. None of the caves were dry, so we had to sit up all night shivering, but they paid us ninety rupees each. After that pilgrimage it rained solid for almost a week. It must have been Bhagwan washing away all the filth left along the trail by the pilgrims."

"One year, over 150 pilgrims made the trek to bathe at the Headwaters," Ram continued. "They spent a night here, and the two huts we had then were so packed that some people had to stand up all night—it was like being on a bus. Two untouchable blacksmiths who came with the party and one woman during her monthly untouchability slept in the dung with the goats and sheep. That was the most erratic procession of folks I've ever seen, young kids and old ladies included. Ram guided while I took up the rear, and if you think sheep are hard to keep in line, that crowd of lowlander pilgrims was even more unmanageable. One old lady, at least sixty-five or so, was breathing so hard she was making *swaā-swaā* sounds and lagging behind before we were even a third of the way to the cave where we should have spent the first night. I said that I didn't think she'd make it. She replied, 'What to do, Babu, I can't turn around and find my way back to the hut now, alone!' This was true. The fog had set in fast and thick. I looked around for a cave and found a large boulder with a crawl space under it just big enough for a person. I left her in there with some flour, told her that we'd be back in a day, and then caught up with the rest of the pilgrims. We didn't make it back there until dusk of the second day, because we had spent so much time doing rituals at the bathing site. She was sick and weaker than ever. The rest of the pilgrims slept under small overhangs and out in the open, and the next morning this old lady's foot had swollen to twice its normal size. The other lowlanders were too tired to carry her, so her relatives offered me a week's wages to carry her back to our hut. My partner took off with the

other pilgrims so that he wouldn't be stuck with her, and I had to carry her all the way back myself. I didn't get so much as a cigarette from those tightwad valley people. That's how some of them operate; they're like a tasty pancake cooked with lots of sugar and butter and salt. No matter how well you grease the pan or how carefully you cook the pancake, there's always a little bit of it that won't come up with the spatula when you want to flip it over. There's always a little bit that just sticks right to the pan."

Raaila joins Ram and Indra in their evening meal of mush and mutton. Indra stokes the fire to keep them warm at least half the night, and they retire under a communal blanket. They awake in the morning to the eerie headache-inducing cracks of rams butting horns in the mist. Ram grabs his cape and stumbles out to see if any lambs have been dropped during the night. One ewe is foaming from the mouth and nose, a symptom of plant poisoning. He finds one newborn alive but cold, and another one that didn't make it.

"I've got my flashlight's house and bulb," grumbles Ram as he unloads the lamb carcass in the corner of the hut, "But I don't have the spices you have to put

Pilgrims Enroute to Headwaters, Gurung Country, Nepal.
Photo by Brot Coburn.

in the flashlight to make it work. Otherwise we could find these newborns at night right when they are dropped."

He prepares an herbal antidote for the poisoned ewe, to be forced down its throat through a bamboo tube. Indra, the churn hanging from his shoulder, wanders out to milk the sheep and goats. He spends an hour strolling casually through the herd, snagging the hind legs of unaware milk ewes. Occasionally he calls Ram to hold a balky ewe.

"Sometimes these ornery animals won't even give milk to their own lambs. One of us has to hold the critter, first while we milk her, then again while the lamb nurses. There's no explaining them, just like there's no explaining the villagers where we come from. Being only shepherds, when we go down to the village, we're treated like sheep ourselves."

Indra and Ram return to the hut with four quarts of sheep milk from forty-odd ewes. Visibly relishing its musty taste, they heat the milk briefly and blanket their mounds of morning mush with it.

"Those sheep are craving salt like gamblers crave alcohol," groans a satiated Indra between licks of his plate. "We should probably feed salt today, even though half our sheep owners haven't yet delivered their share of the salt. That means we'll have to divide the flock just as we did last month and feed only the ones we have salt for. I don't know how they know, but those sheep can tell when we are going to feed salt. They must overhear us talking. How can we keep the flock separated when they know we have a bag of salt hidden in our carrying slings?"

"We also need to move the hut to a new spot," Ram mentions. "The dung is piled up to where we can barely walk through it now. How can we find the time to do all this when cutting firewood, tending sheep, and fetching supplies are full-time jobs? We just have to keep on going, keep on working, without worrying about it. If we think of how much there is left to do, it seems to take longer. We shepherds work to live and we live to die."

13. Going After Wangdu: The Search for a Tibetan Guerrilla Leads to Colorado's Secret CIA Camp

JEFF LONG

There is in Tibet a bizarre and hardy creature called the carabid beetle. Small, black, and wingless, it lives under rocks at seventeen thousand feet and contains an extraordinary glycerol "antifreeze" in its hemolymph. At night the beetle surfaces to hunt less sturdy insects that have frozen on the ice and snow.

It was in the jails of Nepal, in a sink of misery one would not expect to find except in a field hospital, among tortured and unhappy political prisoners and criminals, that I met my first Tibetan guerrilla. He was a cheerful soul, an elderly Khampa with a gold tooth that gleamed in his habitual smile. Fed up with the torpid diplomacy that had, in large part, cost him his homeland and forced him into exile in neighboring Nepal, this rugged fellow had collected a few tattered and meaningless documents and then headed north for a summit conference of his own. Before he could personally communicate his demands to the Chinese, however, Nepalese authorities had apprehended him at the border. We had time to share fruit and some gruff "you-Khampa, me-America" conversation before he was spirited away.

For almost fifteen years, until 1974, several thousand Tibetan guerrillas had taken sanctuary in the caves and huts of Mustang, a cold and arid region at a mean altitude of 15,000 feet (4,600 meters) in northwestern Nepal. Slipping across the Himalayas into their occupied homeland, small bands of these guerrillas would hunt Chinese soldiers to their death, ambush truck convoys, and mine the tortuous Peking-to-Pakistan highway.

Tibetan belligerence to China was at least thirteen centuries old. Moreover, many of the guerrillas were Khampas, a tribe of fierce, seemingly congenital warriors. But even this heritage would not have carried the guerrillas far had it not been for the Central Intelligence Agency. For more than a decade the guerrilla operation was covertly financed, armed, and supplied by the CIA. Between 1959 and 1962 Tibetan warriors were trained at the high-altitude military reservation of Camp Hale, Colorado. What had served the United States Army as the staging grounds of alpine warfare during World War II became the training facility for anti-Communist cadres.

During a climbing expedition to Nepal in 1974 I first heard about these guerrillas. It was said that at the approach to Mustang there was a crude wooden bridge with a door standing in the middle of it. Each night the Khampas locked the door. Beyond that point, Nepal belonged to them. Three years later I heard more tales.

Whisperers anxiously warned me away from the stories, but nearly everyone wanted to talk, too. Darting after slim leads—a crippled monk; an alleged gunrunner; an American "wife" of Wangdu, the guerrilla general; anthropologists; exiles; quasi-diplomats—I came to understand that each new source considered himself the final authority. The guerrillas were still fighting, some said, further west of Mustang or deep inside Tibet. They were counting gold in Katmandu or dying of fever in the jungles of southern Nepal. Wangdu had been shot to death, according to one source. Another argued that it was his twin brother who had been killed. Wangdu still rode the range. Tibet would be won back.

I was spellbound. Twenty-five years old and raised in Colorado, I had all the political poise of an Irish setter flushing butterflies. The mountain I'd come to climb had deeply humiliated my expedition, and there seemed no reason in the world to return to a summer of stone-masonry in the States with life tasting bitter. Tearing up my plane ticket, I let the story of Wangdu and the rumors of a Colorado connection absorb me. Bra-

Tibetan Friends. Photo by M. Tobias.

Sacred Pass, Nepal. Photo by James H. Katz.

vado became a drug. The more I heard, the deeper I probed. Tales of the CIA and guerrillas in my home state accumulated.

Wangdu became the jewel in the lotus. So much legend had encrusted around him that, as befit a guerrilla, the reality had become elusive. For all I knew he'd been captured on that roll of film Harold Ravnsborg had dutifully burned sixteen years ago. I excavated through strata of tragedy, pain, and international duplicity. Wangdu faced the same odds of reconquest of his country as, say, Geronimo once had in our own deserts and mountains. Stealth, horses, and a cache of guns simply pronounced their resistance to the realpolitik, which was supported by the People's Liberation Army, tanks, and Ilyushin jets. Only a simpleton would dare to challenge that kind of muscle. Wangdu had. His simplicity seemed as raw and logical and abrupt as the mountains I'd come to climb. But at the height of my information frenzy, shortly before the Fourth of July, I was arrested and jailed on a smuggling charge.

The arrest piled on top of my failed climb might have overwhelmed me had I not, in my third month of imprisonment and third jail, found myself neighbor to the leaders of the guerrilla movement. There were six of them, seven counting their melancholy Tibetan attendant, who was disfigured by what I presumed to be the scars of severe smallpox. Like me, he slept on the floor of the cell, by the cook fire. Unlike the other guerrillas, he never smiled and never, in my presence, said a word.

There is no small element of J. R. R. Tolkien about the Tibetan experience. Various histories of Tibet tell of lamas that could fly and raise goblets without touching them; even modern-day guerrillas wore amulets that were supposed to render them bulletproof. Once an empire more vast than Kublai Khan's, Tibet had withered in recent times to an ancient feudal kingdom dedicated to spiritual enlightenment. Then the loathsome hordes came pouring in from the East, from China.

It seems genocide is good for about two weeks of front-page newspaper coverage; after that it's time to dredge up new bones. Even during the most brutal moments of her rape, Tibet barely lasted that long in the *New York Times*. Between sixty thousand and one hundred thousand Tibetans died in the fifteen months following the Lhasa uprising in 1959—crucified, burned alive, shot, drowned, starved, hung, disemboweled, beheaded. Thousands of Tibetan children were shipped off to China for proper state indoctrination. The People's Liberation Army troops systematically plundered the monasteries for gold and religious artifacts, and forced-labor camps sprang up. Maps were altered so that the eastern half of Tibet ceased to exist. Decimation, displacement, mass transfer—and the United Nations declined to put the issue on its agenda.

In 1961 a Khampa warrior named Tsering fled the Chinese troops, desperate to save his family from the slaughter in eastern and central Tibet. His one mistake was to ride north into the Chang Thang, a vast arctic desert wracked by subzero temperatures and hurricane-force winds. During the retreat from this Martian landscape Tsering's four children weakened and died. One by one he and his wife laid them out for the scavengers so they could be returned to what he called the "winds of existence." In that manner Tsering relinquished Tibet and then turned south through the Himalayas to the Indian subcontinent. There he joined other refugees. Eventually they would number eighty-five thousand.

Even before these events unfolded, the State Department and the CIA had become fascinated by resistance in the eastern, notoriously warlike portions of Tibet. In February, 1956, several thousand Khampas and neighboring tribesmen, mounted on horseback and armed with swords and guns, slaughtered a Chinese garrison of nine hundred soldiers. Retaliatory air strikes by Chinese jets flattened some three hundred towns and monasteries during the remainder of that year, killing many thousands. Seminomadic survivors—monks as well as peasants, landowners, and wandering bandits—began to organize into a resistance army called Chushi Gangdruk ("Four Rivers, Six Mountains," an ancient name for eastern Tibet). Equally exciting to the American intelligence community was the appearance of an anti-Communist petition authored by guerrilla leaders. With that the guerrillas were in business.

In 1960 a freckled military brat I shall call Christopher was fired upon by troops at Camp Hale. Barely eleven, the boy was old enough to read but still young enough to disclaim any deep understanding of the restricted area signs fixed to barbed wire. So it was that young Christopher, shod in combat boots two sizes too large and wearing a blue parka and a stocking cap, crawled through four strands of barbed wire with his brother and a new toboggan in tow. The snow was deep. The two boys struggled a hundred yards up Cooper Hill before suddenly sharing the distinct sensation that they were being watched. In the tradition of all great escapes, Christopher and his brother dove onto the toboggan and rode hell-for-leather toward the lower road and refuge. At that instant they heard the sound of gunfire—and then they were speeding under the barbed wire and out of the trees.

After the toboggan had slowed to a halt in a distant grove, the boys took stock of themselves. They were cold and the adrenalin was running high. Powdered snow had crusted into masks on their faces, and Christopher had lost his hat, snagging it on the wire. Worse still, he'd ripped his parka. Luckily it was reversible, enabling its owner to change identities in a wink. Thus disguised with his jacket pulled inside out, Christopher and his brother headed for the road, where a truckful of soldiers was not at all fooled by the parka. The boys were questioned at length. That night Christopher was amazed when his father's tirade was directed not at him and his repentant brother but at "those f---ing Chinks in training."

No one could say the boys hadn't been warned. In fact, all of Colorado had been put on notice to steer clear of Camp Hale. In an effort to cloak its covert training of guerrillas in the heart of the Rockies, the CIA orchestrated a marvelous fiction that actually worked. On July 16, 1959, the *Denver Post* carried a front-page story headlined "Atom Unit Making Test Near Leadville." Rear Adm. Edward N. Parker of the Defense Atomic Support Agency hoodwinked the *Post,* deftly wielding denial to suggest that a nuclear bomb had taken up residence at Camp Hale. The top-secret testing program, the admiral divulged, did not include the detonation of nuclear weapons. With a crowning flourish he added, "We don't do what the president tells us not to do." Even a downstream chuckle-head could figure out that the government was trying to goof on him. Of course they were going to blow off a bomb at Camp Hale. The camp was left in peace.

One further, crowning incident nearly spelled international scandal for the CIA. Early on the morning of December 7, 1961, as civilian employees at Colorado Springs' Peterson Field (now Peterson Air Force Base) were sipping their coffee, soldiers armed with automatics, rifles, and machine guns suddenly surrounded the privately operated Kensair Corporation and Maytag Aircraft Corporation air hangars. Without a word of explanation they herded forty-seven civilians into confinement. Before long several of the employees at Kensair saw an army bus drive up beside a C-124 Globemaster on the neighboring air force lot. The bus windows were painted black, but even more ominous was the cargo that stepped off.

"There was fifteen Orientals got out of the bus and onto the plane," Wood recalled. "They were wearing some type of uniform—green fatigues, like the GIs. Each one of these Orientals had a white tag around his neck. As each man got on the Globemaster, someone at the door checked the tag." Meanwhile, Harold Ravnsborg, a Kensair mechanic, pluckily blazed away with his camera. One hour and twenty minutes after the mystery began, the Globemaster departed and the armed soldiers vanished in their jeeps.

The *Colorado Springs Gazette Telegraph* was first to report that civilians had been held at gunpoint. Next the *Denver Post* and the *Rocky Mountain News* carried short articles about a top-secret cargo that had originated at Camp Hale, eighteen miles north of Leadville, Colorado. Wire services then moved the story, and a Washington-based correspondent for the *New York Times* smelled news. Oriental soldiers in the Rocky Mountains? Civilians held at gunpoint? He phoned the Pentagon.

It was as if a U-2 had crashed into the Bay of Pigs. Minutes later the office of Secretary of Defense Robert McNamara was entreating the Washington bureau of the *New York Times* to kill the story. The Orientals were Tibetan, the Pentagon caller confidentially revealed, implying that if this information were disclosed it would be detrimental to the national security of the United States. Those were the golden days of trust in government. The story expired *in ovo*.

Back in Colorado an army officer from Fort Carson had bullied Wood and the other Kensair employees with the same tactic: protecting national security. "He lined us up in my office," said Wood. "We had to hold up our hands and swear we wouldn't talk about it for six months. The army officer had a book with him, and he read the law to us. He was telling us all the things that would happen to us if we talked about it. The guy threatened us; he said we were under the highest secrecy in the world." However, the iron knuckle was quickly candy-coated.

The next day Gen. Charles G. Dodge, the army's chief of information, phoned Wood from Washington and extended his personal apologies for the indignities he had suffered. Although the general carefully neglected to describe the nature of the top-secret project, Wood had already pieced together that "these guys [Orientals] were being trained up at Camp Hale. They were supposed to be shock troops or guerrillas, trained for some damn invasion."

A neat little irony was at play here, though Wood was not to learn about it until years later. As a member of the old Twenty-fourth Combat Mapping Squadron in the United States Army Air Force during World War II, Wood had spent two years flying along the borders of Tibet. Flying back and forth over the Himalayan hump between India and China, Wood had mapped the area that would be the scene of desperate combat between Chinese forces and the same Tibetan guerrillas he had watched board the Globemaster in Colorado Springs.

As for the only tangible evidence of the seizure of Peterson Field—Harold Ravnsborg's film—fear devoured it. After the verbal cudgeling dealt by the army officer in the Kensair office, Ravnsborg emptied his camera and did what any good citizen threatened with federal prosecution would have done. He burned the film.

Wangdu was among the first six Tibetan guerrilla leaders to be trained by the United States. He and five other volunteers were flown to a Pacific island, perhaps Guam or Saipan, where they spent four months learning how to read a map and work a radio. In the fall of 1957 they boarded a small black airplane piloted by an American. Individually equipped with a pistol, a machine gun, an old Japanese radio, $132 in Tibetan currency, and a bracelet containing phials of poison to be swallowed upon capture, the guerrillas parachuted back into their homeland. Four of the six were destined for Lithang in southeastern Tibet. Of the four only one man was ever again seen alive—Wangdu.

The second batch of guerrilla leaders was trained at Camp Hale. The experience was as exotic to the guerrillas as it was to the Americans who later learned of it. "One day Gompo Tashi [the founding father of Chushi Gangdruk] asked me if I could jump from an airplane," one guerrilla was quoted as saying of his training at Camp Hale. "I had never heard of such a thing, but if it would help Tibet's independence I was willing to go. I was also told there was a place where we could learn to use machines with which one man could challenge two thousand men. None of us had ever heard of America except when it was mentioned in Chinese broadcasts at the time of the Korean War. We only knew America was an enemy of China." At first the guerrillas at Camp Hale weren't aware that they were in the United States, but eventually, cued by things such as road signs in English, they caught on to their whereabouts.

After Tibet fell in 1959 the savage guerrilla war that had been floating through eastern and central Tibet found roots and sanctuary in an ancient Tibetan province now annexed by Nepal. Several days' walk north of the 26,250-foot (8,000-meter) barrier of Dhaulagiri and the Annapurna range, the area was Mustang. Magnetized by the promise of American aid, more than 2,000 guerrillas flocked to Mustang. They waited a year. As time passed, the Red Cross reported starvation in the area. Many of the guerrillas practiced shooting with sticks for rifles, and 2,000 tenacious warriors survived by eating boiled shoe leather. Some died for lack of food and shelter. Still they waited. In late 1961 two aircraft dropped enough guns for 475 men, medicine, food, and $1,252 in local currency. Twenty-six Camp Hale–trained Tibetans parachuted in with the supplies, and 12 more Camp Hale graduates walked in from India.

Initially the guerrillas had every confidence that the reconquest of Tibet was at the tips of their trigger fingers. Until the Chinese fortified defenses along the Mustang border, guerrillas would ride horseback hundreds of miles into Tibet, wreaking havoc on isolated garrisons and supply lines. These raids were planned by CIA operatives who sometimes posed as Christian missionaries in northeastern India and on occasion were led by "agency contract mercenaries," according to one former CIA officer. The former agent also observed that these raids "accomplished little beyond giving the Tibetan troops some temporary satisfactions and fanning their hopes that someday they would lead a true invasion of their homeland." At thirty-five cents per pound, the cost of trucking supplies thousands of miles into Tibet was an economic burden for China even without guerrilla sabotage. But China was stubbornly determined to keep Tibet. Coincidentally, this damning obstinance found voice in several mailbags of documents that were captured by the guerrillas and later analyzed by China experts at the CIA's headquarters in Langley, Virginia. In light of China's adamant presence in Tibet, the CIA began to lose interest in the Khampas.

Of what use was Tibet to America? Even at the peak of American trading with preinvasion Tibet, the United States was mainly purchasing yak tails and wool for Santa Claus beards and automobile rugs. Geopolitically Tibet was a gigantic dead zone—backward, xenophobic, and a political nonentity. And though China began stockpiling IRBM missiles and nuclear-capable bombers in Tibet, American national security was not jeopardized.

The United States did score a stunning defeat of communism with propaganda in 1959, when the twenty-three-year-old Dalai Lama "fled" Tibet. During his arduous overland journey, this intelligent and affable young man was seen slipping through the claws of the Red dragon. Unseen were the CIA-trained Khampas who escorted the God-king or their air cover, which

parachuted supplies, maps, and radios for the escape party and strafed Chinese positions. During this fabulous escape, color photographs were taken to show the world that communism was as repugnant to the Third World as it was to the West. But by 1970 that propaganda was more than ten years old. Aside from harassing the Chinese in an increasingly constricted region, the Tibetan guerrillas were useless.

Some of the CIA's "special ops" officers involved in training the Khampas became seduced by their own propaganda. Instructed to encourage Tibetans' hopes for reconquest, some of the agents came to fervently believe in the liberation of Tibet themselves. Special ops agents have been described as a breed apart, often obsessed with a strong need to belong and believe; the extreme cause Tibet represented drew some agents who, even years afterward, would meditate by chanting prayers they had learned from their Tibetan charges. When the CIA lost interest in Tibet, the agents furiously blamed Washington bureaucrats for selling them out. The guerrillas themselves were fatalistic; they understood the withdrawal of support and harbored no hard feelings against America.

Despite its slackening interest the CIA continued to supply the Khampas in the Mustang sanctuary until the late 1960s and to channel funds to them until 1971. After Henry Kissinger's secret trip to Peking in July of that year, all American aid to the guerrillas ceased. Suddenly, after fifteen years of silence, Nepalese newspapers overflowed with tales of blackhearted Khampas stealing, killing, and raping in Mustang. The tales had little or no foundation, but they served notice that the end was not far away.

By 1974, fifteen years into their noble pursuit, most of the guerrillas were in their forties or older. They seemed to have become so infatuated with the notion of finishing their legend in the shadows of their lost nation that when several tigerish young Tibetans arrived from refugee camps in India in the early 1970s, they were sent back after a few months. It was as if the aging warriors were seeking a graceful and solitary decline. Their raids diminished in number and, given the guerrillas' ages, probably in ferocity, too. Nostalgia replaced vengeance, and the guerrillas started investing their funds in small businesses.

China has the memory of an elephant, though. The Khampas in Mustang had served her more than one humiliation, and so the Nepalese government was pressured to do something about the interlopers. Pride fed pride. When the Chinese offered to sweep through Mustang and round up the Khampas for "development projects" in China, the Nepalese heard the whispers of humiliation, too, and took it upon themselves to solve the problem of their fearsome, albeit aging, guests.

Through the spring and early summer of 1974 the Nepalese began to negotiate. The guerrillas were told they could keep, in exchange for their surrendered arms, any land they had settled and any homes in Mustang and that their group would be provided with $150,000 each year for three years for rehabilitation. Those may sound like extravagant concessions coming from one of the poorest nations on earth, concessions being made to one of the smallest armies. But Mustang was a nearly uninhabited area to start with, and a half-million-dollar payoff was a bargain compared to the trade sanctions China was threatening if the Khampa problem was not resolved. Although the terms made sense, they were not sufficiently persuasive to the guerrillas. They had guns, and the Indian government was feeding and supplying them. Why surrender?

In July, 1974, as ten thousand Nepalese troops closed off Mustang, the Dalai Lama sent a twenty-minute tape recording to Wangdu. Huddling with leaders of scattered camps, Wangdu listened as the Dalai Lama greeted his Tibetan patriots. Having gained weapons, the Dalai Lama agreed, it would be difficult for the guerrillas to lay them down. But the world had changed. Asking them to remember that material possessions are secondary to determination, the God-king asked his believers to surrender their guns. The tape was played over loudspeakers at various camps up and down Mustang, and the leaders had to admit that the end was at hand. They would give the Nepalese their guns. There was deep sorrow and bitterness. One of the leaders killed himself. Several other guerrillas slit their throats, jumped from cliffs, or drowned themselves in the river.

In accordance with the agreement with the Chinese, the Nepalese soldiery entered the valley and, camp by camp, began disarming the guerrillas. Camp by camp they methodically reneged on their bargain and began herding the guerrillas southward at gunpoint. The Khampas had been betrayed—first there had been Chinese duplicity, then American abandonment, and now this. Stunned, the outraged guerrillas were powerless to do more than spit on their leaders as they filed by, equally shocked by the betrayal. Lamu Tsering, who had delivered the tape, was rearrested. Rara, Jurme, Tashi Dhondup, Ngadrug, and Palga, all leaders, were arrested and either helicoptered or marched south. These were the men I met in jail. Wangdu was not among them.

On hot, tedious September afternoons I would hunker down against the compound wall and watch kites softly loop and dip high above the prison. One kite always belonged to Tashi, who wielded his elegant weapon from the prison yard. Tashi was a squat, powerful Khampa who sported a sky-blue Maryland Yachting Club cap given to him, he claimed, by a CIA operative more than a decade before I met him. He was a master of kite fighting, utterly dedicated to defeating all comers, most of whom launched their kites from rooftops in Katmandu.

Mornings, Tashi could be found "sharping the knife," as he said, braiding the upper hundred feet of his string and running it through a mixture of glue and powdered glass. He made his own kites, splitting bamboo for struts, then meticulously fastening rice paper to the frame with rubber cement. Yachting cap askew, tongue between his teeth, Tashi seemed eternally youthful. But it took only the slightest breeze to unveil the warrior. A tug of wind and I could practically hear Tashi's blood singing. Like falcons in love with their master, his kites always returned to hand.

All the guerrillas I met were purposeful, patient, vital. Except for the one nameless, pockmarked man who never spoke and never smiled, the Tibetans didn't bother with despair. Before dawn they would be up and about the prison yard, striding vigorously through the cool blue fog. In the midst of my morning pee, 220-pound Rara once or twice sneaked up and ambushed me with a bear hug, shaking me until I'd soaked myself. Whenever one borrowed a book from me, even a dog-eared paperback thumbed beyond its years, it was always returned neatly clothed in a homemade dust jacket, the title inscribed in English and Tibetan. Their cell was made comfortable with beautiful rugs from the Tibetan refugees' rug factory, offerings to national heroes.

For three years the six men and their mute comrade had been imprisoned without trial by the Nepalese authorities. If and when they were brought to court, they had been told, the charge would be "raising arms against the kingdom." Without these very men, however, the guerrillas would never have laid their guns down, and hundreds of Nepalese soldiers and policemen would probably have died. None of these men dwelled on the topic. In view of their continuing imprisonment and because they had taken CIA vows of secrecy, they also declined to discuss their roles in Mustang. As for the fate of Wangdu, what had begun as a feeling of pride in other guerrillas and Tibetans had taken on a shade of envy among my neighbors.

During the surrender in July, 1974, Wangdu had waited at the northernmost tip of the Mustang valley, choosing to reverse standard protocol and hand over his sword last. Possibly he anticipated treachery. By the time word arrived of the betrayal, Wangdu knew it was too late to fight back. Instead, he and thirty-five men immediately mounted horses and climbed out of the stark valley, making their way into Tibet over two high passes. Theirs was not a random flight. For several years India had been recruiting Tibetan guerrillas for their Border Security Force, and Wangdu knew that if he could reach India, his little band would be safe. For the next four weeks, India was his goal.

Back and forth over the high, rugged watershed that forms the Nepal-Tibet border Wangdu and his followers rode and walked their horses. Twice the guerrillas had to retreat into Nepal to escape Chinese soldiers who were dogging their flight, but because the Nepalese terrain was too rough for their horses, they crossed back into Tibet each time. At one point the Nepalese air-dropped a crack unit of soldiers to ambush Wangdu, but the guerrillas simply vanished. Traveling day and night, the group of Tibetans sped for the Indian border.

Half a day short of the mountainous juncture of Tibet, Nepal, and India looms Tinker, a 17,800-foot (5,400-meter) pass. In 1968 nearly five hundred bedraggled refugees froze to death on this pass during a catastrophic mass escape from Tibet. It was in this haunted region that Wangdu sought to slip through the gauntlet of Chinese and Nepalese troops.

In the early afternoon of August 12 the party found itself hemmed in from the north by Chinese troops. Six men were selected to escort Wangdu over Tinker to the Nepal side while the rest stayed behind to fight the Chinese. Scant kilometers short of India, Wangdu and his tiny escort galloped straight into what was, this time, a well-prepared and massive ambush. Of his escort, four were killed on the spot, one escaped to warn his comrades, and one was badly wounded and captured. He watched as Wangdu was riddled with bullets.

The larger group, already engaged in a fire fight with the Chinese, swarmed over the pass and confronted the Nepalese, whom they never considered a danger. En masse they pushed through the ambush and either were picked up by Indian helicopters or rode across the border into the open arms of Indian troops. By sunset that day the last of the guerrillas was either safe in India, property of the Nepalese king, or dead.

The antiguerrilla campaign officially ended with a bright, festive celebration back in Katmandu, at which the king presented more than two hundred medals, certificates, and cash awards. Everyone from the sergeant credited with killing Wangdu to the home minister was decorated. A large tent was erected in which Wangdu's personal effects—his spurs, saddle, revolver, rifle, drinking cup, and amulet—were displayed. Inside the amulet was a picture of the Dalai Lama.

I drove up to Camp Hale recently. The plateau was dark and wet and stretched for miles, neatly littered with rotting concrete foundation walls. Here and there lay brass casings, cold to the touch. From a Ford pickup, the wipers beating back the drizzle and low clouds, Camp Hale seemed ghostlike and haunted. It was therefore no surprise when the Ford was suddenly met by GIs carrying black M-16s. Deeper among the pines and mist was a small settlement of khaki tents and a helicopter. The incident, in the context of my search for Wangdu, was a relic.

Similarly, a 1957 Tibetan-English dictionary is a relic. Ignoring the Bhotia script and Tibetan art, culture, and religion, the dictionary carries such useful entries as the Tibetan equivalent of *mortar, bazooka, drop zone,* and *parachute.* Once a thing passes from utility, it becomes a relic.

I have a large photograph of high-cheekboned Khampas lined up like so many Apaches, a random collection of machine pistols, revolvers, and rifles on proud display. It is a relic. So were the guerrillas I met in jail and later down in India, the men who had lost their heritage and been reduced to laboring on road gangs. Long, long ago, thirteen hundred years past, their nation had swelled to supernova proportions. Now it was a cold, dark star. The guerrillas were a final pulse of light.

People tend to dismiss such relics after a while, presuming that kings and presidents and the Cold War and twentieth-century superpowers are so much more worth remembering. But the past often resides in small and trivial things, too, in obscure photos and obscure people and even in silence.

In Wangdu I had sought entry to the labyrinth of Asia, the Third world, and the CIA, and for a while there, languishing with the Khampa leaders in jail, I was certain I had at last captured Wangdu by recapturing the facts of his death. I was certain I knew everything there was to know, never mind the obscure details.

Then, on my final day and in the final hour before my release, it dawned on me—and later in India it was verified—that the mute anonymous Tibetan was the man who had watched Wangdu die. His smallpox scars were bullet wounds. I had slept beside the one person who could have described every detail of the final moment, but I understood it too late. We never spoke, and, like that, Wangdu had eluded me one last time.

14.   The Image of the Mountain and the Sherpa Landscape

HUGH R. DOWNS

Not so long ago it was the income from Gurkha soldiers serving abroad and the sale of jute products that brought in the bulk of Nepal's foreign earnings. In the early 1970s that all changed. Today it is tourism. What is the image of the mountain for the modern-day sightseer to Everest, and what is that image in the aboriginal Sherpa landscape?

The Himalayas have attracted people for thousands of years, even before there were any Sherpas. Surrounding geological phenomena can be attracted to such massive uplifts because of enormous gravitational forces; people, on the other hand, are attracted because of what a mountain means to them. The different cultural appurtenances brought to a mountain produce correspondingly different meanings. There are many resulting images of the mountain depending on a person's beliefs. It is a curious note for Sherpas, the residents around Mount Everest, that foreign people generally think Mount Everest is important because its peak is higher than that of any other mountain. This is especially curious, even for non-Sherpas, when one considers that there are mountains that are technically more difficult to climb and that there are mountains that present themselves with far more drama, particularly from the Nepal side (Everest is practically hidden by Lhotse and Nuptse). But it is primarily Everest that rises preeminent in the foreign mind. Everest is important to us because it is the highest mountain on the planet.

Hundreds of years before this was known, the western cultures of Europe were moving away from mythological explanations of the world. They transferred the zeal of traditional faith to the demonstrable proofs of the observable method and in so doing let wither the exercises of art. The arcane arts that once investigated natural phenomena slowly became the knowable sciences. In many ways the outsiders who visit Everest could almost seem the devotees of a cult of trigonometry. It is the rare tourist who has actual firsthand experience with Himalayan measurements; most just take it on faith ("Yup, its the highest one around here allright, and we know that 'cause the Elders have triangulated").

Modern men and women are not supposed to be cluttered with the unnecessary baggage of myth or the arcane arts, but how much of this past baggage has really been left behind on the departure platforms of medieval Europe? Do Everest and the Himalayan chain attract foreign visitors merely because of pride in an ability to triangulate the highest and then go there? Or is there some other reason, an attraction that may not have anything to do with our cleverness as geographers?

The words *Everest* and *highest* seem tenaciously linked in English, but let us turn to the languages of the mountain people themselves. Since Everest is not obviously the highest peak, what is it called in Nepal?

In Nepali and other related Indo-European dialects, this peak is called Sagarmatha. Both *sagar* and *matha* are very old Sanskrit words, the first meaning "atmosphere" or "air" and the second a term for the head. The appelation Sagarmatha can mean "head in the sky" or "head inclined towards the sky."

It is interesting that this Sanskritic name was only applied by Nepali speakers in the mid-1950s when the government of Nepal redefined its northern border. This was obviously long after it was known that Everest is the "head" mountain. Before this act of nationalization by the modern (eighteenth-century) Gurkha state, the English name had been used, if any name was used at all.

Unlike their Hindu Gurkhali rulers, the Sherpas are Buddhists who came across the border from Tibet about five hundred years ago. They speak Sherpa, a dialect within the Tibeto-Burman language group, and call the mountain Jo-mo Lung-Ma, "the Goddess of the Air." This is a deceptively simple name; you could literally fill volumes about what this idea implies to a Sherpa. In fact, volumes have been filled in Tibetan literature. We will attempt the parsimony of limiting this intellectual largesse to a few paltry paragraphs.

From its beginnings in the seventh century, the Tibetan written tradition has focused on expressing Buddhist thought. Buddhists maintain that all physical surroundings (including our bodies) are essentially so much dream stuff. Nature, as we see it manifest, is considered a projected image that originates from within the mind. The spoken Sherpa (or Tibetan) language carries inescapable philosophical and mythological associations. The name Jo-mo Lung-ma suggests not only the mountain but also a technique (using the symbol of the goddess) to find that faculty of projection. The speakers of Tibetan dialect who live beside Everest know her by names that intimate the source of being, names that suggest a personal reflection of a psychological adventure.

Not far from Everest is the Sherpa monastery of Thyangboche. The abbot there, Ngawong Tenzin Rinpoche, is fond of handing out a small print of a goddess riding a tiger, titled "Mount Everest God." This goddess is called Migyo Lang Zang and actually is one of a pentad of goddesses considered to dwell on Everest's summit: the Five Sisters of Long Life (Tsering Ched Nga). It is through this symbolic drawing, as if it were a door, that we may pass to examine a little closer another image of the mountain.

Each one of these five sisters is associated with a particular "poison" or defect of the personality; Migyo Lang Zang is associated with the ossified concept of self, or what we might call pride. Her vehicle, the tiger, is a symbol of initiation. The tiger carries the aspirant into the darkness of the forest and then delivers a transformed adept back into the world of light, where life begins again. By starting over, which is all initiation means anyway, one perceives the sense of self as a character in a dream, bound to the ephemeral law of change. To fully appreciate life in this particular way, so say many Buddhists, permits access to an infinite imagination—an imagination unrestricted by either mental prejudices or the physical limitations of the body.

This kind of freedom of creation is also thought of as the fundamentally positive side of life, the source of well-being and prosperity, symbolized in our drawing by the plate of jewels and magic fruit in the goddess's left hand. Her right hand is in a gesture of bestowing, a sign that this is all an open secret; no one binds us to our dream role but ourselves. Ngawong Tenzin Rinpoche has a remarkably different image of this mountain from that of his visitors.

Having no iconography for this mountain except photographs, what about the English name, our symbolic image that suggests this mountain's ultimate glory? We awarded the name of Sir George Everest, a geodesist from Gwernvale, Brecknockshire, Wales, a Victorian bureaucrat. Lest we present Sir George injuriously, it should be understood that he was indeed a remarkable fellow. His name, though, applied to that mountain reveals something of the Western approach to nature in general.

If you call a mountain Everest, you see something very different from a goddess of air. For Nepalese Sherpas the names of forests, rivers, or mountains are usu-

Mount Everest God.

ally intended to elicit some edifying response, like speculation on a goddess. In the United States (which is a country in the West) the intentions behind names given to the natural surroundings are often less than edifying.

The Tetons, for example, received their name because they were once perceived by some concupiscent *crapaud* as swelling mammaries. As unlikely as it would seem that generations would accept an obscure French trapper's libidinous fantasy as a geographical reference, the Tetons remain to this day clearly marked on the maps of Wyoming.

What seems especially vacant about the name Teton is that the association just stops. There is no further meaning brought into the mammary allusion besides "What a set of knockers!" The name operates on only one level and does not pretend to lead or provoke you to any of the less explicitly autoerotic levels of either Gallic or American culture. It remains a ribald one-liner. Well, fair enough; it must have been pretty tough traipsing and trapping the American West in the nineteenth century.

It is always wise to suspend judgment on other peoples' particular world views and not think of different cultures as better than another but to think of them as simply different. Since, as a species, we seem able to accumulate observations in a rather creative way, we are in a particularly good position to include various world views we encounter into our expanding repertoire. How advantageous it would be to marshal a battery of diverse world views (recruited from many different cultures) that could engage the unknown at appropriate moments.

It is sincerely hoped that a planetary mentality like this might continue to edge out the antiquated fears of foreigners and their ways. It used to be that to seriously consider the values of traditional people was "backward." One still runs the risk of "going native," you know, and thereby sacrificing the accumu-

Gadi woman, Zanskar. Photo by M. Tobias.

lated freight of Western Civilization (a term, incidentally, usually described as a miraculous event in ancient Greece). This kind of fear of things foreign is still trembling in, of all places, the foreign aid and development cults; and do not be misled, cults they are, complete with devotees as convinced of the progress to a Pure Land as Sherpas are of air goddesses.

To be sure, simple changes in traditional village life are demonstrably advantageous. But the development cults are notoriously evangelical and all too often drown a different world view in well-intentioned baptisms. A serious interest (or worse still, equipping oneself with aboriginal ideas) can appear to the fearful as heretically burning incense as the idol of the "noble savage."

It is hard to imagine any reasonable soul thinking that nobility is higher in any one part of the world than another. People are people. It does not make much difference whether you drive a car on a freeway or carry an 80-pound (36-kilogram) basket over the mountains; your nobility is an entirely separate matter. One would like to think the valuable contributions of development cultists will be enhanced by their seeing the world through the eyes of the traditional people they profess to help—followed closely by a deeper realization that there is no connection between nobility and technology.

Indeed, there are signs that this understanding is taking place. But where can technical propagandists, or anybody for that matter, begin? Where does anyone start to appreciate the interior design of another culture's mental furniture without forfeiting the equally valuable comforts of one's own intellectual home? Through art, of course.

The art of the Sherpas reveals to us the world they see and also provides us with methods of seeing that we can take away with us—methods of seeing that we can then turn on anything else. But before we can accept this as any sort of law, we must first heed a well-founded caveat: there's a big difference when a European or North American says "art" and when a Nepali, Tibetan, or Indian says "art."

The English word *art* comes from the Latin *artem*, which probably has as its root *ar-,* meaning "to fit." As it is used today, the English *art* usually connotes human skill and is often contrasted with a creation of nature.

The Tibetan Buddhist art of the Sherpas has its roots deep in India. According to this notion of aesthetics, art crafted by human beings has the ability to join the multitude of examples of nature's creativity. A Buddhist image is ultimately designed to double back or remind the viewer of the dream faculty, the inner genius, that produced the image in the first place.

Most Asian cultures (and Medieval Europe, for that matter) believe that mentation does not occur in the head, but rather in the heart. The heart represents an unfathomable vastness, that inner genius out of which infinitely varied forms are drawn by an artist. Considered limitless, it more closely resembles the universal imagination that animates nature. The ideal in Indian art and its progeny is essentially a natural act.

Human skill for a Buddhist artist is developed only insofar as it can serve this imaginative process as a master vehicle of execution. For the craftsman to achieve greatness, he must be good enough to step aside and let the universe stamp its likeness on rock or painting ground.

The images Sherpas paint of mountains are sometimes so highly stylized that westerners would call them more symbols of mountains rather than representations. These paintings are not copies of an exterior or ocular perception; they are mental visions projected into an impressionable material. The painter begins with the inner mentation or visualization from the vastness of the heart.

Everest is deemed real when it makes its appearance inside. In fact, the 29,030-foot (8,848-meter) buckle in the earth's crust, the mountain outside, is more interesting to Sherpas as an act of creation by its audience than as an object separate from its viewers. The reality of the mountain is the urge to create the mountain, an archetype that floats to the surface of the heart in a vision.

When pressed about it, Sherpas are more likely to be interested in what we fancy we see: Do we perceive the mountain as resembling something else, an animal perhaps, or as a maze of routes leading to the top, or as the home of an extraordinary being, rather than a description of the physical reaction on eyeballs? This inner sensation of the mountain is not uncommon throughout Asia. The image of a mountain is, for many, the foundation of their cosmology.

At the very center of the Buddhist universe stands Mount Su-Meru. There are many Sherpa representations of this mountain, often in the porticos of monastic temple complexes, the Gompas. Su-Meru is usually represented as the center of the world, surrounded by four continents at the cardinal points. Out of this central continent rises the highest of all mountains, Su-Meru. It is divided into segments to remind the viewer of the various levels of cognizance described by Buddhist tradition. Its central location emphasizes its role as the still hub about which all things revolve.

The fabulous Mount Su-Meru is a chart of the vast empty space in the heart. Here, rising from the sea of the subconscious, is the very center of everything, the axis of the universe. The more one looks at the paint-ing of Su-Meru, the more one sees a mirror of one's own heart. Sentience itself is a central idea, and all creatures contain the centrality of Su-Meru in them.

In all cultures the mountain, the point where the earth and sky meet, is a privileged place. But instead of being a spot on the earth that is separate and outside of us, the concept of Su-Meru includes us in the scene. In fact, since it is the central axis, we are more accurately Su-Meru than the painted mountain we see outside. The external image, whether mountain or painting, reminds us of our unique place in the scheme of nature.

Mount Su-Meru as the center of the universe should not be dismissed as either primitive geography or as egocentrism. At times modern cosmologies also assume that the individual is the center of the universe. To measure phenomena, the observer must often assume that he is at rest, that he is the still center about which everything revolves.

When the observer analyzes his or her observations, they must take account of this assumption. The observations must conform to a picture of the universe drawn by many observers, each one of whom assumed he or she was at the center. The diagrams of Su-Meru on monastery walls should be understood in a similar way. They are useful models, but one must always remember that everybody else sees himself or herself at the center too. In fact (and you may have to think about this a bit) the multitude of unique loci occupied by all creatures coincides at the summit of Mount Su-Meru.

As the skill of reading Buddhist art increases, a meaning unfolds, just as these symbolic Roman letters are disclosing a message to you now. But Buddhist art has a large part of oneself enmeshed in the art form. Appreciating it is a bit like cleaning dirty mirrors.

Once this kind of contact with Himalayan art is achieved, it is not so easily dispelled. After walking away from a painted image of such a mountain on a monastery wall, a view of the snow giants themselves finds them true offspring of the heart. They are no less awesome for having been conceived in one's imagination, just surprisingly familiar. The painting has influenced the way one sees; the mountains have moved beyond surface appearances to another level of complexity.

Trekkers who find their way to Nepal generally seem gifted with very active imaginations. They seem to harbor a half-buried hope that over the next ridge the people will be dressed in Chinese brocades and look to be forty while nearing two hundred.

Trekkers are not necessarily credulous or naive people, but they do come to Nepal to live out fantasies; trekking is after all a vacation for most. The local outfitters peddle these fantasies often in a rather frank way (Shangri-la is a common name here, and it is usually played for all it is worth).

An arriving trekker had once sent word on ahead with two requests: Which combinations of films and filters would produce the best photographic results in Nepal? and Could she meet a mystic? She was advised to go to the sailboat museum in Connecticut for the latter. As for the former: only God really knows about photography.

Let us hope that if this woman ever did fall into a magic Shangri-la valley she would have enough sense to stay there and get the most out of it, and not dash right out with her Kodachromes to *National Geographic*.

The mountains that attracted our well-meaning trekker are not merely the highest; they had been given a particular significance to her by the people who live beside them. The lure outside Nepal to these mountains stems in part from this significance; the Himalayas mean something—something (perhaps mystical) in addition to their geological wonder.

Muktinath is a remote temple in western Nepal and frequently a destination for the eastern Sherpas. There are actually several temples at the site, but the one of interest at the moment surrounds an emanation of a burning natural gas jet. There are three holes under the main altar of this temple; the right one has fire coming out of a rock, the left one, fire burning on the ground, and the middle one reveals fire burning on top of a flowing spring of water.

A great deal of attention was lavished on this spot; obviously building a temple over this spring and gas emission indicates more than idle curiosity. It means something. In fact what more appropriate symbol could be found to represent the reconciliation of all antithetical elements? Fire and water do not as a rule occur in such comfortable concurrence. The rule usually has them canceling one or the other out. But at Muktinath a great deal is read into this: life and death, man and god, past and future—the whole world of polarized limitations—come together in a privileged spot of atonement.

If you were to compare this small and really unassuming epiphany with breathtaking marvels like the Grand Canyon, Old Faithful, or even the Tetons, you would probably think the shrine at Muktinath, built over a five-inch flame and a trickle of water, was a little dinky. But despite the awe-inspiring presence of American natural phenomena, few people regard them as metaphors of psychological speculation; there is rarely a sense of pilgrimage to them, a reflection of ourselves. Breathtaking North American marvels are great places for the weekend, but nobody is particularly interested in propelling them to eternity.

Industrial societies have taught themselves restraint; they are virtually embarrassed to pay homage to remarkable spots in nature—spots that may bring together the struggling and opposing forces of life like Muktinath or destroy space, like the summit of the world axis. Somehow, though, there has got to be more to nature than simply manipulating it and making it appear different.

Petroleum is manipulated into nylon and silicon into semiconductor chips, and neon is made to glow. Admittedly these and the rest of the avalanche of manipulations are not simple tasks, but performing them seems to provide little ultimate satisfaction. Pushing nature around does not necessarily help us materially, nor has it stilled the restlessness in society or the craving for identity ("Can I take a picture of the mystic when I meet him?").

Obviously, scientific research is of tremendous value; not only is it a lot of fun, but it should also continue with unabated vigour. But when we look back on a solid record of technological success, something is missing. Technology alone (without the fun) gives little sense of our own role in the universe.

The idea of technological automation can all too often simply remove the person. Labor-saving devices can be extremely useful if you have something to do instead of the labor saved. The danger is in the performance of an activity that goes on without you. There has been justifiable concern in many industries that total automation will result in widespread and unacceptable unemployment. Labor saving in this instance can mean throwing the baby out with the amniotic fluid.

The average visitor to Nepal comes from this industrialized background. Many speak quite freely about their insecurities and anxieties, readily admitting that anyone of average intelligence and given the same training would be able to perform their jobs. They themselves do not appear intrinsically important to what they do as a craftsman, say, but more like a warm body, or worse, a cog on a wheel, one about as important as the next.

This feeling of exclusion may very well have cultivated a need for the mirrors of Su-Meru and Everest. This may not be said in so many words; in fact, it may not be recognized at all. But there is an undeniable passion for superlatives.

The trekker who travels from his or her technological village all the way to Nepal is after something more than just exercise. One could, after all, save an enormous amount of money by jogging for a week or so in the local meat locker and emerge with a similar sensation. But that would hardly compare with the Himalayas, now would it? There are no great literary romances of meat lockers, and the usual full-time residents there have failed to produce even one significant mystic. For what it is worth, a famous American mountain climber was actually videotaped once jogging inside a meat locker in the United States to promote her upcoming assault on Annapurna. (The stunt was the television people's idea, not hers.)

Be that as it may, those who forgo the pleasures and safety of meat lockers and who spring for a trip to Nepal seem to be on at least a subliminal pilgrimage where the great peaks emphasize the viewer in the scene, and where a person can appear important, significant, and meaningful even without the elaborate embroidery of Tibetan Buddhist mythology.

One can certainly get carried away with personal emphasis, and it is true that pure self-aggrandizement has been known to be some people's image of a mountain. Thankfully, only a few people take these great wrinkles and trod them underfoot to purely emphasize themselves, but if we are honest we all have a little of this in us. Even simple goals (base camp or the next tea shop) are usually expressions of power. This intensification of self could be a compensation or defense against the exclusion felt in a technical milieu.

Curiously, such an unadorned drive to establish oneself somewhere, anywhere, has led us to cultures that have particularly interesting things to say about this very need. In 1922, C. G. Bruce led an Everest expedition from the Tibet side. The nearest inhabited settlement to his base camp was the Buddhist monastery of Rongbuk, at a height of 16,500 feet (5,000 meters). It is no coincidence that the abbot's name was Ngawong Tenzin Norbu. Rongbuk was responsible for generating most of the Sherpa institutions across the border. Ngawong Tenzin Rimpoche, the present abbot of Thyangboche, is in Rongbuk's direct lineage.

Bruce met with the abbot of Rongbuk several times; what is a coincidence, indeed a delightful one, is that both men recorded their impressions of these meetings. It is fascinating to compare these two accounts, these two world views.

In *Assault on Mount Everest* (1922) Bruce recalls that the abbot's "inquiries about the object of the expedition were intelligent, although at the same time they were very difficult to answer. Indeed, this is not strange when one comes to think how many times in England one has been asked, 'What is the good of an expedition to Everest? What can you get out of it? And, in fact, what is the object generally of wandering in the mountains?' As a matter of fact it was very much easier to answer the lama than it is to answer inquiries in England. The Tibetan lama, especially of the better class, is certainly not a materialist. I was fortunately inspired

Hindustani mountain vagabond. Photo by M. Tobias.

to say that we regarded the whole expedition, and especially our attempt to reach the summit of Everest as a pilgrimage. I'm afraid, also, I rather enlarged on the importance of the vows taken by the members of the expedition. I told the lama (through a translator) that I had sworn to never touch butter until I had arrived at the summit of Everest. Even this was well received. After that time I drank tea with sugar or milk which was made especially for me."

The lama recorded in his *rnam-thar*, or autobiography: "Making use of instruments such as iron pegs, wire ropes and crampons they strove to ascend the mountain. They climbed with the most extreme difficulty. . . . When they had reached about a third of the way up the mountain, one day, with a roar, an avalanche occurred and some men were projected over the cliff face. . . . It was not known whether two big sahebs died. Seven or eight coolies died. . . . I was filled with great compassion for their lot who underwent such suffering on unnecessary work. I organized a very important *bsngo-smon* [prayers, the merits of which are supposedly beneficial to those who have accumulated bad karma]."

The abbot continues when meeting Bruce again: "I asked, 'Are your not weary?' 'Me? I'm all right. A few men died,' he replied and was a little ashamed. I gave him a wooden tubful of breads and a new gold and copper image of Tara; I resolved to pray for his conversion to Buddhism in the future. Then, as he left, as is the custom in Tibet, he took off his hat and said: 'Be seated, be seated,' and so saying went away." *

It is noteworthy that the lama gifted Bruce with this particular Tibetan diety. Tara is the great goddess. She is air. She embodies many of the qualities that the Tibetans ascribe to Jo-mo Lung-ma, the goddess of air herself. Tara is responsible for safe passage from point A to point B geographically as well as the more difficult transitions as we follow a symbol from the surface to its core.

It was as if the lama was offering another approach to the mountain—as if through its image, what the lama considered to be the symbol of the experience of travel, Bruce might at last gain entrance to the world of the mountain. One wonders if Bruce would have made it to the top safely had he really made a vow, had the mountain been for him an honest pilgrimage.

To recognize a pilgrimage spot in nature tends to restrain acts of pollution—whether unnecessarily with the dead bodies of coolies or, more commonly, with toilet paper and assorted camping ejecta—allowing the land to regain its significance as a reflection of oneself. Barring wholesale superstition, myth has the power to restore respect and meaning to a world that may have become slightly sterile or machinelike.

Today the influx of foreigners to the Sherpa community is having dramatic consequences. Young Sherpas generally do not have the same values as their parents. The culture is slowly loosening its fastenings and starting to drift in different directions.

For the Sherpas monastic institutions are their cultural anchors. Here the young receive training in their unusual world view, and the old go to see themselves reflected in a refined atmosphere. These cultural underpinnings were traditionally supported by farmers and high-altitude herdsmen, but no longer.

The structure of Sherpa economics has been radically and, sad to say, irreversibly altered. The dependence on expedition and trekking work has overwhelmed the value of farming and animal husbandry. The exposure to Westerners and their convincing technologies has diverted farmers and herdsmen into other occupations. Any small flutter in the flow of foreigners (political tilts or the not unlikely possibility of a small war somewhere) would leave most Sherpas in the lurch, unable to fall back on ways they have traditionally produced wealth.

Many Sherpas are neither culturally as secure nor culturally as well informed as they once were. With the undermining of support to the Gompas, the indigenous Sherpa collegiate structure, it would appear even fewer Sherpas will be so informed in the future.

Migyo Lang Zang watches from her aerie on top of the world. She watches the tourists gather from all the countries on earth. Every year hordes thousands strong traipse up for a glimpse of Everest; a few are even projected off the cliff faces. Through the rustle of down jackets and the hissing of nylon tents, the outside world forms its image of the mountain. Some who park on the apron of Thyangboche monastery will seek an audience with the abbot Ngawong Tenzin Rimpoche. If they receive the little print of Migyo Lang Zang they may sense her presence and move through the Sherpa landscape.

Kashmiri Hill child. Photo by M. Tobias.

15. The "Abominable Snowman": Himalayan Religion and Folklore from the Lepchas of Sikkim

HALFDAN SIIGER

Before addressing the problem of the Himalayan snowman, it is important to take up some general considerations. The problem is topical because some modern mountaineering expeditions have worked with natives of the region who live by their own nonscientific concepts. While making their way through the high mountain regions, the expeditions came upon some strange tracks in the snow, the origin of which could not be immediately explained. The natives were horrified, and alluded to the snowman as the obvious explanation for the tracks. To the mountaineers this was no explanation, because the snowman had been hitherto unknown to science. Thus, a contradiction between the beliefs of the natives and the outlook of modern science led to the search for the snowman, considered by the mountaineers to be an unknown animal (Gurung 1961).

Despite the numerous expeditions that have explored the region up to the present time, no such animal has been found. The question that therefore arises is whether the problem of the snowman might not be viewed from the angle of local religion and folklore. In such an approach, the question of cultures is very complex. We must distinguish levels of different cultural origin—Tibetan and Lepcha—and at times distinguish various levels within the same culture.

The part of the Himalayan Range in which we are interested is primarily in Sikkim, but we are also concerned with some parts of Nepal. The Tibetan culture which to a high degree influences the northern regions is characterized by two levels: the ordinary old folk culture and the strongly literary high culture of Lamaism. In many respects they are at present so interwoven that we cannot distinguish one from the other, but in other respects a number of features and elements impart a definite imprint of their origins.

The southernmost Tibetan areas have retained an old folk culture with many pre-Lamaist religious features and elements. These areas have various old centers of the pre-Lamaist Bön religion, and they have the big monasteries of Red Sect Lamaism, called *Nying ma pa*.

The culture of the indigenous Lepchas of Sikkim exhibits two religious levels: the original hunters and mountain agriculturists with their priests, priestesses, cults, and mythology, and the later, superimposed layer

influenced by the local lamas of the *Nying ma pa* monasteries and their ceremonies and mythology. Through the centuries, the relationship between these two religions has developed from competition to coexistence to a kind of cooperation (Gorer 1938:186ff.; Siiger 1972:237).

For a study of the problem, we must rely on a number of written sources of varied origins and character. The local so-called Lepcha books, written in Lepcha script, are strongly influenced by Tibetan Lamaism and deal with other questions (Siiger 1967*a*:23ff.). We must, therefore, turn to the material collected in the field by students and anthropologists during the last hundred years or so. For a general evaluation of their publications, I refer to my own book on the Lepchas (Siiger 1967*a*:17ff.). When these publications are used as sources for the study of the present problem, however, we are faced with a special difficulty. Several of these authors use their own spellings of Lepcha words and names, which in some instances may vary from one author to another to such a degree that the same word can be almost unrecognizable. In such cases we must turn to the entire mythological context for an explanation. Even then we are at times left in the dark.

Furthermore, since these authors never collected their material with regard to the present problem, we have to extract a number of scattered and frequently fragmentary pieces of information from the sources in order to elucidate our particular problem. In spite of these difficulties, it seems to me that we can obtain sufficient detail to construct a mosaic, which may then be used to substantiate a tentative hypothesis.

Even so, we must be careful because the influence of Tibetan Lamaism, especially that of the *Nying ma pa,* is obvious in various ways, having left its impression on the mythology and sometimes on the cult ceremonies (Siiger 1972:236).

In both areas—the southernmost Tibetan Himalayas and northern Sikkim—the snowman figures in folklore and, in special ways, in religion.

The common Tibetan term for the snowman, *mu/rgod/mi/rgod,* means "wild untamed man." He is said to be an apelike, hairy creature. This image is also associated with other terms sometimes used for the snowman, such as *gangs mi* ("glacier man"), *mi chen po* ("big great man"), and *mi bom po* ("strong robust man"). The term *mi shom po* ("strong man") is also applied to the snowman (Nebesky-Wojkowitz 1956*a*: 344 fn. 1; 1956*b*: 155ff.).

It is said that this snowman carries a large stone as a weapon and that he makes a characteristic whistling sound. When walking in the high, snowy regions, he leaves very large footprints in the snow. When moving in the forests, he uses all four limbs to swing from tree to tree, but in the open country he generally walks upright (Nebesky-Wojkowitz 1965*b*: 158, 160).

The Sherpas of Nepal conceive of the snowman as an apelike creature who leaves his footprints in the snow. They call the snowman *yeti,* a term used by many Himalayan expeditions, and translated "abominable." The Sherpas avoid meeting the *yeti* because the sight of him portends misfortune (Nebesky-Wojkowitz 1956*b*: 155).

The notion of the snowman as an ape or an apelike creature brings to mind the well-known pre-Lamaist Tibetan legend of the origin of mankind from a monkey and a divine female. But at present no direct connection can be proved (Haarh 1969: 295–97 passim; Waddell 1959: 19). Drawings of the snowman can be found in some picture books that seem to have originated in the Chinese-Tibetan area (cf. Vičck 1959).

Particular parts of the snowman are sometimes used in connection with Tibetan religious or magical rituals. In the iconography of one of the secret aspects of a local protective deity called *rdo rje dbang drag rtsal,* this deity is dressed in the skin of a "wild man," *mi rgod lpags* (Nebesky-Wojkowitz 1956*a*: 251). Adherents of the ancient Bön religion used the blood of the *mi rgod* for certain magical rites. For this purpose the *mi rgod* had to be killed by a sharp weapon or by an arrow, and its blood was mixed with poison and mustard (Nebesky-Wojkowitz 1956*a*: 344).

According to this last instance, the snowman is a real creature, an opinion prevalent among the Tibetans whether they consider him to be dangerous or shy, harmless, and practically extinct (Nebesky-Wojkowitz 1956*a*: 344). A snowman can live very long, a notion that arose from the story of a snowman living on the mountain called *mi go ri* ("the snowman mountain"), and seen limping from a wound he had received during a hunt three generations before (Nebesky-Wojkowitz 1956*b*: 158).

Turning to the Lepchas of Sikkim, we shall approach our problem not directly, but indirectly, that is, via their entire universe, because the snowman seems to be a detail of this great whole. The universe of the Lepchas comprises a huge number of supernatural be-

ings that can be divided into two types: the mostly benign *rǔm* and the hostile *mung.* Some of the supernatural beings constitute families, just as human beings do (Siiger 1967*a*: 112ff., 143ff., 172ff.).

A further investigation reveals that the lives of these supernatural beings can be better understood if we attempt to arrange them into groups according to their connection with the lives and activities of human beings. In this way we may speak of certain complexes, each of which centers on a number of functions or activities in which the supernatural beings as well as the humans play parts. These complexes display, so to speak, a mutual cooperation, and at times even an interdependence, between the two categories of partners. Nevertheless, the supernatural beings still occupy a superior position. Thus one could, for instance, speak of an origin complex, a hunting complex, an agricultural fertility complex, a death complex, and others (Siiger 1968: 277ff.). Some of these complexes are fairly constant because they correspond to fundamental and unalterable conditions of human life; others may change in content and importance according to the varying conditions and development of human society.

In the Lepcha hunting complex, two types of supernatural beings, *rǔm* and *mung,* appear. Twenty-three names have been registered, some of which seem to be variations of the same name, but there may be more (Jest 1960: 133). We cannot account for all of these supernatural beings, because at present some of them are mere names. Some of the names, however, refer to important supernatural beings of whom we have more knowledge. Thus, it emerges that certain characteristics may be emphasized, depending on the mountain zones and the particular animals with which these supernatural beings are associated.

It is interesting to note that in the highest snow regions we meet the snowman whom the Lepchas call *chu mung* ("glacier" *mung*) or *hlo mung* (the *mung* of the higher mountain regions). The name *chu rǔm* may also be found (Nebesky-Wojkowitz 1956*a*: 344; 1956*b*: 158; *Dictionary of the Lepcha Language* 1898: 382*a,* 81*b*). The word "glacier" (*chu*) appears not only in the Lepcha material but also in Tibetan material by the name *gangs mi* (Tibetan: *gangs,* "glacier"). It is obvious that these names are not personal names, but indications of the region with which the supernatural being is associated.

It is further told about this being that the Lepchas worship him as the god of the hunt, the owner of all mountain game, and the lord of all forest creatures (Nebesky-Wojkowitz 1956*a*: 344; 1956*b*: 158; *Dictionary of the Lepcha Language* 1898: 382*a,* 81*b*). Unfortunately, we know nothing more about how the god is worshiped, but it is important to observe that his dominion also includes the animals of the forest region.

The central supernatural being of the hunting complex is *pong rŭm,* also called *pum rŭm* ("chief" or "principal" *rŭm*) (Hermanns 1954:47ff., 30; *Dictionary of the Lepcha Language* 1898:219a). His wife is *shing rŭm* ("goddess of the forests") (Gorer 1938:150, 244).

According to one investigator *pŭm rum/pong rŭm* is also known as *dju-thing* because he is the "lord" or "master" (*thing*) who leads *dju* ("game") to the hunter. As such he is called by different surnames, depending on the species of animals he leads to the hunter: *mo-nom-dju* [chamois and the wild sheep] in the high mountain regions; *se-go-bu-log-dju* [stag and the bear] in the lower hills; and *se-wing-dju* in the lower plains (Hermanns 1954:47ff.).

As the king of all animals and the patron god of hunters, this *rŭm* occupies the most prominent position in the hunting complex with a relationship to both animals and humans.

It is, therefore, no wonder that in ancient times there was an intimate connection between this *rŭm* and the hunters who sought his support and protection. But the *rŭm* was very strict in his demands on the hunters, and the young novice had to go through a period of apprenticeship with an old, experienced hunter in order to learn his duties (Morris 1938:196; Gorer 1938:245).

Once a year all hunters must perform a sacrifice to this *rŭm,* and each time they set out for the hunt they offer a sacrifice, accompanied by a prayer. Having learned the procedure of the animal sacrifice, the young hunter must perform it regularly for the rest of his life. Should he make a mistake, he must repeat the whole ceremony, because the *rŭm* does not tolerate any deviations from tradition (Morris 1938:193ff.; Gorer 1938:244ff.).

When the hunter of Lingthem, northern Sikkim, has killed an animal, he places it on the ground, the head in front with a foreleg and a hind leg on either side and with the singed intestines in the middle. He crouches behind and speaks slowly and softly, gently throwing the singed intestines bit by bit over the animal's head. In Tingbung, northern Sikkim, these bits consist of the head, liver, tongue, ears, and tail of the animal (Morris 1938:193ff.; Gorer 1938:98).

These details concern the common relationship between this *rŭm,* the animals, and the ordinary Lepcha hunter. There are, however, in the Lepcha society some families who, according to their own venerated lineage traditions, have ancient and intimate connections with a supernatural being (Siiger 1967a:112ff.).

This applies to the now almost extinct Salong *pŭ tsho* ("lineage") living in a remote area rather close to Mount Kanchenjunga.

One day the ancestor of this lineage, while walking through the forest, came upon what he thought was a dead bear. He cut it up and ate part of it. When he had done so, *pong rŭm* appeared to him and said that because he had eaten part of *pong rŭm*'s body, he and his children must henceforth serve him, worship him, make offerings to him. Henceforth also the man and his children might eat all animals, even snakes, with impunity. The bear was in reality an incarnation of *pong rŭm,* who for a while was taking a rest outside his incorporeal self (Gorer 1938:56; Morris 1938:194).

This event, which tied the *rŭm* and the lineage into a kind of totemistic relationship, with the bear as the unifying intermediary, gives a profound perspective on the understanding of the ancient hunting complex. At the same time, it adds a new element to the understanding of the personality of *pong rŭm,* that is, his appearance in the form of a bear when seeking a physical manifestation.

The personality of *pong rŭm* and the range of his influence will be further explained when we consider his position within the agricultural fertility complex. The center of this complex is located at the mythical *mă yel,* halfway up the great, commanding Mount Kanchenjunga. Its base shelters the female deity of the origin of mankind, while the great protector god of Sikkim and the Lepchas resides at the summit (Siiger 1968:277ff.).

From the strange *mă yel* beings, sometimes called *rŭm,* living at the *mă yel* place, comes the fertility of the rice, maize, wheat, yams, pumpkins, chilis, and manioc. The *mă yel* beings number seven or nine couples; they are hairy all over, very small, almost like dwarfs, and have huge goiters. This last feature is generally considered to be a characteristic of fertility. They never die; they are children at dawn, grown up at noon, and old in the evening. They have no children (Siiger 1967a:89ff.; Gorer 1938:238ff.; Morris 1938:181, 186ff.).

The most important of these *mă yel* beings are known by name, and one of them is called *mă yel yuk rŭm* ("the high" or "noble god" of *mă yel*) (*Dictionary of the Lepcha Language* 1898:325a). This *mă yel yuk rŭm* is the same as *pong rŭm,* demonstrating the intimate connection of the hunting complex with the fertility complex (Gorer 1938:236).

Moreover, in the legends dealing with the *mă yel* place, it is told that *pong rŭm* has two younger brothers, and that these three together have functions as *sok-po* ("guardians") of the *mă yel* place, the ibexes, and the musk deer. The younger brothers, called Mi-tik and

Tom-tik, are very cruel; Tom-tik is like a bear (Gorer 1938:236).

In these legends about the *mă yel* place there are two points of particular importance. The hunting complex is so closely associated with the fertility complex that we may consider them to be interwoven. The hunting god *pong rŭm* is one of the *mă yel* beings, and as such has the particular *mă yel* name, *mă yel yuk rŭm*.

Because the *mă yel* place provides the Lepcha people with agricultural fertility, the protection of this fertility is, of course, of paramount importance. This obligation falls upon *pong rŭm* and his two brothers, who now guard not only the prominent animals of the high mountain regions, but also the fertility place itself. We also notice that the bear, which in the previously mentioned legend was the incarnation of *pong rŭm*, is here the body of the younger brother called Tom-tik. We cannot account for this difference; it may be due to the fact that *pong rŭm*, as a high-ranking member (compare his *mă yel* name) of the *mă yel* beings, cannot appear in the body of a bear, and that this incarnation has been transferred to his younger brother. In any case, *pong rŭm*, the god of hunting, is also a *rŭm* of the *mă yel* place, and to his ordinary function as guardian of the wild animals has been added the function of supreme guardian of the place of agricultural fertility and its inhabitants, the *mă yel* beings.

In the present Lepcha society there are two factors that are of paramount importance because they have come from the outside world and have caused a fundamental change in the basic material culture of the Lepchas.

The first is the introduction of firearms for hunting.

Petite Dignity, southern Sikkim. Photo by M. Tobias.

They came into use long ago, although some few men in the remote areas still hunt in the ancient way, with bows and arrows. Hunting with firearms has influenced the old habits to such a degree that the ancient rule prohibiting a young hunter from eating the meat of the first hundred animals he kills does not apply to the man hunting with firearms (Gorer 1938:85; Morris 1938:193). As a whole it can be said that most of the ancient hunting ceremonies have become obsolete.

The second factor is the replacement of the old dry rice cultivation with modern wet rice cultivation, a change that took place about the turn of the century. In the wake of this development, the ancient dry rice rituals and prayers have disappeared rapidly, and today only a few old people recall them (Siiger 1967a:91).

In both cases, modern generations have demonstrated by their behavior that they can manage these two means of supplying food without the cooperation of the supernatural beings.

This growth of independence has weakened the bond uniting supernatural beings with humans so that, feeling superfluous, the *mă yel* have withdrawn from the lives of humans and retired to their distant and exclusive abode. In the past, they sometimes helped the Lepchas in difficult situations. Now, the legend informs us, they will return only if the people are on the verge of extinction (Gorer 1938:237; Nebesky-Wojkowitz 1956b:134).

As for *pong rŭm*, the situation is more portentous. The decrease in the worship of *pong rŭm* corresponds to his gradually worsening attitude toward human beings. He became enraged and reacted with persecution and punishment.

Thus, the present relationship between the hunter and the *rŭm* is very strained. If the hunter does not conform meticulously to the rules of sacrifice to the *rŭm*, he can be sure of some kind of retaliation, varying from minor persecutions to full-scale revenge. Hunters who neglect their ordinary ritual duties to the *rŭm* may be pursued by the sinister whistling sound, characteristic of the ominous presence of *pong rŭm*, or they may hear the thump of heavy stones falling, though no falling stones are to be seen. Even the hunter's children may be persecuted (Gorer 1938:245).

The hunter's obligation of an annual sacrifice to *pong rŭm* continues for the rest of his life, even if he has given up hunting. One retired hunter who had neglected his annual sacrificial duties had stones thrown at his orange trees at night. Although he arranged an offering to *pong rŭm* and asked for forgiveness, stating that he would hunt no more, it was in vain. One night he heard his dog barking and whining in a most peculiar way. Going outside, he found it lying dead without any marks on its body (Morris 1938:195; Gorer 1938:245ff.). A keen boar hunter who had killed a dozen wild boars, but did not know the proper way of offering to *pong rŭm* after the kill, was overtaken by the anger of the *rŭm* and killed. Only his bones were found later (Gorer 1938:403). A young hunter, ignorant of the proper way of offering the hunter's sacrifice, asked his maternal uncle to do it on his behalf. But the uncle sacrificed to his own god instead of to *pong rŭm*, and the young man was taken ill and died (Gorer 1938:404).

The once-great and powerful human *rŭm* has turned into a primarily malicious being because the hunters have neglected proper ceremonial sacrifices. In this way his behavior becomes stamped by a psychological pattern similar to that of the neglected children of the great Lepcha goddess of procreation. Motivated by jealousy against the favored human children of the goddess, they turned into evil *mung* constantly persecuting their human brothers and sisters (Siiger 1972:240, 244).

Considering that both *pong rŭm* and *chu mung/rŭm* are supernatural beings belonging to the hunting complex, we encounter the problem of the relationship between phenomena of the natural and supernatural spheres.

There can be no doubt that some phenomena of the Lepcha universe belong distinctly to the natural sphere and others to the supernatural sphere. It is, however, obvious that some phenomena occupy a position in between, or rather, belong to both spheres. Like any other supernatural being, *pong rŭm* can manifest himself at will in whatever sphere he chooses. It may be in a visible shape, for example, a bear, or as the originator of strange, often alarming incidents, signaling his presence and giving humans an admonition or an omen.

In sum, the ancient Lepcha hunting complex comprises many supernatural beings associated with various mountain regions, including the supernatural snowman in the glacier areas. The prominent supernatural being of the hunting complex, who is included in the agricultural fertility complex, has since ancient times preferred the body of a bear as his physical manifestation. Because of modern developments, the Lepchas have increasingly neglected their ceremonial duties toward this being who has, therefore, reacted with jealous persecutions, deeply alarming the Lepchas. Wanderers in the mountain areas, therefore, interpret unusual sounds, tracks, and so on, as omens of activity meant to punish them for their neglect.

Similarly, we might surmise that the people of Nepal might have similar notions about the supernatural world. I am well aware that I cannot at present prove this suggestion, but it seems to me that many corroborating details point in this direction.

The fear, even horror expressed by native participants of the mountaineering expeditions is a horror primarily of the supernatural side of the snowman. To them, the tracks indicated that human beings had come too close to his domain. At any moment he might reveal his presence, either by appearing in the shape of a monstrous and dangerous bear or ape, or in some other physical manifestation.

Based on the foregoing discussion, it would appear that the problem of the snowman would best be studied primarily in the context of religion and folklore and only secondarily as a zoological problem.

16. Mountain Peoples of the Eastern Himalayas: Developments in Arunachal Pradesh

CHRISTOPH VON FURER-HAIMENDORF

The Himalayas are a natural barrier that for centuries separated the civilizations of the Indian subcontinent from the peoples and cultures of the windswept plateaus of Inner Asia. But whereas the Central Himalayas were traversed by a number of trade routes along which caravans of pack animals maintained a trickle of trade between Nepal and Tibet, the tangle of pathless wooded hills stretching from eastern Bhutan to the extreme northeast corner of India served as a refuge for primitive tribal communities. Archaic styles of life and culture could persist in the isolation of such secluded valleys unaffected by the march of progress in neighboring countries. In this region, formerly known as the North East Frontier Agency, and now constituting the Union Territory of Arunachal Pradesh, there are no caravan routes, and the precipitous river gorges breaking through the Great Himalayan Range never permitted trade depending on animal transport except in a narrow strip of country immediately east of Bhutan, the character of which differs from that of all other parts of Arunachal Pradesh. Difficulties of communications, rather than the nature of the neighboring regions of Tibet and India, would seem to be responsible for the fact that the tribal populations inhabiting the mountainous tracts extending between Assam and Tibet remained for centuries untouched by Hindu as well as Buddhist civilization. Their seclusion, caused initially by physical factors, persisted until the middle of the twentieth century because of actions taken by the government of India in the days of British rule. The area situated between the northern fringe of the Brahmaputra plains and the crest of the Great Himalayan range, traditionally regarded as the border between India and Tibet, remained outside the administrative control of the government of Assam, making it for all practical purposes a political no-man's land.

In 1914 there had been negotiations with Tibet and China aimed at defining the Indo-Tibetan boundary east of Bhutan. They resulted in a convention, drawn up by Sir Henry McMahon and initialed by the delegates of Tibet and China, that recognized the ridge line of the Great Himalayan Range as the international frontier, implying thereby that the entire submontane tract lying to the south of it belonged to India. The convention, however, was never ratified, and though official Indian documents had ever since referred to the proposed border as the McMahon Line, no attempt had been made to demarcate the frontier. While Tibet took no steps either to implement or repudiate the convention, China never renounced her claim to the submontane tract. Indeed as late as the 1950s China published maps according to which a large part of the present Union Territory of Arunachal Pradesh was included within the borders of China. What was until then only a diplomatic wrangle between the governments of India and China assumed the proportions of a major international conflict when in 1962 Chinese army units crossed the Himalayan main range in the area of Tawang, close to the border of Bhutan, and occupied a substantial tract of territory which at that time was already administered by India. This invasion not only drew world attention to the region, but also strengthened the Indian determination to extend effective administrative control over the entire tract claimed according to the McMahon convention. When after some months the Chinese withdrew from Tawang and an uneasy peace was patched up, the government of India made tremendous efforts to develop the territory then still called the North East Frontier Agency. How great a challenge this was can be seen if we compare the present situation with the conditions prevailing when in 1944 I first entered a region now known as the Subansiri District.

Village Monastery, Sherdukpen area, Arunachal Pradesh. Photo by I. Simon.

At that time there were no man-made paths, no bridges across the many mountain streams, and above all no established friendly relations with any of the warlike hill tribes almost continuously engaged in fierce intertribal and intervillage feuds. I started from the plains of Assam, and it took me seven days of strenuous trekking through pathless, dripping subtropical forest before I encountered the first signs of habitation and finally entered a wide valley where, at an altitude of some 5,000 feet (1,500 meters), a single tribe known as the Apa Tanis had established themselves and transformed the wilderness into an intensively cultivated rice bowl, with carefully irrigated fields and large settlements of closely packed pile dwellings.

Though it was obvious that here I had come upon a relatively advanced society, communications with the inhabitants of the valley presented considerable difficulties. Encapsuled in their limited environment and knowing little of the outside world, with the exception of their immediate neighbors, the Apa Tanis spoke no other language than their own Tibeto-Burman dialect, and if a stroke of good luck had not enabled me to obtain the services of a man from a neighboring tribe who knew Apa Tani as well as Assamese, in which I was reasonably fluent, my entire visit to the Apa Tani valley would have been abortive. Yet the possibility of communicating through this interpreter removed only one difficulty. Another problem was how to obtain even basic provisions from a people who did not know money and had little use for the Indian coins of which I had brought considerable quantities. Fortunately I had also carried some barter goods, and of these salt, cotton cloth, and tobacco were the most acceptable. Apa Tanis were used to barter, for as skillful cultivators they produced a surplus of rice, and this they traded for cattle and pigs bred by neighboring tribesmen known as Nishis. Living in rugged mountain country very different from the broad Apa Tani valley, the Nishis subsisted mainly by slash-and-burn cultivation, but they were also experienced in the breeding of cattle, and particularly the domestic bison (*Bos frontalis*) locally known as *mithan*.

Though they were economically complementary, Apa Tanis and Nishis were often involved in hostilities, and just at the time of my first visit a violent feud was raging between three Apa Tani villages and a warlike group of Nishis. Several Apa Tanis had been captured and were held as hostages by Nishis intent on extracting from the Apa Tanis' kinsmen as high a ransom as possible.

Neither Apa Tanis nor Nishis recognized at that time any outside authority, but the former had a system of clan heads forming village councils with some judicial powers. Indeed, traditional Apa Tani society was characterized by a high degree of stability. The feeling of tribal solidarity based on community of language and habitat found expression in the unquestioning acceptance of certain forms of social conduct that distinguished the Apa Tanis from all their neighbors. Apart from the division of Apa Tani society into village communities and clans, there was a horizontal division into two social classes of unequal status. The members of the upper class, who married only among themselves, owned the greater part of the land and occupied the leading positions on the village councils. Not all of them were rich, but even patricians of modest means enjoyed certain privileges. Among the commoners there were free men, some of whom had acquired considerable property, but a good many were domestic slaves living and working in the houses of their patrician owners. Slaves inherited by their masters and hence regarded almost like family retainers formed only part of the slave population of the Apa Tani valley. There were many who either had been captured in war or had been bought from Nishis. Though not of Apa Tani stock, such slaves were gradually integrated within Apa Tani society, and their children grew up as Apa Tanis and often married local commoners.

At that time I was in the service of the government of British India, and during 1944 and 1945 I not only collected information on tribal customs and ways of life, but also explored a fairly large region unmapped and unknown to outsiders. Much of my time was spent also in settling feuds not only between Apa Tanis and Nishis, but also between individual Nishis. By establishing some communications between the hillmen and the plains of Assam, the British government laid the foundations for the ultimate development of the

Monpa Yak caravan, Arunachal Pradesh. Photo by I. Simon.

territory. Yet neither I nor anyone else could at that time have imagined the extent to which the life-style of the Apa Tanis and other tribes of Arunachal Pradesh would be transformed within the span of a few decades.

When I returned to the Apa Tani valley for a few weeks in 1962, the scene had begun to change. Tentative steps towards the establishment of an administration undertaken in the last three years of the British Raj had been followed up by the government of independent India. The emergence of an expansionist Chinese regime on the northern side of the Himalayan main range had induced the Indian government to improve communications and to station army units in the Apa Tani valley. At the southern end of the valley modern buildings were constructed to house the administrative headquarters of the Subansiri district, and in this new settlement, known as Ziro, Apa Tanis mingled with the numerous Indian government servants posted to that part of Arunachal Pradesh.

By 1980, when I last stayed among the Apa Tanis, they had undergone a far-reaching transformation. The linking of Ziro by a motorable all-weather road with North Lakhimpur in the plains of Assam had been the main factor in the changeover of the local economy. The Apa Tanis, who had always been enterprising and skillful traders, made full use of the new link with the outside world, and within a few years Ziro became a commercial center of no mean order. Today there are fifty-nine shops at Ziro, all but two owned by Apa Tanis, and these shops, which stock a large range of goods, cater to the needs of the Apa Tanis, the many government employees stationed in the valley, and to a lesser extent also to those Nishi tribesmen who have to pass through Ziro when visiting the plains. The establishment of most of the commercial enterprises has been made possible by the influx of large sums of money, partly by way of government contracts taken by Apa Tanis and partly through the salaries and wages paid to government servants, both Apa Tanis and outsiders. Another source of income is the import of cattle for slaughter as well as for sale to Nishis. The cattle, mainly old bullocks and infertile cows, available at cheap rates in the plains of Assam, are driven along the motor road and usually grazed for some time in the Apa Tani country before being sold to Nishis from neighboring villages.

The old barter system has been almost totally replaced by a money economy. Today many Apa Tanis have accounts at the Ziro branch of the State Bank of India, and the credit balances on some of these accounts exceed one hundred thousand rupees (about ten thousand dollars). There are twelve hundred accounts of local tribesmen, and the majority of these are Apa Tanis.

How can one explain the commercial success of the Apa Tanis, which contrasts so sharply with the dismal economic position of the tribal populations throughout Peninsular India? The principal reason for their ability to take full advantage of the opening up of their country was and still is the virtual absence of competition. The so-called Inner Line policy of the government of India requires even Indian citizens to have permits for entry into Arunachal Pradesh. No outsider is allowed to establish a business in such places as Ziro, and though a few nontribals, such as Assamese and Nepalis, are employed as salesmen in shops owned by Apa Tanis, they do not represent a threat to the local businessmen.

The Apa Tanis are favored even in the granting of public contracts, though in major projects the exclusion of outsiders is not possible because the local tribesmen do not have as yet the experience and resources to take on contracts for such works as bridge building or the construction of modern buildings. Yet even their present share in public works has enabled some Apa Tanis to acquire considerable wealth. It is not unusual for businessmen to own motor scooters, trucks, jeeps, or even cars. Some have electric light in their houses, and a few had telephones installed. Thus, far from proving detrimental to the tribesmen, the protective seclusion of their habitat has proved a boon, and the policy of restricting the entry of potential competitors and exploiters has been fully vindicated.

The spectacular economic development of the Apa Tanis could hardly have taken place if it had not been for the rapid educational progress among many sections of the tribe. The first primary schools were established in the 1950s. At first Assamese was the medium of instruction, and this was later changed to Hindi. However, an agitation among Apa Tani and other tribal students and politicians in favor of English brought about a second change, and today English is the official medium of instruction and the language of the administration. In the high school at Ziro, housed in excellent buildings, Apa Tani boys and girls study side by side with Nishis as well as some of the children of nontribal government employees. Many of the students have gained admission to such universities and colleges as those of Pasighat, Dibrugarh, Gauhati and Shillong, and some have gone as far as Calcutta and Delhi. In 1978 there were already 33 Apa Tani graduates, and among these were several gazetted government officials, one pilot in the Indian Air Force, and two medical practitioners. The number of Apa Tanis in gazetted posts was 15, and that of men in nongazetted posts and in the defense services and police was 342. Compared to developments among tribal populations of Peninsular India, the progress these figures reflect is little short of miraculous.

The fortunes of an educated elite and the material progress of successful traders must not be taken as an indication that Apa Tani society as a whole is in a state of turmoil and rapid alteration. In some spheres of tribal life there has been relatively little change, and traditional values and practices persist with only minor modifications. One of these spheres and obviously a very important one is that of land use and agriculture. The Apa Tanis have already been extremely industrious and skillful cultivators of rice on irrigated terrace fields. Those fields were tilled by hand with the help of iron hoes and various wooden implements, and there was never a question of using plows and animal traction. Even when government experimented with the introduction of plows and plow-bullocks, the Apa Tanis stuck to their traditional methods and continued to grow their staple crops of rice and millets in the same way as they had always done. On the other hand, they readily adopted the cultivation of newly introduced vegetables, both for their own consumption and for sale in the market of Ziro. Indeed, this is one of the ways in which women can earn the cash required for the purchase of various novel commodities.

There is, however, one change in the Apa Tanis' agricultural economy. Previously men and women took equal shares in the cultivation of the land, and labor gangs working on the rice fields consisted usually of both young girls and young men. Now, many such gangs are made up only of girls, and men working on the fields are mainly middle-aged or old. Young men prefer to engage in trade, government employment, or contract work.

Another change, which may not be for the better, is the replacement of the products of local crafts by imported machine-made goods. Weaving, a craft in which Apa Tani women were expert, has declined, largely because mill-made cloth, obtainable in the Ziro bazaar, is cheaper than the much superior handwoven textiles. Moreover, college-educated men tend to dress in shirts, trousers, pullovers, and sometimes tailored coats. Similarly, iron pots have replaced the earthen pots which used to be made by Apa Tani women.

The basic structure of Apa Tani society has withstood recent economic changes remarkably well. The division of the tribe into two hereditary classes has remained unaltered, but slavery was abolished in the early 1960s and the former slaves have been absorbed into the mass of free commoners. The endogamy of the two classes persists as an ideal, and many patricians still consider mixed marriages objectionable. In practice, however, such marriages take place and are tolerated, though they create for the spouses some difficulties in the performance of rituals. Some of the educated young Apa Tanis advocate the liberalization of marriage rules to permit even unions between Apa Tanis and members of other tribes, such as Nishis. A few such marriages exist already, but the couples do not live in Apa Tani villages, where they would still encounter opposition and exclusion from ritual performances, but have settled either at Ziro or even outside the Apa Tani valley.

The most important factor in the development of social conditions is the establishment of peace not only within Apa Tani society, which was always well ordered, but also between Apa Tanis and their martial neighbors. Raiding, kidnapping, and the holding for ransom of hostages are things of the past, and today Apa Tanis can travel far afield in the pursuance of trade without running any risk to their life and freedom. Disputes within villages, or between inhabitants of different villages, are settled by councils derived partly from the old system of clan representatives and partly of elected members of village *panchayats*, the smallest units in the new system of grass-roots democracy.

In 1978 full-fledged parliamentary democracy was introduced into Arunachal Pradesh, and several Apa Tanis contested a seat in the Legislative Assembly. The winner in the contest was the son of one of the richest and most prominent Apa Tanis, who was once a famous war leader and later devoted his organizational talent to building up extensive business interests. His son, who belongs to the educated elite, attained the position of speaker in the Legislative Assembly.

Thus, modernization has affected many aspects of Apa Tani life, and there is every prospect that this relatively small tribe with a total population of under fifteen thousand will make a significant contribution to the development of the Subansiri District and possibly the whole of Arunachal Pradesh. Unlike many other tribal people who suddenly came face to face with the modern world, Apa Tanis have retained their self-confidence and optimistic outlook. Even in the towns of the plains one can recognize Apa Tanis by their proud bearing and a certain swagger with which young men stride through the motley crowds of Assamese and other Indians.

17. The Wanchos and Mon-pas: Two Portraits from Arunachal Pradesh

IVAN SIMON

The mountainous territory known as Arunachal Pradesh comprises five districts with a total area of just 32,200 square miles (83,500 square kilometers). Its outer boundaries coincide with the international borders of Bhutan on the west, Tibet on the north, and Burma on the east. Its inner boundaries, extending over an appreciably shorter distance, touch Assam, and a small part of Nagaland in the extreme southeast. The total population of the territory at the census of 1971 was 467,511.

The considerable land area and the low population may suggest to map scanners that the territory is virtually a *Benensraum* for excess populations elsewhere. Closer acquaintance reveals a different picture. Although 13,100 square miles (34,000 square kilometers) of the total area consists of land above 10,000 feet (3,000 meters) in altitude, only some 50 percent of the remaining lower regions is arable. The principal concentration of population is therefore crowded into the lower hills and valleys contiguous with the plains of Assam.

Arunachal Pradesh, until 1971 known as the North East Frontier Agency, is the home of a remarkable variety of tribes falling into two broad camps, according to the more obvious aspect of their life and culture—the northern zone comprising lamaistic (Buddhist) tribes of western Kameng, and the southern zone of Siang, Tirap, and Lohit districts, with its agro-pastoralists. The habitat of the former group is largely alpine in character. The people are experts in animal husbandry and are skillful weavers, fashioning for themselves clothes of wool while textiles are usually of cotton for the rest.

Tirap District in the southeast is the home of three major tribes: the Wanchos, the Noctes, and the Tangsas. The Wanchos form the largest single group, with a population of 28,650 as of 1971. They inhabit the area contiguous to Nagaland and the plains of Assam. To their southeast lies Burma, in the border areas of which many of their kinsmen live. A virile race of admirable physique, the Wanchos were until recently formidable headhunters. In British days their homeland was included in what was known as the Unadministered Area, where they lived with practically no interference unless they committed some act that threatened the

peace of people living in administered territory. There are still people living who probably look back with nostalgia to the earlier though precarious days, when a man's worth rested wholly on his having taken or assisted at the taking of a human head, and those symbols of past exploits—the tattoo marks on the face and ornaments of brass or wood representing a human head—are displayed with unmistakable panache. The human skull was supposed to contain soul power, and its acquisition would contribute to the prosperity and welfare of the village to which the victor belonged. Suitable rites were always performed over heads so taken and picked clean of all tissue matter before being placed in the principal youth dormitory of the village (*pa-nu*). Certainly these relics of the past are even today treated with the utmost reverence, even awe, and no unauthorized hand may touch them. Some of these skulls show perforated or cleft crowns, indicating all too obviously the manner in which the victims were dispatched.

The main occupation of the Wanchos, as indeed of most of the tribes of Arunachal Pradesh, is agriculture. Like the majority of the tribes, particularly those of the nonlamaistic groups, the Wanchos adopt what is called in this part of the country *jhumming,* or shifting cultivation, which involves the cutting down of trees and brush in a selected area and burning the dry vegetation thoroughly. This slash-and-burn method, though destructive, has certain short-term compensations in that the ash and charred deposits supply nutrients for the crops to be grown, and the burning destroys soil pests and weeds. The heavy task of forest clearing and disposal of all but the heaviest pieces of debris is done by men. Actual planting is mostly done by women, who dibble in seeds of hill rice, or Job's Tears at a later period, and in time attend to weeding work using crude but efficient homemade tools for the purpose. Naturally, with this method the land cannot retain optimum fertility for over two years, and new fields then have to be cleared afresh, the old patch being left to recover its natural vitality as far and as fast as it can by reverting to a wild state.

Even fifteen years ago most Wanchos were innocent of clothing. Yet they comported themselves with a total lack of self-consciousness even in the presence of outsiders, and the standard of morality among them was certainly of a very high order, at least in those days. With the intrusion of "civilized" norms, the old values are bound to erode. Invidious comparisons will invariably be made, and the outcome may well be a sense of being odd and "improper." Indeed, the sight of a young miss in long skirt or slacks and wearing her hair long (in the past, the privilege of ladies of the higher class) is by no means rare in the Wancho society of today.

The Wanchos, and also the Noctes, expose their dead on raised platforms erected in cemeteries that are in fact extensions of the respective villages, and people do not seem to be aware of the oppressive effluvium that emanates from a putrefying corpse. There may even be, one suspects, a sense of comfort at the near presence, even in that state, of one who has been a member of the community. The fact that in the last stage of decomposition the skull is detached from the cadaver and installed in the house, after the purification rites, suggests that, though no longer among the living, the dead person's soul power remains behind, a potential source of blessing for the family. For this reason the Wanchos are acutely concerned that nothing should happen to disturb the transition from physical existence to one on a higher plane. It was their sense of outrage at what they considered to be an insult to a recently dead chief by some laborers belonging to a Survey of India team, who not only passed disparaging remarks but actually struck at the grave effigy, that led the people of Ninu in 1875 to attack the camp and massacre the entire team of about eighty men, including the leader, Lieutenant Holcombe.

The Mon-pas (population 28,209) inhabit the entire western section of Kameng District up to the border of Bhutan. There are three main groups: the Southern or Kalangtang Mon-pas, the Central or Dirang Mon-pas, and the Northern or Tawang Mon-pas. Except for a small area in the plains, the area traditionally accepted as the home of the Mon-pas is one of towering mountains, some of them over 18,000 feet (5,800 meters). The average altitude is approximately 9,500 feet (2,900 meters). The higher peaks are covered with snow during winter, and winter starts early in the central and northern parts, snowfall beginning around September and coming to an end about the end of April. Vegetation is of the temperate variety, pine in the lower hills, gradually replaced by oak, magnolia, dwarf rhododendron and spruce as the altitude increases until at about 15,000 feet (4,600 meters) trees no longer can grow. Flowering plants like the alpine gentian, primula, and blue Himalayan poppy (*Meconopsis*) thrive at these heights and in this climate to

Miji Headman, Arunachal Pradesh. Photo by I. Simon.

thrill the traveler who chooses the right season for his travels. Altogether, the area is beautiful—towering peaks, awesome cliffs, green alpine meadows, farms connected by narrow footpaths that skirt the edge of sheer gorges.

High as they are, the mountains of the Central Mon-pa area mark the lowest and southernmost limits of the pasturelands for yaks. The Mon-pas are experts in animal husbandry and the controlled breeding of different breeds of cattle for specific purposes. They have even used the *mithun,* that shy, hard-to-tame animal so greatly valued by the eastern tribes, into these experiments, obtaining the animals when quite young and allowing them to grow up among domesticated cattle. Love of animals is an outstanding characteristic of the Mon-pas; their cattle, sheep, and ponies certainly look well cared for. Working in shifts, the yak herdsmen spend much of their time each year in the mountain pastures, their movements being controlled by that of their animals, which seek the cooler heights in summer. Yaks provide the people who live at higher altitudes with all their requirements of butter and cheese, which are regular items in their diet. The butter is usually churned with tea liquor and salt to make a very nourishing drink for those who like their tea to taste like that. The cheese is sometimes dried hard and cut into cubes to be used as needed on long journeys. They undoubtedly provide much-needed calories in this cold climate.

The main occupation of the Mon-pas is, however, agriculture. In spite of the poor soil, they manage to make their farms quite productive by a judicious use of animal manure and leaf compost. Barley is the principal crop, the flour being an important article of food. Barley is also much used in the distilling of the highly potent local liquor. Beans and potatoes are also grown.

The Mon-pas naturally use a lot of wool in their weaving. They do their own carding, spinning, and dyeing. The men habitually wear a loose, buttonless coat with generously overlapping folds that they secure at the waist with a belt, using the recesses for keeping small articles. They wear trousers that do not quite touch the ankles, tucking them into hand-stitched knee-high leather boots that, despite being generally heelless, do not appear to handicap traveling up and down the often slippery hill tracks. Younger women generally prefer medium-length frocks and open-fronted jackets

for everyday wear, although older matrons affect the Tibetan style of dress. Both men and women wear the hair-cap (*kong-shhum*) which usually has five projecting tufts around the rim, although the *mago-thimbu-shhum* of the people of the higher altitudes near the border has as many as twenty tufts.

Many Mon-pa families have secondary occupations. Their women make beautiful carpets, rugs, and seat covers. The dragon motif is popular and is brought out by a harmonious use of colors that reveals artistry of a high order. This skill in the blending of colors is also seen in Mon-pa paintings, whether on a grand scale as in their murals or in religious *tankas*. The art of painting may have had its beginnings in the monasteries, but it has certainly spread out to the masses. Wooden utensils of delicate finish are often turned with crude-looking tools, the motive power for the unsophisticated lathes being provided by small boys working the treadles. The blocks of wood (usually birch) are usually steeped in boiling water and then dried to prevent warping and cracking before being shaped. The finished products, lacquered and painted with beautiful designs, make effective decorative pieces for the living room. Indigenous paper, exclusively used by monk-

Aka children, Arunachal Pradesh.

scribes, is manufactured from the bark of a species of laurel, and incense sticks, which are used in their rituals, are obtained from by-products of the juniper. The manufacture of these articles is restricted to a few localities.

Religion has undoubtedly played a definitive part in shaping the character and temperament of the Mon-pa people. Whatever their station in life, their bearing and manners belie a superior culture.

One can at most make an intelligent guess about how long the Mon-pas have been Buddhists. Monastic lore affirms that the great Indian monk Padma-Sambhava (Lopon Rimpoche to the Mon-pas), who introduced Buddhism into Tibet in the eighth century A.D., visited the Mon-pa area afterwards and laid the foundations of that faith there. Several places in western Kameng are associated in local traditions with the name of the monk. It is possible that by the twelfth century, Buddhism had already replaced the old Bon-po religion in the Mon-pa country. The local people remember with pride the fact that the Sixth Dalai Lama, Tsangyang Gyatso, was a Mon-pa, born near Urgye-ling or Urgyanling Gom-pa a few kilometers below Tawang, the site of the great Lamaist monastery believed to be the largest south of the Himalayas. This monastery is very much alive today. Standing on a commanding site covering a few acres, the whole complex, surrounded by a high wall that gives it the appearance of a fort, is visible from a great distance. The monastery is believed to have been constructed about A.D. 1645 under the inspiring leadership of the monk Mera Lama. There is an aura of antiquity about the place, from the heavy wooden gates and the cobbled courtyard to the chapel from which one may hear the murmur of monks at prayer. The library possesses hundreds of volumes of sacred texts, each set securely bound between two decorative wooden slabs, as well as documents of a secular character—records and accounts of historical importance. Discipline and strict observance of protocol mark the deportment of the inmates, whether ordained hierarchy or novices.

Although the practice of sending up one child from each family for the priesthood seems to be losing favor, there did not seem to be any dearth of aspirants at the time of my last visit to the monstery in the fall of 1979.

For Arunachal Pradesh, the pace of progress during the past thirty years has been very rapid, more rapid than has been the experience of any other tribal area in northeast India. It is not impossible that some communities, in particular those of remote areas, find the transition from a state of comparative non-control to one of organized polity unsettling. The prohibition of head-hunting in Tirap was at first considered a threat to the prosperity of the community: Did not the acquisition of heads constitute an accretion of soul power? Similarly, the abolition of slavery in those areas where it was prevalent was looked upon as quite an unreasonable interference. It may be remarked that the type of slavery or, perhaps better, serfdom practiced in the territory is a far cry from the kind of slavery that implies harsh treatment, confinement to barracks, and breaking up of families. The serfs in most cases lived a life hardly different from that of their masters; they moved freely and they had free access to the masters' houses, where they often ate and slept. True, they had to keep their place, but otherwise there was little for them to complain about. An Apa Tani master might, and often did, send his serfs to the plains of Assam to sell his goods and bring back the articles that he needed. Incidents there—serious incidents in the Bangni and Tagin areas—have been symbolic of the reaction of untouched communities to what they considered were threats to their way of life. What might be termed the government's policy of paternalism, a refusal to overreact to sporadic disturbance of the peace and treatment of each such situation in isolation, has obviously paid dividends, as evidenced by the fact that over this period of thirty years the government has had to tackle only the two serious incidents mentioned. On the credit side, it has established peace and security for everybody. There are many people who recall that there was a time when it was unthinkable for people to travel out of their villages except in strong, well-armed groups. The great majority of the tribal people are simple, unsophisticated, and as yet untouched by the less pleasant features of "civilization." There is no doubt, however, that with the improvement of communication there is bound to be a change in the situation, but the built-in safeguards that each community has evolved over the centuries to protect itself from upsetting influences could still be effective. The Inner Line regulations preventing uncontrolled influx from outside, in any case, offer added protection. It would seem that the greater dangers are those posed by more subtle influences which may well lead to a shedding of old values that have certainly contributed to the development of a character marked by strength, self-reliance, honesty, and truthfulness—traits that still distinguish most tribal people in this part of the world. The adoption of a money economy in place of the old one, based on capital stock like land, cattle, and the like, has resulted in affluence for many. This has proved unsettling in many tribal communities elsewhere, as wealth among them often creates an inordinate urge to get more and more of it somehow. Again, there have been a number of important developments leading to change in the traditional social arrangement; among them is the institution of elected councils at all levels and the erosion of the authority of the councils of adults, in the function of which maturity and experience are counted as desirable qualities.

The people of Arunachal Pradesh, however, have this advantage: they have the experiences of other communities to guide and warn them. Conservatives may deplore the rapidity with which the winds of change have impinged upon the life of the people of this mountain arcadia, but it is helpful to reflect that the right people to try out experiments with a view to securing for themselves a fuller life are often themselves.

PART FIVE   EAST ASIA

FOW

MONGOLIA

Tien Shan

Beijing

Kunlun Mountains

Mount
Su-Meru
(-Kailasha)

Himalayas

TIBET

NEPAL

CHINA

4 •Pemakod

1

3
Yunnan

•Kweilin

BURMA

2

LAOS

THAILAND

VIETNAM

CAMBODIA

JAPAN

Tokyo

5

East Asia

MOUNTAIN COMMUNITIES

1. Huang, Nung, Mak, La, Ning, Lao
2. Hmong, Lisu, Lahu, Karen
3. Miao-Yiao
4. Tibetans
5. Ainu

18. The Tribal Whirlpool: Mountain People in the People's Republic of China

CHRISTOPHER L. SALTER

Wherever it may be, they like to burn off the fields,
Round and round, creeping over the mountain's belly.
When they bore the tortoise and get the "rain" trigram,
Up the mountain they go and set fire to the prostrate trees.
Startled munjacks run, and then stare back;
Flocks of pheasants make *i-auk* sounds.
The red blaze forms sunset clouds far off,
Light coals fly into the city walls. . . .
They drop their seeds among the warm ashes;
These, borne by the "essential heat" (*yang*), burst into
  buds and shoots.
Verdant and vivid, after a single rain,
Spikes of trumpet vine come out like a cloud.
The snake men chant with folded hands;
Neither plowing nor hoeing involve their hearts.
From the first they have found the temper of this land,
Whose every inch holds an excess of "essential cold" (*yin*).
                       [Schafer 1967:54–55]

With the graphic poetry of Liu Yü-hsi of the early ninth century, major elements of the life of the mountain people of China are conjured up as images of land use and technology. Add to that imagery an observation of an early-twentieth-century adventurer Harry Franck—"High mountains and swift rivers naturally make the southwest a racial garden, a tribal whirlpool, almost as bad as New York. . . . This part of China [is] an ethnological maelstrom" (Franck 1925:497–99)—and we see the potential for isolation, conflict, and cultural interaction. Finally, we can make the scene contemporary with a quote from Joan Robinson: "Once, when the People's Liberation Army was carrying out maneuvers in the mountains [of southwest China] smoke was seen billowing up from the virgin forest, and there was found a community of hunters, dressed in skins, with a language of their own, but no known history" (Robinson 1975:21). An irregular blend of swidden agriculture, cultural separation, and occasional continuing isolation then sketch in the fundamental elements for this speculative paper on the mountain peoples of the People's Republic of China.

The mountainous regions of China may be divided into five regions. In the far southwest, the high plateau of Tibet exists as one semiautonomous region (Region I). To the north, the mountain peoples of the Kunlun and Tien Shan massifs and lesser ranges of Xinjiang comprise Region II. In North China, west of the North China Plain, lies the Taihangshan, which guides the Yellow River south and then penetrates into China's northeast. These mountains in Region III have a moderately dense population, but it is made up primarily of Han people and not aboriginal mountain folk so much as impoverished peasants who have slowly been pressed onto this marginal land through a combination of personal and demographic misfortunes. Region IV is the pair of islands to the east of China—Taiwan in the north and Hainan in the south—and these both have mountain people who are non-Han and who have maintained persistent independence and cultural individuality notwithstanding the high population densities of the adjoining agricultural and urban plains. Finally, Region V embraces the broken plateaus and well-forested mountain systems of southwestern China, ranging from the Sichuan Basin and Yunnan in the west to the coast of China and from the hills surrounding the Canton lowlands through the Fujian massif to the Changjiang Delta. This area has the largest population of non-Han mountain folk, living either in traditional mountain settings or upland brigades and villages into which they have slowly been forced during the past decades, even centuries.

Tibet is covered in another section of this volume. The scattered upland settlements in Xinjiang are politically and bibliographically in the shadow of the increasingly Sinicized lowland and valley settlements of the non-Han nomadic peoples (Krader 1963:1–32). These mountain people come the closest to paralleling European transhumance upland patterns.

Region III is important for our concerns because it is the home of the model village for China from 1964 to 1977. During that period, millions of Chinese agriculturalists were transported on tourist pilgrimages to the mountain village of Dazhai (Tachai) in the Taihang Mountains in Shanxi Province, sixty miles southeast of the provincial capital, Taiyuan. This is the only time in Chinese history that lowland villagers from throughout China proper were tutored in farming practices with a montane model (Salter 1976, 1978). Although the resident population of Dazhai is fully Han, the terraces, irrigation, cropping patterns, agricultural organization, and political consciousness were standard assignment for brigade and commune representatives from non-Han and Han regions alike for more than a

Northern China. Photo by M. Tobias.

decade. Although the revolutionary tour circuit does not include Dazhai any longer, stone terraces in all China's provinces attest to the landscape influences this mountain community has had. It has played a role seemingly far out of proportion with the five hundred villagers it has resident on the flanks of the mountains of Xiyang Hsien.

The Kaoshan people of Taiwan and the Li-Miao of Hainan (the islands of Region IV) have both been objects of considerable government policy for the past three decades. In Taiwan, the mountain zone has been basically closed to Han Chinese with the exception of a cross-island highway that requires mountain passes for transit. At the same time, the Joint Commission for Rural Reconstruction has steadily promoted plans that would bring the mountain aboriginals into closer and more productive contact with the lowland Han culture of the island (Salter 1970).

A combination of rapid economic growth with associated vocational opportunity in the lowlands and continuing pressure by government officials to stop swidden fires of slash-and-burn agriculture in the uplands has led to a steady migration stream out of the high-lands. In addition, Taiwan has had an unusual demographic situation with a large population of single males, many of whom would not consider marrying a Taiwanese. This population is the retiring military men of the Nationalist forces who came to Taiwan from mainland China in the late 1940s. Because of Taiwanese alignment with the Japanese during the Sino-Japanese War, these men paid special interest to the mountain tribes, who had a history of continuing conflict with the Japanese during their fifty-year tenure in Taiwan from 1895 to 1945. This marital and cultural union of Nationalist Chinese and young aborigine women served as an additional influence in the assimilation of this mountain minority into the Han majority.

On Hainan Island, various campaigns to introduce productive stands of rubber led to considerable forest clearance and planting of rubber trees. The Li and Miao of the southeastern part of the island were involved in some of this. In a larger sense, the general expansion of official Han interest in the island, with its productive agricultural base and iron and coal deposits, has led to further Chinese interaction with the montane as well as lowland minority peoples.

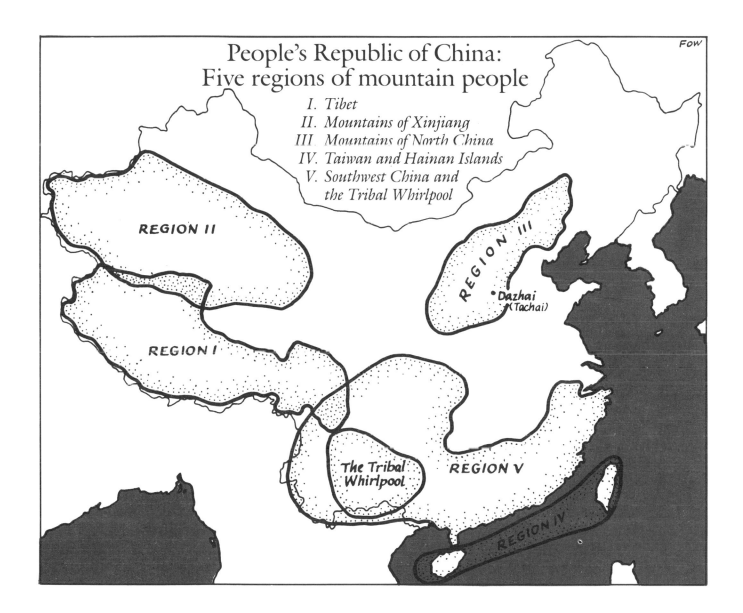

People's Republic of China:
Five regions of mountain people

I. Tibet
II. Mountains of Xinjiang
III. Mountains of North China
IV. Taiwan and Hainan Islands
V. Southwest China and
the Tribal Whirlpool

REGION II

REGION I

REGION III

•Dazhai
(Tachai)

The Tribal
Whirlpool

REGION V

REGION IV

Fow

The real zone, however, of significant mountain population is Region V, or the ranges and valleys of southwestern China. In the three provinces of Sichuan, Yunnan, Guizhou, and the Guangxi-Zhuang Autonomous Region, there is approximately 20 percent of China's total population, but nearly 50 percent of the non-Han total (*Illustrated Atlas of China* 1972:36–37). And a large—but indefinite—percentage of this population either resides in mountain settings or has economic or cultural interaction with the non-Han who live in the ranges.

The determination of exact numbers, percentages, and statistical trends plagues the student of China, and particularly the student of mountain peoples. Individual Chinese and non-Han peoples have traditionally been disinclined to produce exact figures on family size, livelihood, or farm production because of the potential for the taxman to follow the census taker. When Han Chinese officials have been responsible for getting such numbers from the mountain population who happen to reside in their administrative district, there has been much delegation of responsibility, casual estimation, and probably fabrication of numbers. In a detailed breakdown of the best census the Chinese have done, Theodore Shabad divides the non-Han populations into 150 language groups (the nearly universal criterion in China for Han and non-Han differentiation) and locations (Shabad 1972:39–43). By location of these autonomous regions, *chou, hsien,* and *hsiang* on the map of China, one can estimate that 79 of the non-Han locales have mountain population and that nearly 20 million of the 1953 census of 37 million non-Han Chinese were located in montane environments (Shabad 1972:38–53).

A further analysis of this contemporary figure of 3 percent to 4 percent of the non-Han population of China who live as mountain people will produce yet additional perspectives. Professor Herold Wiens—in one of the few scholarly studies on the southern reaches of China that includes detailed discussion of the non-Han population—sketched out the economy and setting of 361 tribes in this fifth region. Of the 361 tribes, 205 were characterized as having either a "mountain-habitat" or as farming with "fire-field agriculture" (Wiens 1967:49–54).

This region is further described by a geographer who traveled considerable distances in China when such a mode of research was still possible. George Cressey (1934:371) describes the region in this way: "The Southwestern Tableland is the most diverse region in all China in its human make-up. Only about half the population consists of real Chinese and the remainder is made up of a great variety of primitive

Kweilin, China. Photo by M. Tobias.

peoples. The Chinese themselves are all immigrants from other provinces and are chiefly found in the plains and in the more accessible valleys from which they have driven the original inhabitants. . . . [The non-Han generally] live in the mountains where they eke out a simple living as herdsmen, hunters, and primitive peoples. Cressey goes on to approximate the population density for this region at one hundred people per square mile in the mountainous areas (Cressey 1934: 373), while Wiens estimates densities for the mountain folk to be about twenty per square mile (Wiens 1967:331). Such variance even in the works of serious students of the Chinese scene seems to be customary in dealings with mountain peoples.

Two phenomena appear to be responsible for the increasing interest the Chinese have taken in the study of and dealings with their minority peoples. Although these non-Han amount to only 6 percent of the nearly billion people China currently has, "this six percent of the population occupies between 50 and 60 percent of China's territory" (Kraus 1979:269). Kraus goes on to point out that "many of the more primitive groups of southwest China are mindful of the long process by which Han settlers have occupied rich agricultural land, forcing minority peoples to retreat to mountain area" (1979:269). The combination of new economic and political pressures on the Chinese to make fuller and more productive use of their natural resources and China's own wish to be seen as a government that is supportive of minority rights has dictated Beijing policy for at least a decade. A thorough and provocative study done by June Teufel Dreyer traces the governmental relations between the Han and non-Han through three decades of somewhat erratic policy development (Dreyer 1976), while Wiens and Schafer carry it back centuries, even millenia (Wiens 1967; Schafer 1967).

In this century, one of the mountain resources that was most important to lowland China was the opium poppy. Like mountain folk all over the world, these various groups realized reluctantly that they did have some need for items of the lowlanders' technology and marketing. They also realized, however, that by the time a farmer hired two days' transport for the grains or fruits from his field, the drayage cost equaled the value of the farm produce. Just as corn liquor solved this problem for the Appalachian farmer in the United States, the sap of the opium poppy overcame the bulk transport constraint in southwestern China. By the turn of the century, Region V was the prime producer of opium in China. "It was estimated in 1923 in Yunnan that the poppy occupied two-thirds of the cultivated land during the winter season" (Cressey 1934:375). A good sense of the relative importance of this upland crop three-quarters of a century ago is given in the two-volume work by Sir Alexander Hosie (1914). This abundant growth of the poppy in most of the region, in small, upland plots as well as isolated valleys, continued actively into early revolutionary era.

Between the active efforts at suppression of the poppy in 1910 and the even more powerful government intervention in the 1950s, one especially interesting book came out on the mountain people of this region. It was the work of a sociologist at Yenching University in Beijing. His monograph, *The Lolo of Liang Shan* (*Liang-shan I-chia*), came from a field exploration Professor Lin Yueh-hua undertook in 1943. In that short work he compiled a clearer picture of the material and social components of the Lolo (more accurately called the I or the Nosu) culture. These peoples reside in the complex folds of the mountains that thrust up in the border regions of Sichuan, Yunnan, and Xizang.

In a short but detailed monograph Lin points out that the I live by a modified swidden farming system and that "every Lolo family has its own cultivated field, which constitutes its basic property. The wealth of a black Lolo household, however, is measured by the herd of animals it owns. Domesticated animals consist largely of sheep and goats, pastured by household slaves. The sheep pen is inside the walls of the house" (Lin 1961:90). Continuing, he points out that not only do the I have "white" I slaves, but they also take slaves from among the local Han Chinese who fall into their hands. "Black" Lolo are the traditional leaders, while the so-called "white" Lolo have traditionally been subjugated, have served as slaves to the black Lolo, and have a lower class status. The colors come from creation lore that speaks of "Black-bone and White-bone Lolo." These Chinese workers cultivate *sawah* (paddy rice) in the valleys while the I continue to be most concerned with productive upland cultivation of buckwheat, maize, vegetables, and—in 1943—the opium poppy. The black I do not farm, but rather give over their time to matters of animal husbandry. Lin believes this pattern emerged because "animal husbandry was originally the main economic activity of the black Lolo and . . . the Lolo were formerly a pastoral people. It was only after the conquest of the white Lolo and the capture of the Han-Chinese as slaves that the black Lolo started farming by forcing the conquered people to cultivate the land. Most of the white Lolo were originally Han-Chinese who, having lived in the Lolo territory for many years, forgot their Han Chinese ancestry and considered themselves as Lolo" (Lin 1961: 85–86). Although anyone who has spent any time reviewing Chinese images of their own nation would argue that any amount of time could truly cause immigrants to "forget their Chinese ancestry," Lin does develop an interesting sequence in the colonization and cultural development in this area of 10,000- to 14,000-foot (3,000- to 4,300-meter) mountains and steep-sided valleys. It is just such an area as this that Franck was alluding to when he spoke of the tribal whirlpool in the high mountains and swift rivers.

Government policies toward the mountain people in Region V varied from General Stillwell's efforts with the Burma Road in the 1940s to the early PRC reflection of Soviet policies toward minority peoples (Dreyer 1976:1–60). It was only in the 1950s that the Chinese began to see the vital necessity of securing their borders and making themselves more visible as a nation not only tolerant of, but also supportive of, minority cultural development. With concerted efforts to relocate Han populations in the border areas—although the inner Asian margins of Xinjiang were more influenced by this than were the southwestern Region V borders—the Chinese realized that a policy toward China's non-Han had to be developed.

There was, however, a fundamental contradiction to be overcome. If the mountain people were to be allowed, nay, encouraged to flourish with the continued use of their indigenous languages and customs, then what role could the Chinese from the crowded eastern seaboard play in fomenting economic reorganization and development of the region? And, at the same time, if the mobility managers of the Chinese government were intent upon sending educated urban youth into the non-Han territories of valleys and mountains alike, what possible incentive could be used? One of the solutions to this clash of peoples and place was the introduction of lowland, machine-assisted cultivation in place of traditional upland swidden farming patterns. The increased presence of the Chinese, with their barefoot doctors, new skills in animal care, and interest in the creation of institutes for the education of the national minorities, began to work in a progressive fashion to bring some of the populations down to the valleys and take some of the Han technology and patterns up the slopes.

One of the best windows on the process of culture change in the whirlpool is the continuing series of articles on the improvement of the material culture of China's minority peoples in *China Reconstructs* and *China Pictorial*. In these short, formula articles two facets of the mountain scene are generally stressed. First, there is discussion of the government's promotion of traditional indigenous cultural patterns. Second, it is announced in what ways agriculture has been modified to include irrigation, permanent field farming, some minor mechanization, and reorganization of the labor force. The inevitable outcome of such a transformation is higher productivity coupled with greater self-esteem. The following is an example of such an article focusing on a mountain group on the northern margin of Region V:

> In the old society crops had been grown with the primitive slash-and-burn method. There were few fields and little water. In 1964 Chairman Mao had called upon agriculture to learn from Tachai (Dazhai). Lota's members began to level hills to make fields, dig wells and cut canals through the mountains. Today water flows down the slopes to irrigate terraced fields. Rice fields are 80% irrigated. Within five years grain output increased one-and-a-half times. . . . Every year since 1970 over 600,000 people in the Tuchia-Miao Autonomous Prefecture have taken part in basic farmland improvements. [Tuchia-Miao Autonomous Prefecture 1978 : 35]

The cultural implications are profound for a transition from traditional swidden agriculture with its asso-

ciated self-sufficiency and multicrop planting pattern to the development of *sawah* beds with demands for permanent field preparation and single-crop production. There is a need for a much higher level of community organization and cooperation. There is new labor needed for the engineering of the pond, canal, and dam networks. And, perhaps most significantly, there is the establishment of a higher need for interdependence between the rice grower and other sectors of the agricultural and the merchant population. All of these changes have a greater likelihood of leading to more rapid acculturation into the Han society than to perpetuating the cultural autonomy of the montane minority.

In the example cited above from the Tuchia-Miao article, note also the invocation of the slogan, "In Agriculture, Learn from Tachai (Dazhai)," which communicated a message of political as well as agricultural moment. For at least a decade, the mountain habitat of the Dazhai brigade was being used as a standard by which farming communities throughout China measured their productivity and cooperative efforts in improvement of their farming base. It had relevance for all mountain peoples, non-Han or Han. The range of experiences noted in this spring of articles drawn from the tribal whirlpool area includes additional instruction from the experience of Dazhai ("A Visit to the Greater Miao Mountains" 1976), a tour of more than five hundred minority people (all in their native costumes) to Beijing to meet Premier Hua Kuo-feng in addition to visiting Dazhai (Wang 1979), the agricultural shift away from swidden to the growing of irrigated rice ("The Shui People—A New Life" 1976), the replacement of virgin forest with cash crops (Latsch-Heberer 1978), and the introduction of some mechanized farming (Zhi 1980). Change appears to be universal.

Clearly, variations occur in the specifics of each mountain-people case, but the general progression toward new productivity in agriculture, greater involvement in the cash economy, and steady improvement in the relations between the Han Chinese and these upland minorities is the news that comes from China. The continuing difficulty outsiders have in gaining access to the mountains of Region V for field research makes these images less broadly based than is ideal, but even with the limited perspective available, it is clear to see that the mountain peoples of China are more involved in lowland-upland interaction than has ever been the case before. Such a situation will probably lead to the curious occurrence of a short-lived fluorescence of native cultural expression and aboriginal independence, followed by increasingly rapid "Hanification."

The inevitable linkages of single-crop *sawah* agriculture weave a network around all aspects of mountain life. Cultural exchanges built around the transfer of hand-embroidered capes for transistor radios have historically led to the disappearance of the hand loom and the implacement of a community (brigade) television set. Notwithstanding the uphill gradient characteristic of the mountainous regions in China, the eventual outcome is bound to be cultural assimilation of all but the most fiercely independent and geographically isolated non-Han peoples. Perhaps the only significant difference in China is that assimilation of 6 percent of a base population of approximately one billion means that some sixty million people are to be absorbed. The magnitude of that reality alone suggests that Region V, particularly, will continue to afford mountain settings for culturally distinct mountain people for some time to come.

19.   Beyond Cathay: The Hill Tribes of China

GARY SNYDER

The lands south of the Kiang (Yangtze) are broad and sparsely populated, and the people live on rice and fish soups. They burn off the fields and flood them to kill the weeds, and are able to gather all the fruit, berries, and univalve and bivalve shellfish they want without waiting for merchants to come around selling them. Since the land is so rich in edible products, there is no fear of famine, and therefore the people are content to live along from day to day; they do not lay away stores of goods, and many of them are poor. As a result, in the region south of the Yangtze and Huai rivers no one ever freezes or starves to death, but on the other hand there are no very wealthy families.

—SSU-MA CH'IEN, THE GRAND HISTORIAN
(D. 90 B.C.)[1]

These people of the south, though the same race as the northern Chinese, were once considered barbarians, "monkeys with caps on." Now they are thoroughly assimilated, and most are fully accounted as civilized. Only in remote enclaves in the hills does some trace of the vast precivilized southern Chinese world survive.

The source of the wealth of the Chinese state was the labor of the masses applied to cultivation of millet and rice. To the northeast of the northern Chinese heartlands (the lowlands along the Yellow River) the land climbs and the rainfall drops off. It is a high grassland and semidesert unsuited for agriculture. The south, difficult though it seemed, was convertible to agriculture up all the valleys and branches, so China expanded south. By A.D. 605 a grain transport canal system from the Yangtze north to the capital was completed, and southern China gradually began to become the most productive part of the empire. Over the centuries the lowland-dwelling natives were converted to Chinese ways, their Chinese names put on the tax lists, and the ethnic past forgotten, or Hua (the old term for heartland Chinese) immigrants simply overwhelmed them with their numbers. However, the specialized agricultural system that was so appropriate in the lowlands had less economic use for the hills. Hundreds of upland islands of non-Hua culture survived as scattered forest communities in which hunting and gathering was combined with slash-and-burn farming. They did not give up easily; within the area of Hupei-Shensi-Honan-Anhwei, the very center, there were over forty insurrections of tribal peoples between A.D. 404 and A.D. 561.[2] South of the Kiang, or Yangtze, watershed and west in Kweichow and Yunnan there are some very

large populations that are mostly non-Chinese, known nowadays by such names as Yi, Pai, Tai, Miao, Yao, and Lisu.

Much of this southern landscape is over three thousand feet high and rises in western Yunnan and Szechwan as high as fifteen thousand feet. The southeastern part has the heaviest rainfall in all China—as much as ninety inches a year on the hills. In Kweichow, the main home of the Miao people, the protected forest of Wumong Mountain gives us a sample of what the southwestern forest was all once like: walnuts, alders, dogwoods, tulip trees, liquidambar, beech, evergreen oak, chinquapins, and members of the laurel family such as cinnamon and sassafras. Outside such protected areas the later successional pines are now dominant.[3]

In T'ang and Sung times the non-Hua peoples of the south were collectively called the Man, the "Man" of Marco Polo's "Manzi," the area in his travels south of what he calls "Cathay." *Man* is the word translated into English as "barbarian." The oldest name for the area, in Medieval Chinese pronunciation, is Nam-Ywat, which in modern Mandarin is Nan-Yueh—"South Yueh"—and in another modern pronunciation (the "south" reversed) "Vietnam." In the politics of T'ang times this southern region included the whole southern Chinese coast, and the major city was Canton; the territorial boundary was south of the delta of the Red River, south of Hanoi, where Chinese cultural influence was finally brought up against the cultural influence of India—the Cham empire. *Ywat* probably means "ax"; the southerners were people of the "stone ax." In Vietnam the surviving hill tribes, essentially of the same lineages as those farther north, are now called "montagnards." These many peoples speak languages of the Sino-Tibetan family: Tibetan, Burman, Tai, Yao, and Miao. The tribes were called Huang, Nung, Mak, La, Ning, Lao. On the southwestern border of Yunnan a few peoples spoke a Mon-Khmer language.

Traveling through the south in the thirteenth century, Marco Polo writes of the freedom of the women and constant rumors of violence and brigandage.[4] Some of this may have been heard from prudish and patriarchal Chinese. He describes a rich life: "The traveller enters a country of great mountains and valleys and forests, through which he makes his way for twenty days towards the west. . . . The people are idolaters, living on the fruits of the earth, on wild game and domestic animals. There are lions, bears, and lynxes, harts, stags, and roebuck, besides great numbers of the little deer that produce musk."[5] (It seems unlikely he saw lions.)

The Hua people regarded the tribal Man as semi-animals, whose speech resembled the chatter of monkeys. There was a totemic legend of a dog ancestor among the Miao, the Nosu, or Lolo, now called Yi by the Peoples' Republic that had a "pine tree ancestor." Such legends only confirmed this view for the conquerors. Yet the Hua found the Man women beautiful. There was a regular trade in girls of the southern tribes who were sold as concubine-slaves to wealthy Chinese of the north. The fighting courage of the men was also acknowledged—"They love swords, and treat death lightly."[6] The Chinese scorned them for their occasional cannibalism and head-hunting and then sent against them the sadistic general Yang Szu-hsu, who built a pyramid of the bodies of natives he killed in A.D. 722 and reputedly took scalps and peeled the skin from the faces of prisoners.[7]

In spite of uprisings and struggle there were also periods of peaceful trade between the tribesmen and the Chinese. The government policy of "controlling barbarians with barbarians" meant sanctioning the authority of some chiefs over others, and in return receiving tribute: kingfisher feathers, elephant tusks, and rhinoceros horn.[8] In China, as in North America and Siberia, when natural peoples get caught in a trade relationship with a civilization, it is the wildlife which suffers first.

Liu Yu-hsi was exiled in Kwangtung in the ninth century. Edward Schafer translates his "Song of the Man":

"Sakya coming out of his mountain retreat," painted by Kato Moriuke, Kano School, Japan, 1632, after earlier Sung Dynasty work by Liang K'ai (Chinese); 42cm x 30cm, oil on silk. Tobias Private Collection.

The speech of the Man is a *kou-chou* sound
The dress of the Man is a *pan-lan* linen.
Their odorous raccoons dig out the sand rats;
At seasonal periods they sacrifice to P'an-hu.
Should they meet a stranger riding a horse,
They are flustered, and glance round like
startled muntjacs.
With axes at their waists they ascend the
high mountains,
Proposing to go where no old road exists.[9]

Assimilated Man individuals were scarcely distinguishable from Hua Chinese, and some rose to local power as merchants or administrators. Perhaps the most famous aboriginal half-breed in Chinese history is the sixth patriarch of the Ch'an sect, Hui-nêng. Hui-nêng's father was Hua, but his mother was an aboriginal— possibly a Lao. His biography apologetically says, "Although he was soaked and dyed with the airs of the Man and the customs of the Lao, they were not deep in him."[10] According to one legend, Bodhidharma himself came into China by way of the southern port of Canton. (In the territory of the Miao nation, now called Kweichow, early Buddhists carved images on the cliffs in the southern style of Javanese and South Indian art.)[11] The "Southern School" of Ch'an, which may have started with Hui-nêng, is notorious for its vivid rejection of received forms and ideas and its demand that we look directly into the ground of Mind without preconceptions. Perhaps the earthy and independent lives of the indigenous peoples, through Hui-nêng, contributed to the force and flavor of this still flourishing school of Ch'an/Zen.

(The most prized of all incenses used in the temples of the Far Eastern Buddhist world is from resinous aloe wood, called *jinko* in Japanese. Its smoke pervades the high-ceilinged head temples at Founders Day ceremonies in Kyoto even today. It was obtained in trade with the isolated aboriginal Li people of Hainan, who got axes, cereals, silks, and hatchets in return.[12]

Today, the People's Republic of China has made almost half of Kweichow province, where three million Miao are living, into an autonomous district. The whole province of Kwangsi, home of seven million Tai-speaking Chuang, is also autonomous. Yunnan has a number of autonomous districts for the Tibet-Burman hill people. Mainstream Chinese and Christian missionaries alike have been jolted by the Miao. An American traveler of the twenties wrote: "Every village had its club-house where the girls gathered nightly to sing and dance, and where the youths not of their own but from neighboring villages came to try them out as possible wives."[13] The women wore brilliant multicolored blouses, jackets, and skirts—"red perhaps predominating in the intricate patterns, but no conceivable combination of colors barred. Evidently there was nothing worn beneath the short, pleated skirts that swung so saucily as the girls walked . . . cut so conveniently for hoeing corn on a steep hillside."[14] The Miao distilled their own alcohol and had a supposedly spectacular orgiastic festival, called "Fifth of the Fifth," up until recently.

It is significant that the mountain forests, much altered in the past few centuries, were protected and replanted more by the local mountain people than by the economically dominant Chinese, at least before the PRC took over.[15] The way the tribes saw their wild hills as home, and the wildlife as fellow beings, is apparent in their magical folklore term for the tiger: in myths and tales he is called "Streaked Lad."

20.   The Japanese Mountains: Crowds, Convenience, and the Sacred

ROYALL TYLER

This book is about mountain peoples. Are the Japanese a mountain people like the others represented here? I wonder. They are not exactly a mountain culture, since from the beginning most of them have done their best to live on whatever little plains or valley bottoms they could find. Besides, their culture is too vast and too rich to qualify them as a mountain people in any strict sense. From their low places, however, the Japanese have always seen mountains, and these mountains—even the very small ones—have certainly stood very large in their thoughts.

There have of course been since ancient times hunters, woodcutters, remote mountain villages. Still, the perception of the mountains as another world, the abode of numinous beings, has many deep roots in Japan. Anyone, I am sure, can understand that. Cults centered upon sacred mountains were the real core of Japanese religion for a very long time. There exist beautiful icons of mountains as, in effect, manifestations of pure enlightenment. Indeed, in centuries past there may have been in Japan well over a thousand religiously significant mountains.

Times have changed. Folk beliefs and practices that even urban Japanese suppose to have died out in their country are still in some places very much alive. Nonetheless, the tide of the modern world is high, and it is still rising. In the old poetry, man and maid often assured each other that their love would last "till the waves wash over Pine Mountain." Well, on the summit of some Pine Mountains the waves are already breaking. When the convoy of tour buses roars into the mountaintop parking lot, the outrage has much to do with infidelity, or with that particular sort of disrespect that masquerades as appreciation.

Let me speak of what I know best, and tell you about the Omine Range. No mountains in Japan have been more honored.

From Yoshino, a storied village just south of the Yamato Plain, the chain of peaks runs down to the dark hills of Kumano nearly to the sea. The highest peak rises just short of two thousand meters, but the slopes are steep, the valleys narrow. From some spots you can see four or five waterfalls, blooming like flowers on the mountainside. Only once in every few hours of walking do you find a place both level enough and clear enough for a small tent. *Sasa,* a tough sort of dwarf bamboo, springs up thickly everywhere, and pushing through it on the trail, you are soaked long after the rain has passed.

One of the peaks in the Omine Range was called in times past Kane-no-mitake, "Golden Mountain." Some said that there lay stored in Kane-no-mitake all the gold that was to transfigure the world at the coming of Miroku, the Buddha of the Future. On this mountain first appeared Zaō Gongen, the lord of the range, an awesome deity whose temple at the summit is active still.

The Golden Mountain is now called Sanjō-ga-take, and it remains for a while yet inviolate. In fact there continues in force on Sanjō-ga-take an ancient prohibition, and women may not approach it. The boundary of the forbidden zone keeps shrinking in toward the mountain, however, and I doubt the restriction will last forever. Reader, do not applaud, though you be a woman, a scholar, and a veteran of El Capitán. The ban has its reasons, and its lifting will not throw open to you the mysteries of the mountain. It will only confirm that the mysteries are lost, dissolved into our future's murky air.

They are fading even now. Pilgrims still make ritual ascents of Sanjō-ga-take, but where once they walked in proud procession all the way from Kyoto, they now ride air-conditioned buses and trains to Yoshino itself. A time-saver, no doubt. People are so busy, and the summers are so hot. Not that these ritual climbs are a casual practice, but they now come packaged in foil, as it were. On Ontake, another sacred and much higher mountain, a road has been laid to the very summit, and devotees now ride happily upward in comfort. It sounds like sense, but it is nonsense. Instant pilgrimage: your mountaintop pops up for you, seasoned with gods and magnificent vistas, like a full-course frozen dinner from a radar range.

Speaking of radar, there is the example of Misen. Several peaks in the Omine Range are actually higher than Sanjō-ga-take, and Misen is one of them. Its name is a Japanese version of Su-Meru, the central mountain of the Buddhist cosmos. At the top of Misen is a shrine to Benzaiten, a goddess of water, of music, of wealth, and of wisdom. Beside the shrine is a *goma* site: a place for working the rite of fire. Over shrine and *goma* hearth, however, loftier than the trees, stands now the inevitable microwave relay tower.

Two friends and I went over Misen in the fall of 1978. Since one of us was a woman, we had not followed the regular pilgrimage route by way of Sanjō-ga-take. We arrived in the late afternoon. Clouds had erased the celebrated view. Indeed, what with the wet skies and the wet *sasa*, we were very damp. To our astonishment we found, looming out of the mist, an enormous, brand-new shelter hut. It contained huge piles of bedding and could probably sleep 150 people. No doubt it is often crowded in summer. The Japanese travel in large groups, and they love hiking. Those hikers can even telephone home now from the top of Misen. What would you have done? We did not pitch our tent in the rain. We paid our money, right there on Mount Su-Meru, and slept, just the three of us, in spacious, modern ease.

South of Misen we crossed Hakkayō-ga-take, the highest point in the range. Alas, the clouds were still thick. There was a mysterious tentlike structure on the narrow summit among the pines.

Then came several hours of true magic. We entered indeed another world. By peak and saddle we walked the narrow ridge, through a realm as alive as the minds of the immortals. Up there the fairies dance or sigh, according to the weather, on every stone and leaf. The rocks, the copious moss, the light, seemed as pristine as interstellar space, though as rich as the eons of earth. We passed over the sharp summit of Shaka-ga-take (named for the Buddha Shakyamuni) and came down, by the late afternoon, to a saddle called Jinzen.

It was quite inexpressibly beautiful. This was where, in an earlier day, the highest initiation was given: the initiation into the realm of enlightenment. The rite included a re-creation of the world. En no Gyōja, the arch-wizard of the Japanese mountains, is said to have lived here. Trickling from a rock face nearby is a tiny spring, and before it, wonderful to tell, there is a stone monument to En no Gyōja's beard. The trees and grass were green and gold with the setting sun. We saw a shabby hut and a little Buddhist chapel. The space was busy with people. It was a team of ecologists.

These ecologists were doing a survey. No doubt the structure on Hakkyō-ga-take had been theirs. A commendable purpose! But they had their gear strewn all over the chapel as well as the hut. They were catching the water of the spring in big pans and cooking dinner in the obvious place for the *goma* fire.

We put up our tent some distance from them and passed an extremely strange night. There were spirits abroad. They invaded our sleep with dreams the like of

Japanese Pilgrim. Photo by James H. Katz.

which we had never dreamed before. Beings crackled and panted and thumped outside. At times we lay awake expecting some Shape any minute to loom in the tent door, or to crush the tent entirely. They might well have been unhappy, these spirits, displaced and little honored as they were, with snoring, well-intentioned bodies all over the very chapel floor.

Near Jinzen is a fork; you can go on south along the ridge or drop down toward the east out of the range. Later I walked most of the trail to the south, and I found there more microwave towers, and high tension lines, too, not to mention a road passing through a tunnel under a low point in the ridge. But this time we, like most pilgrims and hikers, turned left and headed down.

Down toward the road. For there are roads pressing in upon the Omine Range. Despite the extraordinary ruggedness of the terrain, there are excellent north-south roads, with regular bus service, along the valleys both to the east and to the west. The next big, obvious thought is to put a road down the middle: a skyline drive. Though the area is a national park, I see no reason not to suppose that someone is already dreaming of the project. Similar roads exist by now elsewhere in Japan. The tourists and Sunday drivers seem not to mind the astronomical tolls.

And there are the lumbering interests. I know a man who, in the name of a religious corporation, owns three small hills in the mountains north of Kyoto. Being sacred ground, his hills are not logged; hence they have upon them some valuable timber. The man says the local lumber men have a very beady eye upon his woods. As for Omine, there are lumber roads snaking into the mountains from both sides, and south of Jinzen I walked straight through several logging sites. Around Sanjō-ga-take I have seen, affixed to trees along the trail, appeals from an environmental group to halt such invasions. But I wonder if it can be done.

We headed down, as I said, toward the road. The road I mean is the bus route. The way was very steep indeed. At last we came to Zenki, a place that used to be a thriving religious community and that used to provide support for hermits in the area of Jinzen and Shaka-ga-take. Now, alas, only one man lives there. Zenki will survive as a vestige a while longer, but more than that I do not expect. Then some way past Zenki we got to the logging road.

We had ten kilometers of that road. It was hot and flat and hard. Crews were clear-cutting whole hills along the way, probably preparing them for tree farming. Lumber was being hauled out on creaky cables overhead. At the bottom of the gorge there was still the river, swift and clear, and tumbling sometimes in spectacular falls.

Then the river grew slow and fat. It widened, it stilled. Somewhere down there was a dam. Streams leaping down the hillside sank and died. Drifts of wood chips floated on the stagnant waters, and here and there along the unnatural shore were inexplicable encrustations of little fishermen. Apparently some boat was making the rounds, delivering them to their inaccessible spots and picking them up a few silent hours later. I checked the map: over the mountains to the west, in the noble Totsugawa Gorge, was another such

reservoir. Wood chips and the bloated corpses of rivers: Omine was surrounded. At the bus stop we stuck coins in the soft drink machine and guzzled like any idiots ice-cold, semifruit juice, its flavor too blatantly good to be true.

Such are the signs of the times. There is plenty of life in Omine yet. The crowds are growing, though, and the various pressures, while knowledge and practice of the old religion are wearing thin. I have heard of a man doing the practice of the thousand days' pilgrimage from Yoshino to Sanjō-ga-take (one round trip per day, no mean feat). No doubt he must push through the packs of hikers. I myself have not seen such practice in the Omine Mountains, but on Mount Hiei I met someone like that. He is a brave man.

Mount Hiei is at the northeast corner of Kyoto. It is a venerable religious center with a sometimes turbulent history. Even now the woods are deep in places, and wild monkeys roam there. There are still temples scattered over the mountain. There is also, however, a first-class road to the top, up which roar streams of buses and cars. The view, it is true, is splendid, so much so that the very summit of Mount Hiei is a paying amusement area at the center of which rises, mushroom-shaped, a futuristic tower. The tower of course contains a restaurant, and studded round its circumference are speakers blaring upbeat pop.

The monk I speak of has recently completed the thousand days' circumambulation of the mountain. In the final period of his practice he was walking 50 miles (80 kilometers) a day. People waited along his route to be blessed. Yet the mountain is decapitated, as it were, its head replaced with that of some monstrous child's toy robot. I regard the achievement of this monk with mingled awe and horror. Perhaps I am not sure that he is not a ghost.

Such things are familiar to all, of course, in general if not in detail. The vision of mountains as sacred cannot be lost from the human mind, but each sacred mountain, one by one, can be lost to the vision. I trust there will always be in this world enough unblighted mountaintops for a few wild men to sit upon, but such erosion of a whole tradition, with all its teaching, its rites, and its lore, is a sad thing. Peace be to the spirits of Omine and of all the mountains in Japan. May they still find, when their need is pressing, acceptable refuge.

PART SIX SOUTHEAST ASIA

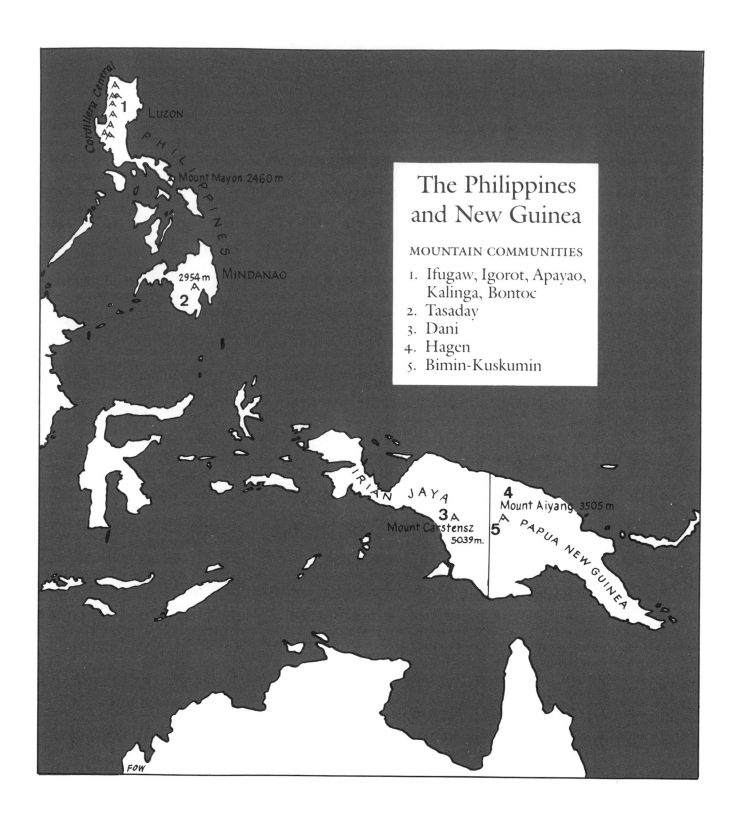

The Philippines
and New Guinea

MOUNTAIN COMMUNITIES

1. Ifugaw, Igorot, Apayao,
   Kalinga, Bontoc
2. Tasaday
3. Dani
4. Hagen
5. Bimin-Kuskumin

21.   The Igorots of the Philippines

THOMAS A. MARKS

Long ago there were human beings on the earth. They were not Igorots, and times were hard, for the earth was flat, and thus, no matter how fast they ran, hunters could not catch the game they sought. Hunger spread. Then came the great flood, which covered the land.

When the waters receded, all had changed. Where before the land had been flat, now it was an unending succession of peaks and valleys. On one peak a man had survived, on another a woman. Eventually they found one another, and from their subsequent union came the Igorots, the mountain people. They hunted and grew rice in the mountains that had been created for them.

So do Igorot legends record the origin of the mountain people in northern Luzon of the Philippines. They

Igorot hunter. Photo by Tom Marks.

are not as precise in explaining the presence of the lowland Filipino population, but there is a story that they were once Igorots. In a storm they were washed downstream and were unable to climb back up to their mountain home. Having hurt their heads in the descent, they eventually forgot their language and their customs.

Thousands of years passed, and mountain people and lowland people walked along separate paths, each group developing its own unique life-style. Lowland ways changed rapidly under the sway of foreign rulers, first the Kastila, or Spaniards, then the Americanos, or Americans. Following World War II, a free nation of the Philippines was declared, ruled by lowlanders.

All the while, life in the mountain fastness was as it had been for centuries. "Modernization," whatever its form or source, held no attraction in the Igorot world, where life, with its countless customs and rituals, was itself a sacred gift from the heavens. "Government" did not exist, save for irregular meetings held by groups of villagers concerned about some issue. Furthermore, although there were a number of distinct ethnolinguistic "tribes" that labeled themselves Igorots—the Benguets, Bontocs, Ifugaos, Kalingas, and Apayaos, each of which in turn had its own "subtribes"—these bodies did not function as integral units at any level. Instead they merely held in common certain cultural and linguistic characteristics, and each tribe made its home in a fairly distinct geographical area, often giving its name to the province that the authorities formed about it.

Despite the length of time they had been in place when the Spanish arrived, and the fact that they had in many cases developed viable fixed forms of cultivation, the Igorots remained but clusters of scattered villages. The most salient feature of their collective culture was head-hunting, which was connected with both religion and revenge. An injury to a member of the family or village normally required retribution in kind, death being answered with death, and those who took several enemy heads not only achieved the desired revenge, but also acquired all of the manly attributes of the deceased: courage, virility, and so forth. The only manner in which this process could be arrested was through the formation of peace pacts between rival villages or groups. At any one time hundreds of such pacts might be in force throughout the mountains.

No inventory of such pacts was ever made. Neither were Igorot numbers precisely determined, though figures estimated within the last decade give the following tribal strengths: Benguet, 25,000; Bontoc, 50,000; Ifugao, 120,000; Kalinga, 60,000; and Apayo, 16,000. The village was the basic political unit and was headed by a chief selected by his fellow tribesmen because of either his wealth or his leadership ability. Society was patrilineal, and the oldest living male was the head of each family. The purpose of marriage was procreation, and a union generally did not achieve permanency until pregnancy occurred.

Villages consisted of from several to a hundred houses, located at altitudes between 2,000 and 7,000 feet (600–2,100 meters). Narrow upland valleys limited communication, so each village was basically a self-contained unit. Trade existed, but subsistence agriculture was the rule. A majority of the Igorots practiced variants of swidden, or "slash-and-burn," agriculture, although this practice was not accompanied by the migratory aspects found among many other Southeast Asian hill peoples. Rather, crop or field rotation was practiced to insure that the soil would be suitable for the crops of rice that formed the mainstay of the Igorot diet. The watershed was zealously guarded. Several tribes, notably the Ifugaos, had over the centuries wrested from the mountains elaborate agricultural terraces, and in places these covered entire mountains. The terraces had come to figure in Igorot mythology and religion and in many cases were thought to represent "stairways to heaven." In every home a rice granary guardian, a carved statue unique to each family, stood guard over the product of the stairways, the life-giving rice.

To add variety to their rice diet, the Igorots also grew lesser crops and practiced some hunting. The major measure for introducing meat into the diet was not hunting, however, but religious ceremonies, wherein pigs and chickens were killed as sacrifices.

Just as religion ruled the provision of meat in the diet, so it also controlled, together with custom, all aspects of Igorot life. The hill people, contrary to many writings of early observers, did not practice monotheism. In fact they worshiped a pantheon of gods numbering in the hundreds but arrayed in very definite classes. The noted anthropologist Roy F. Barton at one time listed 1,240 Ifugao gods, with seven classes still to go. Missionaries introduced the term *Apo-Dias,* or Supreme Deity, in the belief that the Igorots had a concept to match. They did not, and an Igorot lived in a world of spirits and gods, even having a function and

Igorot statuary. Photo by Tom Marks.

needing solicitation and/or appeasement. These deities were not so much objects of worship as they were sources of power.

While not worshiped as such, the primary source of power for the mountain people was the mountains themselves. For it was from the Cordillera Central, the great chain of mountains occupying the interior of northern Luzon, that the Igorots took their identity and even their very name. There on the slopes and peaks they buried their dead, performed their rituals, and lived in a world totally unlike that of the lowlanders.

Yet as the decade of the 1980s began, this life-style was gravely threatened, for at last the lowlanders, those who had hurt their heads and thereby forgotten their language and customs, had succeeded in climbing back up the slopes. Their aim, however, was not to partake again of the gifts offered by the peaks.

Instead, the martial-law government of President Ferdinand Marcos, determined to reduce the dependence of the Philippines on foreign oil, was endeavoring to push ahead with plans to tap the vast hydroelectric potential of the mountains, to push ahead with plans to construct a series of dams along the Chico River. These dams, if completed, would flood the heart of Bontoc and Kalinga land. The massive construction project, destined to become the largest hydroelectric complex in Southeast Asia if completed, had turned into a battle for the survival of a way of life.

Government promises of resettlement for dislocated people had all the trappings of the American government's policies concerning Indian reservations. Eventually activists of all stripes, including the communist New People's Army (NPA), became involved on the side of the mountain people. Troops of the Philippine Constabulary (PC) were called in, to be followed later by regular army forces, but both only succeeded in inflaming the situation with their abuses of the people. Violence followed. The assassination of Kalingan chief

Igorot man. Photo by Tom Marks.

Macli-ing on April 24, 1980, only served to fan further the flames of rebellion.

That the Igorots would resist the assaults upon their mountains and their way of life was a foregone conclusion. They had always done so. Records of their tenacity dated from 1565, when the Spaniards came to the islands. While they were able to conquer the lowland areas with relative ease, the Kastila nevertheless found the mountain regions quite a different matter. There, as the Igorots even now point out, men had not damaged their gall bladders, as the lowlanders obviously had when they were washed downstream. Mountain people had good gall bladders and thus the courage to fight the Kastila.

Though the Kastila had guns, most of their soldiers were lowlanders. With their bad gall bladders and lack of knowledge of the mountains' secret defiles and dangers, they were driven back. Unable to penetrate further than the Baguio gold mines, a point reached by the expedition of Don Alfonso Martín in 1624, the Kastila left the "Ygolots," as Don Alfonso called them in his reports, to themselves.

Punitive expeditions continued throughout the eighteenth and nineteenth centuries with the ultimate goal of establishing a permanent Spanish presence in the mountains. These attempts were only partially successful, and in 1868 a large revolt broke out against the occupiers. Still, the occupation effort was pushed forward with vigor and continued until 1898. *Occupation* was a term to be read loosely, however, since the Spanish presence was small and limited to a few major centers. An 1881 royal decree attempted to force the Igorots into towns and to make them wear clothes—the men used only a G-string, the women a skirt, and both sexes frequently adorned their bodies with tattoos. This effort at urbanization and "civilization" failed, as did similarly minded efforts at changing mountain ways.

Resistance was continuous. To die in battle was not the end of all things, for each mountain person was a double self—a physical self and a spiritual self. Only the former was subject to death. While the physical self was alive, the spiritual self lived therein, though it sometimes left for a time and wandered about. After death, the physical self ceased to exist, but the spiritual self joined the souls of the ancestors. There it still engaged in those activities it had practiced before the death of the physical self, such as watching over the family or resisting the interlopers. Communion with these ancestral spirits was carried out through human mediums. Propitiation occurred through sacrifices.

These sacrifices were a key part of Igorot life and accompanied every phase of the annual cycle. Among the most important was that which occurred at death, a ceremony that over the centuries had resisted all inroads of "civilization." The body of the deceased was placed in a death chair, and sacrifices began. An adult's funeral ultimately required eighteen pigs and eleven chickens. After a period of time, during which the body was carefully tended—unless it was that of a murder victim, in which case it was neglected, or the victim of a beheading, in which case it was abused—the body was carried to a burial cave. Young males vied with one another to do the carrying, for it was considered enormously fortunate if the carrier was smeared with the juice from the rotting body. He thereby inherited all good luck, successes, and virtues from the deceased. Death, then, far from being simply a calamity or a time of mourning, served as a source of renewal for individuals and the community at large.

Individual tribes had their unique death rituals. The Ifugaos, for example, after a year or so collected the remains of the deceased, washed the bones, and placed them in a blanket. The bundle was then kept beneath the eaves of the home. In contrast, the Bontocs interred their dead permanently in burial caves near their homes; and young children were buried in the yard itself of the family compound. Myriad details in the process of burial were dictated by custom and taboo, all to ensure that the spiritual self entered the spirit world properly. Certain of these ancestors had come to assume a position in the pantheon of Igorot deities and were worshiped as sources of power. Thus, as generation succeeded generation, the mountains were mother to the continual regeneration of a symbiotic relationship between the living and the dead. All dwelt together as had their ancestors, and as would their children.

When the dead were buried, battle resumed, for an absence of fear concerning death was not the only force at work. The fight also provided an opportunity to increase the spiritual force and productivity accruing to the community in still another way, because with combat came the taking of heads. Head-hunting in the Igorot world possessed religious significance, providing as it did both a means of redressing an imbalance in the division between right and wrong—that is, revenge—as well as a method for adding to the collective cosmic stock of a group. In addition there were the individual rewards to be gained, as the victor assumed the merits and strengths of the beheaded. Tattoos often served as a symbol of heroism in this endeavor, and frequently the amount and designs of the tattooing depended upon the head-hunting prowess of the bearer.

Head-hunting, then, played a central role in Igorot life and was accorded a major role in agricultural and other ceremonies. Even in those areas where the authorities established order, and where the missionaries made inroads, head-hunting, while forbidden, was retained in ritual form. There came to be two ways of taking a head: the actual act and a ritual one. Ritual consisted of magical performances and short prayers by which the gods of war and their emmissaries were commissioned to do what the Igorots themselves could no longer do. Occasionally this took the form of an elaborate sacrificial performance in which a phase of a head-hunting expedition was simulated. One such Ifugao example was accompanied by a chant that called on the spirits to strike down the tribe's enemies and that included the words: "for we can no longer go to their abodes, for now there is *ulchin* [peace and order enforced by the government]."[1]

Ulchin particularly reigned after the change in colonial rulers brought American administrators to the Philippines in 1898. Head-hunting did not again become widely practiced, despite a relapse of sorts during World War II, when members of the Japanese occupation forces became fair game. Still, the central role of the practice was not to be totally dislodged, and village feuds all too often were punctuated with beheadings and ritual murders. These practices continued during the era of independence.

Initially the new lowland government was cautious and even benevolent in its dealings with the Igorots. Over the years the mountain people were allowed to lead their own lives as they saw fit, and even the exploitation of the mountains' mineral wealth, though it changed the lives of many individuals who went to work in the mines, was not carried out in such a fashion as to threaten Igorot culture. It was not even until 1968 that a special agency, PANAMIN (Presidential Assistant on National Minorities), was formed to deal

Corrugated roofing among the Igorot. Photo by Tom Marks.

specifically with the problems and "development" of minority peoples such as the Igorots.

Regrettably, by 1975, when increased opposition of the Kalingas and Bontocs to the Chico River dams helped to bring about the final collapse of President Marcos's Commission on National Integration (CNI), PANAMIN was put in charge of all non-Muslim minorities. This automatically created a conflict of interest, as PANAMIN sought to please its employer, the president, by paving the way for dam construction, as well as other development projects, while simultaneously looking to the welfare of its charges. "Divide and conquer" tactics; formation of village militias, which created mutually antagonistic groups within the mountains; resettlement plans designed to turn mountain people into lowlanders; a failure to protect the long-established rights of the Igorots to their land; and finally the introduction of government troops into the Igorot areas—all served to end forever the splendid isolation that the mountain people had for so many years fought to protect.

Soon the politics of organization replaced the "non-politics" of the mountains; ambushes of government soldiers replaced rituals that called upon the gods to smite the foes. For the first time representatives of different tribes met to develop strategies to counter the common threat to their mountain way of life. For the government's plans, if allowed to run to their logical culmination, involved nothing less than the death of the Igorot people in the affected areas scheduled to be flooded by the Chico River dams. Once carried out, such a course could easily be repeated when other circumstances so dictated.

Gone would be the stairways to heaven, the graves of the ancestors. The mountains that had been created for the Igorots would be taken away as they had been formed, by a great flood.

Yet now the flood would come not from the heavens but from the lowlands. And its purpose would not be creation, but instead the destruction of the Igorot way of life. This no man with a strong gall bladder could accept. Better to fight and, if death called, to join the ancestors in the world of the spirits.

22. Tasaday

JOHN NANCE

One gray day not so long ago a tiny group of nearly naked people picked up their babies and a few prized stone tools and followed a mysterious stranger into the jungle. They left behind their ancestral caves in the rain-forested mountains to meet, they hoped, a legendary man who would bring them good fortune.

They hiked for three days, sleeping at night huddled together beneath giant palms and ferns. They were in an unfamiliar part of the forest and worried whether they were on the right path. Some wanted to turn back.

The people, who called themselves the Tasaday (Taw-saw-dai), had debated at length whether to make this journey. Some had anxiously recalled an ancestral prophecy that to leave the caves would put them in grave peril. But others invoked another prophecy of Tasaday fathers that said someday a great man would come and save them from life's suffering.

The mysterious stranger, who had met them some time earlier and brought magical tools and knowledge, urged them on. His name was Dafal, and he was a trapper and trader who lived beyond the mountains. He was one of the rare outsiders to venture far into the thickly jungled interior. More prudent folk stayed away, believing the dark mountains were haunted by ghosts, savage spirits, and wild beasts. The wily Dafal, however, was undaunted and during a hunting foray met the Tasaday. He paid several more visits later and finally invited them to come meet a man of great power and wealth who would help them.

The people looked thin and poor, Dafal had thought, and could use help. When he had first seen the Tasaday, they had no metal or cloth, wore only leaves, and made their tools of wood and stone. They did not know how to kill or eat the pig and deer and monkey, and they did not plant crops. Also, they were troubled by having lost contact with two similar groups in the mountain rain forest. They had always intermarried with those others because people were not supposed to find mates within their own group.

Although Dafal spoke a strange language, the Tasaday understood enough to convince them that it was worth taking risks to meet his "good man." Dafal told them: "He'll come out of the sky and bring you wonderful gifts." Birds, the Tasaday's favorite creatures, also flew out of the sky and sometimes brought messages from the Owner of the Forest, an invisible power who resided high above the treetops beside the sun, "the eye of day."

So, despite their fears, the Tasaday decided that everybody should go with Dafal "to see with all of our eyes, and to hear with all of our ears if this is truly the good man of our ancestors' legend."

Their first great surprise came before they met him. On the third day of hiking they reached the end of their world. The mountains stopped. The forest stopped. The land swept away to a distant horizon. The people were frightened and ran back into the forest. They had no idea there was such flatland. Dafal persuaded three men and two boys to come forward again, and from a knoll they gazed in wonder across the open spaces toward a new world—toward the unknown. The people called it "the place where the eye sees too far!"

As the men and boys stood trembling, Dafal suddenly pointed into the sky and shouted, "here he comes!"

The Tasaday searched the sky with their eyes but saw only a speck, like an insect, moving toward them. They watched it grow larger and larger until it loomed overhead, not an insect or a bird, but a gigantic creature with a shrill voice and breath so powerful that it ripped leaves from the trees. It hovered, then screaming and blowing dropped to the ground. The Tasaday fell in terror. One young man, named Balayam, believed all of them would die. "The Tasaday are finished," he thought, "finished!"

And so the mountain people discovered the modern world. It was June, 1971, when the sleek jet helicopter landed on the knoll in the province of South Cotabato, on the island of Mindanao in the Philippines. As the people lay on the ground, their "good man" stepped from the aircraft, and part of the Tasaday's journey was indeed finished—but another part had just begun.

Their journey of three days had transported them through thirty thousand years of technological time—from the Stone Age to the Space Age. It also started me on a journey, lesser than theirs, but like them I did not know when it would end or where it was going.

I met the Tasaday as a journalist, a reporter and photographer for the Associated Press who had spent several years in Southeast Asia, including more than two covering the Vietnam War. I visited the Tasaday ten times, the first shortly after they met the screaming helicopter in 1971 and the last in 1974, after the forty-six thousand acres of forest which the government had set aside as a Tasaday preserve was put off-limits to all but a few authorized visitors.

In the period 1971–74, a considerable number of observers, including journalists and at least ten social scientists, visited the Tasaday. Their visits were sporadic and usually brief, the longest one lasting about three weeks. All of the scientific researchers have rued the short duration of visits and the paucity of data they were able to obtain, but nonetheless they have been able to produce published documentation. (A bibliography in the Notes section of this book provides those sources.) Consequently, we have significant information about the Tasaday that offers a glimpse of these folk who one scholar described as having been "as close to nature as any people known in modern times."

At their first meeting with the outside world, the Tasaday totaled only twenty-six persons. Until meeting Dafal some indefinite time earlier, their way of life corresponded to the period popularly called the Stone Age. The Tasaday's main tools were made of stone and wood—from fingernail-sized stone flakes to large stone pounders to beveled-edge scrapers with wooden hafts fastened with vines. Digging sticks were important tools. Unlike many such peoples, the Tasaday did not have bows and arrows, spears or traps. They had no use for such items because they did not hunt the larger animals of the forest and had no human enemies to fight. They said all persons in the forest were *kakay*, "friends."

The Tasaday had no cloth, pottery, or wheels. They maintained no domesticated animals, did not practice agriculture, and were gatherers who relied on plants for most of their food. They did catch by hand and eat the tiny crabs, fish, and tadpoles in their stream and said the largest creature they had ever killed was a frog. They also enjoyed grubs dug from rotting logs. Among their most important productions was fire, made by spinning a wooden drill.

The society, of course, represented their adaption to a ruggedly mountainous tropical rain forest that protected them at the same time it isolated them. It provided sufficient food, harbored few dangerous animals and no threatening peoples, and had no harsh extremes

Stone-age Sanctuary—Members of the Tasaday group fill the
mouth of their main habitation cave in a mountain rain-forest
of Mindanao, Philippines.

of weather—save frequent rainstorms and occasional earthquakes. The forest covers several hundred square miles of Mindanao Island in the southern Philippines, just a few degrees above the Equator. It spreads along the island's southwest flank from Saragani Bay up to Moro Gulf and inland to the Alah River.

The tropical climate keeps the air humid and the soil moist. Dark green jungle with trees 200 feet (60 meters) high covers the jagged mountains, whose peaks rise up to 5,000 feet (1,500 meters) above sea level. Home for the Tasaday is in a narrow valley with steeply sloping sides. Their main shelters are three caves on the western slope, some 500 feet (150 meters) above the valley floor, along which flows a clear stream. The morning sun shines into the mouths of the caves—daylight usually comes about 6 A.M. and darkness about 6 P.M.

The surrounding profusion of life includes more than two hundred plants for which the Tasaday have names. Many trees, palms, vines, shrubs, ferns, roots, herbs, and grasses are used for food, fuel, medicines, clothing, implements, and entertainment.

The most prevalent animals include a wide and colorful variety of birds, monkeys, pigs, deer, squirrels, rodents, reptiles, and countless insects. The creatures most feared are venomous snakes, which have taken Tasaday lives; most revered are certain birds, which the Tasaday say herald good news and warn of dangers.

The Tasaday say their ancestors lived in the forest as far back as anyone knows. Two other groups—named the Tasafeng and Sanduka—lived in other parts of the forest. The Tasaday's ancestors told them to stay close to their own particular area; it was safe to travel in daytime, but at night they should return to their caves, which protected them from darkness, rain, lightning, and other dangers. Ancestors also warned that traveling too far could bring sickness, sent at least sometimes by the "Owner of the Forest," a supernatural deity who resided in the sky above the forest.

These ancestral edicts surely help account for the Tasaday's lack of knowledge of the outside world. Their valley with the caves is less than 30 miles (50 kilometers) from the edge of the forest, where, on a nearby plain, is a village of people called Manubo Blit. The nearest town is about 50 miles (80 kilometers) from there; the nearest city, Davao, some 100 miles (160 kilometers) east; and Manila, the Philippines' capital, some 700 miles (1,100 kilometers) north.

Linguistic researchers have verified more than nine hundred Tasaday words and have compared their language with related dialects. It is linked to Manubo, a local subfamily within the much larger Malayo-Polynesian family that is spoken by all Filipino and many other Pacific peoples. Linguists say that the Tasaday's dialect appears to have split off from the nearest known dialect between four hundred and eleven hundred years ago.

The 1971 Tasaday population of twenty-six was in six nuclear families related by blood through the adult males. The adult women had married into the group from the Tasafeng and Sanduka. The Tasaday say they lost contact with these groups—apparently in the 1960s—for unknown reasons and have not been able to find them. This has created a serious social problem, because the Tasaday have no steady supply of mates for their young men and women. They do not allow marriage within the group (an incest taboo) and say they are monogamous. ("A man and woman marry and stay together until their hair turns white.")

The oldest Tasaday were a man and wife who appeared to be in their late fifties or sixties. Age was uncertain because the Tasaday did not keep track of months, seasons, or years. The next oldest couple appeared to be in their late forties or fifties, and three other couples were in their twenties and thirties. There was a widower in his thirties, and the oldest bachelor was about twenty. The remaining fourteen Tasaday (twelve boys and only two girls) ranged in age from a few months to teens.

The social structure was that of a group, not a band or tribe. The Tasaday had no chief or formal leadership hierarchy. Individuals did, however, have activities in which they specialized (treating snakebite, for instance), or excelled (catching fish, digging edible roots, finding firewood, and the like), or were influential (superior because of experience, strength, intelligence, persuasiveness, creativity, and so on).

Men and women appeared equally free to express themselves on matters of importance. Both worked and cared for the children, who accompanied parents throughout the day. Children were taught early to share food and toys, and to look after one another. Fighting and bickering were discouraged by a variety of techniques, rules, and beliefs. The group evidently put high priorities on unity, sharing, cooperation, discussion, consensus, and the avoidance or rapid dissolution of hostility.

They also took care in dealing with their environment, being careful not to destroy a plant when harvesting the edible portion. For instance, in digging *biking,* an edible tuber, they always replaced the leafy top in the ground so it would grow again. They did not hunt the deer, pigs, monkeys, or birds and only recently learned to trap such creatures for food. Nonetheless, they appear to have had sufficient food. When first contacted by outsiders, most of the people were thin but in reasonably good health.

Still, human life was precarious. Sickness and death, storms and earthquakes, injuries and pain presented profound mysteries. Phenomena such as dreams were important and contributed to what appears to be the foundation for a religion of animism and an afterlife in which their dead ancestors survived. We have, however, only sketchy information about their religious beliefs and have only fragments of Tasaday folk tales and creation myths. We may conclude, though, that a significant role was played by the "Owner of the Forest," the invisible spirit or godlike entity the Tasaday said was responsible for the forest and who influenced such phenomena as the weather and human health. Several Tasaday said the Owner sent storms and sickness as punishment when people violated rules of behavior. Some Tasaday also spoke about lesser spirits, witches, fairies, and so on, who had influence in particular parts of the forest.

The Tasaday said death occurred when a person's living part left his body. One Tasaday described this living part as "the seer of the dream." They said that when death appeared certain, the dying person was carried by relatives to a distant, rarely visited place and left alone to die. This was so that the departing spirit would not lure away the spirits of living Tasaday.

During the period of my visits with the Tasaday, I left my job with the Associated Press and since then have spent much of my time telling about the Tasaday in some form or another, in conversation, lectures, articles, books, and films. Sometimes the story focuses on the events, at other times on the group, and still others on one individual—perhaps Balayam, a brilliant bachelor who had "cold insides" because he had no mate, or on Lobo, a bold and beautiful boy who dazzled the outsiders and became so spoiled he was severely punished. Or I might tell about the "good man," a colorful and controversial Filipino millionaire named Manuel Elizalde, Jr., who had graduated from Harvard University.

After fourteen years of telling and retelling, one would think I would be finished with the story. But no, I'm as fascinated as ever. I sometimes wonder why I can't seem to let the story go. I have not seen the Tasaday for more than a decade, but not a day goes by that I do not think of them.

I have received sketchy second- and third-hand reports over the years from people who have seen them, usually for only a day or two. I'm told the Tasaday are fine, but I often wonder what will happen to them, and I think about this or that individual and how he or she is faring. I'm told also that logging is a continual threat to their forest and that there is danger that their area may be entered by warriors retreating from the violent factional fighting that flares up in the surrounding region.

To think that violence could provide the next major event in the Tasaday's journey is alarming—and ironic. Translators of their unique dialect could find no words in Tasaday speech for fighting, war, enemy, or weapon. The Tasaday claimed they never said anything bad about another person. They avoided hostile confrontation and appeared to have developed a strategy for survival in which a key element was peaceful cooperation. One aspect of this strategy was expressed in times of difficulty by the invocation of a Tasaday appeal for unity: "We must remember to call all men one man, and all women one woman." This ideal made one man's pain everyman's pain. For two persons to fight or throw stones in anger threatened everyone's well-being. Violent disagreement could easily destroy the entire society.

In some ways the Tasaday group reflected ideas expressed by anthropologist Marshall Sahlins in writing about more ancient hunters and gatherers. Sahlins said that "in adapting to the perils of the Stone Age, human society overcame or subordinated such primate propensities as selfishness, indiscriminate sexuality, dominance and brute competition. It substituted kinship and cooperation for conflict, placed solidarity over sex, morality over might. In its earliest days, it accomplished the greatest reform in history—the over-

Stone Age Boy
with Bird in Hand—
Lobo, a young boy of the
Stone-Age Tasaday people,
plays with a bird.

throw of human primate nature, and thereby secured the evolutionary future of the species."

But at the same time the Tasaday's call to unity also invited rigid conformity to certain group values. We may have seen this at work in the case of Lobo, who became the spoiled darling of the outsiders and behaved in ways unacceptable for a Tasaday boy. He was nearly left alone to die when, some Tasaday adults said, the Owner of the Forest made him ill for harming a sacred plant.

These are but facets of a larger story that vibrates on many levels, is many stories. It is for children or mature scholars and may be as simple or complex as we make it. It contains the raw stuff of fairy tales and epics, of legends and mythology. It is a saga of adventure and exploration—equal in Tasaday measure to the travels of Odysseus, Columbus, or the astronauts. It is also fantastic, as if H. G. Wells's time machine hurtled us backward through history. Simultaneously, it is anthropology, disclosing a way of life that has virtually vanished from the earth.

The Tasaday offer us a view of humanity at a stage when such things as society, technology, and religion were in their infancy. The forest people embrace new things and ideas, and we see familiar human predicaments unfolding: they take up steel knives and it is too easy—for us—to see that tool as a potentially lethal weapon. They did not yet see it so.

On another plane, the people and their lengthy isolation afford us an opportunity to look into a totally self-contained social and environmental system, to ponder what it means to be human, the foundations of culture, the effects of sudden change, and the rise and resolution of conflict. Most significant, it invites us to look at ourselves and our own societies and to wonder who we may have been, are now, and shall become.

These are not new ideas, of course; learning about ourselves from others is fundamental to anthropology. But the Tasaday do offer metaphors and connections that seem particularly apt to our modern world. Perhaps we can see our own problems in fresh ways through the Tasaday lens. The introduction of steel knives in their world matches the impact of computers in ours. New medicines and political ideas cause revolutions in both societies.

The Tasaday's handling of aggression, mentioned earlier, connects with a crucial twentieth-century issue: two Tasaday could not throw stones in anger because it threatened the entire group. For us, as technology shrinks the planet into a global village, two angry nations can no longer hurl their biggest stones—nuclear bombs. It threatens the whole world.

Echoing the Tasaday's appeal for unity ("all men one man, all women one woman"), Margaret Mead said after America's atomic attack on Japan: "The bomb has made us one, in a way we have never been one before. We must find news ways of living together."

This is one reason I have titled some recent work about the Tasaday "A Message from the Stone Age." In discussing the Tasaday with widely varied groups, from kindergarten classes to university seminars and senior citizens' retirement groups, the expressions of interest are often intense. Sometimes it is merely a romantic longing for simpler times or the attraction of the exotic, but often it goes deeper.

A possible clue to this interest came recently from novelist Ivan Doig, who remarked in a published interview that the late writer and teacher John Gardner had said there were only two good stories: "Somebody took a journey, and a stranger rides into town."

Reading that, my mind flashed to the Tasaday: Dafal came into the forest and took the people on a journey to "the place where the eye sees too far."

Gardner's two elements had always figured prominently in my telling of the Tasaday's story, but I had not consciously recognized these deeper implications.

Again the Tasaday invite us to ponder ourselves and our human connectedness. We grapple with a paradox: each of us is unique, but we are all more alike than different. And if we can see ourselves in the Tasaday—a people seemingly as remote from modern society as any on earth—how can we not see ourselves in our neighbors? That, too, is a message from the Stone Age.

After a twelve-year absence, I visited the Tasaday for six days in 1986. They retained much of their Tasaday character, but had changed remarkably in their economic and social strategies. Through Sindi, the Manubo Blit wife of Balayam, the Tasaday had linked with the Blit through many marriages (population had risen to approximately sixty persons), had become active hunters, were learning Blit slash-and-burn agriculture, and were preparing to start their own cultivation of crops. The Tasaday said their complex of three caves remained a home base, although they were spending more time deeper in the rain forest and also outside with the Blit, who supplied them with such things as metal, cloth (most Tasaday had acquired clothing), and tobacco (many had become smokers), as well as new ideas. The Tasaday appeared healthy and flourishing, although protection of their forest from encroaching outsiders was a continual problem. Dr. Jesus Peralta, head of anthropology for the Philippine National Museum, said it was amazing to see the Tasaday go from gathering to trapping, to hunting, and soon to planting—a process that traditionally spanned many generations, "happening before your very eyes in a single lifetime."

23. The Erosion of a Sacred Landscape: European Exploration and Cultural Ecology among the Bimin-Kuskusmin of Papua New Guinea

FITZ JOHN PORTER POOLE

There was a time, not long ago, when Europeans came to look for our sacred place of the ancient black oil. My father, ritual elder of the Watiianmin [clan] before me, was very worried and angry. He told me that the sacred oil was given to us long, long ago by the great ancestor Afek when our [human] ancestors first appeared upon the land. . . . He told me that the sacred oil was the "root" of the taro and the pandanus, the "skin" of the pig, and the "semen" of the great cassowary. He told me that Europeans must never take the sacred oil from us. . . . [If they should take the oil,] he said that the great ancestor Afek would rise in anger from the ancestral underworld and would unleash the terrible thunder and lightning of her rage. Then, he said, great fires, fierce winds, and torrential rains would sweep through the mountains and valleys. The bounty of the land would be destroyed and washed away forever. . . . The people would sicken and die. . . . Afek's children would be no more. . . .

— BOSUUROK, PARAMOUNT MALE RITUAL ELDER OF THE WATIIANMIN CLAN OF THE BIMIN-KUSKUSMIN

In 1964 an ominous shadow passed over the land of Bosuurok's people and threatened to disrupt not only much of their traditional way of life but also the very foundation of their "natural" world. An Australian patrol penetrated the remote southeastern corner of the West Sepik Province of Papua New Guinea in search of a natural oil seep that was rumored to exist in the territory of the Bimin-Kuskusmin people.[1] Despite Bosuurok's protests and attempts to mislead the patrol, a small sample of the oil was collected and taken away. To the Australians, the find proved to be of no commercial value, and the oil was soon forgotten. To the Bimin-Kuskusmin people, however, the European "discovery" of this sacred substance at an important ritual site long enshrined in their mythology was seen as an omen of impending cataclysm. And, by ritual and other means, the Bimin-Kuskusmin tried valiantly to protect themselves and their sacred land against further threats of European exploration. The oil became the focus of this defense against intrusions of the *tabaarasep* (Europeans) into domains of ritual importance and has remained the major symbol of the European erosion of a sacred landscape. The extraordinary symbolic value of this oil (*kiimning*) in Bimin-Kuskusmin narratives of the cultural significance of historical encounters with Europeans is appropriate. For Bimin-Kuskusmin, as Bosuurok noted, "The oil is our blood, our semen, our bone, our heritage from our ancestors . . . our life."[2]

This essay is an attempt to explicate some of the cultural significance of this historical event in terms that make sense of Bosuurok's anguished account of it. This explication must examine some central features of how the remote, small population of Bimin-Kuskusmin—a people of the mountainous hinterland of Papua New Guinea—viewed the impact of European exploration upon their traditional way of life and upon the contours of their known world. It must probe the Bimin-Kuskusmin cultural construction of history and of ecology from the perspective of an anthropologist. But this essay is also a personal account drawn from the intense experience of living among the Bimin-Kuskusmin for over two years.[3] And it is colored by hues of not only intellectual curiosity but also strong affection for the ways of a people struggling to understand and to cope with new beings and forces in the high valleys of their homeland.

Every anthropological analysis is guided by certain theoretical predilections that inform the selection and organization of the ethnographic data to be presented. For purposes of this essay, I adopt the view that humans perceive their "natural" world through a culturally constituted lens of beliefs, knowledge, values, and purposes.[4] It is in terms of such cultural images that they act upon—and indeed see themselves as acted upon by—"nature." The study of such cultural maps or cognized models of a society's territory is often labeled ethnoecology or perhaps ethnogeography, for it deals with those learned and shared notions that a people hold to be true and put to philosophical or pragmatic use in regard to their environment. Often, the structures, processes, and attributes of "natural" phenomena are invested with sacred significance, and unseen beings and forces are thought to move the world in ways detailed in myth and perhaps affected by ritual. Beyond the apparent surface of the landscape there are hidden topographies known best to ritual experts but cognitively and emotionally salient to all. It is perhaps in this sense of the intertwining of "natural" and "supernatural" orders that the cultural significance of oil among Bimin-Kuskusmin is best expressed.[5] And Bosuurok's interpretation of the significance of the

European "discovery" of Bimin-Kuskusmin oil is cast in dense, intricate cultural idioms that must be delicately unraveled to reveal the subtle contours of a sacred topography.

About one thousand Bimin-Kuskusmin dwell in a remote, rugged, ecologically diverse, heavily forested, mountainous area in the extreme southeast of the Telefomin District of the West Sepik Province of Papua New Guinea. From headwaters in this mountain fastness, the great Fly and Sepik rivers begin their meandering southerly and northerly descents from the central cordillera of New Guinea toward the distant sea, which is beyond Bimin-Kuskusmin traditional reckoning and cultural imagination.[6] Bordered to the west by the formidable Strickland Gorge and on all other flanks by massive ranges, the two main Bimin-Kuskusmin valleys have remained relatively isolated and beyond the pale of European exploration until quite recent times.[7] This tiny territory—the Place of the Center (Abiip Mutuuk)—has been the pivot of their cultural construction of the world and the focus of their social traditions for more than a millennium.[8] Indeed, by their own reckoning they have occupied this land since primordial times, when their original ancestors gave birth to the first humans who founded the autochthonous clans of the contemporary Bimin-Kuskusmin.[9] Speaking a Mountain-Ok (non-Austronesian) language, they discuss with pride and enthusiasm their historical priority, ritual superiority, military supremacy, and cultural uniqueness in the region. But networks of trade, alliance, warfare, intermarriage, and ritual relations bring them into various kinds of contact with other tribal groups of their immediate region and beyond.[10] In their mythology, their known world, encompassing all *fiitep* ("humans") and some semihuman creatures at the periphery, is bounded and covered by the canopy of the sky, which is linked to the earth by great pillars of limestone and massive trees just beyond the farthest extent of human experience.[11] Beyond the pale there is a boundless and frightening realm of rocks and craters, torrential floods and ever-burning fires, violent landslides and earthquakes, and hideous monsters and giant fungi. There is—or was thought to be until recently—no safe passage between the known world and this bleak outer realm.

In the early part of this century, the great divide between the orderly, known world and the chaotic outer realm was breached in some unfathomable way, and an anomaly appeared on the landscape. The form of the pale-skinned, strangely clothed, fiercely armed European was seen by distant peoples in the far mountains. The Bimin-Kuskusmin have known something of Europeans at least since the German Kaiserin-Augusta-Fluss Expedition (1912–14) penetrated the Telefomin area to the west. Some folktales present images of strange beings with weapons that held both thunder (*kimaan*) and lightning (*bamning*) in the region before that time, and these stories may represent the early wanderings of Malay bird of paradise hunters from the Dutch colony of Nederlands Nieuw Guinea.[12] The first sightings of the Europeans raised puzzlement and then fear and anxiety among Bimin-Kuskusmin as the strangers' patrols circled ever closer to their land and as tales of insult and violence against persons and property increased. But first direct contact with the strange *tabaarasep* was limited to a very few individuals in 1957. At that time, few patrols ventured far from the distant government station at Telefomin. With the opening of the Oksapmin patrol post to the north in 1961, however, more frequent expeditions of exploration began to probe the periphery of Bimin-Kuskusmin territory from time to time. And the pace and extent of contact with the peculiar beings began to increase.

On the eve of my initial fieldwork in 1971, nevertheless, such contact remained markedly limited. Most Bimin-Kuskusmin had never seen a European, except perhaps at a great distance. Some stone tools were still in regular use, and only a little European paraphernalia beyond steel axes and machetes was in evidence. Familiarity with mission and government custom was slight. Yet the European was viewed with the ambivalence of both fear and curiosity. All encounters with Europeans and accounts of their movements, activities, and customs were carefully scrutinized for their hidden significance, and diviners sought to fathom the secret meaning of such events by ritual means. The vividly remembered search for the sacred oil was a recurrent theme of these intense discussions. Once, when a patrol accompanied by a geologist was traveling near the northern boundary of Bimin-Kuskusmin territory, my friend Maakeng noted poignantly,

> The patrol officer comes now along the track. He tells no one where he goes, what he wants. Some say that he holds a great secret, searches for hidden things of great power as once before. Another European comes with him to gather rocks. He tells them [the Oksapmin people to the north] that he wants to learn of unseen things beneath the ground. [The realm of ancestral spirits is below the ground.] . . . Men came in my youth to find our sacred black oil. They too collected rocks from the land. And then they took away the rocks and some of the oil forever. Then our taro grew poorly, and many of our children became weak and ill. Some died. The ancestors were very angry and would not help us. Do the Europeans now seek our sacred crystals too? The European takes rocks from caves. [Large crystals found in limestone caves are thought to be animate, sentient, and highly sacred.] . . . Both the oil and the crystals join the above and the

below [the abodes of the living and the dead]. To take them from us would destroy our land, our sacred things, our people. . . .

The revered oil is located below a small ridge toward the eastern end of the mountain range that separates the northern and southern Bimin-Kuskusmin valleys. This central chain of mountains is the spine (*daang kuun*) of the land. The oil is its marrow (*kuun yoor ok*). In a deep hollow, hidden by dense stands of trees, there is a tiny clearing in the midst of which a steady trickle of viscous black oil seeps through a rock crevice. The sluggish flow of oil is caught in an elaborately carved bamboo tube, which guides it into a large, circular depression below. The depression is lined with clay and encircled by sacred red *Cordyline* plants.[13] A large clay sacrificial hearth within a miniature hut stands to one side. Several shrines, each containing pig, human, and cassowary skulls, have been constructed near the edge of the clearing. Immediately above the oil seep there is a very tall shrine in which large and sparkling crystals are kept.

At this great ritual center the clearing is periodically cleaned of all forest debris. Men plant new areas with red *Cordyline* shoots within the clearing and decorate the shrines with ocher and cassowary plumes and boar tusks. When the oil is collected at special times in the annual cycle of rites, ritual experts roast marsupials in the hearth and present sacrificial morsels to the ancestral skulls and to the crystals. Ancestral spirits are said to return then from their underworld abode and to increase the flow of sacred oil. Such occasions are times of solemnity and liturgy, for this ritual site links all Bimin-Kuskusmin, living and dead, in a common bond with the land and its resources. And the precious oil is thought to represent the source of fertility, growth, renewal, and change for all faunae, florae, and humans that dwell on the land of the Place of the Center and even beyond to the farthest reaches of known human settlement. The highly valued Bimin-Kuskusmin oil is a unique resource in the region, with significant implications for the rituals, peoples, and lands of all ethnic groups in the Mountain-Ok area.

From the ridge top above the hidden oil seep one can look down into the awesome, windy abyss of the Strickland Gorge, with its great river roaring so far below, or across the misty, forested panorama that stretches eastward from the gorge far into the Southern Highlands and Western Highlands provinces. Somewhere beyond the distant horizon, the canopy of the sky bends earthward to enfold the known world, and the mighty Strickland River curves toward the sky and into the rolling clouds to supply the abundant rain that nourishes the lush vegetation. But in the immediate foreground, the male hunting preserves of the Bimin-Kuskusmin extend along the near flank of the Strickland. Only adult men who have endured the ordeals of the decade-long, ten-stage cycle of male initiation rites may venture into this domain or approach the sacred site of the oil.[14] Near the lip of the great gorge there is a slender but ever widening belt of tall, tufted swordgrass where men drive feral pigs and marsupials by fire and by drum in collective hunts. This zone, at the eastern edge of the Place of the Center, is wind-swept, hot, and dangerous. Fires move through the sun-dried grass at often frightening speed, sometimes trapping the unwary hunter. Scorpions and death adders abound. In the open grassland, the stalking hunter may fall prey to arrows shot from ambush by enemies from across the Strickland or from the land of the Oksapmin to the north, for poachers sometimes invade this area in search of Bimin-Kuskusmin game. But as one travels westward up the steep valley floors, the arid grassland gives way to the dense, dark, humid tropical rain forest.

Bimin-Kuskusmin claim that the grassland is a recent phenomenon that is neither an integral part of their ancestral terrain nor under their ritual control. The sun-baked soil around the clumps of grass is cracked and friable. When the heavy rains fall, rivulets of water soon erode the land and form gullies in which new grasses will take root. Tall shade trees will no longer grow there, and the poor soil will not sustain food crops. Even the animals hunted in the grassland are known not to dwell there, for their lairs and young are found only in the forest. Many older men note despairingly that their generation has seen this barren zone gradually widen and similar grasses begin to appear in the regenerative growth of gardens turned to fallow in the higher areas. They suggest that the hidden, dendritic network of underground capillaries radiating from the oil seep throughout the Place of the Center no longer infuses the grassland with dark, rich, moist soil. And they point to the patches of tufted grasses in abandoned garden sites that will not be reclaimed, that no longer yield an abundance of fine, large taro or sweet potato tubers. It is said that the semen (*maiyoob gom*) of the founding ancestor Afek—represented by the sacred oil—does not nourish the grassland, and repeated fertility rites have failed to replenish the soil by reestablishing a connection between these blighted areas and this life-sustaining substance. Once an integral part of Bimin-Kuskusmin territory, the desolate but ever-expanding grassland now encroaches upon the Place of the Center and causes a gradual deterioration (*maafaagamiinaam*) of this sacred land.

For Bimin-Kuskusmin, remembered history provides a possible explanation for this ominous desolation. In the 1930s, the first Europeans ever to enter the Place of the Center crossed the Strickland Gorge from the east—within "sight" of the oil—and traveled northward along the edge of the gorge, where the greatest expanse of grassland is now to be found. Some men suggest that this early patrol pointed their strange weapons toward the sacred oil and that thunder and lightning erupted from these "thunder bows" (*wanuuk kimaan*). The ritual elder Trumeng notes that other forms of malevolent European magic harmed the oil and the nearby land when this patrol passed along the flank of the gorge. More of the invasive grasses are said to have appeared in gardens and groves since the Europeans came to take samples of the oil in the mid-1960s. Indeed, when I first arrived in their land, the Bimin-Kuskusmin were loath to allow me to see the sacred oil seep or to enter garden sites and pandanus groves until I had been properly transformed by their rites of initiation.[15]

Encompassed by the underground flow of oil and firmly under ritual control, the majestic rain forest stands in vivid contrast to the desolate grasslands. The high canopy of large-buttressed trees is dense and interlaced with mats of epiphytic mosses and ferns, with delicate climbing orchids in their midst. Within this canopy there is little sunlight on the most cloudless days, and the interior microclimate is one of lower temperature and higher humidity. Here an uneven, two-tiered canopy unfolds in the dank, dappled twilight of the inner rain forest. A profusion of bamboos, palms, and countless other rain forest trees provides a living lattice for the dense network of climbers, epiphytes, parasites, saprophytes, and strangling plants that obstruct human passage at every turn. There is a steady, monotonous dripping of moisture from the intertwined foliage, from which leeches hang in abundance and drop to the forest floor. Beneath the lowest tier, a complex undergrowth of mosses, lichens, mushrooms, creepers, vines, nettles, ferns, and magnificent orchids forms an intricate carpet over the spongy, rotting layers of forest debris. A host of insects, worms, crustaceans, lizards, and rodents burrow busily in the decaying forest floor. A myriad of small streams gurgles through the tangled underbrush, and sparkling forest pools capture the diffuse sunlight filtered through the ascending canopies above. Above these forest waters may sometimes be seen an enormous filigree spiderweb, fluttering gently in a soft breeze and sparkling silver in the rays of sunlight.

On occasion there is a sudden break in the interwoven tentacles of forest growth. One comes unexpec-

tedly upon a small clearing laboriously hewn out of the surrounding jungle and finds well-tended stands of semicultivated banana, breadfruit, manioc, fruit pandanus, sago, and other wild (*kuut*) crops. Each tiny clearing has a rough shelter built amidst the food trees and perhaps a small shrine. Wooden devices encircle tree trunks, and clusters of feathers are hung from tree limbs to prevent fruits and nuts from falling prey to the numerous animals and birds that raid these crops. But often a few banana trees are left unprotected at the edge of a clearing in order to attract giant fruit bats, which are snared or shot with arrows from ambush. Despite these efforts to claim a place in the vast rain forest, however, the massive, dense, encompassing jungle dwarfs these valiant human endeavors to gain a foothold in its dark expanse. Indeed, when these clearings are left untended for even a few months, the always encroaching growth of forest vegetation quickly obliterates almost all signs of human domestication. And the men who brave the forest to create these tiny islands must risk its considerable dangers in isolation when they reside there.

In mythology and social experience, the rain forest is a cornucopia of a truly bewildering variety of game, food plants, *materia medica*, and ritual ornaments. It provides the special woods and fibers for the manufacture of a vast assemblage of bows, arrows, clubs, and other technological and ritual implements. Varied bird feathers and animal skins for brilliant headdresses,

Ancestral skulls, surrounded by roasted marsupials, are the focus of sacrifices at a small shrine near the oil seep when oil is being collected for ritual purposes.

drums, amulets, and cult house ornaments come from hunting in the forest. Feral piglets are captured there to replenish the domestic herds kept at higher altitudes near the areas of human settlement.[16] But danger also lurks in the form of poisonous centipedes, snakes, and spiders, and of malaria-bearing mosquitoes. The lethal rush of a wounded wild boar may find the hunter cut off from escape in the dense underbrush. And if one becomes sick or wounded, one is too far from human settlements to seek help. Myriad legends tell of hunters lost forever to the great forest.

The rain forest is portrayed, nevertheless, as a place of serenity, mystery, and plenty—a primordial order of the world of long ago. Old men, no longer able to endure a journey into the jungle, talk nostalgically of their youthful experiences in this sacred domain. Great hornbills, frightened by the passage of hunters, take wing over the high canopy with an eerie booming sound. Large black or white cockatoos shriek shrill warnings from the high branches, and numerous parrots and lorikeets flit through the lower canopies. Bowerbirds and brush turkeys hover near their huge, mounded ground nests, and iridescent birds of paradise cry and flutter their lacy plumes in the stillness. Giant iguanas, startled by the unfamiliar sound of human voices, crouch motionless on rotting logs and then rush headlong into the safety of darkness. Massive pythons rest on heavy tree limbs, awaiting the unwary pig or marsupial on faint game trails below. Smaller emerald green pythons slide silently through the underbrush in search of lesser game. Exquisite moths and tree frogs cling to the moist vegetation in the lower reaches of the forest, and varicolored butterflies float through the more sunlit heights of the upper canopy. And the great cassowary—the magnificent and mysterious image of the founding ancestor Afek—glides silently like a phantom through its murky forest domain.

From the central massif in its midst, the rain forest is thought to be dominated—physically and ritually—by the ritual center of the oil seep. In mythology, the sacred site of the oil is depicted as the nucleus of a vast, radiating complex of underground pathways that link the forest to it and to the ancestral underworld. When all of the Place of the Center was once rain forest long ago, the great, hermaphroditic ancestor Afek inseminated the land through the rock crevice from which the oil now flows. Afek's semen promoted fertility in the dark, rich soil so that her progeny would never want for food and other essentials of human life. After Afek founded the original clans of the Bimin-Kuskusmin and taught the human ancestors the secrets of all ritual knowledge that could be imparted to mortals, the great

ancestor entered the ancestral underworld to reside deep beneath the oil seep. At times of ritual activity on this site, Afek's semen pours forth to replenish the vital supply of sacred oil upon which so much depends.[17] At the height of ritual intensity in these performances, Afek is said to return to the great forest in the guise of a giant cassowary and to ensure the abundance of this domain through the semen believed to be scattered in the fertile droppings of the cassowary. Thus, Afek, as the great cassowary, is called the "mother of the game animals," "parent of the flowering trees," and "father of the sacred oil." Afek's name may never be uttered, nor may the great cassowary ever be killed, in the rain forest domain.

There are recognized seasons when animals are mating and nurturing their young, eggs are hatching, seeds are sprouting, and fruits are maturing in the forest. At such times male adepts at ritual conduct elaborate sacrifices at the shrines that surround the sacred oil seep. Women and children are forbidden to enter the rain forest when these sacrifices are held, and there is a general taboo on men's hunting and trapping there. It is a time of renewal and replenishment. As the sacrifices take place at these shrines, initiated men carry bamboo tubes of oil to clan cult houses in the higher residential areas and to isolated shrines scattered throughout the vast forest and surrounding mountains. Oily smoke rises from seemingly disparate points of further sacrifices throughout the landscape of the Place of the Center, but all are connected by the underground labyrinth of the pathways of Afek's semen. And all are involved in promoting the fertility of the forest, for each shrine and cult house is deemed ritually responsible for ensuring the propagation and growth of some particular set of faunae and florae. All adult males invest much time and energy in their ritual devotion to the richness of the rain forest landscape, and the sacred oil is the center of these ritual performances.

The male ritual participants rub themselves and their pregnant wives, newborn children, domestic pigs, and hunting dogs with sacred oil to ensure bodily and ritual strength and to prevent illness—especially scabies, which mars the skin and must be treated with oil. Their glistening skins are signs of the efficacy of these ritual undertakings and the regeneration of life in the wild and domestic domains. Oil-soaked mashed taro is forcibly fed to domestic boars in order that they may grow fat and their skins may shine in health. In the consecrated taro gardens and nut pandanus groves of the higher altitudes, ritual experts bury bamboo tubes of oil to promote growth,[18] for oil is the "root" (*kiimkiim*) of the taro and the pandanus, as well as the "skin" (*kaar*) of the pig. In the rain forest, men harvest wild honey from great rotting trees, for honey is another manifestation of Afek's semen and will promote the spiritual growth of men with glistening skins. Before the season of renewal is complete, the ritual elders finally congregate at the ritual center of the oil seep to gather up the sacred crystals from the tall shrine there. With reverence and muted chanting they bear the precious stones to tiny shrines throughout the forest and halt to anoint each shrine with oil. When the crystals are returned to the ritual center, men may again begin to hunt and to trap, and women to gather the flourishing bounty of the forest. Their ritual "work" is done. Now the ancestral spirits will guide their passage, and benign forest spirits will bring them no harm. And Afek's presence will be felt throughout the renewed forest.

As one climbs westward from the oil and the encompassing rain forest, one slowly emerges from the dank microclimate into the more open, mixed "montane" forest at the lower limits of human settlement. After passage through a somewhat transitional zone, one notes the appearance of two forest canopies: a towering formation of massive broad-leaved trees and conifers, and a lower tier of tree ferns, shrubs, saplings, pandanuses, and *Casuarina* trees. Near present and ancient residential and garden sites, the heavy forest gives way to small clearings and brief expanses of grasses and reeds. Heavily eroded footpaths crisscross the landscape and expose gnarled root systems. Log or vine bridges appear at stream and river crossings. The houses of hamlets are strung along defensible ridge tops. Below, women and children tend well-fenced sweet potato gardens or forage for a variety of wild foods in forest and stream. Domestic pigs wander between the hamlets and gardens in search of young shoots and earthworms or the succulent tubers in an unfenced sweet potato garden. Groups of boys romp through the nearby woodlands in search of food or sport. At night, the torches of witches are said to flicker on distant, uninhabited ridges, and malevolent spirits are known to wander abroad. In these settlement areas, adult men may tend sparse stands of nut pandanus or hunt for the scarce game that avoids human habitation, but their daily activities often take them to the higher or lower forest and its greater abundance. In the hamlets, however, men reside, shape political events, plan economic ventures, oversee domestic affairs, and concern themselves with the weighty matters of ceremonial exchange and ritual. On the territory of every clan a cult house forms a ritual center for male activities. There, fertility and other rites are conducted under the auspices of clan elders, and bamboo tubes of oil are stored for purposes of ritual and of trade.

In these settled areas of gardens and hamlets, the expanding grasslands are again thought not to be under ritual control, and signs of chaos begin to loom in the domestic realm. Indeed, ominous comparisons are made between the recent advent of local grass in these areas and the more distant and earlier desolation of the edge of the Strickland Gorge. The more recently invasive grass and a new variety of bee are said to be the unfortunate consequences of the European "discovery" of the sacred oil. Some men claim that this devastation began in the time of their forefathers, when Europeans were first sighted in the region, and that the appearance of the grasses and bees has been dramatically rising only since the oil was taken from their land. Bimin-Kuskusmin maintain that the grass is a sign that the underground flow of oil no longer encompasses some parts of their landscape, and some elders note that the new and vicious bee produces no honey. It may be recalled that both oil and honey are manifestations of Afek's semen and sources of the fertility and vitality of the land. There is much anxious discussion in men's houses about what has happened to the oil and the land, what can be ritually done about it, and what the future holds for their destiny as a people.

To restore this damaged land, special rites are now held in every clan cult house, and ritual experts periodically sprinkle oil on the grassy sites throughout the residential and garden areas. But all agree that these acts have not renewed the fertility of the soil, and that the grasses are increasing. Some elders say that the appearance of the bee is associated with the flight of game from the settlement areas, for the aggressive bee is believed to be a dangerous kind of "forest spirit" (*kwanuuk anengmotiir*) that attacks game animals. Perhaps, as Bosuurok suggests, the demon bee is in the vanguard of a recent invasion of deadly *anengmotiir* that have brought new illnesses and many deaths.[19] Sacred oil has also been used in new rituals created to destroy the bees and to ward off the new illnesses. In both old and new kinds of ritual undertakings, larger and larger amounts of oil are taken from the tiny trickle in the mountains. Some oil is diverted from traditional rites of fertility to cope with the new changes in the environment, and there is much concern about the consequences of weakening traditional ritual emphases in this manner. In addition, these new ritual uses of a finite supply of sacred oil not only are believed to have accomplished little, but also have had profound consequences for the regional trade, exchange, and ritual relations of the Bimin-Kuskusmin.[20]

The Bimin-Kuskusmin hold an areal monopoly over the oil and the secrets of its ritual use, for there is no other known source within the region. All other ethnic groups with whom the Bimin-Kuskusmin interact, and some groups beyond their immediate networks of relationships, highly value the sacred oil and the secrets of its use for ritual and curative purposes. By Bimin-Kuskusmin reckoning, the sacred oil promotes fertility, growth, health, and ritual efficacy among all known peoples and their lands, although the underground flow and major secrets of the oil do not extend beyond the Place of the Center.[21] Indeed, they often gave me quantities of oil when they thought I was weak or ill, but forbade me to take any oil beyond their realm into the outer world of new and unknown dimensions. Normally, vast amounts of oil are collected from the ritual center and stored in bamboo tubes for regular expeditions of exchange and trade, and this sacred substance brings in return a panoply of ritual treasures from other groups throughout the region and beyond.[22] As a consequence, the Bimin-Kuskusmin have been notably wealthy in sacred bird of paradise plumes, dugong tusks, wallaby bones, crocodile ribs, monitor lizard skulls, turtle carapaces, pearl-shell discs, stone adzes, ancient mortars and pestles, a variety of small shells, and other rare ritual valuables within their area. Their regional prestige has been measured by such unusual wealth and by their command of the precious oil and the efficacy of the powerful rituals that are linked to its use.

As ever-increasing amounts of sacred oil are devoted to dealing with new phenomena within Bimin-Kuskusmin territory by ritual means, however, the extent and frequency of external trade and exchange in the sacred substance are declining. And Bimin-Kuskusmin recognize that they must suffer the economic and political consequences of this decline while other groups must face ecological, ritual, and therapeutic uncertainties as a consequence. Indeed, reverberations of the Bimin-Kuskusmin interpretations of the European "discovery" of the oil and its ritual consequences are felt throughout their known world, and rebound on the delicate fabric of Bimin-Kuskusmin economic, political, and ritual relations with other peoples. At night in the men's houses, heated arguments may focus on the appropriate balances between internal ritual use and external trade or exchange of the oil, and much is at stake in these difficult deliberations. Yet, the subtle linkages between the sacred oil and the "natural" and "supernatural" landscape are always of primary consideration and extend far beyond other economic and political concerns. It is the future of the people and the land of the Place of the Center that is of primary importance, and the landscape is now in a delicate and threatened balance.

As one ascends from the valley settlements into the steep surrounding mountains, there is a greater frequency of *Lithocarpus* and oak, broad-leaved trees, tree ferns, and climbing bamboos. As the density of the montane forest increases, the undergrowth proliferates in a carpet of terrestrial orchids, climbing epiphytes, filmy ferns, flowering rhododendrons, creeping vines, stinging nettles, and scrambling shrubs. Along limestone ridges and outcroppings the forest growth becomes markedly stunted or blighted, and jagged karst formations jut through this sparser foliage. Myriad streams, springs, caves, sinkholes, rock outcroppings, crevices, cliffs, and other "natural" features of the lower and mid-montane terrain are identified with ancestral events in myths that add sacred contours to the landscape. Lightning-scarred trees and places of landslides—all signs of Afek's power—are remembered for the mysterious, "supernatural" events that have occurred there in the course of a lifetime. Tiny knolls and forest glades are vividly recalled as the sites where a hunter crouched in fear when the whistle of a witch, the rumble of an earthquake, or the howl of an anguished spirit—perhaps in the guise of a bird—was heard in the vast stillness. The montane forest is a realm of great ritual importance and intense spiritual presence.

In this domain, the animate, sentient, sacred crystals are ritually harvested from deep limestone caves, and other caverns serve as ossuaries for the carefully tended ancestral skulls. The dead are placed upon high burial platforms in these mountain forests, where the echoes of the chanting and wailing of ritual mourning resound eerily through the trees. At deep sinkholes the spirits of the dead find passage to the ancestral underworld, and ancestral spirits return through these passages to haunt and to bless this domain. At times of sacrifice, hunters seek the sacred marsupials and megapode eggs here. Great eagles and hawks soar overhead and nest in the high branches and cliffs, but snares and arrows doom the less wary of them for the ritual value of their feathers in headdresses. And as in the rain forest far below, the great phantom cassowary lurks always in the wooded background, for Afek's semen flows to this mystical, fertile, forested landscape. But here, with solemn ritual preparations, hunters may dare to kill Afek's symbolic image on special occasions if they draw no blood, or to gather a single egg from the terrestrial nest of the bird. They must then enter ritual seclusion and daub themselves with the yellow mud of funerary mourning, for they have killed the incarnation of their greatest ancestor to bring its awesome strength and power to the land and people of the Place of the Center.

Throughout these mountain slopes are scattered the ritually important nut pandanus groves, taro gardens, and hunting shrines of initiated men, and women and children may not linger long in this forest of ancestral spirits (*kuut ser kusem*). At regular intervals and times of crisis, the ritual elders conduct fertility rites among these crops and hunting shrines and place bamboo tubes of oil and of semen deep in the soil.[23] Such liturgical acts are said to renew the vital connection between these remote gardens, groves, and shrines and the distant oil seep, for the underground flow of oil is thought to reach into this mountain fastness. Indeed, there is no sign of the malignant grasses or bees in this domain. And fine pandanus nuts and taro tubers are believed to glisten with oil and semen and to strengthen in body and in spirit those who eat them. Near the hunting shrines the marsupials are said to be fat and fertile and to provide meat that drips with oily fat in the sacrificial and domestic cooking fires. But there is a deeply felt sense of precariousness within the forest that has emerged in recent times. Diviners have detected ominous signs of the entrails of marsupials that the land may be barren in the future. And powerful ritual acts and barriers must now be constructed to ensure against damage to the delicate "natural" and "supernatural" balance of the mountain forests.

Since the European "discovery" of the sacred oil, many shrines of a new kind have appeared in the taro gardens and pandanus groves, around the traditional hunting shrines, and along the lower ridges of the mountain slopes. Each is decorated with cassowary skulls and plumes in homage to Afek, and each contains a hollow cassowary egg filled with the sacred oil—Afek's semen. Whenever blighted crops or sick animals are observed in the forest, frightening omens are seen by diviners, or Europeans are believed to be active in some mysterious way in the region, sacrifices to Afek and other ancestral spirits are conducted at these shrines. And drops of precious oil are sprinkled over the ritual fires. When these shrines are active, all harvesting and hunting in the forest is forbidden. Diviners search the landscape for more promising omens of ritual success, but the signs often remain ambiguous. Tiny protective amulets of cassowary claws and bones are buried on the mountain paths that European patrols follow into the Place of the Center, and these objects are said to ensure that the patrols will not wander from these trails and come upon the most sacred features of the surrounding forest. When the patrols must cross water on their passage into the Place of the Center, Bimin-Kuskusmin elders may hide tiny crystals beneath the bridges or pour oil into the upstream currents. Such magical techniques are said to "blind" the Europeans to all sacred phenomena, for the implications of the "discovery" of the oil are viewed as a general threat that could recur in other sacred matters. Thus, as ritual barriers or shrines are erected along the lower slopes to impede the ascending grasses and bees, ritual constructions are also placed along the mountain crests that mark the northern, southern, and western frontiers of the Place of the Center to discourage the passage of patrols.

These high frontiers are an uncultivated wilderness—cold, dank, misty, and windswept. As the ascent toward the mountain summits becomes steeper, the montane forest begins to intergrade with the high moss forest. Where the moss forest prevails, the vegetation drips steadily as the perpetual mist of the cloud belt penetrates the thick undergrowth and condenses on the foliage. The underlying rock formation is largely a thick veneer of old, heavily decomposed limestone, from which occasional jagged crevices, clusters of rock spikes or karst, and odd-shaped nodules emerge. Landslide, tree fall, and erosion expose large areas of rock surface, which are soon covered with slippery masses of roots, lichens, mosses, ferns, and layers of rotting debris that turn to rich humus. This sodden carpet often hides deep, treacherous sinkholes, many of which are said to be passages to the ancestral underworld and are marked with ritual emblems. The rough-barked, moss-covered trees include new associations of beeches, oaks, conifers, and numerous other broad-leaved, high-altitude species, with a lower canopy of diverse *Elaeocarpus, Saurauia, Dacrycarpus, Schefflera, Amaracarpus, Papuacedrus,* and other varieties. The undergrowth presents a welter of young saplings, sprawling shrubs and vines, and *Cyathea* ferns. From the limbs of trees of the middle tier hang drooping, variegated masses of mosses, epiphytes, and bryophytes. From these fibrous clumps protrude several species of *Grammite* ferns, climbing orchids, and spiny *Calamus* palm tentacles. On all sides, slippery decay, cold winds, dripping moisture, sharp thorns, stinging nettles, jagged rocks, sheer cliffs, clinging roots or vines, treacherous holes, and other, more "supernatural" dangers crowd in upon the fearful traveler.

In the midst of this stark wilderness, men sometimes come to collect wild pandanus nuts and acorns and to hunt for marsupials, birds of prey, bats, and the occasional cassowary that inhabit this area. Women and children may gather frogs and toads and edible plants while passing along the higher trails, but they are afraid to veer from the track or remain long in this forest. Men, too, fear and avoid the eerie moss forest, for the warrior spirits (*aiyepnon*) of men whose violent deaths in battle remain unavenged capriciously attack travelers in the deep woodlands. A variety of harmful forest spirits and occasional witches (*tamam*) or sorcerers (*biis* or *kiimon*) roam abroad and seek their mortal prey. The *finiik* spirits of dreamers wander here, and the spirits of the dead pass through the moss forest in search of the sinkhole passages to the underworld. Both kinds of spirit may injure or kill the living. And *khaapkhabuurien* spirits of the recently deceased may seek deadly vengeance on living men before they evaporate into the swirling mists of the moss forest. When men do venture into this dangerous domain, they often wear protective cassowary-bone amulets and the powerful cassowary-plume headdress. If they should see a cassowary or its droppings among the trees, they would know that the great Afek was guarding the bearers of her ritual emblems. But only isolated tentacles of the underground flow of sacred oil—Afek's semen—penetrate into this remote frontier of the Place of the Center.[24]

In recent times ritual elders have journeyed to the moss forest to build and to tend tiny hidden shrines that are said to shield the sacred topography of the Place of the Center from European intrusions. Near the major paths on the mountain summits, cassowary-bone daggers are buried in the ground in triangular patterns pointed toward approaching patrols. At the base of these magical triangles, hollow cassowary eggs filled with oil are also buried. The shrines are said to thwart the efforts and desires of patrols to enter the land, and to keep the Europeans from "seeing" any sacred phenomena of major importance. The ritual elder Trumeng suggests that these shrines must be constantly renewed with new oil in order that "the power of Afek's semen will flow out toward the Europeans. Then they will find the mountain steep and hard. Their legs will be sore. They will stumble and fall. They will see only the dark mists of the forest ahead. . . . They will feel the cold of the winds. The trail will fade before them. They will turn back. . . . They will not come to the place of the center. . . . They will not again find the sacred oil. They will not take the sacred, hidden things." But the Europeans do come, and their intrusions always bring some sense of fear and a memory of a time when they saw a ritual cornerstone of the Bimin-Kuskumin cosmos and took away some sacred oil. For more than half a century, Europeans have been crossing into the known world from the outer, uncharted realm and have been moving slowly but relentlessly toward the Place of the Center and the revered oil seep.

Before the turn of the century, Luigi d'Albertis explored the upper reaches of the Fly River to the far south, and H. C. Everill charted the junction of the Fly and the Strickland. But these events of European history made no mark on Bimin-Kuskusmin oral traditions. Tales of bizarre men with terrifying weapons spread through the region long ago, and it is possible that Malay hunters may have crossed the Dutch border to the west in search of bird of paradise plumes. In 1910 a German-Dutch expedition journeyed into the border region near Atbalmin to the southwest, and the Bimin-Kuskusmin knew of a strange presence in this distant place. These vague, early impressions of new beings in the world only became focused, however, when the Kaiserin-Augusta-Fluss Expedition approached the western Telefomin area from the north. The expedition research anthropologist, Richard Thurnwald, traveled alone to the Telefomin plateau and then on to Feramin to the immediate west of the Place of the Center. He spent the night at Feramin, where he left steel tools and felt a sense of profound awe before rejoining his comrades. Bimin-Kuskusmin did not encounter Thurnwald, but ritual elders soon went to Feramin to acquire in trade some of these wondrous artifacts and to hear accounts of the strange "white skin" (*kaar yemur*). The European was thought to have been some kind of spirit never before seen, perhaps from the ancestral underworld. The steel implements were judged to have great power and were ceremonially installed in cult houses. Over the next four decades, more European items gained in trade would be added to this sacred store of modern relics. Yet some men began to ask if these new, miraculous phenomena were a threat to the integrity and efficacy of traditional rituals.

Between 1913 and 1924, Bimin-Kuskusmin learned of European patrols from the south moving between the Fly and Strickland rivers, but no contact was made with nearby peoples known to the Bimin-Kuskusmin. Between 1926 and 1928, however, C. H. Karius and I. F. Champion launched the famed expeditions of the North-West Patrol. The first expedition explored the Fly headwaters and fought brief battles with Faiwolmin warriors to the southwest, crossing the southern trade routes of the Bimin-Kuskusmin several times. Awed by accounts of guns and killings and in fear, the Bimin-Kuskusmin abandoned a planned trading expedition to the south and sent emissaries to the Faiwolmin to learn more of these strange events. Faiwolmin

Bosuurok (on right) and his brother survey the blight of the slowly encroaching grassland during a fertility rite intended to reestablish a connection between the infertile grassland and the powerful oil—the "semen" of the ancestor Afek. As a ritual elder, Bosuurok wears a headdress adorned with Raggiana Bird of Paradise plumes and carries a ritual drum.

tales of thundering, flashing weapons and bleeding, dying men brought panic to the Place of the Center upon the return of the emissaries, and the massive war ritual houses were activated as men armed for the defense of their territory. As the second Karius-Champion patrol then passed through nearby En-kaiakmin and swept toward Telefomin and far beyond into the upper Sepik plains, the terrified Bimin-Kuskusmin stood poised for an apocalypse that never came. They anxiously dissected all rumors of the twisting movements of the patrol out of an intense fear that it would suddenly turn toward their land, but then they heard of the mysterious danger moving far beyond their realm. Divinations did not foresee its return. Almost a decade passed before Europeans again threatened the land and the people of the Place of the Center. Bimin-Kuskusmin only vaguely recall the distant excursions of the Strickland-Purari Patrol (1935),

the Fox Brothers Expedition (1936), and the Archbold Expedition (1936–37) near the border of their known world. But, as yet unbeknownst to them, that world would never be the same in the wake of increasing exploration of their remote mountain domain.

In 1935–36, as a prelude to placing an airstrip at Telefomin, considerable aerial reconnaissance took place in the region. At that time the Bimin-Kuskusmin had a direct and frightening experience with new forces far beyond their ken. Late one morning a low-flying plane roared across the Strickland from the east and along the course of the Takiin River in the northern Bimin-Kuskusmin valley. At treetop level, the plane traversed the length of the Takiin and then retraced its course to disappear over the Strickland. Many Bimin-Kuskusmin were in gardens and hamlets beneath its path. In the ensuing panic, hamlets and gardens were abruptly abandoned, and people subsisted on foraged, raw food for weeks in the deep forest. The war ritual houses were readied, and sentries kept watch on the mountain perimeter of the Place of the Center. Runners sped along the trade routes in all directions to gather news of similar "attacks" on other groups and found that sightings of planes in recent months had been widespread. To prepare for further "attacks," and to summon ancestral power for communal protection, endless sacrifices were held in sacred caverns, and pandanus nuts were scattered in the forest to encourage Afek's symbol, the great cassowary, to destroy the plane. From the oil seep, bamboo tubes of oil were carried into the deep mountain forest to anoint the bodies and the weapons of warriors preparing for battle. War leaders prepared their plans of defense. Women and children gathered forest foods to withstand a siege. Ritual experts day and night intoned their solemn chants for the victory of the people and the welfare of the land. Intense terror was felt throughout the Place of the Center, but the fearsome plane did not return. Intertribal councils met to determine the significance of this "shadow of the sky" (*takhaak abiir*), but it remained a mystery.

In 1936–38, following this period of reconnaissance, the J. Ward Williams Expedition proceeded up the Fly River and across the formidable Hindenburg Wall to the Telefomin plateau to clear an airstrip. Within a week, a light aircraft soared onto a rough landing strip at Telefomin, and exploratory patrols—supplied by airdrops—began to fan out from this base through the region in search of mineral wealth. The new appearance of planes and the strange gathering of rocks were of concern to the ritual elders of the Bimin-Kuskusmin, as were the collections of faunae and florae acquired by the 1938–39 Archbold Expedition, but the patrols remained far to the west, north, and south. By that time the Bimin-Kuskusmin were pondering the significance of detailed reports of European paraphernalia and behavior. New artifacts were sometimes recognized by comparison with the treasures of trade that had been accumulating in the cult houses. The planes were said to be alive and dangerous, perhaps a species of monstrous forest spirit or flying-fox bat, and sacrifices were performed to appease them. Reports of skirmishes, insults, sacrileges, and lootings of gardens were frequent among groups having experienced the passing of patrols, but tales of the more benign powers and human kindnesses of Europeans circulated too. With much ambivalence, some elders expressed considerable curiosity about European ritual powers and sacred objects, for stories of planes, radios, guns, watches, mirrors, and other marvelous phenomena were told and embellished throughout the region. From myths of their sacred origins, Bimin-Kuskusmin elders recalled that

Afek's lastborn son returned with the great ancestor to the underworld to learn great secrets of ritual power and to be given mysterious and sacred objects that were not imparted to the human ancestors at the time of creation. Perhaps Afek's prophecy of the eventual return of this favored son to the world of the living had now been realized in the advent of the Europeans. But fears of sacrilege and bloodshed soon returned.

In 1938–39, a part of the famed Hagen-Sepik Patrol passed from the Western Highlands toward Telefomin, and crossed the Strickland Gorge near the ritual center of the oil seep. From hiding in the nearby forest, the hunter Gaaktiin breathlessly watched the Europeans supervise the construction of a bridge across the great gorge. From afar, he was unable to see the fabled white skin (*kaar yemur*), but he noted the strange, "two skin" (*kaar arep*) appearance of clothing on these new beings. As the patrol turned northward along the flank of the Strickland toward the land of the Oksapmin, Gaaktiin followed the toeless footprints at the distance and then ran to bear the startling news to the high settlement areas. He said that the Europeans had pointed in the direction of the sacred oil, and the elders questioned him about what kinds of magic the strange Europeans might have planted near the rain forest and the oil seep. That day the ritual experts brought sacred oil to sanctify the newly constructed bridge and to obliterate the strange footprints. They decreed that the oil seep should now be guarded and that travel in the rain forest should be banned. Soon rumors from the Oksapmin told of the killing of men and pigs and the burning of hamlets and gardens as the patrol passed through that neighboring land. Many Bimin-Kuskusmin men came to view the bodies of the dead and the devastated settlement areas to the north, and their reports of the carnage wrought by bullets aroused new terror in the Place of the Center. Once again, the war leaders assembled to announce plans of defense, but the patrol passed to the northwest without further incidents.

One of the recommendations of the Hagen-Sepik Patrol was the establishment of an administrative center at Telefomin to assist in the exploration and control of the vast area west of the Strickland. Before such plans could be implemented, however, Japanese forces landed at Rabaul on far New Britain in 1942, and they soon controlled the north coast of New Guinea. In that same year, a party of expatriate civilians at Wewak on the north coast were threatened by advancing Japanese forces and began an arduous journey up the Sepik and ultimately through the central mountains toward the south coast of Papua. For several months they camped on the Telefomin Plateau. As news of their presence traveled to the Place of the Center, Bimin-

Kuskusmin recalled harsh memories of the bloody Hagen-Sepik Patrol and readied an attack force to assist the Telefomin people in driving the strangers from their land. But these new Europeans were reported to be friendly, frightened, exhausted, and often sick and to pose no threat. Soon they departed to the south. Indeed, the ferocity of World War II in New Guinea passed almost unnoticed in these mountains until 1944, when masses of men and materiel were suddenly airlifted to the old landing field at Telefomin to create a military airstrip. Although the workers soon departed and the landing strip was rarely used, a permanent government station was finally established at Telefomin. During the construction of this airfield and thereafter, some Bimin-Kuskusmin men ventured to the forested edge of the Telefomin Plateau to watch the Europeans, for the elders had come to believe that these strange, feared beings were now a feature of their world and must be understood.

Following the war, patrols from Telefomin began an extensive exploration of the region, but none approached the frontiers of the Place of the Center until the early 1950s. Despite general alarm among the people when these patrols were abroad, the patrols never encountered any Bimin-Kuskusmin nor entered their territory. Rumors persisted of the increasing abuses of people and of local resources by patrol personnel, especially in the Telefomin region. Resentment and anger rose steadily throughout the area, reaching a peak with the defilement of a major cult house. Then in 1953 the Telefomin people launched a sudden and massive attack on the new despised Europeans and indigenous police, killing many police and all of the European officers. After the lone missionary radioed the alarm, a detachment of police was quickly flown to the plateau to quell the uprising, and numerous arrests of persons and retaliations against property soon occurred. Alerted by the Telefomin to these dark events, some fearful Bimin-Kuskusmin traders in the area witnessed many of the attacks and retaliations and returned to their homeland with the alarming news. The Bimin-Kuskusmin thought the raids against the Europeans to have been proper under the circumstances. But as allies of the Telefomin people, they assumed that government forces would soon turn eastward to take revenge upon them. They readied their war ritual houses and weapons, positioned sentries in the mountain passes, and waited for the inevitable attack. None came. In the following several years, a geological survey to the south and an ornithological expedition to the west caused concern among the ritual elders over the delicate "natural" and "supernatural" balances of the region, for it was known that these patrols took some specimens from the earth and the forest. The elders wondered if harm had been done to the landscape and if Europeans had taken revenge in this way. More patrols circled ominously closer to the frontiers of the land. Then, without warning, a severe epidemic of influenza spread eastward from the Telefomin plateau and struck the Place of the Center, and many people died in its wake.[25] The curers were helpless in trying to cope with this new illness. At last, it was thought, the Europeans had taken their vengeance. And their power was awesome.

After the epidemic, trade and ritual relations with the Telefomin people began to weaken, for Bimin-Kuskusmin feared to travel near the European presence on the plateau. Apparent but unfathomable associations among the new illness, the grass, the bee, and the advent of the Europeans were being noted with fear by the elders. And ominous changes in the topography along the Strickland and in the settlement areas were now observed. New rites were created and abandoned in a frenzied attempt to cope with these signs of ecological malaise. But the Bimin-Kuskusmin could no longer avoid the feared European, for he was even then approaching their frontiers. In the autumn of 1957, R. T. Neville and R. Aisbett led a large patrol from Telefomin across the Hindenburg Wall to the very edge of Bimin-Kuskusmin territory. Early on the morning of October 23, the patrol descended rapidly into the northern Bimin-Kuskusmin valley and frightened a woman and her children, who fled. The patrol left trade salt nearby and sent its Telefomin interpreters to find adult men. Soon, three men—all war leaders—arrived to guide the patrol to an uninhabited clearing, where a camp was made for two days. More war leaders appeared, and the ritual houses of war echoed faintly with the sound of drums in the distance. The Europeans exchanged marvelous treasures for simple food but spoke insultingly of local custom, warfare, weaponry, and other matters. A constable was designated to demonstrate the power of a rifle by shooting a local tethered pig, but he missed at close range, much to the amusement of Bimin-Kuskusmin bowmen.[26] The patrol stayed close to its camp. On the final day, the ritual elder Bosuurok led the patrol into the northern mass forest, beyond the frontiers of Bimin-Kuskusmin territory, and to the descending path toward the land of the Oksapmin. Unknown to the Europeans, hundreds of heavily armed men had been moving silently through the forest on either side of the patrol during all of its progress through the Place of the Center.

This first-contact patrol was the subject of intense discussion and elaborate divination for many months. Every remembered detail of the encounter was scrutinized for possible omens of hidden significance. Yet this patrol had been peaceful and, in retrospect, was not feared. Indeed, it had been controlled in its activities by ritual and by the constant presence of many hidden warriors. During the next several years, patrols ranged widely among the Oksapmin and to the west, but none returned to the territory of the Bimin-Kuskusmin. In 1961, with the establishment of a government post in the Tesin Valley of the Oksapmin, however, exploration of the perimeter of the Place of the Center intensified, and a few patrols entered the northern valley to examine the terrain and settlements and to conduct population censuses. In 1962 the Australian Baptist Missionary Society built a mission center in the Tekin Valley of the Oksapmin, but its pastors did not yet venture far from that base. In 1964 a patrol entered the southern valley of the Bimin-Kuskusmin for the first time, but few people were ever encountered. These peaceful patrols aroused little fear and much curiosity, for no patrol had done violence to the land or to the people. No one suspected that a major catastrophe was about to occur that would erode an already fragile sacred landscape.

In 1964, A. Marks had heard rumors while on patrol

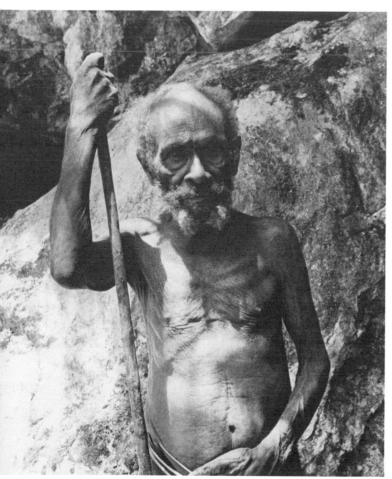

The ritual elder Trumeng examines the sacred oil seep (behind him) after an exploration patrol has passed to the north.

among the Oksapmin about the existence of oil within Bimin-Kuskusmin territory, and this betrayal by enemy Oksapmin groups has never been forgotten or forgiven by Bimin-Kuskusmin. In that same year, Marks led a patrol from the Oksapmin post into the northern valley of the Place of the Center and let it be known that he had come to see the source of the oil. While the patrol camped, anxious meetings of ritual elders took place in the cult houses to devise a plan to protect the sacred oil from this sudden intrusion. An initial feigning of ignorance about such matters was swiftly brushed aside by the patrol officer, who had seen traded bamboo tubes of oil among the Oksapmin. Finally, after much discussion, the elder Bosuurok was selected to lead the patrol on a long, meandering route through the rugged mountains for four days. Through a fearful Oksapmin interpreter, Bosuurok always continued to deny that the oil existed. Ultimately, after a long and wearing trek, the patrol abandoned its stated mission and returned to the government station. But, unbeknownst to the Bimin-Kuskusmin, Marks realized that he had been misled and recorded his suspicion in his patrol report.

The threat to the oil was devastating. Ever since the early Hagen-Sepik Patrol had passed along the Strickland below the oil seep, the ritual elders had placed this major sacred center under constant, protective guard. By now they knew that some order of ecological misfortune was upon the land, but they believed that the damage could be remedied through ritual uses of the oil in the blighted areas. The oil itself and its underground flow remained largely unimpaired. Suddenly, and through the treachery of the Oksapmin, the Europeans had learned of the oil and had come in search of it, but perhaps Bosuurok's ploy had discouraged their search. The elders were soon to learn otherwise. Once again in 1964, P. J. Lancaster launched a second attempt to find the oil seep that Marks had failed to discover. Lancaster's patrol moved southward from the Oksapmin station into the rugged mountains between the northern and southern valleys of the Place of the Center. Once again Bosuurok used the same strategy of deception, but this patrol kept its own pace on the meandering track and did not tire. Finally, Lancaster assured Bosuurok that he knew of the existence of the oil beyond any doubt and that further deception would bring dire consequences for the Bimin-Kuskusmin people. And Lancaster promised that the precious oil would not be damaged or stolen, that only a tiny amount would be taken in exchange for much wealth, that the sacred site would remain undisturbed, and that the wily Oksapmin would never learn of its location.

Bosuurok met with all other ritual elders of the

Bimin-Kuskusmin for more than a day. Finally, the paramount ritual leader of the ranking Watiianmin clan, Bosuurok's father, the greater elder Kiirep, voiced the consensus of an anguished statement and said,

> For the many seasons of my life, the European has been at the edge of the world. With pale skin and thundering weapons, he has come closer and closer to our midst. We always knew that he had great power, power to kill us all. . . . Once we believed that he was the great Afek's son come back from the place of ancestors, but his power is not that of Afek. Now, he wants to take her sacred semen. Will the cassowary flee from our forests? Will the land be swept away by great rains? Will our gardens be strong? Will we hunt where we have always lived? Make the European hear your speech. Talk clearly. Then, he must take only a little [oil]. . . . Some may die. . . . We must give the oil if we are to live with the European. . . .

For another whole day Bosuurok tried to explain to the European something of the sacred importance of the oil and of the land of the Place of the Center to all Bimin-Kuskusmin, living and dead. Then, with no remaining recourse, Bosuurok and Lancaster alone slowly descended through the forest to the ritual center of the oil seep. Bosuurok filled the small container with the precious substance and they returned to the camp. Lancaster gave ax heads, machetes, knives, salt, tobacco, and tinned meat in exchange for the oil, but Bosuurok himself would not touch the new wealth. On the journey from the rain forest he had tried to de-sanctify (*aiyem-baniim-khraaniin*) the sacred oil, but he feared that he had not succeeded.[27] On the next day, the patrol traversed the northern valley and climbed through the moss forest, taking the oil away from the Place of the Center forever. Bosuurok returned to the ritual center to check the vital flow of the sacred oil and to make sacrifices at the shrines.

When I left Bimin-Kuskusmin territory in 1973, I parted last and most sadly with Bosuurok. He stood and smiled and embraced me with wise words, for he knew that I would not return before his death.[28] He was a splendid, forceful elder who was known throughout his land and lands beyond as a man of great and sacred power. In the graceful and measured cadences of the oratory of important men, he expressed the great strength and beauty and sensuality of his beloved homeland with rare eloquence and compassion. He knew well that the pace of change was quickening in his world and that his aged generation would perhaps be the last to follow the long ritual trail of Afek's sacred cassowary through the labyrinths of the steamy rain forest to the misty heights of the moss forest at the edge of his domain. He saw the mission and the government seeking to wrest the young from ancient traditions, as Europeans had once torn a sacred substance from his beloved land. In both contexts of change, he acutely saw and deeply felt the delicacy of the fabric of knowledge and emotion that had long bound together the "natural" and "supernatural" strands from which his world was woven. He told me that the sacred oil was like a shining, black thread that reflected the rainbow canopy over the great waterfall pool where the phantom cassowary comes to drink at dawn and dusk. Its vital flow underlay the variegated, sacred contours of the land and bound together the rich bounty and the strong people of the Place of the Center and the world below. It was the semen of Afek which had created and sustained the Bimin-Kuskusmin since the beginning of time. For Bosuurok, in his declining years, his myths and rituals would grant him solace against the erosion of this sacred landscape, for, like the phantom cassowary, he was a creature of the subtle hues of the deep forest, and not of the open, barren grasslands of the new era.

24. Dialectical Dreaming: The Western Perception of Mountain People

MICHAEL TOBIAS

In mountain oases of Ahaggar, deep in southern Algeria, earthworms have survived from Pleistocene times while surrounding desert fauna have repeatedly been wiped out. Despite its rigorous environment, the mountain promotes persistence. Little wonder, then, that the earliest villages in human history were all in the highlands. In Europe, it took the technological drainage of marshes to fuel resettlement in the plains. In Mesopotamia, the first prairie towns sprang up beside sophisticated irrigation works. But the sacred water was all of the mountains, as were the annual rituals atop ziggurats, meant to inspire the flow of water. Human thoughts, even in the long aftermath, leaned nostalgically towards the high places. This Ice Age spirituality continued into the Stone Age. At Çatal Hüyük, in Anatolia, a single, lonely wall painting depicts the volcano Hasan Daği, which rears its wild countenance far behind town. Obsidian was quarried there. But more important, lovers stole away on hot summer nights to bask in the mountain's cool breezes, a refreshment akin to religion.

Nature has fostered a wellspring of thought in mountains. Fifteen million years ago the dryopithecine great apes, traversing East Africa's Rift Valley, must have savored the cool air as well. And before them, arboreal shrews cultivated sensory acuities that later marked Cro-Magnon curiosity as it thrilled to what few precious moments of sheer vertigo were left it.

The earliest domesticators fourteen thousand years ago were mountain folk at the Spirit Cave in northern Thailand, and later in the Andes and Zagros ranges. With modest density of population there was a scarcity of dialectic, of history, of contention and warfare. Among lean and tenacious, healthy, blushing mountain people there has grown up a rare and invaluable quality to humanity.

But mountains awarded little obvious gain, only fringe ideas, habitats, beliefs, and customs marked by peripheral, solitary peoples with mute pasts and right-brain preferences. Whether it be Inca or Tibetan gold, Yunnan musk, highland *Meconopsis* (blue poppy), sullen statuary, cat's-eye, resplendent *thankas,* or slaves, the mountains have, despite their relative poverty, provided perilous incentive for that stream of flatlanders who have heard rumors, myths, fables, unimaginable surveyor's gab. Such tales first spelled out the fate of mountain people, whose once impregnable fortresses and noble paucity have nearly fallen to the investment of outside forces. To be sure, the Chinese have invited back the Dalai Lama on their terms. But life in the Himalayas could never be the same.[1]

There was once an abundant security in mountain life—aesthetic, religious, and agricultural satisfactions that exceeded the turmoil, brick, and monoculture of the lowland world. There was indeed a spiritual purchase up high: invigorated animism, winter nights, sparkling noons, the chimes and wind flutes and lowing of highland heifers. There were T'ang poets, Sung landscapists, *hsien* wizards with feathers, shamans denuded in the snow, and whole villages—tens of millions of carousing family folk—firmly in the tide and fecundity of creation, all in absence of Norelco shaving cream, oil refineries, and barbed wire fencing. The warm, providential intimacy of long houses, yurts, hogans, caves, and gumpas exerted magical influence over all those who managed to get in from the outside. But magic only affects the heart of believers. The plains dwellers had big bellies but soft blood and little faith. There was bound to be conflict. All peoples, in all times, have been leery of philosophy. Majestic thought abounds in the highlands—not the noteworthy stuff better suited to a fourteenth-century Paris or nineteenth-century Heidelberg, or Princeton's fusion laboratories, but processes of interaction and reverence that characterized *Homo sapiens* aboriginally and continue to do so today among hundreds of millions of survivors still in touch with the beginning of mankind, systems of interrelationship that coddled our ancestors in inaccessible nooks and valleys. Such havens gave birth to sufficiency, allometry, human scale—to all of those traits we now seek desperately to reacquire.

The image of mountain people is what concerns us here: how it evolved; what mind-sets were fueled by outsiders; why western civilization came to suspect serpents, then saints, then shepherds under every rock; and where this increasing humanization of nature led the historical imagination.[2]

ROMANTICISM AND THE MOUNTAIN
EXPERIENCE

Before 1800 numerous translations of Horace-Benedict De Saussure's celebrated *Voyages dans les Alpes* (1796) appeared throughout western Europe. Other mountain accounts by Mark Beaufoy (*Annals of Philosophy*, 1817), the Polish poet Count Malczewski, Jeremiah van Rensselaer, W. Coxe, T. Martyn, Pinkerton, G. W. Bridge, and Gottlieb Runer flooded the journals and book-buying market, as well as the lecture circuit. Gavin De Beer cites more than seven hundred individuals who traveled through and wrote of the Alps before 1816, the time when Percy Shelley founded legends about Mont Blanc as a transcendental image. More important, both Shelley and Byron complained about the "goitered idiots" who dwelt on the lower alpine slopes. By the industrial era that very sentiment had entered the working vocabulary of social psychologists who stated resolvedly that alpine peoples were short, brown, broad-headed, with a limited mentality, and antiprogressive, their only attributes—a love of labor and frugality—apparently condemning them to slavery and stupidity. Symptomatic of this view, Mary Shelley gives us Frankenstein's monster, a mere "figure of a man" who "descends" the Mer de Glace.

These Alps were invested with "ghostly grease and rancid religion" (Swinburne) but little admiration for locals. English tourists fired their rusty howitzers in appreciation of the scenes (to Ruskin's great horror), while others got down on their hands and knees and prayed. ("Unable to take my eyes from the mountains, I threw myself on the ground and drank in, gasping, the enchanting spectacle" [Sir Archibald Alison, *Some Account of My Life*, 1883]). Wordsworth's *Descriptive Sketches Taken during a Pedestrian Tour in the Italian, Grison, Swiss and Savoyard Alps,* published in 1793; Humboldt and Bonpland's *Personal Narrative;* and Humboldt's later two-volume study of the Andes had a profound effect on the matrix of mountain images throughout the nineteenth century. Asia had special pertinence toward this effect. In Kotzebue's *Account of His Banishment to Siberia* (three volumes, 1806), Mountstuart Elphinstone's *An Account of the Kingdom of Caubul and Its Dependencies in Persia, Tartary, and India* (London, 1815), and H. T. Colebrooke's *On the Height of the Himalaya Mountains* (Calcutta, 1817) we have all the trappings of science merging with mythology. Ruskin had said that one derives the feeling, the longing of infinity in "no more than such a mere luminous distant point as may give to the feelings, a species of escape from all the finite objects about them." Earlier, Edmund Burke had suggested that "Greatness of

Tibetan mendicant. Photo by M. Tobias.

dimension is a powerful cause of the sublime. . . . an hundred yards of even ground will never work such an effect as a rock or mountain of that altitude. . . . A perpendicular has more force in forming the sublime, than our inclined plane; and the effects of a rugged and broken surface seem stronger than where it is smooth and polished." Our ancestral bush apes, with a higher concentration of retinal rods than cones, passed on the affinity for climbing along branches. The eye has not changed appreciably since the diversion from *Ramapithecus,* who was largely a tree dweller. And in no more favorable light than that enshrouding mountains are we able to glean the evolution of an idea. The Romantic Era had come full swing, from religious cosmography, the adoration of the saintly figure, to those displacement activities by which the mountain landscape was abstracted.

THE EMERGENCE OF ALPINE
LANDSCAPE PAINTING

By the nineteenth century the demonology of mountains had been eroded, replaced by the sheer resplendence of the Picturesque passions, topographical poetry, and the new interest in Orientalia, with its tradition of *shan-shui* mountain-water aesthetics. Arnold Boecklin's *Petrarch Beneath Mount Ventoux,* Camille Corot's *Homer and the Shepherds,* and the Barbizon euphoria of Jean-François Millet confirm the disappearance of the saint. Geological time is now peopled with biological space. Gauguin's *Brittany Landscape: Swineherd with Yellow Pigs* (1888) celebrates the angiosperms amid a pastoral ideology, replete with hedgerows, neatly cropped hills, and the unforbidding regularity of inclines. Such sentimentality has little power to seize the imagination, but caters instead to the comforts of the farmer. Painters such as Francois Diday, Alexandre Calame, John Brett, Edward Lear, and John Ruskin are each concerned to provide portals through which we might glean evidence of the tranquil alpines. And this epoch of serenity is further contrasted by the Romantic temperament in Joseph Turner, Caspar Friedrich, and John Martin, all of whom treat the mountain as a transcendent symbol lingering in the visceral reality, where people travel, pay thrall, and die. The visual codes of nineteenth-century Europe were utterly determined by the oxymorons of pictorial approach: desolation and lavish beauty. And this conflicting enthrallment was carried over into America.

Environmental determinism, sociobiology, nurture-nature complexes of the psyche, all tax the intellect beyond patience when confronted with the richness of response that landscape has elicited in certain parts of the world. The Himalayas enraged the sympathies and ardor of British lonely-heart explorers who doted, dared, and by battlement style or political sinecure managed to intrepidly cross the wastelands north of India, bringing home portfolios of artwork and lore that have inspired, in the twentieth century, the very notion of Shangri-la. Similarly, on a more religious stratum, the Andes bore down on the Incas, who buried some of their dead high up in the glaciers and constructed pyramidal prayers, borrowing from nature's own architecture. In America it was the Rocky Mountains that played merry hell with the senses, fostering dreams come true and dreams shattered, dividing cultures and spawning that great hope that brought down the Eastern establishment, at least as far out as Denver, and then coaxed it further West.

The painter and literateur were as crucial to this migration as the U.S. Geological Survey. As presented in the extraordinary work *The Rocky Mountains: A Vision for Artists in the Nineteenth Century* (Patricia Trenton and Peter H. Hassrick), early American landscape painters actually *taught* Easterners how to see and think about mountains. *View of Boston* (John Smibert, 1738) and *Fairmont and the Shuylkill River, Philadelphia* (William Groombridge, 1800) are two early examples of pastoral in the United States that first instituted the practice of seeing nature according, more or less, to *its* rules. Such works employed familiar surroundings to accomplish their task—a boat here, a farmstead there. In England, two hundred years had gone into the dispensing of such security, in the gardens of William Kent and the ravishing lyrics of the wilderness poet Colcridge. But in America there was to be a schism,

every bit equal to that of European Romanticism: a vision divided between the serene and the apocalyptic sublime; between a Hamilton on the banking side of town and a Jefferson across the way in the wild radish patch.

Imagine then the rousing storms that accompanied the first sightings of the Rockies. The painters minced nothing; they sought eagerly to present a tantalyzing world vision more impressive than that of the Alps, and they succeeded.

Samuel Seymour, a painter assigned to the Major Stephen Long expedition, was the first known artist to depict the Colorado Rockies, say Trenton and Hassrick. His *Distant View of the Rocky Mountains* (1820) is rather extraordinary, combining elements of traditional German romanticism with the later work of George Catlin, the Indian documentarist. Seymour sees rarified, glacial crags, over-exposed, across the quiet, lumbering prairies where bison roam in orderly array. Indians stand on a foreground hillock, watching over their territory with patriarchal confidence. They do not yet notice that they are being observed by outsiders, so that the bucolia remains intact, for the time being. Major Long had urged his artist-for-hire to portray a vast land that would, for all time, remain the haunt of wildness. Such was the dread and the thrill that first issued from the land. Thomas Doughty, Titian Peale, Karl Bodmer, and Alfred Miller all followed the lead of Seymour, occupying themselves with the presentation of paradise, and perhaps no more glamorously, gauzily, than in Miller's *Stewart's Camp, Wind River Range, Western Wyoming* (1865). The components are replete: haze, sentiment fused with verticality, the rangy Indian at peace with every bush and moat.

Military and railroad surveys brought along other perspectives to the accumulating vision of the Rockies handed down by artists to the insatiable public eye. Here was the mid-nineteenth-century projection of wealth, of Horace Greeley's "West," of the lavish possibilities of manifest destiny, in Richard Kern's inherently resource-concerned sketches, John Mix Stanley's eye for settlement sites, and Gustavus Sohon's use of topography to illustrate military predicaments out in the wilds. The boundary surveys employed draughtsmen whose purpose in coming along was in fact divided. On one hand they had joined up to record a track West, to depict authentic experience useful for the construction of quarter-section maps and the staking out of industrial prizes. But they were genuinely stricken with the beauty, which they could not help but convey. So we get a Joseph Heger drawing the Wasatch mountains in the summer of 1858. Heger was a graduate of West Point, served with Company K of the First Regiment of Mounted Riflemen. He and twenty-five others followed Captain Randolph March from Fort Union to Camp Floyd, Utah, to deal with the Mormon crisis, such as it was. In so doing, Heger accomplished twenty-four drawings in pencil, recording the troop's movements. His impressions are remarkable, unexpected. "Near the Summit of Wahsatch Mts., July 30th/58, Pencil" has about it the intelligence and ambition of Leonardo's own earliest sketches. That's right, Leonardo Da Vinci. And in his enthusiasm Heger provided an insight into the Green River valley that will not, can not, dissipate from recall. Similarly, John Young edified the Timpanogos River canyon, James Alden glorified the Kintla Mountains, Ransom Holdredge placed a Sioux Camp in the Rockies adjoining God itself. Laramie, Greeley, the Platte River, Georgetown Creek, Chicago Lakes, Raton Pass, the La Poudre, and Valley of the Chugwater all assume legendary grace, places of timeless relish that came throughout nineteenth-century exploratory America to dominate the mind, as scholars like Rod Nash and Hans Huth have pointed out.

Perhaps John Kensett's *In the Heart of the Rockies (Bergen Park, 1870)* and George Caleb Bingham's *View of*

Pike's Peak, 1872 best characterize the symptom of veneration at work in the West. The colors, as reproduced in the work by Trenton and Hassrick—the frosting of snow, sophisticated dabble of oil, incline of shrub, salience of bark, poignance of cloud—all contribute to this inventive opulence of landscape, of seeing more clearly. Here was the painter's access to revelation, as it was played out in the early years of mountain settlement. Today these testaments should help us to hold on where destinies seem increasingly threatened and the legacy of high mountain America ignored, or trammeled.

These early eighteenth- and nineteenth-century portraitures of nature were concerned with periphery and showed the extent to which human occupancy could teeter, but lent no credibility to the flirtation.

The true mountain man—the American Indian—emerges from this maelstrom of vertical sensation. Bierstadt's *Sunset Light, Wind River Range of Rocky Mountains* (1861) and Catlin's numerous noble renditions of Plains Indians, often surrounded by cliffs, highlight an era that was absorbed with possessing whatever the West had to offer. Traffic in furs led fiercely independent men and women into Ute country, where bears figured more prominently than bison

The British entering Nagaland, mid-19th century. Courtesy of
Gordon Means.

and where the water snows again amplified the religious character of fourteen-thousand-foot peaks. Bierstadt paid particular tribute to such views and to the indigenes who inhabited those mountains.

Ultimately, the mountain rhapsodist reverts to the original abstraction. In Ferdinand Hodler, August Macke, Thomas Hart Benton, Hartouzian, Thomas George, Milton Avery, John Marin, to name a few, we see no person. Georgia O'Keefe's New Mexico mountains, saturated in pale or lambent hues and glossy textures, have more to say about meandering crows than about residents. Only Segantini implants dark hooded figures beneath the Alps, as Brueghel had done. Ernst Kirchner, in his luscious *Shepherds in the Evening, Sertig Path* (both 1937), and early *Winter Moon Landscape* (1919), endorses the notion of Alpine pastoralists, but so attenuated, so reduced to stick-figure color, as to suggest a triumph of art over empathy, albeit an uneasy one.

One meager tradition stands out which is contrary to this historical abstraction: Nicholas Roerich, Himalayan explorer, writer, and painter of the 1930s, and others like him, painted primitive, telling watercolors of the Tibetan and northern Indian population. As far back as the 1850s, pen-and-ink graphics, as seen in the exotic spate of Himalayan archives available at various university libraries and explorer clubs, captured the lonely, noble, affable character of Asian montagnards. By the early twentieth century that vision was a photographic one, and what rings clear is the tassled, ragged, spartan, yet loving condition of Mongolian herders and Tibetan yakmen. There are perhaps no better photographic documents of this type than those of Kingdon-Ward, taken in the 1920s, many of the photographs made by his sole companion, Lord Cawdor. They range across Pemakod, in Southeastern Tibet, Yunnan, and the Upper Mekong, Irrawady, Salween, and Tsangpo rivers, the most inaccessible, mysterious mountain area on earth. With the photographic vision, however, such places and peoples entered a new phase of popularity. Just as Yosemite suffered the subsequent invasion by those who had been photographically titillated, so more remote spots witnessed an upswing in tourists, mountain climbers, and anthropologists.

THE RISE OF ETHNOGRAPHY

The Roman essayist Varro had first described the Scythian mountain regions as characterized by "inhospitable solitude." For Lucretius, such regions were the home of all primitives, whom he lauded as preferable to the degraded Roman citizen. "The people are necromancers," said Marco Polo of the Asian mountain people he encountered, "and by their infernal art perform the most extraordinary and elusive enchantments that were ever seen or heard of." The *Ebstorf Mappa Mundi* (thirteenth century) was the first widely recognized ethnographic cartography. Roger Bacon was able to write in *Opus maius* "in accordance with the experience of writers on nature and of travellers respecting the places and races of the habitable world." Many visitors had described trips to the mountains of the Holy Land. One such was Felix Fabri, who referred to hairy mountain women accustomed to traveling naked, in bands, with tamed lions working for them; these creatures would attack unsuspecting pilgrims from behind rocks; it is difficult to know whether Felix enjoyed such encounters or not. The Crusader Jacobus de Vitriaco wrote about the customs of those peoples he encountered in the Middle East; Giovanni di Plano Carpini (*Historia Mongalorum*), Willem van Ruusbroek (*Itinerarium*), and Johannes de Monte Corvino, an Asiatic missionary, all described Central Asians in detail, following Marco Polo's *Book* (1399).

The ethnographer Ramon Pan accompanied Columbus; Matteo Ricci, a sixteenth-century missionary, went into China and Antonio Malfante (fifteenth century) into Africa, while Bernardino de Sahagun journeyed early on among the Aztecs. Battitista Ramusio edited a collection of travel essays in the sixteenth century; Pierre Bayle and Montaigne both asserted the benefits of diverse peoples and customs; and William Temple, in *An Essay upon the Origin and Nature of Government* (1672), offered a climatological explanation for the diversity of cultures and "unequal course of imaginations."

Joannes de Laet (1593–1649) compiled extensive travel writings, Johannes Scheffer composed the first ethnographic treatise, titled *Lapponia,* in 1673, and Edward Brerwood speculated that American Indians migrated from Siberia through Alaska in his *Enquiries Touching the Diversity of Languages and Religions* (London, 1635). Hugo Grotius and Jean Bodin used travel accounts to establish a relationship between culture and geography. Much of these accounts derived from Samuel Purchas's twenty-volume *Purchas His Pilgrimes: Containing A History of the World in Sea Voyages and Land Travels by Englishmen and Others;* from Richard Hakluyt's *Voyages* (twelve volumes, published in the late sixteenth century); from the *Liber Peregrinations* of Jacopo Da Verona; from the fifteen-volume *Monumenta Henricina;* and from the *Annual Letters* of the Jesuit missionaries.

In all this frenzy, mountain people retain a special favor. Bodin's *Six Books of the Republic* survey governments throughout the world with an eye to natural en-

Lamayuru Monastery, Ladakh. Photo by M. Tobias.

vironments and deterministic aspects: "In the same climate, altitude, and latitude and the same degree we can see the different consequence of highlands in comparison to lowlands." Montesquieu would write, "Lack of fertility of the soil makes people diligent, sober, tough at work" (*Spirit of Laws*). In his *Histoire naturelle,* Georges-Louis Leclerc, Count de Buffon (1707–88), presented his own theory of environmental determinism with regard to mountain people of northern Tartary, suggesting that they were "robust and uncultivated." Johann Gottfried von Herder (1744–1803) believed that "nature has drawn determinant lines round her species." He acknowledged "laws of nature" that were beautiful and said, "The most ancient hierarchy upon earth reigns on the mountains of Tibet; and that the nearer to Asia, the more firmly established the government and customs."[3]

Where did Herder get such a notion? St. Cacella and J. Cabral had gone from their Catholic Mission in Bengal into Bhutan in 1626. Other Jesuits had penetrated China, India, and Burma throughout the seventeenth century. Missionaries had gone to the Philippine highlands in 1581 and the Andes as early as 1571.

Thirty years before a Peruvian mission, the Zapotec ruler Santiago de Guevea was pictured seated in a temple adjoining a central mountain. In one of eighteen oval toponyms within the depicture, a mountain has the head of a happy villager. Could such portrayals—seen in Tibetan panorama paintings—have given rise to this European interpretation of culture? The ordered hierarchy of Bodhissatva configurations, in Potala *thangkas,* amid the backdrop of Mount Su-Meru and its heavenly circumspections, could have rendered just such a commentary.

Warren Hastings, in charge of the British East India Company, sent George Bogle in 1774 on an offcial British mission to the Panchen Lama at Bkra shis lhun po. Nine years later, Samuel Turner led a second mission. Their reports, in the context of the previous Jesuit letters and the long-time sentimentality of theologians on the subject of Asian paradise, may have influenced Herder. Martin Dobrizhoffer's monograph on the South American *Abipones* (1783) made a strong case for primitive highlanders. Herder is perhaps the greatest Romantic philosopher; he elucidates the primitive nature poetics of Homer, McPherson (Ossian), and

Shakespeare and develops an uncanny affection for genetic origins and primitive, spontaneous poetry, which he likens to religion. His masterpiece, *Ideen zur Philosophie der Geschichte,* grapples with the connection between human evolution and the environment. Here he contests Kant's anthropology by placing human beings firmly in the ebb and flow of Nature, whereas Kant had discerned human development merely in terms of rational free will. How different Herder's feelings were from those of others of his era can be understood by comparing them to David Hume's concepts. Hume flatly denied any importance of the natural environment, in favor of moral and cultural determinants.

Hobbes, Locke, Rousseau, and Montesquieu were all steeped in the anthropological literature of their eras. Hobbes had read of the warring tribes in America, and one can follow Locke's political development by cross-checking his eclectic readings; Montesquieu's own booklist was compassed by Orientalia, while Rousseau was enamored of Indian tales from Central America. One of the greatest nineteenth-century sources of such information came from the continuing missionary writings published in Lyons between 1819 and 1854 in thirty-four volumes: *Lettres édificantes et curieuses: Écrites des missions étrangères, avec les Annales de la propagation de la foi.* Graphic illustrations, such as Dufour's work on Cooke's *Voyages,* further weighted the image pool of savagery.

The early history of exploration in Tibet and the writings which resulted came to exert a profound influence on Westerners. Tibetan landscape lent its inhabitants the full vocabulary of superlatives, such that Shangri-la came to assume the proportions of previous millennarian aspirations.[4]

TIBETAN EXPLORATION

In the 1830s the Maharaja of Jammu annexed all of Kashmir, including Ladakh, and Alexander Cunningham went in shortly thereafter for a year, subsequently publishing a comprehensive study of the region that is still considered the definitive text. No heart of darkness ever proved so consistently ravaging as the splendor and desolation of the western Himalaya in the nineteenth century. The dozens of clandestine commercial, survey, and political missions that debouched into the high-altitude deserts and wild ravines of Kashmir, Ladakh, Baltistan, Kafiristan, Wakhan, and Eastern and Western Turkestan held one inestimable spur in common: the remoteness of the places and peoples. What few journeyors had skirted the tracts before the British Great Game left scarcely any records of those regions. Chinese Buddhist monks, such as Hiuen Tsang, had come in the sixth and seventh centuries seeking manuscripts from northern Indian monasteries and ascetic communities. Marco Polo crossed the Pamirs in 1274 but left all of three pages of notes. Jesuit missionaries, such as Fathers Azeveda, Desideri, and de Goes, traveled through Tibet in the seventeenth and eighteenth centuries, their data figuring in the nebulous maps of Rennel and d'Anville. François Bernier and George Forster had made it to Srinagar in 1663 and 1783, and George Bogle had crossed much of the country in 1774. But their diaries left large gaps: the Himalayan cultures were obscured by reports of warring raja states and furtive mixtures of Mongol, Turanian, and wayfaring Aryan. The whole region remained cloaked in impenetrable unresolve.[5]

When William Moorcroft, disguised as a *saddhu* in 1812, set off after Tibetan goat wool for the East India Company, he had all of two sources to follow: Polo's brief remarks and Elphinstone's itinerary. "Mooztagh, or Kurrakooram" had just appeared on maps. Moorcroft climbed the Niti Pass in Garhwal, went on to Gartok and Manasarowar to the source of the Sutlej. In his remarkable book, *A Journey to Lake Manasawara in Undes, a Province in Little Tibet,* he describes his guide as a "pundit" who leads him "up rocks nearly perpendicular, and on which irregularities, for the toe to hang upon, were at a most inconvenient distance." Creeping on hands and knees, they attain the Niti Ghati, skirting tremendous gapes to "appal the stoutest heart." His affection for the guide, and the guide's people, is borne out.

In 1819, searching for stallions, Moorcroft made it through the Pir Panjal, spent a month in a beggar's house, continued to Kulu, over the Rohtang into Leh (two months), met the Hungarian itinerant scholar de Koros (the first and only Tibetan scholar of the Romantic Era), and continued up to Bukhara. Moorcroft and his two companions would die mysteriously in the deserts south of Bukhara.

After them came Victor Jacqemont, a botanist and friend of Stendhal who in every way met the Byronic prototype. Following a turbulent love affair with an opera singer, seeking solace in the ultimate wilds, he arrived in Calcutta in 1829 dressed all in black. Two years later, following a stint in Lahore, he ended up in Srinagar, where he poured out 346 letters, romanced the women, and died the following year of heat and fever in Bombay.

Joseph Wolff, Godfrey Vigne, and Alexander Gardiner all founded legends, and each one embodied that characteristic madness that the Rousseaus had earlier ennobled. Take Wolff, for example. A disciple of Jesus, originally Jewish, his early romps had taken him throughout German monasteries. In 1823 we hear of him in Jerusalem and deathly ill; in 1824, sick in Baghdad; in 1825, prostrate with typhus in the Caucasus before being rescued and nurtured back to life in a Georgian sanitorium; in 1827, shipwrecked in Cephalonia; in 1828, with dysentery in Cairo; and in 1829, attacked by pirates near Salonica. Wolff's *Researches and Missionary Labours, 1831–34,* appeared in 1835. The book was strewn with errors, but what legacy its successors inherited was the fact of Wolff's animated passage through the Hindu Kush, over snowdrifts and for hundreds of miles, *naked,* down into Kabul, an apparition.

Vigne was to catch the first sighting of Nanga Parbat from the Gurais Pass in 1835. He then pressed on and by early September of that year obtained a glimpse of Baltistan "through a long sloping vista formed of barren peaks, of savage shapes and various colours, in which the milky whiteness of the gypsum was contrasted with the red tint of those that contained iron— I the first European that had ever beheld them (so I believe), gazed downwards from a height of six or seven thousand feet upon the sandy plains and green orchards of the valley of the Indus at Skardu, with a sense of mingled pride and pleasure of which no one but a traveler can form a just conception."

Alexander Gardiner was less direct. The greatest, most controversial of nineteenth-century Asian explorers, he was the first westerner to visit Yarkand, Gilgit, to cross the Karakoram Pass, and reach Kafiristan. He traversed the Kun Lun, Karakoram, Pamir, Tien Shan, Hindu Kush, and Pir Panjal before maps acknowledged the names of the very mountain ranges. Well ahead of his times, he kept scarcely any notes of his adventures: consequently, for nearly a century, his unrivaled wanderings were discounted as fraud. Wrote the Asian geographer, Sir Henry Yule: "But amid the phantasmagoria of antres [countries] vast and deserts idle, of scenery weird and uncouth nomenclature, which flashed past us in the diary till our heads go round, we alight upon these familiar names as if from the clouds; they link nothing before or behind; and the traveller's tracks remind us of that uncanny creature which is said to haunt the eternal snows of the Sikkim

Hemis Monastery, Ladakh. Photo by M. Tobias.

Himalaya and whose footsteps are found only at intervals of forty or fifty yards." A wonderful man, that Gardiner. Indeed, such was his story. When he died peacefully in Srinagar in 1877, at the age of ninety-one, the American-born mystic had already, like Moorcroft, inspired an age of exploration over terra incognita, into those *bolors,* half-revealed highlands, which drove the British Raj crazy.

Britain was competing for Asian trade against Russia, and the Chinese and Muslims in Turkestan were being none too cooperative. In their quest for a trade route between Leh and Yarkand, innumerable men were enigmatically massacred. When Dr. Thomson climbed the Sasser-La above Nubra, he needed no trail other than the numerous human skulls that littered the way. Such forebodings could break a man. John Wood, singly seeking the source of the Oxus, would decry the wretched solitude along those desolate banks of the legendary Sir-i-kol. Others maintained the veneer of stability that would later mark the Victorian expeditions. When Lieutenant Henry Haversham Godwin-Austen, with the Kasmir Survey, traversed the furthest reaches of Baltistan, making up the Panmah Glacier to a "desolation of desolation," failing to score a route over the Mustagh Pass, he acknowledged the dreaded portents, the crashing avalanche, but then proceeded smoothly up the Baltoro, climbed 2,000 feet (600 meters) up Masherbrum, and sighted, at toppling distance, Conway's Golden Throne, K2. Austen died in 1924, still a forceful, venerable voice in mountaineering circles. And it was the avenue of mountaineering that opened up the encounter between two cultures.[6]

ECOLOGICAL ANTHROPOLOGY

"It is not uncommon, I have been frequently told, in the Highlands of Scotland for a mother who has borne twenty children not to have two alive," wrote Adam Smith in 1776 (*Inquiry into the Nature and Causes of the Wealth of Nations*). The rigors of mountain life have been debated. Most often, those anthropologists eager to seize upon qualities of the "primitive" have consistently voiced negative values associated with it. James Frazer's infamous *507 Questions on the Customs, Beliefs and Languages of Savages* (Cambridge, 1907) fairly summarizes the bias. Edward Tylor's *Primitive Culture* (1871) had first set down the systematic approach to understanding such peoples. In 1927, John Murphy, in *Primitive Man,* cited the state of "primitive" as meaning, "when he began to be human." George Murdock's *Our Primitive Contemporaries* (1934), Franz Boas's *Mind of Primitive Man* (1938), Margaret Mead's *Primitive Heritage* (ed. 1953), and Lewis Cotlow's Twilight of the

Primitive (1971) each chronicle the modern escalation of an image one would have assumed overcome in the last century. Even currently there is tremendous inadequacy in the conception of the term *primitive*. Note C. R. Hallpike's *The Foundation of Primitive Thought* (Oxford University Press, 1979): "In primitive society the expression of individual experience is very limited. While interior states such as motives, feelings, and knowledge are recognized, their manifestations are assessed on the basis of behavior; and while this behavioural assessment is often highly sophisticated, we find no elaborate terminology for the development of this awareness into the ability to express any of the finer shades of private experience such as the educated in our society take for granted (in the work of novelists, for example). . . . Only in a society whose world-view can be explicitly generalized is it possible . . . to separate belief from action." This rings sadly of the white Harlem schoolmarm who carps over her students' speaking differently from herself.

Paul Radin's *Primitive Man as Philosopher* is one isolated example of an earlier work that empathetically grasped the magnitude of elegance and insight characteristic of those cultures we find it more convenient to simply label "primitive." Radin's fascination with "simulacra," the psychical, spiritual masks which the Winnebago, Oglala, Dakota, and Maori fashion, is a theme central to psychoanalysis. Why then, one must ask, has such analysis missed its mark in the anthropological arena? I would offer a simple explanation. The Western mind-set, stemming from the fullest range of cultural artifice—the city with its amenities, the mandate of manifest destiny, agricultural abundance, cheap energy, the transgression of family and sexual constraints, the breakdown in pair-bonding, frenetic mobility, the publishing industry and subsequent popularization of photography, and tourist regimes and their absorption in material distractions—has polarized anthropological analysis, rendering black or white categories that do not hold to the subtler grays of reality or tell us much about anyone, least of all about ourselves, which should be the overriding concern of anthropology.

There have been past efforts to get at the empathy I referred to above. Humboldt and Bonpland's *General Comparative Geography* (1852) strove to identify integrity in diverse peoples, to solicit the genius of place. Other attempts were the later determinism of Karl Ritter, Friedrich Ratzel, and Maximilien Sorre; of Ellsworth Huntington in the United States (*The Human Habitat,* and *Environmental Basis of Social Geography* with Fred Carlson); and of Alfred Hettner, Benjamin Lee Wharf, Theodore Kroeber, and Morris

Swadesh, the last three men attempting to resurrect the American Indian by identifying facets of his language that were complex, expressive, and edifying. More recently, George Steiner, in the second chapter of his monumental book *After Babel,* has summarized some of those findings. Peter Matthiessen's *Snow Leopard* also distinguishes qualities of thought amongst Hopi and Sherpa which stress greater complexity and nomenclature than that illustrated in western languages and natural sciences of today. Ellenore Dark's *The Timeless Land* had much the same to say about the Australian aborigine. In Harold Conklin's dissertation, "The Relations of Hanunoo Culture to the Plant World" (Yale, 1954), the Hanunoo mountaineers of Mindoro Island are shown to know about fifty soil types, 1,500 useful plants, and 430 cultigens. This deep structure totemism, based upon ecological relationships that carry over into interpersonal affinity, more closely voices the kind of organization that Herder was searching for, the very legacy of preindustrial know-how throughout the world that is still exercised by way of economic and cultural acumen by some estimated 10 percent of the world's human population.

Isaiah Bowman, director of the American Geographical Society in 1916, wrote of Peruvian Indians: "Most of the luxuries and comforts of the Whites mean nothing to the Indian. . . . The machine-made woolens of the importers will probably never displace his homespun llama-wool clothing. His implements are few in number and simple in form. His tastes in food are satisfied by the few products of his fields and his mountain flocks. There he has lived for centuries and is quite content to live today. . . . Finally, he is not subjected to the white man's exploitation when he lives in remote places. The pastures are extensive and free . . . and he need have no care for the morrow, for the seasons here are almost as fixed as the stars" ("The Geographic Basis of Human Character," in Bowman's *The Andes of Southern Peru,* published by the American Geographical Society of New York and based upon the Yale Peruvian Expedition of 1911 along the Seventy-third Meridian. Bowman was referring to the plateau Indians near Antabamba and Salamanca in the Arma Valley.).

Such softness may astound us, or elicit sighs of nostalgia in today's world. But before World War I, mountain people were, in fact, remarkably isolated. As the political barriers broke down, the western image of them remained unattuned to hardship, languishing instead on the sheer romance, the "Heidi complex." With no other environment were indigenes so closely identified in terms of economy, life-style, personality, even religious beliefs, as mountain people with their mountains. L. A. Waddell's *The Buddhism of Tibet, or Lamaism* (W. H. Allen, 1895) had much to do with this espoused symbiosis. Writings by Ekai Kawaguchi, Giuseppe Tucci, Marco Pallis, Lama Govinda, and Alexandra David-Neel have furthered the logic, with specific reference to Tibetans, who have always been esteemed in proportion to their special position at the zenith of all mountain ranges. It is a humanistic logic, full of the love these writers share for mountain people.

And in fact the basis for modern mountain anthropology seems indeed rooted in this passion. But what moves it is the alluring applicability of techniques—science—and the awareness of tremendous, adverse pressures on highland populations. An early work in this light was C. W. Hobley's *Eastern Uganda* (Anthropological Institute of Great Britain and Ireland, 1902). He writes: "Like most other mountainous regions in Central Africa, there are, however, practically no permanent human habitations in any part of the country which has an altitude of over 7,000 feet. . . . The fact is that the climatic conditions of the last 1,500 feet are such that tropical cereals like dhurra (mtama) and the eleusine grain (wimbi) will not flourish, and this alone is I consider sufficient to effectually check any further movement to higher altitudes" (referring to Bantu Kavirondo, Nilotic Kavirondo, Nandi, and Masai.) Roderick Peattie's *Mountain Geography* (Harvard, 1936) defined *mountain* as any great locus of dramatic or unexpected uplift that takes root in the imagination of the people who inhabit it, live near by, or have, at least one time, seen it. This definition voiced, early on, the symbiosis that environmental anthropologists have now come to adopt as the most central issue within highland populations. A year after Peattie's book, Griffith Taylor (*Environment, Race and Migration*) expressed the sentiment of a whole generation of historians by suggesting that Central Asia was the center of human evolution, based upon the geologic and paleontologic evidence—rapid animal development following tremendous mountain-forming activities, and the slow Himalayan transition from Paleolithic to Neolithic times, assuming continuous human development. Such views were intuitively arrived at a century before. From his readings of Himalayan and Andean exploration as presented in *Blackwood's, The Edinburgh Review,* and the *Quarterly Review,* Percy Shelley believed mankind's origins to have taken root in a secret vale of Kashmir, and this belief he articulated in his tragedy "Prometheus Unbound" and in his epic poem "Alastor." There was a sense that the Himalayan impenetrabilia fostered the mythologic wellspring, and this sense, as we have shown, grew up gradually and was accredited by Genesis. The variation of updrafts and diurnal downdrafts, the amount of ozone and increased electric currents in the air at high altitude acting as stimulants, may not have been facts, in themselves, scientifically addressed, but the fervor of mountain storms—of mountain life—was revered. Mountain people were suspected to be our original progenitors. More recently, the fossil record indicates that Neanderthal man might have emerged from the French Alps. In *Our Evolving Civilization* (London, 1946) Taylor went on to say, "The alpine foldings during the last few million years are . . . responsible for the evolution of man himself."[7] Persistent hopes that the yeti may turn out to be the last vestige of Upper Paleolithic Himalayan culture is yet another clue to our perennial belief system. The wildness Westerners have adulated intones the most complete desire to *become* that which we have perceived. In the Middle Ages, writers depicted instances of castaways mating with animals. In the Renaissance, the mute stones were given light, brought to life. In the Romantic Era, hapless wayfarers explored the corners of the mountainous planet, bringing back extraordinary data. By the twentieth century, social scientists were willing to extend the metaphor of wildness to the inhabitants. It was a troubling conclusion.

The sentiment of wild people sharing the planet has about it the "refugium" concept, Pleistocene islands in which the mountain offers a laboratory for the study of its ecosystems, islands in time where divergent evolution has occurred. Larry Price has stated that the Himalayas gave rise to all the world's arctic and alpine plants because they were dry during the Pleistocene. In his *Ethnographic Atlas* (University of Pittsburgh Press, 1967) George Murdock says that a thousand years of cultural isolationism is the basic criterion for determining divergent evolution. Tibet, high Andean valleys, New Guinea plateaus—such regions satisfy the isolationist demands and have, as a result, attracted the explorer. Because of their isolation, mountain people have only recently witnessed the influx of anthropologists that inland, subcontinental populations have known. As a consequence, the time frame for mountain anthropology has corresponded with the twentieth-century recognition of ecology.

As early as 1932 the American Geographical Society's publication *Pioneer Settlement* (No. 14, edited by W. Joerg) examined the hydroelectric and tourist possibilities of Patagonia. It called for the first international mountain zone of beauty, with the realizaton that it would be attractive to tourists, income from which would fuel subsequent development in the local farm and ranching provinces. Carl Troll coined the term *geoecology* in 1938. In 1940 the concept of comparative geography of high mountains was developed.

This geography applied principally to environmental factors of mountain landscapes (that is, frost and nival climates). Since 1965, Troll's work has been promoted by UNESCO. In 1968, the International Geographical Union found the New Commission on High Altitude Geoecology. International symposia took place in 1966, 1969, 1972, and so on continuously thereafter. This network of international concern (see "Meetings on the Topic of Mountain Environment," by Charles Bailey, *Nepal Studies Association Bulletin Nos. 16/17,* p. 13) has brought to the attention of governments throughout the world the severe nature of mountain ecological problems. Intercultural dilemmas have been less easily treated. Survival International, under the inspired leadership of Tenison, Bentley, and others, for lack of funds has dealt primarily with Amerindian populations of the jungle. Concern in India for energy-related problems has superseded more delicate issues of cultural maintenance in such areas as Arunachal Pradesh. In Nepal, the thorough bungling of the Khampa crisis resulted from adverse political pressures of the superpowers.

In 1948 the Refugee Economic Corporation in New York published a curious document that seems, in my mind, to synopsize the age-old menagerie of archetypes that Westeners have attributed to mountains and their supposed Edenlike potentials; a repertoire of attributes that colors the anthropologist's approach, be it neoevolutionist, neofunctionalist, or what have you. Entitled *Quest For Settlement: Summaries of Selected Economic and Geographic Reports on Settlement Possibilities for European Immigrants* and released in modest, obscure fashion following the revelations of Auschwitz, a large proportion of the "possibilities" were in mountain areas. Such choices included the San Pedro Mártir Mountains of northwestern Baja California; the Alta Verapaz Highlands and Pacific Volcanic Range foothills of Guatemala; the Valla de Diquis mountains and Cordillera Brunqueña of Costa Rica; the "vast unoccupied western slopes of the Andes (Ecuador) between 4,000 and 10,500 feet" (where "settlers will be able to raise practically all their food requirements and cash crops such as bananas, sugar cane, and yucca in the lower altitudes, vegetables and fruit in the middle altitudes, and sheep and cattle in the higher altitudes. Settlement is impractical on the Cordillera slopes below 4,000 feet because of malaria hazards."); the lower slopes of Kilimanjaro and Meru; the Livingston Mountains and Matengo Highland of Tanganyika; the Interior Highlands of South-West Africa; the highlands of Madagascar; and the mountains of North Island, New Zealand. On the surface, it seems perfect, all this recommendation—vertical zonation, blessed climate, tropical tubers. Indeed, the scientific record indicates a healthier, more pollution-free locale for human habitation on high. Communitas, hardihood, vigor—these are the presumed attributes. As early as sixty thousand years ago, Shanidar IV man, in the Zagros mountains, was buried in a circle of grape hyacinth, bachelor's button, hollyhock, and yellow-flowering groundsel. Carbon 14 dating, bone analysis, relative entropy mapping, survivorship, cluster analysis, computer-based biotope analysis—these paleoecological methods have enabled us to determine climate, circumstance, and to some extent culture from the gravelly hillsides and jaw-ware of the past. In the case of Shanidar, we have deciphered the first glimpse of *conscience* at work in human history. And it is alpine.

From palynological scrutiny of cave middens in central Nevada, hearth inquiries at Choukoutien, near Peking, to Paccaicasa Cave in Peru, such evidence has enthralled us at the early prospects of seemingly unlimited mountain experience—be it quartzite manufacture or remnants of a once lavish diet. We can read into such discoveries a precarious social and economic balance that obtains throughout all highland communities. While the balance is always changing, mountain cultures have tended to bear exquisite witness to selective homeostasis.[8]

Thomas Wolfe, in *The Hills Beyond,* describing Appalachian ruins, first intoned the coming course of events, a fatalism now emphasized in upland anthropology: "The whole region had been sucked and gutted, milked dry, denuded of its rich, primeval treasures; something blind and ruthless had been here, grasped and gone." We have seen this pattern to be synonymous with what Frederick Jackson Turner meant by the frontier instinct, and its accompanying ills. A brief survey of major mountain groups through the world—the scattered four hundred million individuals—and their present dilemmas, should help indicate the magnitude of conflict confronting mountain people today.[9]

New Guinea: the Gadsup-Agarabi, Auyana-Usarufa, Awa, Tairora, Gende, Siane, Gahuku, Kamano, Fore, Hagen, Wahgi, Jimi, Chimbu, Enga, Lembun, Huli, Mendi, Wiru, Karam, and Duna-language-speaking highland groups. The major pressure on these collectives has arisen as a basic result of outside intervention and then sudden political independence.

China: the Monguor, Salar, Turki (in Tsinghai and Kansu); the Kiao in Kweichow, Hunan, and Yunnan; the Yao of Kwangtung and Kwangsi; the Lahu and Akha of Yunnan. There are over two hundred mountain tribes in China. Massive efforts are underway to fully detribalize them. Only southeastern Tibet has thus far remained immune.

Taiwan and Hainan: The Kaoshan people and the Li and Miao struggle for their aboriginal rights.

Philippines: The Igorot, Tasaday, Bontoc, and Kalinga grapple with their government's disregard of highland cultural integrity.

Malaysia: the Orang Asli; the Lionese mountaineers of Central Flores; Solorese on the slopes of Solor-Larantuka; the Alor-Pantar; the proto-Malay and Papuan southern Moluccans; thirty ethnic groups in the high, densely forested mountains of Halmahera; the interior groups including Alfur, Ternatana, Tidorese, Loloda, Tobelorese, Galelarese, Sahu, Pagu, and Nodole; fewer than one hundred Toala mountain people in the southwestern Celebes; the Batak in Sumatran mountain valleys near Lake Toba; the Idahan and Kelabitic Murut of interior Borneo; Punan-Penam mountain nomad hunters and gatherers scattered throughout southern Borneo; the Semang, Senoi, and Jakun of the central mountain chain in Malaya. The pressures borne upon them derive principally from outside industry, largely oil and timber multinationals.

Southeast Asia: the Burmese Sino-Tibetan Naga, Chin, Garo, Lutzu, Nakhi, Minchia, Kachin, Kadu, Lolo, Lisu, Lahu, and Akha; the Yao-Miao hill tribes spread throughout northern Vietnam, Laos, and Thailand, including over fifty tribes. Two-thirds of the mountain regions of Vietnam are occupied by two million minority, tribal peoples who have suffered intensely from racism and were pawns in the war and ongoing political mayhem.

India: Isolated hill clans alone account for some forty million highlanders. In Mizoram (Manipur) live the Manipuri, Mizo, and Chin; in Central India, the hill Maria of Bastar; the Khonda and Oriya of the western Orissa Hills. Mountains of the Western Ghats have the Badaga Kodagu of Coorg, Puliyar, and Paniyar, and the Toda of the Nilgairi Hills, who number under one thousand. The Chenchu of the Amrabad Hills live in leaf shelters. Other hill tribes exist in the jungles above Chittagong in Bangladesh. The essential threat to these groups can best be described as assimilation.

Transhimalaya: The eighteen hundred miles include the Kinner, Garhwali, Kalash Kafir, Balti, Lepcha, Guji, Ladakhi, Kashmiri, Burusho, Bhotia, Pahari, Magar, Minaro, Gurung, Chetri, Tamang, Sherpa, Newar, Kiranti, Drukpa, Wancho, Aka, Apa Tani, Miri, Padam, Minyong, Shimong, Tagin, Rami, Pasi, Rai, Byan, Thakali, Chomi, and Sulong. Topsoil erosion, inflation, tourism, declining wood supplies, food-fuel competition, flooding, migration to the lowlands—these are the primary pressures constituting an ecological plight in the Himalayas.

Afghanistan: The *powindah,* or trading, Pashtun nomads between the Hindu Kush and Koh-i-Baba Range, and between the Koh-i-Sangan and Amu Darya steppes and deserts of Khash, Dasht-i-Margo, and Registan—divided into the Ghilzai of East Afghanistan and the Durrani of South and West Afghanistan—compete with the Hazara peasants who use the same upland slopes for farming. The Tajik, Hazara, Uzbek, Turkoman, Nuristani; the Wakhi and Kirghiz, who have been politically displaced to a nearly untenable file of land. Between Afghanistan and Pakistan exist the Kohistani, Gumar, and Pathan in Swat, the Durrani and Khalji on the Afghan side, and the Yusufak and Afridi in Pakistan; the Marri, Bugti, Baluchi, Brahui, Luni, Kakar Pathan and Khetran of Baluchistan; the Kalash Kafir—all uprooted in the wake of Soviet invasion.

Bangladesh: Throughout the Chittagong Hills are many Buddhist tribes that are distinct from the Bengali hill tribes—the Marma, Chakma, Mru, and Morung. Their livelihood—albeit impoverished by Western

(narrow) mind-sets—seems more or less assured for the time being.

Iran/Iraq: the Rowanduz and Jaf Kurds who winter on the Mesopotamian and Mosul plains, then head up into the Taurus Mountains in summer to roam the slopes of bushy oak, spiny grass, and herb; the Basseri, Lur, Qashqai, and Bakhtiari of the Tang gorges in Iran's Zagros. There is competition for land with lowlanders, and the ever-encroaching factor of assimilation.

Turkey: the Yayla mountain pasturage near the Black Sea, where the Yuruk graze their flocks. By the 1930s, most pastoral nomadism in Turkey ended as peasant expansion deprived them of their winter quarters and then of their summer *yaylas,* finally forcing most of them off the mountain. Now, the majority of Turkish mountain people must live off the plains.[10]

Soviet Union: the Chechen of the Central Caucasus; the Ingush, Karachayev, dispersed Circassians; the Daghestani, Ossete, Armenians, Kurds of Eastern Anatolia, and the Kalmuk shepherds. As in China, their traditional way of life has been comprehensively

"Moses Contemplating Mount Sinai and the Burning Bush,"
Icon from St. Catherine's Monastery, Tretjakov State Gallery,
Moscow. Photo by M. Tobias.

altered, sedentarized. The Soviet Kirghiz are no longer able to move between summer and winter pasturage. M. Mirrakhimov and I. Ibraimov estimate a current population of forty-five thousand Tajik highlanders inhabiting the Tien Shan and Pamir ranges. Several hundred collective farms—the *kolkhozy*—have been established by the government, along with telephone lines, television, airports, and dutiful cadres of educators. Write Mirrakhimov and Ibraimov:

> Tien-Shan and Pamir villages are now inconceivable without planned building, brick houses (instead of the yurts of the past), schools, hospitals, cinemas, clubs and, of course, macadam or earth roads. . . . In other words, life in these mountains is not significantly different from that in other villages in the USSR. All this by no means signifies that life in the mountains has become a pleasure. . . . On the whole, highlanders tend to be excessive in everything, and the effect of this excessiveness is not always positive. They like to eat and drink much, dress strikingly (even if they cannot afford it or it is out of place). As concerns their intellectual tastes, they mostly prefer oral to printed information, which may be related to the fact that at high altitudes printed information is rather difficult to grasp, as confirmed by psychologists studying these problems. . . . But, luckily, highlanders have sufficient grounds to think optimistically of the future of their mountains, since the State has taken the concern of protecting wild nature of Tien-Shan and Pamir into its own hands. . . . There is no reason for panic as yet. [Correspondence with the editor.]

Syria: The Alawi still manage to maintain an integrated, traditional mountain life.

Bulgaria/Albania: The Wallachians of Bulgaria (Karakachani)and Gheg of Albania have each retained their own traditional life-styles to date.

Sinai: The Tiaha in the north, comprising the Tarabin, Tiaha, Heiwat, and Azazimeh, and the Towara in the south, comprising Suwalhe, Wulud Sayyid, Rahamy, Quraish, Awarme, Aleiqat, Mzeine, Wulud Sulaiman, Beni Wassel, and the Jebeliyeh at St. Catherine's Monastery (Sons of the Nazarenes), collectively amount to under twenty thousand—a number remarkably unfluctuating throughout history, despite the onslaught of successive warlords: Egyptians, Israelites, Nabateans, Moslems, Crusaders, Pilgrims, Allied troops, Egyptians, Israelis, and again Egyptians. The Bedouin still wander brazenly free throughout the dioritic masses. Yet their indomitable future is precariously linked to Camp David and the burgeoning tourist industries of Israel and Egypt.[11]

Africa: the Dogon in northern Nigeria and Mali; the Ait Atta, Arbaa, and Sai Atba tribes between the Sahara and Tell Atlas; the Teda of the Tibesti Massif; Beni Mguild, Zaian, Bougueman, Messaoud, Ait Ougadir, and the Ait Lias of the Central Moroccan Middle Atlas; the Tuareg of the Ahaggar and Ajjer

massifs, in conflict with Fulani cattle herders in the Air Mountains; the Ovimbundu, Akwambundu, and Bakongo of the food-growing central highlands of Angola; the Jewish Falash of northwestern highlands near Gondar and throughout the Tigre Mountains of Ethiopia; and the various peoples of the Rift regions (See Colin Turnbull's contribution)—Ik, Tussi, Amba, Konjo, Pare, Kikuyu, Teita, and Pokot. Poverty, overpopulation, and political turmoil are afflicting all of the African mountain tribes. In some cases, efforts by governments to protect animal life have meant the dispossession of tribal lands in the mountains. This is not an easy conflict, to be sure.

Mexico: the Tarahuamara in southwest Chihuahua; Chinantec in the Oaxaca mountains; Tarascans in the mountains of Patzcuaro. Poverty on all sides has managed to insure the inviolate stature of these pastoralists until now.

Latin America: To a lesser extent the same may be said for Costa Rican highlanders, though the latter scattered populations face competition for their food from the mountainous national parks established in Costa Rica.

South America: two million Aymara and Quechua in the Bolivian Andes; the Canari of Ecuador; the Peruvian Buca; Caingang and Bororo of the eastern Brazilian highlands; over one million Maya in stricken Guatemala—all fraught with war, oppression, in some cases genocide.

Europe: assorted Alpine villages in France, Switzerland, Italy, Liechtenstein, Andorra, Germany, Austria, the Romansch district, and the shepherds of Sardinia with their *codice barbaricino*. The European highlander, like the American, has of course been largely won over to the technological culture of his respective nationale. At least the Swiss government has made a concerted effort to retain key vestiges of mountain life, both for agricultural and tourist reasons, paying subsidies to montagnards to enable them to continue more or less their way of life (see article by Jack Ives).

In summary, the current census of mountain peoples throughout the world indicates extreme attrition, resulting from some key causes. In the northern Caucasus, Ossete, Ingush, and Karachayev peoples have been migrating to the lowlands as a result of hunger and of the alluring, intensive urbanization of the plains.[12] In the Yugoslavian highlands, Muslim Slav sheepherders are also seeking alternative employment in the lowlands. The same is occurring amongst Rumanian-speaking Vlahs.[13] These alterations are occurring in the wake of economic disruptions. Traditional *systems* of exchange have been broken (the circle of life violated). The young, and then their parents, must seek alternatives. Thus, we see an entire hotel business being developed in Nepal by sherpanis, the wives of the sherpas who have gone down to Kathmandu to sell themselves as trekking guides and porters. In a mountain village in Ionia, an entire population has abandoned its stronghold and moved to Athens.[14]

Throughout Swat, Gilgit, and Chitral, an immense tourist industry is perpetrating the full-scale erosion of innumerable mountain groups. (See contributions by Pat Emerson and Schuyler-Jones.) An "*image de marque*" fashioned from antiquarian, British heritage misconceptions, by the government tourist bureau in Pakistan, has utterly masked the contemporary reality of mountain life, with its forced poverty, erosion, deforestation, and extinction of mountain species, encouraging more than forty expeditions that trudge annually up the Baltoro glacier, affecting the economics and spirituality of life through the Hindu Kush and Karakoram ranges.[15] In Luristan the mountain people witness a total breakdown of their previous agropastoralism as a result of official corruption and landowners' de facto control.

The logic of governments in dealing with mountain indigenes appears inflexible. The more bureaucracy, apparently the better off mountain people are presumed to be. Note the outcome of the Arab League Educational, Cultural and Scientific Organization meeting in Khartoum in 1972. The Rezigat nomads of Sudan are castigated for presuming their full freedom to wander about with children and animals from horizon to horizon (as they have *always* done). Now, however, such wandering is determined to be in sudden violation of the Land Settlement and Registration Ordinance of 1925, which requires twenty years of "continual possession" of land before possession is guaranteed. In other words, nomads are intrinsically illegal; they do not conform. "The nomads' contact with government officials will necessarily raise their standard. . . . The present government [of Sudan] is interested in settling nomads and plans large-scale sugarcane cultivation. . . . UN assistance is expected." In fact, Maurice Strong, secretary general to the UN Conference on Human Environment at the time, delivered an opening address to the Arab League's meeting. On the plateau of Kenya, highland cultures face ecologically imbalanced lands. The Kenyan government cites the indigenes themselves as guilty of practicing poor management of resources. But in fact it is the long-term dominance of capitalist modes from the outside that has resulted in the distortion of local economies stemming from a reliance on unsuitable monocrops favored by neocolonial powers.[16] When a culture has managed to reject that outside influence, and its government-stultifying mandates, we are liable to see spectacular, if infrequent, results. The Boran herders of northern Kenya have developed intensely spiritual restrictions against the killing of all mammals, as well as numerous insects, reptiles, plants, and birds. They live in relative harmony with their highland surrounding.[17]

The mountains contain watersheds that directly influence half the world's population, and therefore it is in the lowlanders' interest to see that traditional mountain life is sustained in all its previous ecological integrity. The IUCN World Conservation Strategy cites the protection of such resources as a critical global priority. Ten percent of the world's population inhabits those watersheds. For all of their intrinsic beauty and fascination, their cultures and livelihoods, their know-how, genes, and special genius, are on the rapid wane, caught up in the tragic hourglass of this century. In most cases the highlanders are denied protective legislation, accessible medical aid, or those basic amenities and subsidies that lowlanders more routinely enjoy. Organizations that deal in mountain problems are by no means adequate to the task. The United Nations University, the International Bank for Reconstruction and Development, U.S. AID, the Swiss Association for Technical Assistance, UNESCO's Man and the Biosphere Program, and, most recently, the International Mountain Society, in association with the Institute for Arctic and Alpine Research, are some of the major concerned groups. The principal focus of all their efforts involves integrated hill development projects, hazard studies, land degradation assessment, emigration, and research on damage to downstream food-producing systems. In most cases social scientists offer technical solutions, such as a way in which to bolster food-grain yields or amplify energy flows in rural communities. Such efforts are largely inspired ones, conservationist, hopeful to preserve a way of life that *feels* ancient and important to us—we who have made pilgrimage from cities of learning, cities of discontent, our heads all aswarm with science and altruism and sabbatical leaves of one sort or another.

ARCHETYPES

In uncovering the various mind-sets—mythologic, Biblical, semiotic, the compulsion to discover paradise, the ethnographic, romantic, and scientific—what have we seen? Much of the information presented here is meant to suggest the collective unconscious, replete with its storehouse of motivations—metaphors that have galvanized the conquistadors and geographers alike, and in so doing, have actually defined the mountains and their inhabitants.

Today, we have disabused ourselves of very few of these metaphors. As scientists, we know how to delineate fact, but nonetheless *feel* the same dream of coming home to the mountains. As wanderers, tourists, mountain climbers, we are compelled by the salient edge of a mountain against any weather, filled with the glory of possibility and the irreplaceable sensation of something beyond, something hidden and waiting (Kipling). This might be romantic nonsense, but it persists for the reason that some people simply *love* mountains and mountain people, not for what they are, or are not, but for what they symbolize, while others prefer the highlander and his surroundings for no other reason than the abandonment to dirt, to scent, to rarified air and rarified customs that prevail in a village at 15,000 feet (4,600 meters)—the kinaesthesia, the commons, and the ever-rejuvenated pulse. In the intellectual hubbub of imagery, it is easy to forget the *fact* of real human beings living up there. They have not engendered the imagery, nor do they live it. Their lives are compassed by all the same complaints, suffering, and joys that exist down below. There may be a greater scale, proportion, and balance to their technological means and ends, imposed by their environment, but there is no less industry. These very constraints endow them with all the vigor for which they have been justly idealized. But it is no paradise for the vigor alone. True enough, there is something like a Methuselah factor in the Vilcabamba Valley, throughout the Sierra Madre, the Carpathians, and behind Rakaposhi in Hunza. These centenarians might very well be the limited source for all such idealization.

It is important to hold on to our myths and archetypes, but only if they can allow us to better identify and gauge the crises that threaten to strangulate highlanders—from destruction of their watersheds to their lack of representation in their governments (see Georgina Ashworth's contribution) and their poor access to health care, transportation, energy, and communications. These benefits of the city will always trickle down in various degrees. It is up to mountain people themselves to create their own destiny, of course. By understanding our own homage to them, and the motivations that press for homage, we should come more honestly to adjust our sights as well as the demands of an overweening world.

TENZING

There is the nearly pathetic anachronism of his coming of age, a culture shock he has gracefully maneuvered. Ever since he led Hillary to the top of Everest, he has been shuffled around the globe as guest of one alpine club after another, called upon to rehash the old epic, to smile famously. His teeth are those of a twenty-year-

Tenzing Norgey. Photo by M. Tobias.

old. This Tenzing attributes to the salt he has rubbed on them since childhood.

For eighteen years he tended yaks in Khumbu, during a time when Nepal was as sealed and alluring as is Pemakod today. Born in 1914, Tenzing was reared in the shadows of Everest, the mountain that the Sherpa say is "too tall even for birds to fly over." It was Tenzing's dream to climb it, and on the seventh expedition he did indeed.

By then he had already moved to Darjeeling, looking for work. He still resides there, overlooking Kanchenjunga, an admitted alien in both Nepal and India, between two worlds. For all of his mountainy humor, there is some bitterness in Tenzing. The Indian government, explorers' clubs, tour agencies, the press, other Indian mountaineers, tea and airline companies—the list goes on—have all exploited his joie de vivre, an innocence that Tenzing has, admittedly, learned to exploit. He seems troubled while reflecting on the burden of his good luck. A Tibetan Stein Erickson, neither reading nor writing, he conceals bewilderment with a charm that Eric Shipton first noticed back in 1936 when he hired Tenzing to porter instead of other more qualified Sherpa.

He wears a white sports car cap, a red wind jacket, woollen knickers, a Norwegian pullover. Huge sunglasses give him the slight seriousness of a World War I fighter pilot. Like most Sherpa he is stout, thick-footed, somewhat bowlegged, barrel-chested, with a reddish throat thinly latticed by wrinkles acquired on myriad glaciers. His eyes are dark and mottled with color. In jeans from Italy he looks, somehow, emaciated.

Tenzing speaks a random English, at times studied, alarmingly eloquent, and all with the effeminate, Sir Edmund Backhouse kind of inflection, that of a Mandarin or French montagnard. His timidity can be unnerving, and his raucous, immediate affability seems to survive from the gentleness of prehistoric times. He laughs at the slightest provocation, out of control like Polynesian youngsters, like children who have not been forced to read books, take dancing lessons, or not say *shit*. Once I asked him what the funniest event in his life had been. He frowned, then burst out: "My meeting with Krushchev!" "Krushchev?" I asked. "Yes. A man with a thousand chickens in his stomach!" Tenzing cried, curled over in hysterics.

Tenzing believes he could climb Everest until he is eighty. After that, maybe not. "Mountains give little trouble to older men once they are used to them," he says. For twenty years, as one-time director of the Himalayan Mountaineering Institute, with a base camp beneath Mount Kabru in Sikkim, he has seen more high-altitude action than most mountaineers. To say that high-altitude peoples are more fit than we is of course wild understatement. It is no secret that the cardiovascular, respiratory, and skeletal systems are greatly benefited by thin air and rough terrain. At eighty-four, Tenzing's grandmother made the difficult two-week trek from Thami to Darjeeling. Tenzing himself, over seventy now, has a robustness that one simply does not witness in the lowlands. He breathes an energy that seems to defy the law of entropy.

He is as legendary a figure throughout Asia as Mohandas Gandhi. Dogs know to come begging for food from him. Seeing two caged yaks in a New York zoo, Tenzing whispered words from the old Tibetan breviary; he relates that the yaks turned anxiously towards him, remembering. Tenzing is also turned toward the hearty folklore of his haunting grounds, fast disappearing. The Sherpa have become consummate merchants of their wilderness. He was the first to do so. Mean-

while, the language of the Sherpa, the farms of their upbringing, their whole way of life is sadly on the decline. Tenzing cannot help but blame himself in part, and this may be his peculiarly western tragedy. Still, he is a hero. Children happily assail him on the street. His large home in Darjeeling abounds with medals and gifts and worldly letters that he cannot exactly read. Letters from kings and from astronauts.

Tenzing manages to flirt with his double-bind situation. His children speak five and six languages. His third wife, Daku, is a keenly beautiful woman of great power. Tenzing supports his family by leading mountain tours. Yet the tourist influx is a primary onus to him. Like the rest of us, he seems to suffer from that ineluctable paradox of loving his mountains too much, while needing money. He sees Bhutan as one of the last possibilities for medieval mountain preservation. Though even Bhutan has sniffed out the dollar sign since the mid-1970s, when Tenzing and I journeyed there together at the front of an incoming queue. The price per head was then $150 a day. Grossinger's or Caesar's Palace can cost that much. Needless to say, Bhutan is worth it. But is the price worth itself? Tenzing did not think so. Nor did I. But there we were.

He walks like a mystic. I followed him for a month, peeing in the deodar when he did, running when he did, taking the similar course through boulder fields and snowdrifts. The man was a Himalayan monarch. He has tracked the Zen ten thousand miles. My hope was to assimilate something of his grace, his easy-breathing exuberance, which seemed to merge his spirit with that of the black bears and oxygenless days.

Nothing! I was locked into my particular way of negotiating steepness, of looking straight ahead, and down, of greeting villagers. There was nothing *peripheral* to my approach, whereas his gaze was tigerlike, all over, his walk a stroll of self-possession, reason for being there, fully commensurate with the broad surroundings. He possessed a rare perspective, I now realize, no doubt deriving from his unusual purgatory of experience and allegiances and inner mystery. Not an enviable place to be, perhaps. But I wanted it; torn, ignorant, wanting the left and the right. Tenzing seemed capable of commanding the cross-cultural evocations in himself; something of a mobile Joe Conrad, a mountaineering V. S. Naipaul, unassimilable, on the fringe, yet squarely in the heart of life, an alpine U Thant.

Perhaps it is the quality of mountains, the nurturing of intelligence year in and year out beneath their grandeur that has endowed Tenzing, simply, with this sobering ability to confront two worlds. He manages, and there is no one who will not be caught up in the splendor of his embrace; a homecoming of hugs, some instant of affection from the primeval past, with a coup de grace; a feverishness proclaiming impossible juxtaposition. Tenzing pulls it off, with modesty.

He does not sit still. After some twenty-five major climbing expeditions, he is more gung-ho than ever. He discusses his climbing feats with the calm unheroics of a tailor or elevator operator.

I do not think he has ever hammered in a piton. He certainly does not take technical matters very seriously. It is the snow that captivates him, the snow's gleam. His are the big mountains. His peaks are those of the Vedas, the Sutras, the Old Testament. If there is true ecology in the world, it is in the fact that Tenzing climbed Everest first, and surely foremost. Tenzing is indispensable to that mountain. Their greatness is the same greatness.

I remember getting snowbound with the old Sherpa in his tent, along the high ridge to Sandakphu. I was using Hillary's sleeping bag, the deflated one from the first Everest ascent in 1953. By now it had completely lost its loft, suffered unguessable trials and washing machines. Tenzing's children were with us in the tent, bent on mad goosing late into the blizzardy night. In the cold, battering high altitude, I lay entranced beside this family of mountain people. I had never seen such total happiness and comfort in all my life. Tenzing *was* the mountain, and this realization affected me profoundly.[18]

The Contributors

Georgina Ashworth is a leading advocate of minority rights and British editor of the publication *World Minorities*.

Joe Bastien is a professor of anthropology at the University of Texas at Arlington and author of two books. He has lived for several years among mountain communities of Bolivia.

Gerald Berreman is a professor of anthropology at the University of California at Berkeley with numerous publications to his credit. Berreman has worked extensively throughout northern India.

Broughton Coburn, author of *Nepali Ama* and former UNESCO representative at Mount Everest National Park, is currently the World Wildlife Fund representative in Nepal and spends his spare time walking throughout Tibet.

Robert Coles is professor of psychology at Harvard Medical School and winner of a Pulitzer Prize for his extraordinary *Children of Crisis*.

Hugh R. Downs is an expert on Nepalese painting and an author. Downs has lived for the past five years in central Nepal.

Pat Emerson, a sociologist and linguist with the South Asia Studies Program of the University of Washington, Seattle, has spent much of her time living in the Karakoram Range.

Daniel Feldman has long been involved in the American Indian movement and has worked extensively for the Black Hills Alliance.

Christoph von Furer-Haimendorf is professor emeritus of Asian anthropology at the University of London. His books include *Tribes of India: The Struggle for Survival* and the classic *Sherpas of Nepal*.

Kenneth Hewitt, a Canadian geographer at Wilfrid Laurier University, has written widely on human ecology and the mountains and has lived with the Kalash Kafir community.

Jack D. Ives is president of the International Mountain Society, Boulder, Colorado.

Schuyler Jones has been an Oxford don since 1970 at the Pitt Rivers Museum. His many expeditions have taken him throughout Africa, South Asia, and Afghanistan. He is the author of several books.

Jeff Long was in a Kathmandu jail cell for many months interviewing Tibetan refugees. He is a world-class mountaineer and journalist. His book *Outlaw* was published in 1985.

Larry Lowendorf is a professor of archaeology at the University of North Dakota, with special expertise in the area of American Indian prehistory.

Thomas Marks, a political scientist based in Hawaii, is a prolific writer with special expertise in East Asian outback cultures.

John Nance is a photo-anthropologist who made one of the earliest connections with the Tasaday tribe. His books include *The Gentle Tasaday* and *Discovery of the Tasaday*.

Fitz John Porter Poole, a professor of anthropology at the University of California, San Diego, in La Jolla, Poole is one of the very few people to have visited the Bimin-Kuskusmin. He is completing monographs on cultural images of children and childhood rites of passage.

Robert Rhoades is a human ecologist who works in Lima, Peru, with the International Potato Institute.

Bruno de Roissart, a Belgian ethnographer, has lived with mountain groups in the Algerian Hoggar, the Upper Moroccan Atlas, and the Bolivian Andes.

Kit Salter, professor of geography at UCLA, specializes in China, where he is a frequent visitor.

Halfdan Siiger is a Danish anthropologist whose work on the Lepcha of Sikkim represents one of the earliest groundbreaking studies ever conducted in the Himalayas.

Ivan Simon, a former editor and administrator in the Assamese state government of India, has conducted survey work throughout the Eastern Himalayas.

Gary Snyder, a Pulitzer Prize—winning poet at the forefront of ecopolitics, took his early training in anthropology and oriental studies.

Colin Turnbull is professor of anthropology at Georgetown University. His books include *The Forest People, The Mountain People,* and *The Human Cycle.*

Royal Tyler is professor of Oriental languages and religion at the University of Oslo. Dr. Tyler lived in Japan for a considerable time and did extensive work on the symbolism of sacred mountains.

Notes and References

Editor's Note: The notes and references follow the order of the book and are listed by chapter number. No uniform citation system has been imposed, since each article is independent of the others and each citation system is appropriate to the matter it supports.

CHAPTER 2

References Cited

Bowers, Alfred W.
1950.   *Mandan Social and Ceremonial Organization.* The University of Chicago Publications in Anthropology. Chicago, Illinois: University of Chicago Press.
1965.   *Hidatsa Social and Ceremonial Organization.* Smithsonian Institution Bureau of American Ethnology Bulletin 194. Washington D.C.: Government Printing Office.

Catlin, George
1967.   *O-Kee-Pa, A Religious Ceremony and other Customs of the Mandans.* Ed. John Ewers. Lincoln: University of Nebraska Press.

Chamberlain, Von Del
1982.   *When Stars Come Down to Earth: Cosmology of the Skidi Pawnee Indians of North America.* Anthropological Papers #26. Los Altos, Calif.: Ballena Press.

Conner, Stuart W.
1982.   Archaeology of the Crow Indian vision quest. *Archaeology in Montana* 23 (3): 85–127.

Eddy, John A.
1974.   Astronomical alignment of the Big Horn medicine wheel. *Science* 184(4141): 1035–43.

Gilmore, Melvin R.
1930.   The Arikara tribal temple. *Papers of the Michigan Academy of Science, Arts and Letters* 14: 47–70.

Grey, Don
1963.   Big Horn Medicine Wheel Site, 48BH302. *Plains Anthropologist* 8 (19): 27–40.

Irving, Washington
1961.   *Adventures of Captain Bonneville.* Ed. Edgeley W. Todd. Norman: University of Oklahoma Press.

Lowie, Robert H.
1918.   Myths and traditions of the Crow Indians. *Anthropological Papers of the American Museum of Natural History* 25, pt. 1: 1–308.
1922.   The religion of the Crow Indians. *Anthropological Papers of the American Museum of Natural History* 25(2): 309–444.
1956.   *The Crow Indians.* New York: Holt, Rinehart and Winston.

Medicine Crow, Joseph
1962.   Crow Indian buffalo legends. In Symposium on Buffalo Jumps, ed. C. I. Malouf and S. W. Conner, pp. 35–39. *Memoir No. 1.* Missoula, Montana: Montana Archaeological Society.

Mehrer, Emery La Dean
1980.   The Huff Site, a reconstruction of past lifeways. In Topics in Environment and Archaeology, *Nebraska Anthropologist* 5: 92–106. (Anthropology Student Group, Dept. of Anthropology, Univ. of Nebraska, Lincoln.)

Simms, S. C.
1903.   A wheel-shaped stone monument in Wyoming. *American Anthropologist,* n.s. 5: 107–10.

Wilson, Michael
1981.   Sun dances, thirst dances, and medicine wheels: A search for alternative hypotheses. In *Megaliths to Medicine Wheels: Boulder Structures in Archaeology.* Proceedings 11th Chacmool Conference, Archaeological Association of the University of Calgary, pp. 333–70.

Wood, W. Raymond
1967.   *An Interpretation of Mandan Culture History.* Smithsonian Institution Bureau of American Ethnology Bulletin 198. Washington D.C.: Government Printing Office.

Woolworth, Alan R.
1956.   Archeological investigations at Site 32ME59 (Grandmother's Lodge). *North Dakota History* 23 (2): 79–102.

CHAPTER 3

References

1. In 1980 an organization of Indians, ranchers, and environmentalists known as the Black Hills Alliance used legal action to successfully halt uranium mining in the Black Hills. However, the judgment affects only Union Carbide Corporation. Several other corporations have uranium exploration leases in the Black Hills.
2. **Richard O. Clemmer,** "Black Mesa and the Hopi," Joseph G. Jorgensen, et al., eds., *Native Americans and Energy Development* (Cambridge, Mass.: Energy Resources Center, 1978), p. 17.
3. **Edward Dozier,** *The Pueblo Indians of North America* (New York: Holt Rinehart and Winston, 1970), p. 31.
4. Ibid., p. 63.
5. **Clyde Kluckhohn** and **Dorothea Leighton,** *The Navajo* (Cambridge: Harvard University Press, 1946), pp. 35ff.
6. Figures from the Albuquerque office of the Bureau of Indian Affairs, 1976. The seventeen pueblos are Acoma, Cochiti, Isleta, Jemez, Laguna, San Felipe, Sandia, Santo Domingo, Zia, Nambe, Picuris, Taos, Papaque, San Idlefonso, San Juan, Santa Clara, and Tesuque.

7. **Guy R. Stewart,** "Conservation in Pueblo agriculture," *Scientific Monthly* 51 : 201.

8. **Richard VanValkenburgh,** *A Short History of the Navajo People* (Window Rock, Ariz.: U.S. Department of the Interior, Navajo Service, 1938), p. 4.

9. **Winona LaDuke,** "The Council of Energy Resource Tribes: An Outsider's View In" (unpublished manuscript, 1980), p. 26.

10. **R. J. Clifford,** *The Cosmic Mountain in Canaan and the Old Testament* (Cambridge, Mass.: Harvard University Press, 1972), pp. 3 ff.; Mircea Eliade, *The Myth of the Eternal Return,* trans. Willard R. Trask (New York: Pantheon Books, 1954), p. 12.

11. **Leland C. Wyman,** *The Red Antway of the Navajo* (Santa Fe: Museum of Navajo Ceremonial Art, 1965), pp. 115 ff.

12. *Indian Claims Commission,* docket no. 229, p. 900; **Karl W. Luckert,** *Navajo Mountain and Rainbow Bridge Religion* (Flagstaff: Museum of Northern Arizona, 1977), p. 50.

13. **Frank Mitchell,** *Navajo Blessingway Singer* (Tucson: University of Northern Arizona Press, 1978), p. 219.

14. **Leland C. Wyman,** *Blessingway* (Tuscon: University of Arizona Press, 1970), p. 4.

15. **Alfonso Ortiz,** *New Perspectives on the Pueblos* (Albuquerque: University of New Mexico Press, 1972), p. 142; **Alfonso Ortiz,** *The Tewa World* (Chicago: University of Chicago Press, 1969), p. 19.

16. *Book of the Hopi* (New York: Penguin Books, 1977), p. 166.

17. **Ortiz,** *New Perspectives,* p. 211.

18. Recent discoveries in the field of archaeoastronomy indicate a tremendous degree of precision in the abilities of Native American astronomers to determine the solstices and equinoxes.

19. The ritual prototype of the Mountain Soil Bundle belonged to first man, according to Navajo mythology. It was known as the Magic Corn Bundle and contained the power and materials to produce the Inner Forms. **Frank Waters,** *Masked Gods,* p. 167; **Washington Matthews,** *Navajo Legends* (New York: American Folk-Lore Society, 1897), p. 34; **Mitchell,** *Blessingway,* pp. 20 ff.

20. **Maude Oakes,** *Where the Two Came to Their Father,* Bollingen Series I (New York: Pantheon Books, 1934).

21. From an address delivered at Dartmouth College, 1972.

22. **Ortiz,** *Tewa World,* p. 25.

23. **Mitchell,** *Navajo Blessingway Singer,* p. 178.

24. (New York: Signet, 1977), pp. 97–98.

25. **Mitchell,** *Navajo Blessingway Singer,* pp. 201–202.

26. *Navajo Times,* March 15, 1979, p. B-11.

27. **Marcia Keegan,** *The Taos Indians and Their Sacred Blue Lake,* (New York: Julian Messner, 1972), n.p.

28. **William Brown,** "The Rape of Black Mesa," *Sierra Club Bulletin,* August, 1970.

29. **Clemmer,** "Black Mesa and the Hopi," p. 17.

30. Ibid., p. 20.

31. **Brown,** "Rape of Black Mesa."

32. **Peter Matthiessen,** *Indian Country* (New York: Viking Press, 1984), pp. 315 ff.

33. Ibid.

34. **David Harris,** "The Last Stand for an Ancient Indian Way," *New York Times Magazine,* March 16, 1980, p. 79.

35. **Gladys A. Reichard,** *Navajo Religion: A Study of*

Symbolism (Princeton: Bollingen Foundation, 1950), pp. 19–20.

CHAPTER 5
References

Bandelier, Adolf F.
1910.   The Islands of Titicaca and Koati. New York: The Hispanic Society of America.

Bastien, Joseph W.
1973.   *Qollahuaya Rituals: An Ethnographic Account of the Symbolic Relations of Man and Land in an Andean Village.* Latin American Studies Program at Cornell, Monograph 56. Ithaca, N.Y.: Cornell University.

1976.   "Marriage and Exchange in the Andes," *Actes du XLII Congrès International des Américanistes* 4 : 149–64.

1978.   *Mountain of the Condor: Metaphor and Ritual in an Andean Ayllu.* American Ethnological Society Monograph 64. St. Paul: West Publishing Co.

n.d.*a*   "Land Litigations in an Andean Ayllu from 1592 until 1972," *Ethnohistory.*

n.d.*b*   *Medicine, Malnutrition, and Morbidity in the Andes.* Austin: University of Texas Press.

Cárdenas, Miranda, Raimundo de
1979.   *Provincia Bautista Saavedra.* La Paz: EDOBOL.

Girault, Luis
1972.   Personal conversation at the Musée de l'Homme in June.

Garcilaso de la Vega
1961.   *The Incas.* Ed. Alain Gheerbrant. New York: Avon Books.

James, Preston E.
1959.   *Latin America.* Indianapolis: Odyssey Press.

Kaatan manuscript
1904.   Copias de documentos de 1880–1904 por custodio Angeles, notario de Provincia Muñecas. Chuma.

La Barre, Weston
1950.   "Aymara folktales." *International Journal of American Linguistics* 16 : 40–45.

Murra, John V.
1972.   "El 'control vertical' de un máximo de pisos ecológicos en la economía de los sociedades Andinas." In *Visita de la Provincia de León de Huánuco en 1562.* Ed. John V. Murra. Huánuco, Peru: Universidad Nacional Hermilio Valdizan.

Oblitas Poblete, Enrique
1968.   *Il idioma secreto de los Incas.* La Paz: Editorial "Los Amigos del Libro."

1969.   *Plantas medicinales en Bolivia.* La Paz: Editorial "Los Amigos del Libro."

1978.   *Cultura Callawaya.* La Paz: Grafica Alba.

Stark, Louisa R.
1972.   "Machaj-juyai: Secret language of the Callahuayas." *Papers in Andean Linguistics* 1 : 199–227.

Thomas, R. Brooke
1972.   "Human adaptation to a High Andean energy flow system." Ph.D. diss., Pennsylvania State University.

Troll, Carl
1968.   *Geo-Ecology of the Mountainous Regions of the Tropi-*

cal Americas. UNESCO, 1966. Kommission bei Ferd. Bonn: Dummlers Verlag.

Tschopik, Harry

1946. "The Aymara." In *Handbook of South American Indians* 2:501–73. Washington: Smithsonian Institution.

Wassén, S. Henry

1972. *A medicine-man's implements and plants in Tiahuanacoid tomb in highland Bolivia*. Etnologiska Studier, Monograph 32. Göteborg: The Ethnographic Museum.

CHAPTER 9

Notes

Ethnographic and related studies of the Kalash and Kafiristan include **K. Jettmar,** ed., "Cultures of the Hindu Kush," In *Selected Papers for the Hindu Kush Cultural Conference: Moesgard, 1970,* Vol. I of *Beitrage z. Sudasiens forschungen,* Sudasiens Inst. Heidelberg (Wiesbaden: **Franz Steiner Verlag,** 1974); **A. R. Palwal,** "History of Former Kafirstan," *Afghanistan: J. Historical Soc. Afghanistan* (Kabul) 21, no. 3 (1968): 48–66; 22, no. 1 (1969): 6–27; 22, no. 2 (1969): 20–43; 23, no. 2 (1970): 21–52; 23, no. 4 (1971): 24–36; 24, no. 2 (1972): 10–17; **S. Jones,** *An Annotated Bibliography of Nuristan (Kafiristan) and the Kalash Kafirs of Chitral, Hist. Filos. Medd. det. Danske Videnskabernes Selskab* 41, no. 3; and **L. Dupree,** *Nuristan:* "'The Land of Light' Seen Darkly," American Universities Field Staff Reports, South Asian Series, vol. 15, no. 6, pp. 1–24.

1. The terminology and meanings employed here are discussed at length in the first chapter of **M. Eliade,** *The Sacred and the Profane: The Nature of Religion,* trans. W. R. Trask (New York: Harcourt, Brace and World, 1959), 256 pp.
2. **P. Graziosi,** "The wooden statue of Dezalik, Kalash divinity, Chitral, Pakistan," *Man* 61 (1961): 169–51.
3. See **Eliade,** *Sacred and Profane.*
4. The matters referred to here can be found in, for example, G. de Santillana and H. von Dechend, *Hamlet's Mill* (Boston: Gambit Inc., 1969), 505 pp; **M. Elaide,** *The Myth of the Eternal Return,* trans. W. R. Trask, Bollingen Series, vol. 46 (New York: Pantheon Books 1954); **J. G. Fraser,** *The Golden Bough: A Study in Magic and Religion,* abridged edition, (London: Macmillan, 1922), 756 pp. For material on ring dances, see E. L. Backman, *Religious Dances in the Christian Church and Popular Medicine,* (London: Allen and Unwin, 1952), 364 pp.; and C. Sachs, *World History of the Dance,* trans. B. Schonberg (New York: Norton, 1937) ch. 3, pp. 144ff.
5. For a description of old Kafiristan immediately before its "warring independence," see G. S. Robertson, *The Kafers of the Hindu Kush* (1896; recently reissued by Oxford University Press).

CHAPTER 10

Notes

1. The Kashmir cease-fire line that has been disputed between India and Pakistan for thirty-three years and three wars is the southern boundary of the region. The Sink-

iang province of China forms the northeastern boundary.
2. Pakistan-American Expedition to Paiyu, 1974. Masherbrum La, until then unexplored, opened up a route from the Baltoro Glacier on the north side of the range into the Hushe Valley on the south side.
3. **E. F. Knight,** *Where Three Empires Meet* (London, 1895).
4. According to Ybgo Fateh Ali Khan, rajah of Khapalu (and Hushe), only the people of the Karakoram valleys keep their animals in this fashion in winter. The Dards of Gilgit to the west pen their animals in roofless enclosures. The Ladakhis to the east herd them on the open slopes. Hence, the source of their name and of the region: *Balti*—Baltis and Baltistan.
5. The most important animal in this agro-pastoral society is the *hYak*–common cow hybrid. The male, *dZo,* is a plow and harvest animal. The milk of the *dZmo,* the female, is especially rich in butterfat.
6. *Apo* means "grandfather" (*api,* "grandmother") or anyone over forty years old, whichever state comes first.

CHAPTER 11

Note

*An earlier version of this essay appeared under the same title, as IWGIA Document 36, Copenhagen: International Work Group on Indigenous Affairs, 1979.

References cited

American Anthropological Association

1983 *Professional Ethics: Statements and Procedures.* Washington, D.C.: American Anthropological Association

Bahuguna, Vimala

1975 "Contribution of Women to Chipko Movement." *Indian Farming* 25:69–71.

Berreman, Gerald D.

1962 "Pahari Polyandry: A Comparison." *American Anthropologist* 64:60–75.

1968 "Is Anthropology Alive? Social Responsibility in Social Anthropology." *Current Anthropology* 9:391–96.

1969b "Urgent Anthropology in India." In *Urgent Research in Social Anthropology,* Transactions of the Indian Institute of Advanced Study, Simla, Vol. 10, pp. 1–13.

1971 "Ethics, Responsibility and the Funding of Asian Research." *Journal of Asian Studies* 30:390–99.

1972 *Hindus of the Himalayas: Ethnography and Change.* Berkeley: University of California Press.

1973 "The Social Responsibility of the Anthropologist." In *To See Ourselves: Anthropology and Modern Social Issues,* ed. Thomas Weaver, pp. 5–61. Glenview, Ill.: Scott, Foresman and Company.

1975 "Himalayan Polyandry and the Domestic Cycle." *American Ethnologist* 2:127–38.

1978 "Ecology, Demography and Domestic Strategies in the Western Himalayas." *Journal of Anthropological Research* 34:326–68.

1983 "Identity Definition, Assertion, and Politicization in the Cultural Himalayas." In *Identity: Personal and Sociocultural,* ed. Anita Jacobson-Widding, pp. 289–319. Atlantic Highlands, N.J.: Humanities Press.

Bodley, John H.
1975   *Victims of Progress.* Menlo Park, Calif.: Cummings Publishing Co.

Condominas, Georges
1973   "Ethics and Comfort: An Ethnographer's view of His Profession" (Distinguished Lecture, 1972). *Annual Report of the American Anthropological Association, 1972,* Washington, D.C., April, 1973, pp. 1–17.

Crawley, F. R. (Producer)
1970   "The Man Who Skied Down Everest." (Japanese Everest Ski Expedition, 1970). A Crawley Film Production.

Dogra, Bharat
1983   *Forests and People: Efforts in the Himalayas to Reestablish a Protective Relationship* (Second, revised edition). New Delhi: Bharat Dogra.

Eckholm, Erik P.
1975   "The Deterioration of Mountain Environments." *Science* 189 : 764–70.
1976   *Losing Ground: Environmental Stress and World Food Prospects.* New York: W. W. Norton.

Elwin, Verrier
1957   *A Philosophy for NEFA.* Shillong: North-East Frontier Agency.

Food and Agriculture Organization
1977   "Forestry in Uttar Pradesh: The Hugging the Trees Movement." *Ideas and Action Bulletin, No. 116.* Food and Agriculture Organization of the United Nations, Freedom from Hunger Campaign, pp. 20–21.

Frankel, Francine R.
1971   *India's Green Revolution: Economic Gains and Political Costs.* Princeton, N.J.: Princeton University Press.

Illich, Ivan
1969   "Outwitting the 'Developed' Countries." *New York Review,* November 6, 1969, pp. 18–22.

India News
1976   "More Mountaineers Visit India." *India News,* July 9, 1976. Washington, D.C.: Information Service, Embassy of India.

Majumdar, D. N.
1962   *Himalayan Polyandry.* New York: Asia Publishing House.

Mamdani, Mahmood
1972   *The Myth of Population Control.* New York: Monthly Review Press.

Marriott, McKim
1957   "Technological Change in Overdeveloped Rural Areas." In *Underdeveloped Areas,* ed. Lyle W. Shannon, pp. 423–33. New York: Harper and Bros.

Mills, C. Wright
1961   *The Sociological Imagination.* New York: Grove Press.
1964   "On Knowledge and Power." Reprinted in *Power, Politics and People,* ed. I. Horowitz, pp. 599–613. New York: Ballantine Books.

Mountain Gazette
1975   "Mountain Notes." *Mountain Gazette* (Denver, Colorado), Oct., 1975.

Nair, Kusum
1961   *Blossoms in the Dust: The Human Factor in Indian Development.* New York: Frederick A. Praeger.

News INDIA
1975   "Himachal Pradesh: Furore over Parmar's Book on Polyandry." *News INDIA* (Air India International Publication), July, 1975, p. 10.

O'Brien, Conor Cruise
1966   "The Counterrevolutionary Reflex." *Columbia University Forum* 9, no. 2: 21–24.

Overseas Hindustan Times
1975   "Feminine Wrath Over C.M.'s Book." *Overseas Hindustan Times,* May 22, 1975, p. 3.
1976a   "Down Trishul on Skis in 90 Minutes." *Overseas Hindustan Times,* May 27, 1976, p. 16.
1976b   "Trishul Skiing Triumph," by H. P. S. Ahluwalia and N. Kumar. *Overseas Hindustan Times,* July 1, 1976, pp. 8–9, 14.
1976c   "Tourist Train Around Dal Lake." *Overseas Hindustan Times,* September 2, 1976, p. 16.
1976d   "Stress on Tourism." *Overseas Hindustan Times,* Sept. 30, 1976, p. 10.

Parmar, Y. S.
1975   *Polyandry in the Himalayas.* Delhi: Vikas Publishing House.

Rowell, Galen
1977   *In the Throne Room of the Mountain Gods.* San Francisco: Sierra Club Books.

Royal Anthropological Institute News
1974   "Comment: Mountaineers and Sherpas." *Royal Anthropological Institute News,* No. 5, (Nov./Dec., 1974), pp. 1–2.

Saberwal, Satish (ed.)
1968   "Academic Colonialism: A Symposium on the Influences Which Destroy Intellectual Independence." *Seminar,* No. 112 (Dec., 1968). New Delhi.

Schumacher, E. F.
1973   *Small is Beautiful: Economics as if People Mattered.* London: Blond and Briggs Ltd.

Sharma, Hari P.
1973   "The Green Revolution in India: Prelude to a Red One?" In *Imperialism and Revolution in South Asia,* ed. Kathleen and Revolution in South Asia, ed. Kathleen Gough and Hari P. Sharma, pp. 77–102. New York: Monthly Review Press.

Srinivas, M. N.
1969   "Some Thoughts on the Study of One's Own Society." In *Social Change in Modern India,* pp. 147–63. Berkeley: University of California Press.

Statesman
1973   "The Himalaya are in Danger: Symposium on Conserving the Himalayan Environment." Reprinted from *The Statesman* in *The Himalayan Journal* 32 (1972–73): 180–82.

Wolf, Eric R., and Joseph G. Jorgensen
1970   "Anthropology on the Warpath in Thailand." *New York Review of Books,* November 19, 1970, pp. 26–35.

CHAPTER 14

Note

*The words of both C. G. Bruce and Ngawong Tenzin Norbu are quoted from Alexander W. Macdonald, "The Lama and the General," *Kailash* 1, no. 3 (1973; Kathmandu, Nepal: Ratna Pustak, Bhandar, Bhotahity).

CHAPTER 15

References

B. F. Kirtley has written a very interesting survey essay, Unknown hominids and New World legends, *Western Folklore* 23 (1964): 77–79, on the general question of hominids in folklore. I would like to thank Professor Alan Dundes, University of California, for drawing my attention to this article.

De Nebesky-Wojkowitz, René
1956a *Oracles and demons of Tibet: The cult and iconography of the Tibetan protective deities.* The Hague: Mouton.
1956b *Where the gods are mountains: Three years among the people of the Himalayas.* Trans. from the German by Michael Bullock. London: Weidenfeld and Nicolson.
Dictionary of the Lepcha language
1898 *Dictionary of the Lepcha language.* Berlin. (Compiled by G. B. Mainwaring; revised and completed by Albert Grünwedel. Printed and published by order of Her Majesty's Secretary of State for India in Council.)

Gorer, G.
1938 *Himalayan village: an account of the Lepchas of Sikkim* 1st ed. London: Michael Joseph.

Gurung, H. B.
1961 Aspects of the snowman: Fact and fiction. *Himalayan Journal* 23: 171–75.

Haarh, Erik
1969 *The Yar-Luṅ dynasty.* Copenhagen: G. E. C. Gad.

Hermanns, Fr. M.
1954 *The Indo-Tibetans.* Bombay: K. L. Fernandes, Bandra.

Jest, Corneille
1960 Religious beliefs of the Lepchas in the Kalimpong district (West Bengal). *The Journal of the Royal Asiatic Society* 124–34.

Morris, J.
1938 *Living with Lepchas: A book about the Sikkim Himalayas.* London, Toronto: William Heinemann.

Siiger, H.
1967a *The Lepchas: Culture and religion of a Himalayan people.* Part one. Results of anthropological field work in Sikkim, Kalimpong and Git. Ethnographical Series 11, Part 1. Copenhagen: Publications of the National Museum.
1967b *The Lepchas: Culture and religion of a Himalayan people.* Part two. (Lepcha ritual texts and commentary by Halfdan Siiger. Phonetic transcriptions of Lepcha ritual texts with introduction by Jørgen Rischel.) Ethnographical Series 11,
Part 2. Copenhagen: Publications of the National Museum.
1968 Himalayan mountain cults: From the Lepchas of Sikkim. *Ethnology* 2: 277–79.
1972 "A Himalayan goddess of procreation: From the Lepchas of Sikkim," in *Studies in the history of religion (Supplements to NUMEN) 22.* Leiden: E. J. Brill.

Vlček, E.
1959 Old literary evidence for the existence of the "snowman" in Tibet and Mongolia. *Man* 59: 133–34.

Waddell, L. A.
1959 *The Buddhism of Tibet or Lamaism.* 2d ed. Cambridge: W. Heffer and Sons.

CHAPTER 18

References

Cressey, George B.
1934. *China's Geographic Foundations.* New York: McGraw-Hill.

Dreyer, June Teufel
1976. *China's Forty Millions: Minority Nationalities and National Integration in the People's Republic of China.* Cambridge, Mass.: Harvard University Press.

Franck, Harry A.
1925. *Roving through Southern China.* New York: The Century Co.

Hosie, Sir Alexander
1914. *On the Trail of the Opium Poppy.* London: Georg Philip & Son.

Illustrated Atlas of China. 1972. Chicago: Rand McNally.

Kolb, Albert
1971. *East Asia.* London: Methuen.

Krader, Lawrence
1963. *Peoples of Central Asia.* Uralic and Altaic Series, Vol. 26. Bloomington. Indiana University Press.

Kraus, Richard C.
1979. "Social Affairs." In *The People's Republic of China,* ed. Harold C. Hinton, pp. 259–84. Boulder, Colo.: Westview Press.

Latsch-Heberer, Marie-Luise
1978. "A Trip to Yunnan." *China Reconstructs* 27, no. 12 (December): 26–31.

Lin, Yueh-hua
1961. *The Lolo of Liang Shan.* New Haven, Conn.: HRAF Press.

Robinson, Joan
1975. "In the Deep Southwest." *New China* 1, no. 3 (Fall): 21–23.

Salter, Christopher L.
1970. "The Geography of Marginality: A Study of Migration, Settlement, and Agricultural Development in the Rift Valley of Eastern Taiwan." Dissertation, University of California, Berkeley.
1976. "The Role of Landscape Modification in Revolutionary Nation-building: The Case for Mao's China." *China Geographer,* no. 4 (Winter): 41–59

1978.   "The Enigma of Tachai: Landscapes and Lore."
         The China Geographer, no. 9 (Winter): 43–62.
Schafer, Edward H.
1967.   *The Vermillion Bird: T'ang Images of the South.*
         Berkeley and Los Angeles: University of Califor-
         nia Press.
Shabad, Theodore
1972.   *China's Changing Map: National and Regional
         Development, 1949–1971.* New York: Praeger Pub-
         lishers.
         "The Shui People—A New Life." 1976. *China Pic-
         torial,* July, pp. 36–39.
         "The Tuchia-Miao Autonomous Prefecture."
         1978. *China Reconstructs* 27, no. 7 (July): 34–39.
         "A Visit to the Greater Miao Mountains." 1976.
         China Pictorial, January, pp. 35–37.
Wang, De
1979.   "Strengthening Unity, Exchanging Experience."
         China Pictorial, February, pp. 14–17.
Wiens, Herold J.
1967.   *Han Chinese Expansion in South China.* New
         Haven, Conn.: The Shoe String Press.
Zhi, Exiang
1980.   "The Jinuos: China's Newest Nationality." *China
         Reconstructs* 29, no. 2 (February): 55–61.

CHAPTER 19

Notes

1. **Ssu-ma Ch'ien,** *Records of the Grand Historian of China,*
    trans. Burton Watson (New York: Columbia University
    Press, 1961), Vol. II, p. 490.
2. **Edward H. Schafer,** *The Vermilion Bird* (Berkeley: Uni-
    versity of California Press, 1967), p. 16.
3. **C. W. Wang,** *The Forests of China* (Cambridge, Mass.:
    Harvard Botanical Museum, 1961), p. 147.
4. **Marco Polo,** *The Travels of Marco Polo,* trans. R. E.
    Latham (New York: Penguin, 1958), pp. 142–44, 146,
    148.
5. Ibid., p. 140.
6. **Schafer,** *Vermilion Bird,* p. 58.
7. Ibid., p. 60.
8. **Chia-ting Chi,** *Key Economic Areas in Chinese History*
    (London: Allen and Unwin, 1936), p. 109.
9. **Schafer,** *Vermilion Bird,* p. 54.
10. Ibid., p. 92.
11. Ibid., p. 91.
12. **Edward H. Schafer,** *Shore of Pearls* (Berkeley: Univer-
    sity of California Press, 1969), p. 80.
13. **Harry A. Franck,** *Roving through Southern China* (New
    York: Century, 1925), p. 493.
14. Ibid., p. 494.
15. **Schafer,** *Vermilion Bird,* p. 167.

CHAPTER 21

Note

*****Frances Lambrecht,** "The Main Factors of Resistance to
Culture Change in Ifugaoland," in *Acculturation in the

Philippines, ed. Peter G. Gowing and William H. Scott
(Quezon City, Philippines: New Day Publishers, 1971),
pp. 83–89.

CHAPTER 22

References

Elizalde, Manuel, Jr., and **R. B. Fox.** "The Tasaday Forest
    People." Mimeographed, Smithsonian Institution Center
    for Short-lived Phenomena, 1971.
————. "The Tasaday Project: A Research Design." Mimeo-
    graphed, PANAMIN Research Center, 1971.
Fernandez, Carlos, II, and **Frank Lynch.** *Tasaday.* Pan-
    amin Foundation Research Series No. 1 (1972); also pub-
    lished in *Philippine Sociological Review* 20, no. 2 (October,
    1972).
Llamzon, Teodoro. "The Tasaday Language So Far." *Phil-
    ippine Journal of Linguistics* II, no. 2 (December, 1971), with
    "Comments" by Richard Elkins.
Lynch, Frank, and **Teodoro Llamzon.** "The Blit Manubo
    and the Tasaday." *Philippines Sociological Review* 19, nos.
    1–2 (January–April, 1971).
Nance, John. *The Gentle Tasaday.* Harcourt Brace Jovano-
    vich, 1975.
Salazar, Zeus. "Footnote on the Tasaday." *Philippine Journal
    of Linguistics* II, no. 2 (December, 1971).
————. "Second Footnote on the Tasaday." *Asian Studies* II,
    no. 2 (August, 1973).
Yen, D. E., and **John Nance,** eds. *Further Studies on the Ta-
    saday.* PANAMIN Foundation Research Series No. 2
    (1976), a collection of six papers: Robert Fox on Tasaday
    stone technology; Carol Molony, with Dad Tuan, on the
    language, including an eight-hundred-word vocabulary;
    D. E. Yen and Hermes Gutierrez on the useful plants;
    D. E. Yen on plant names; D. E. Yen on the subsistence
    system; and Hermes Gutierrez on a new species of lily.

CHAPTER 23

Notes and References

Notes

1. At the time of field research (1971–73) the Bimin-
    Kuskusmin people dwelt in the United Nations Trust
    Territory of New Guinea under the administration of
    Australia. In September, 1975, the United Nations Trust
    Territory of New Guinea and the Australian External
    Territory of Papua became the independent nation of
    Papua New Guinea.
2. The references to blood, semen, and bone implicate fun-
    damental Bimin-Kuskusmin notions of the constitution
    of human nature, the person, and the self (see Poole
    1976, 1981, 1982).
3. Field research among the Bimin-Kuskusmin was gener-
    ously supported by the National Institutes of Health,
    the Cornell University–Ford Foundation Humanities
    and Social Sciences Program, and the Center for South
    Pacific Studies of the University of California, Santa
    Cruz. The New Guinea Research Unit, Research School
    of Pacific Studies, Australian National University and

the Department of Anthropology and Sociology of the University of Papua New Guinea provided valuable assistance. The Bimin-Kuskusmin people, however, are owed the primary debt of gratitude for myriad acts of tolerance and kindness and for much empathy and wisdom.

4. For further elaboration of these theoretical issues, see, for example, Frake 1962; Huber 1979; Pataki-Schweizer 1980; and Rappaport 1979 (cf. Downs and Stea 1973; Gould 1972; and Gould and White 1974). For exemplary studies of matters of ethnoecology or ethnogeography in Papua New Guinea, see Huber 1979 and especially Pataki-Schweizer 1980.

5. The Bimin-Kuskusmin, however, do not draw a conceptual distinction between "natural" and "supernatural" in any way that is readily aligned with Western notions of the contrast. For a particularly insightful discussion of the complex cultural constitution of the "natural" interwoven with an analysis of ethnographic materials from New Guinea, see Strathern 1980.

6. With the recent advent of plantation labor recruiting among Bimin-Kuskusmin, a few young men have visited some of the coastal areas of Papua New Guinea and have returned with tales of wondrous things near the great "salt river" (*ok yoor bang*). But the sea remains a mystery that is detached from their integrated view of the world. Indeed, the only analogies that seem to facilitate their understanding of this phenomenon are drawn from their recognition of a salt spring and large rivers within their territory and of Lake Kopiago to the east across the Strickland Gorge and beyond the range of their normal travels.

7. Although the traditional Bimin-Kuskusmin view of the farthest extent of "human" groups is limited to within about a hundred-mile radius at most, their trade networks ultimately extend far into the Highlands provinces to the east, across the frontier of Irian Jaya to the west, and to the northern and southern coasts. Present knowledge of the complex interlinkage of trade routes in Papua New Guinea is based upon examination of the probable subregional origins of both recent trade items and ancient archaeological finds, as well as careful ethnographic surveys of ongoing trading activities (see Hughes 1977).

8. The assessment of the longevity of Bimin-Kuskusmin settlement in their present territory is based on fragmentary data of the following kinds: dating of archaeological excavations of early settlement sites; dating of the linguistic divergence of the Bimin-Kuskusmin language from cognate areal languages; dating of the kind, size, and density of vegetative regenerations in areas where slash-and-burn agriculture has been practiced over generations; and the convergence of certain claims embedded in various ethnohistorical traditions.

9. There are several genres of Bimin-Kuskusmin myths of origin. The most elaborate and ritually significant versions detail the emergence of the first human ancestors within their present territory. Other and more fragmentary classes of myth suggest migrations from the Highlands to the east, from Irian Jaya to the west, and from the lower course of the Sepik River to the north into what is now Bimin-Kuskusmin territory.

10. For a general ethnographic survey of the area, see Barth 1971, 1975.

11. For further discussion of the Bimin-Kuskusmin map of their known world and the human, semihuman, and nonhuman beings within it, see Poole 1983.

12. Nederlands Nieuw Guinea has since become Irian Jaya, a province of Indonesia.

13. Several varieties of red *Cordyline* plants are used to establish powerful sacred boundaries around ritual sites to warn and guard against intrusion and to provide a purification of the site.

14. For a description and analysis of some features of the Bimin-Kuskusmin male initiation ritual cycle, see Poole 1976, 1982.

15. In order to study matters of secret myth and ritual, I was required to pass through a special and highly condensed version of the most advanced stages of male initiation—a procedure that is akin to that used to initiate adult emigrants who have returned. Once initiated in this fashion, I was believed to possess an appropriate and respectful "understanding" of sacred phenomena and to be less prone to harming the Place of the Center (see Poole 1982).

16. Feral boars do not often roam at the higher altitudes of human settlement, and domestic boars are castrated to keep them docile and to protect the populace from both "natural" and "supernatural" harm. It is said that in the past, before the appearance of the noxious grasses and bees near the hamlets and gardens, feral boars were plentiful in the settlement areas and frequently impregnated domestic sows.

17. Ultimately, however, Afek's supply of semen is limited. Indeed, once expended, neither ancestral nor human semen is replenished except insofar as it is recycled in the births and deaths of the great cycle of intergenerational renewal within the Bimin-Kuskusmin community. Thus, any human semen or *sacred* oil that permanently disappears from the Place of the Center and into a social group with whom the Bimin-Kuskusmin have no relations of ritual reciprocity can never be replenished and is lost forever to the community.

18. In the ritual consecration of these gardens and groves, bamboo tubes of human or wild boar semen are also buried.

19. Since the mid-1950s, the Bimin-Kuskusmin have suffered several severe epidemics, notably of influenza, with very high mortality rates. Many people suspect that there is some association among these new illnesses, the coming of Europeans, the "discovery" of the oil, and the appearance of the new varieties of grasses and bees.

20. It should be noted that all oil passing beyond the Place of the Center has been ritually stripped of its greatest and most secret powers and is no longer truly sacred (*aiyem*), although it may still promote the efficacy of the ritual endeavors of other peoples. One great tragedy of the oil taken from the Place of the Center by the Europeans was that this oil was not fully desanctified.

21. Ideally, all lore concerning the most sacred nature and use of the oil is restricted knowledge exclusively of the paramount male ritual elders of the original Bimin-Kuskusmin clans.

22. Such expeditions are always organized under the aus-

pices of ritual experts, and the oil may never be traded or exchanged directly for ordinary items of wealth. In time, Bimin-Kuskusmin came to understand that the apparent marvels that they had accepted from the Europeans in exchange for the sample of sacred oil were merely ordinary items of trade.

23. Usually wild boar or marsupial, but sometimes actual human semen is used in these ritual contexts. These forms of semen are symbolic representations of Afek's ancestral semen, which is the source and the symbol of the sacred oil.

24. A sign that the moss forest is largely beyond the pale of ritual control, moral influence, and spiritual intercession is said to be that it is a favorite haunt of men intent upon suicide by hanging. And witches and sorcerers, who are outside of the moral order, are thought to have taken many victims in this isolated domain. Yet the most powerful ritual elders perform important rites in this high mountain area.

25. Fearing an attack on their military and ritual future in the form of young males, Bimin-Kuskusmin protectively gathered together little boys in the war ritual houses, leaving little girls dispersed among their hamlets of residence. When the epidemic of influenza struck, it severely reduced the population of young boys in particular.

26. In 1969 another patrol launched a more impressive firearms demonstration by shooting a hole through a line of warshields.

27. The procedure of desanctification should properly be performed in secret, for witnesses not in possession of appropriate ritual status and knowledge would defile the proceedings and destroy their efficacy.

28. Indeed, in 1978 word came that Bosuurok was dead. He had been placed in his great cult house amidst the clan ritual objects during his dying, and his passing was marked by the elaborate funerary ritual and mourning befitting a paramount male ritual elder of the ranking Watiianmin clan.

References

Barth, F.
1971. "Tribes and Intertribal Relations in the Fly Headwaters." *Oceania* 41:171–91.
1975. *Ritual and Knowledge among the Baktaman of New Guinea.* New Haven: Yale University Press.

Downs, R., and D. Stea (eds.).
1973. *Image and Environment.* Chicago: Aldine Publishing Company.

Frake, C. O.
1962. "Cultural Ecology and Ethnography." *American Anthropologist* 64:53–59.

Gould, P. R.
1972. "On Mental Maps." In *Man, Space, and Environment,* ed. P. W. English and R. C. Mayfield, pp. 260–82. New York: Oxford University Press.
———, and R. White.
1974. *Mental Maps.* Harmondsworth: Penguin Books.

Huber, P. B.
1979. "Anggor Floods: Reflections on Ethnogeography and Mental Maps." *Geographical Review* 69:127–39.

Hughes, I.
1977. *New Guinea Stone Age Trade.* Terra Australis 3. Canberra: Department of Prehistory, Research School of Pacific Studies, the Australian National University.

Pataki-Schweizer, K. J.
1980. *A New Guinea Landscape.* Anthropological Studies in the Eastern Highlands of New Guinea 4. Seattle: University of Washington Press.

Poole, F. J. P.
1976. *The Ais Am.* 5 vols. Ann Arbor: University Microfilms International.
1981. "Transforming 'Natural' Woman: Female Ritual Leaders and Gender Ideology among Bimin-Kuskusmin." In *Sexual Meanings,* ed. S. B. Ortner and H. Whitehead, pp. 116–65. Cambridge: Cambridge University Press.
1982. "The Ritual Forging of Identity: Aspects of Person and Self in Bimin-Kuskusmin Male Initiation." In *Rituals of Manhood,* ed. G. H. Herdt, pp. 99–154. Berkeley: University of California Press.
1983. "Cannibals, Tricksters, and Witches: Anthropophagic Images among Bimin-Kuskusmin." In *The Ethnography of Cannibalism,* ed. P. Brown and D. Tuzin, pp. 6–32. Washington, D.C.: Society for Psychological Anthropology.

Rappaport, R. A.
1979. "On Cognized Models." In *Ecology, Meaning, and Religion,* ed. R. A. Rappaport, pp. 97–144. Richmond, Calif.: North Atlantic Books.

Strathern, M.
1980. "No Nature, No Culture: The Hagen Case." In *Nature, Culture and Gender,* ed. C. MacCormack and M. Strathern, pp. 174–222. Cambridge: Cambridge University Press.

CHAPTER 24

Notes

1. The first Indian pilgrims to be admitted to Lake Manasarowar (Mapam) in many years came back with dismal reports of vast desecration and monasteries reduced to rubble. The eight large monasteries surrounding the lake, in view of Mount Su-Meru (Kailasha, or Di Se), that existed before the Chinese invasion have all been blown up. A lonely prayer flag was seen to issue from the resurrected rock crannies of a makeshift *gompa.* See *New York Times,* Sunday November 1, 1981.

2. See **Paul Gayet-Trancrède's** *Hommes, cimes et dieux: Les grandes mythologies de l'altitude et la légende dorée des montages à travers le monde* (Paris: Arthaud, 1973).

3. *Ideen zur Philosophie der Geschichte der Menschheit,* in *Werke,* ed. H. Meyer, trans. T. Churchill (London, 1803), pp. 267–68.

4. See *Readings in Early Anthropology,* ed. J. S. Slotkin

(New York: Wenner-Gren Foundation, 1965); and *Natural Environment and Society in the Theory of Geographical Determinism* (Prague: Charles University, 1969).

5. The first intrepid Britisher to reach Lhasa as a tourist was Thomas Manning, who walked in unannounced one day in the fall of 1811. His journal notes reveal a cantankerous fellow not without his sense of humor and easily persuaded by Tibetan civility, which he comments upon. "I was extremely affected by this interview with the Lama," he wrote afterwards. "I could have wept through strangeness of sensation." How similar this is to the occasion of Carl Jung's own first encounter with an American Indian in which Jung actually did break down and weep.

6. For much of this section I am greatly indebted to John Keay's fine study, *When Men and Mountains Meet* (London: John Murray, 1977).

7. Recent type-c virogene analysis indicates that man's ancestors during the Pliocene evolved in Asia, not Africa. It is startling evidence, an environmental imprint on primate cellular DNA and coming quite possibly from mountainous northern Burma. See R. E. Benveniste and G. J. Todaro, "Evolution of Type C Viral Genes: Evidence for an Asian Origin of Man," *Nature* 261 (May 13, 1976): 101–107.

8. The supposedly stable, conservationist strategies of some mountain tribes have been recently questioned. See J. Smith's "Man's Impact upon Some New Guinea Mountain Ecosystems," in *Subsistence and Survival: Rural Ecology in the Pacific,* ed. T. Bayliss-Smith and R. Feachem (New York: Academic Press, 1977), pp. 185–214; and Hagen's "Man and Nature: Reflections on Culture and Ecology," *Norwegian Archaeological Review* 172, no. 5(1): 1–22, in which Hagen presents material indicating that man has been a negative ecological presence on the Hardangervidda mountain plateau since the earliest Stone Age. This negative value, associated with primitive life, was first evoked in George Marsh's *Man and Nature.*

9. The following material is, in part, gleaned from Robert Brain's *The Last Primitive Peoples* (New York: Crown Publishers, 1976); the Yale University Human Relations Files; George Murdock's *Ethnographic Atlas;* the two-volume *Minority Rights* work; and contributions to *Mountain People.* See also N. J. Allen's "Fourfold Classifications of Society in the Himalayas," in J. Fischer, *Himalayan Anthropology* (The Hague, Netherlands: Mouton, 1977).

10. See **Douglas Johnson,** *The Nature of Nomadicism* (Chicago: University of Chicago Press, 1969).

11. See **Henry Fields,** *Contributions to the Anthropology of the Faiyum, Sinai, Sudan, and Kenya,* (Berkeley: University of California Press, 1952); as well as Carl Ritter, *The Comparative Geography of Palestine and the Sinaitic Peninsula,* trans. W. Gage (New York, 1866).

12. **G. Volkova,** "Migrations from Mountain to Plain in North Caucasus in the 18th–20th Centuries," *Soviet Ethnography,* no. 2 (1971): 38–47.

13. **I. Matley,** "Transhumance in Bosnia and Herzegovina," *Geographical Review* 58, no. 2 (1968): 231–61.

14. **G. Burgel,** "Island Mountains in Greece: The End of a World—the Example of Karya on Leucade," *Réchèrches Geographiques à Strasbourg,* 3 (1977): 91–99.

15. **R. Ali** and **R. Ferras,** "Tourism in Pakistan: Potential and Projected Image," *Société Languedocienne de Géographie Bulletin* 10, no. 4 (1976): 313–33.

16. **Ben Wisner,** "Man-made Famine in Western Kenya: The Interrelationship of Environment and Development," *African Environment,* special report 5 (1977): 194–215.

17. **H. A. Isack,** "An African Ethic of Conservation," *Natural History* 85, no. 9 (1976): 90–95.

18. Tenzing died in May, 1986, the same month he climbed his mountain.

Index

Mountain People,

designed by Bill Cason, was set in various sizes of Galliard by G&S Typesetters, Inc., and printed offset on Simpson Lee's 60-pound Modified Antique Coronado Opaque by Thomson-Shore, Inc., with case binding by John H. Dekker & Sons.